Intelligent Databases:
Technologies and Applications

Zongmin Ma
Northeastern University, China

IDEA GROUP PUBLISHING
Hershey • London • Melbourne • Singapore

Acquisition Editor: Michelle Potter
Senior Managing Editor: Jennifer Neidig
Managing Editor: Sara Reed
Development Editor: Kristin Roth
Copy Editor: Nicole Dean
Typesetter: Jessie Weik
Cover Design: Lisa Tosheff
Printed at: Yurchak Printing Inc.

Published in the United States of America by
    Idea Group Publishing (an imprint of Idea Group Inc.)
    701 E. Chocolate Avenue
    Hershey PA 17033
    Tel: 717-533-8845
    Fax: 717-533-8661
    E-mail: cust@idea-group.com
    Web site: http://www.idea-group.com

and in the United Kingdom by
    Idea Group Publishing (an imprint of Idea Group Inc.)
    3 Henrietta Street
    Covent Garden
    London WC2E 8LU
    Tel: 44 20 7240 0856
    Fax: 44 20 7379 3313
    Web site: http://www.eurospan.co.uk

Library of Congress Cataloging-in-Publication Data

Intelligent databases : technologies and applications / Zongmin Ma, editor.
    p. cm.
  Summary: "This book integrates data management in databases with intelligent data processing and analysis in artificial intelligence. It challenges today's database technology and promotes its evolution"--Provided by publisher.
    ISBN 1-59904-120-0 (hardcover) -- ISBN 1-59904-121-9 (softcover) -- ISBN 1-59904-122-7 (ebook)
  1. Database management. 2. Expert systems (Computer science) 3. Artificial intelligence. I. Ma, Zongmin, 1965-
    QA76.9.D3I54826 2006
    006.3'3--dc22
                        2006019125

British Cataloguing in Publication Data
A Cataloguing in Publication record for this book is available from the British Library.

Intelligent Databases:
Technologies and Applications

Table of Contents

Preface

Computer-based information technologies have been extensively used to help many organizations, private companies, and academic and education institutions manage their processes and information systems hereby become their nervous center. Information systems are used to manage data. The explosion of massive data sets created by businesses, science and governments necessitates intelligent and more powerful computing paradigms so that users can benefit from this data. This information needs to be summarized and synthesized to support effective problem solving and decision making. Various techniques have been proposed for intelligent data processing and analysis in the area of artificial intelligence (AI). Machine learning, for example, would implement various forms of learning, in particular mechanisms capable of inducing knowledge from examples or data.

Databases are designed to support the data storage, processing, and retrieval activities related to data management in information systems. Database management systems provide efficient task support and tremendous gain in productivity is hereby accomplished using these technologies. Database systems are the key to implementing data management. Data management requires database technique support. Database technology is typically application-oriented. With advances and in-deep applications of computer technologies, in particular, the extensive applications of Web technology in various areas, databases have become the repositories of large volumes of data. It is very critical to manage and use the worth data resource for effective problem solving and decision making. The research and development of intelligent databases are hereby emerging as a new discipline and are receiving increasing attention. The knowledge discovery in databases and data mining has witnessed it.

By means of database technology, large volumes of data can be stored in databases. Meanwhile large volumes of data in databases can be handled by means of AI technology and database systems should provide task support for such information processing. The next generation of information systems will be built based on intelligent databases to support various problem solving and decision making. So the study of intelligent databases is a field that must be investigated by academic researchers together with developers and users both from database and AI areas. This book focuses on two major issues of intelligent databases, namely, intelligent information processing in databases and intelligent aspects of database systems, and presents the latest research and application results in intelligent databases. The different chapters in the book have been contributed by different authors and provide possible solutions for the different types of technological problems concerning intelligent databases.

Introduction

This book which consists of 11 chapters is organized into two major sections. The first section discusses the issues of intelligent information processing in databases in the first eight chapters. The next three chapters covering the intelligent aspects of database systems comprise the second section.

First of all, we take a look at the problems of the intelligent information processing in databases.

Most algorithms and approaches dealing with data mining in general and especially those focusing on the task of association rule mining have assumed all items to be only positively correlated, and looked only into the items that remained finally in a shopping basket. Very few works have proposed the existence of negative correlations between items, based though on the absence of items from transactions rather than on their actual removals. Kouris, Makris, and Tsakalidis look into mining that takes into consideration valuable information from rejected items and propose various alternatives for taking the specific items into account efficiently. The authors finally provide experimental evidence on the existence and significance of these items.

Outlier detection is an important research issue in data mining fields. The number of cells in the cell-based disk algorithm increases exponentially. The performance of this algorithm decreases dramatically with the increasing of the number of cells and data points. Zhao, Bao, Sun, and Yu find that there are many empty cells that are useless to outlier detection. They propose a novel index structure, called CD-Tree, in which only non-empty cells are stored, and a cluster technique is adopted to store the data objects in the same cell into linked disk pages. They test the performance of the proposed algorithms.

In the field of data mining, developing an efficient mining algorithm that can incrementally maintain discovered information as a database grows is quite important. Deletion of records in databases is commonly seen in real-world applications. Hong and Wang propose an incremental mining algorithm for maintenance of association rules as new transactions are inserted. The authors first review the maintenance of association rules from data insertion and then attempt to extend it to solve the data deletion issue. The concept of pre-large itemsets is used to reduce the need for rescanning the original database and to save maintenance costs. A novel algorithm is proposed to maintain discovered association rules for deletion of records. The proposed algorithm doesn't need to rescan the original database until a number of records have been deleted.

Inductive databases have been proposed as general purpose databases to support the KDD process. Unfortunately, the heterogeneity of the discovered patterns and of the different conceptual tools used to extract them from source data makes difficult the integration in a unique framework. Meo and Psaila explore the feasibility of using XML as the unifying framework for inductive databases, and propose a new model, XML for data mining (XDM). They show the basic features of the model, based on the concepts of data item (source data and patterns) and statement (used to manage data and derive patterns). They make use of XML namespaces (to allow the effective coexistence and extensibility of data mining operators) and of XML-schema, by means of which they define the schema, the state and the integrity constraints of an inductive database.

Although data warehouse and geographical information system technologies are very useful in the decision making process, they are usually used separately. Integrating these two technologies coins new terms: spatial datawarehouse (SDW) and spatial OLAP (SOLAP). By using SOLAP, users may enhance their capacity to explore the underlying dataset once spatial methods incorporated into OLAP ones may be used. Sampaio et al. propose an integrated architecture for a SDW, including a formalized data model for SDW, a SQL extension query language which enables spatial roll-up and drill-down, optimization techniques which improve performance of complex spatial queries by pre-storing spatial aggregates, and a prototype, *MapWarehouse*, which validates the ideas proposed.

Data mining has the capability for classification, prediction, estimation, and pattern recognition by using manufacturing databases. Databases of manufacturing systems contain significant information for decision making, which could be properly revealed with the application of appropriate data mining techniques. Oke demonstrates the application of decision tree, a data mining tool, in the manufacturing system. Decision trees are employed for identifying valuable information in manufacturing databases. Practically, industrial managers would be able to make better use of manufacturing data at little or no extra investment in data manipulation cost. The author shows that it is valuable for managers to mine data for better and more effective decision making.

Zarri evokes the ubiquity and the importance of the so-called "narrative" information, showing that the usual ontological tools are unable to offer complete and reliable solutions for representing and exploiting this type of information. Then the author supplies some details about Narrative Knowledge Representation Language (NKRL), a fully-implemented knowledge representation and inferencing environment especially created for an "intelligent" exploitation of narrative knowledge.

The main innovation of NKRL consists in associating with the traditional ontologies of concepts an "ontology of events", in other words, a new sort of hierarchical organization where the nodes correspond to n-ary structures representing formally generic classes of elementary events like "move a physical object", "be present in a place" or "send/receive a message". More complex, second order tools based on the "reification" principle allow one to encode the "connectivity phenomena" like causality, goal, indirect speech, co-ordination, and subordination that, in narrative information, link together "elementary events". The chapter includes a description of the inference techniques proper to NKRL, and some information about the last developments of this language.

A major goal for database research has been the incorporation of additional semantics into the data model. Classical data models often suffer from their incapability of representing and manipulating imprecise and uncertain information that may occur in many real-world applications. Therefore, fuzzy set theory has been extensively applied to extend various data models and resulted in numerous contributions, mainly with respect to the popular relational model or to some related form of it. To satisfy the need of modeling complex objects with imprecision and uncertainty, recently many researches have been concentrated on fuzzy semantic (conceptual) and object-oriented data models. Ma reviews fuzzy database modeling technologies, including fuzzy conceptual data models and database models. Concerning fuzzy database models, fuzzy relational databases and fuzzy object-oriented databases are discussed, respectively.

In the second section, we see the intelligent aspects of database systems.

Wolff describes some of the kinds of "intelligence" that may be exhibited by an intelligent database system based on the SP theory of computing and cognition. The author introduces the SP theory and its main attractions as the basis for an intelligent database system: that it uses a simple but versatile format for diverse kinds of knowledge, that it integrates and simplifies a range of AI functions, and that it supports established database models when that is required. Then with examples and discussion, the author illustrates aspects of "intelligence" in the system: pattern recognition and information retrieval, several forms of probabilistic reasoning, the analysis and production of natural language, and the unsupervised learning of new knowledge.

Integrity constraints are a key tool for characterizing the well-formedness and semantics of the information contained in databases. In this regard, it is essential that intelligent database management systems provide their users with automatic support to effectively and efficiently maintain the semantic correctness of data with respect to the given integrity constraints. Martinenghi, Christiansen, and Decker give an overview of the field of efficient integrity checking and maintenance for relational as well as deductive databases. It covers both theoretical and practical aspects of integrity control, including integrity maintenance via active rules. The authors outline new lines of research, particularly with regard to two topics where a strong impact for future developments can be expected: integrity in XML document collections and in distributed databases. Both pose a number of new and highly relevant research challenges to the database community.

Information systems, including their core databases need to meet changing user requirements and adhere to evolving business strategies. Traditional database evolution techniques focus on reacting to change to smoothly perform schema evolution operations and to propagate corresponding updates to the data as effectively as possible. Adopting such posterior solutions to such changes generates high costs in human resources and financial support. Bounif advocates an alternate solution: a predictive approach to database evolution. In this approach, ones anticipate future changes during the standard requirements analysis phase of schema development. The approach enables potential future requirements to be planned for, as well as the standard, determining what data is to be stored and what access is required. This preparation contributes significantly in the ability of the database schema to adapt to future changes and to estimate their relative costs.

Acknowledgments

The editor wishes to thank all of the authors for their insights and excellent contributions to this book and would like to acknowledge the help of all involved in the collation and review process of the book, without whose support the project could not have been satisfactorily completed. Most of the authors of chapters included in this book also served as referees for chapters written by other authors. Thanks go to all those who provided constructive and comprehensive reviews.

A further special note of thanks goes to all the staff at Idea Group Inc., whose contributions throughout the whole process from inception of the initial idea to final publication have been invaluable. Special thanks also go to the publishing team at Idea Group Inc., in particular to Mehdi Khosrow-Pour, whose enthusiasm motivated me to initially accept his invitation for taking on this project, and to Kristin Roth, who continuously prodded via e-mail for keeping the project on schedule. This book would not have been possible without the ongoing professional support from Mehdi Khosrow-Pour and Jan Travers at Idea Group Inc.

The idea of editing this volume stems from the initial research work that the editor did in past several years. The assistances and facilities of University of Saskatchewan and Université de Sherbrooke, Canada, Oakland University and Wayne State University, USA, and City University of Hong Kong and Northeastern University, China, are deemed important, and are highly appreciated. The research work of the editor has been supported by the *Program for New Century Excellent Talents in University* (NCET-05-0288) and by the *MOE Funds for Doctoral Programs* (20050145024).

Finally the editor wishes to thank his family for their patience, understanding, encouragement, and support when the editor needed to devote many time in the edition of this book. This book will not be completed without their love.

Zongmin Ma, PhD
Shenyang, China
January 2006

Section I:

Intelligent Information Processing in Databases

Chapter I

Uncovering Hidden Associations Through Negative Itemsets Correlations

Ioannis N. Kouris, University of Patras, Greece

Christos H. Makris, University of Patras, Greece

Athanasios K. Tsakalidis, University of Patras, Greece

Abstract

Most algorithms and approaches dealing with data mining in general and especially those focusing on the task of association rule mining have assumed all items to be only positively correlated, and looked only into the items that remained finally in a shopping basket. Very few works have proposed the existence of negative correlations between items, based though on the absence of items from transactions rather than on their actual removals. In this specific chapter we look into mining that takes into consideration valuable information from rejected items and propose various alternatives for taking the specific items into account efficiently. Finally we provide experimental evidence on the existence and significance of these items.

Introduction

In the last years we have witnessed an explosive growth in the amount of data generated and stored from practically all possible fields (e.g., science, business, medicine, and military, just to name a few). However the ability to store more and more data has not been followed by the same rate of growth as the processing power for evaluating and analyzing it and therefore much of the data accumulated remains unanalyzed still today. Data mining, which could be defined as the process concerned with applying computational techniques (i.e., algorithms implemented as computer programs) to actually find patterns in the data, tries to bridge this gap. Among others, data mining technologies include association rule discovery, classification, clustering, summarization, regression, and sequential pattern discovery (Adrians & Zantige, 1996; Chen, Han, & Yu, 1996; Fayad, Piatetsky-Shapiro, & Smyth, 1996). Mining association rules especially from large databases of business data such as transactions records has been the "hottest" topic in the area of data mining, probably due to its large financial interest. This problem has been motivated by applications known as market basket analysis, which find items purchased by customers; that is what kinds of products tend to be purchased together (Agrawal, Imielinski, & Swami, 1993). Practically, the goal of this task is to find all frequent itemsets above a user speci-fied threshold (called support) and to generate all association rules above another threshold (called confidence) using these frequent itemsets as input. This type of information could be used for catalogue design, store layout, product placement, target marketing, and so forth. The prototypical application of this task has been the market basket analysis, but the specific model is not limited to it since it can be applied to many other domains, for example, with text documents (Holt & Chung, 2001), census data (Brin, Motwani, Ullman, & Tsur, 1997), telecommunication data, medical images, and more. In fact, any data set consisting of "baskets" containing multiple "items" can fit this model. Many solutions have been proposed in the last few years using a sequential or parallel paradigm, experimenting on factors such as memory requirements, I/O scans, dimensionality reduction, and so on.

The specific problem was first introduced by Agrawal et al. (1993) and an algorithm by the name AIS was proposed for effectively addressing it. Agrawal and Srikant (1994) have introduced a much more efficient solution, and two new algorithms by the names Apriori and AprioriTid were proposed. Algorithm Apriori has been and still is a major reference point for all subsequent works. Most algorithms and ap-proaches proposed thereafter focus on either decreasing the number of passes made over the data or at improving the efficiency of those passes (for example, by using additional methods for pruning the number of candidates that have to be counted). Toivonen (1996) proposed a sampling algorithm that required only a pass over the data but at the cost of generating a large number of candidate itemsets that have to be counted (false positives). Brin, Motwanti, Ullman, et al. (1997) proposed algorithm DIC that reduced the number of passes made over the database and at the same time did not suffer from the problem of generating too many candidate itemsets as the work of Toivonen (1996). However its application on synthetic data was not a large improvement. Park, Chen, and Yu (1995a) proposed algorithm DHP that managed to reduce the number of candidate itemsets (especially the 2-itemsets which are critical for performance) by employing a hash table structure. Han, Pei, and Yin (2000) proposed algorithm FP-Growth that managed to alleviate the multi-scan problem and improved the candidate generation process by making use of a compact tree structure for representing frequent patterns. The specific algorithm requires only two full I/O scans of the dataset to build the prefix tree in main memory and then mines this structure directly. Among other things studied in association rule mining are: (1) incremental updating (Cheung, Han, Ng, & Wong, 1996; Lee, Lin, & Chen, 2001), (2) mining of generalized and multi-level rules (Srikant & Agrawal, 1995; Han & Fu, 1995), (3) using multiple minimum supports (Liu et al., 1999a; Wang, He, & Han, 2000), (4) mining of quantitative rules (Srikant & Agrawal, 1996), (5) parallel algorithms (Agrawal & Shafer, 1996; Park, Chen, & Yu, 1995b), and so on.

Lately it has been widely accepted that the model of association rules is either over-simplified or suffers from several omissions that cannot nowadays be considered insignificant (Liu et al., 1999a; Kouris, Makris, & Tsakalidis, 2005). For example, treating the itemsets as mere statistical probabilities and neglecting their real significance, or handling them as Boolean variables and not taking into consideration their exact number of appearances in every transaction, leads to fragmentary and dubious results. In this chapter, we deal with such another important omission, and more specifically with the existence and great significance of negative correlations and relationships between items in a database.

Definition of Association Rule Mining

We give a formal description of the problem of finding association rules based mainly on the statements made by Agrawal et al. (1993) and by Agrawal and Srikant (1994), as well as based on what has been repeated in many works that followed (Brin et al., 1997; Park et al., 1995a; Savasere, Omiecinski, & Navathe, 1995; Srikant & Agrawal, 1995). Let $I=\{i_1,i_2,...,i_m\}$ be a set of literals called items, with m considered to be the dimensionality of the problem. Let D be a set of transactions, where each transaction T is a variable length set of items such that $T \subseteq I$. Since the quantities of items bought in a transaction are not taken into account, each item is a binary variable representing if an item has been bought or not. Each transaction is associated with a unique identifier, called its TID. Consider X to be a set of items in I. A transaction T is said to contain X if and only if $X \subseteq T$. Each itemset has an associated measure of statistical significance called support, which is defined as the fraction of transactions in D containing the specific itemset.

An association rule is an implication of the form $X \rightarrow Y$, where $X,Y \subset I$, and $X \cap Y = \varnothing$. X is called the antecedent and Y is called the consequent of the rule. The rule $X \rightarrow Y$ holds in the transaction set D with confidence c if $c\%$ of transactions in D that contain X also contain Y. The rule $X \rightarrow Y$ has support s in the transaction set D if $s\%$ of transactions in D contain $X \cup Y$. In other words, the support of the rule is the probability that X and Y hold together among all possible presented cases. The confidence of a rule on the other hand is the conditional probability that the consequent Y is true under the condition of the antecedent X. The problem of discovering all association rules from a set of transactions D consists of generating the rules that have a support and confidence greater than a given threshold. The association rules mining task can be decomposed into two main steps:

1. Generate all frequent itemsets that satisfy *minsup*.
2. Generate all association rules that satisfy *minconf* using the frequent itemsets as input.

The step that is particularly computationally expensive is the first step due to the number of possible itemsets that have to be counted. The second step on the other hand is fairly straightforward but can nevertheless present difficulties at few situations (e.g., when the number of frequent itemsets or the number of discovered rules is too big).

Negative Association Rules

Whilst the positive association rules handle the existence of items within the transactions, the negative ones deal also with the absence of items. For example a positive association rule would handle all transactions containing beers and chips and would generate all corresponding association rules. An approach dealing with negative association rules on the other hand would also consider rules such as: those that buy beer buy also chips, but not dry fruits (*beer* $\rightarrow$ *chips* $\wedge \neg$ *dry fruits*), or those that buy beer but not wine buy also chips (*beer* $\wedge \neg$ *wine* $\rightarrow$ *chips*). The measures used for determining the strength of a correlation and for pruning the insignificant ones are again the support and confidence metrics.

A generalized negative association rule can include various negated and positive items (i.e., items existing and items absent from transactions) either in its antecedent or in its consequent. An example of such a rule would be: $A \wedge \neg C \wedge \neg F \wedge W \rightarrow B \wedge \neg D$. However the obvious insurmountable obstacle created by such contemplation is the number of possible itemsets that would have to be generated and counted as well as the number of rules created, since apart from the existing items we would have to consider all possible absent items and their combinations. Most approaches thus far have made various assumptions in order to come to approximate solutions, working on subsets of the problem of generalized association rules. For example considering rules where the entire consequent or antecedent could be a conjunction of similar items (i.e., negated or non-negated), or considering negative rules only in the infrequent items. Nevertheless the absence of an item from a transaction does not necessarily imply direct negative correlation between items, but could be attributed to factors such as mere luck or coincidence.

Motivation

Our work deals with efficient discovery and maintenance of negative association rules. When we talk about negative association rules we mean association rules that model negative relationships between itemsets; that is rules implying that the occurrence of some itemsets are characterized also by the removal of others.

Negative association rules can be useful in market-basket analysis to identify products that conflict with each other or products that complement each other and can also be very convenient for the building and maintenance of classifiers that base their classification model on association rules. Many other applications would benefit from negative association rules; for example in Brin, Motwani, and Silverstein (1997) it is mentioned that fire code inspectors trying to mine useful fire prevention measures might like to know of any negative correlations between certain types of electrical wiring and the occurrence of fires. As has already been mentioned, a major weakness of the classical association rules model, if we try to extend it in order to capture and record negative association rules, is that it can not model efficiently the negative associations that may exist between a set of different items, since in this case the number of possibilities would increase exponentially. Moreover, some of these patterns may not even appear in the transactions. The reason for this is that while generating candidate itemsets in association rules mining, it would be necessary to consider not only the positive patterns, but also the negative ones since each positive pattern of length k gives rise to $O(k)$ negative patterns, making the search space exponentially larger. Hence, the problem is quite difficult and we need to come up with a subset of the negative association rules that could be of special significance to the data miner.

The main contributions of this work are as follows:

1.   We try to face the difficulty in phrasing negative association rules by exploiting the information provided to us by items that are removed from a transaction; we call these items negative items and treat them as independent and autonomous entities.

2.   We present a set of algorithms for dealing with these "negative" items, in the association rule mining discovery process.

Hence, trying to formulate the model more typically, we are following the notation described in the section Definition of association rule mining with the following differences: (1) the set $I=\{i_1,i_2,\ldots,i_m\}$ of literals is expanded to a larger set $I'=\{ i_1,i_2,\ldots,i_m, {}_-i_1,-i_2,\ldots,-i_m \}$ where $-i_k$ designates a negative item, (2) each transaction can contain various items from the set I and it can also contain negative items, where the presence of a negative item designates the removal of the respective item.

Our purpose is to come up with meaningful association rules that can also contain negative items. The presence of a negative item in a rule carries the same semantic as that described in the previous section entitled *Negative Association Rules*.

Problem Statement

Current electronic shops and their corresponding database systems only keep track of sold items in every transaction. More specifically they store for every transaction a unique transaction identifier (noted as *TID*), the date and sometimes even the exact time of the purchase and finally the unique ids (in the form of bar codes) of the items purchased. The systems used up to now did not store something regarding items that inserted a specific basket but for some reason were removed during the subsequent purchases by the customers. These items, though, contain valuable knowledge that is unfortunately neglected by current approaches and systems. As we will show later in this chapter, items present not only positive influence and correlations to one another but also negative influence (i.e., the presence of one item influences negatively the presence of another one). For example, suppose that a customer of an electronic shop has already put items A, D, E, and F in his basket. The system now based on these items decides to propose item I to the specific customer, who then decides to remove product D from it. This is some indication that items I and D are in fact negatively correlated, or maybe that there is some conflict with one or more items already present in the specific basket. The question now is how can one quantify that information and subsequently how can it be used effectively?

The answer to the first part of this question is fairly simple and can be derived from a simple statistic analysis of the data gathered during these removals the same way it was done for frequent itemsets. More specifically, does this situation appear more than some number of times or does it satisfy some specific criterion (e.g., like the support threshold)? The second part of the question is not so trivial and must be addressed through the application or the nature of the system where such a procedure is operated. According to Kleinberg, Papadimitriou, and Raghavan

(1998), "a pattern in the data is interesting only to the extent in which it can be used in the decision-making process of the enterprise to increase utility". So the utility of extracted patterns (such as association rules and correlations) in the decision-making process of an enterprise can only be addressed within the microeconomic framework of the enterprise. To put it in a more practical way, are we operating for example inside a retail firm where the first priority is usually the maximization of the net profits or in some other form of organization or application with different priorities and goals?

In this work current systems are expanded in order to be able to collect information that was left unused, and to deliver new information to the data miners. In order to provide a better presentation of the proposed technique, we use as a working example throughout this chapter the case of a retail firm selling commercial goods to its customers, which primary goal is to maximize the profits made. Both approaches that are proposed below have as an essential part the storing of items that were initially in a shopping basket but were removed from it. They differ in the way this information is stored and processed by the end users. Such information is only available in a Web store, or more generally in a store servicing its customers entirely electronically since it is very difficult to keep track and to store such information in a physical shop.

The remainder of this chapter is organized as follows: in the first section, *Relevant Works*, we give a brief overview of two approaches which serve as basis for our proposals. In the following two sections we propose first an approach for handling these items that is based on the classic two stepped model of mining association rules and then, *Indexing Negative and Positive Items*, an alternative approach based on the use of information retrieval techniques in solving such problems. The experimental methodology as well as its results are given in the *Experimental Results* section and we conclude with the final section where we discuss some issues and highlight future research directions.

Relevant Works

Despite the fact that the existence and significance of negative association rules has been recognized for quite some time, comparably a very small percentage of researchers have engaged with it. To our knowledge Brin, Motwani, and Silverstein (1997) were among the first that have brought up and addressed the existence of negative relationships between items, by using a chi-squared test for correlations derived from statistics. Subsequently Savasere et al. (1998) and Yuan, Buckles, Yuan, and Zhang (2002) have proposed two similar approaches, which tried to discover strong negative associations depending heavily on domain knowledge and predefined taxonomies. Another work was that of Wu, Zhang, and Zhang (2002), which used, in addition to the support and confidence measure, a measure for more efficient pruning of the frequent itemsets generated called *mininterest*. Thiruvady and Webb (2004) proposed an extension of Generalized Rule Discovery — GRD algorithm (Webb, 2000) for mining negative rules. The proposed algorithm did not require the use of any minimum support threshold, but rather the specification of any interestingness measure along with a constraint upon the number of rules that would be finally generated. Finally Antonie and Zaiane (2004) proposed an algorithm for finding generalized association rules, where the entire antecedent or consequent consists of similar items (i.e., only negative or only positive items), thus generating only a subset of negative rules that they refer to as confined negative association rules. In their work they used, in addition to the minimum support and minimum confidence measures, the correlation threshold as a third parameter. In the same context can also be considered works dealing with unexpected patterns (also known as surprising patterns), where the negative items can be thought as such patterns (e.g., Liu, Lu, Feng, & Hussain, 1999; Hwang, Ho, & Tang, 1999; Hussain, Liu, Suzuki, & Lu, 2000; Suzuki & Shimura, 1996; Suzuki, 1997; Padmanabhan & Tuzhilin, 2000, 1998). Last but not least is the most recent work of Arunasalam, Chawla, and Sun (2005) that propose an efficient algorithm for mining both positive and negative patterns in large spatial databases (i.e., databases where objects are characterized by some spatial attributes like location or coordinates).

Our proposal, despite the fact that we also try to discover the existence of negative relationships between items, deviates and in a sense extends these works. Instead of considering rules stemming from itemsets where the absence of an item implies a negative relationship we consider itemsets where the conflict between items is recorded in the form of an item removal. In this way: (1) we transform the problem into a form that can be handled, without incurring an exponential increase in the search space, (2) we can handle the negative associations rule problem by using classical techniques, just by handling each negative item as an autonomous item. Below we briefly present two classical data mining approaches, described because they serve as a basis in our proposals for solving the specific problem.

Algorithm MSApriori

Apriori-like algorithms that use the single minimum support measure for all items in a database cannot assess the differences that exist among the various items (with most important the widely varied frequencies between them). Frequent items are not always important whereas the rare ones are sometimes very significant (e.g., when they present very large profits). Setting the support to a large value rules out all such rare itemsets while when setting it to a low value, not only the significant rare data but also all other data that satisfy the low minimum support would also be discovered, and the rare itemset problem where all the data satisfying the minimum support become associated with one another would take place (Mannila, 1998). Liu et al. (1999a) suggested algorithm MSApriori in order to identify all rare but important itemsets along with the frequent itemsets without encountering the problems just described.

To encompass the importance of data, Algorithm MSApriori employs minimum item support (*MIS*), the minimum support of each data item. A very important itemset will enjoy a small *MIS* value while an unimportant one a large value. That way we try to make sure that important itemsets will be identified irrespectively what their frequency is as compared to the frequencies of other itemsets in the database. The *MIS* for every 1-itemset i is expressed as *MIS*(*i*), and is calculated using the following formula:

$$MIS(i) = \begin{cases} M(i) & M(i) > LS \\ LS & Otherwise \end{cases}$$

$$M(i) = \beta \cdot f(i)$$

equation (1)

Where $f(i)$ is the actual frequency of an item in the dataset, *LS* is a user defined lowest minimum item support allowed and β is a parameter that controls how the *MIS* values should be related to their frequencies. Algorithm MSApriori also works level-wise, i.e., by finding the frequent itemsets at every step then using these frequent itemsets to generate the candidate itemsets of the next step, finding the frequent ones and so on. All higher order itemsets now (i.e., k-itemsets, where $k>1$) take as MIS value the least MIS value among the MIS values of the data items that compose an itemset. Namely, the minimum support for itemset $i_{1,2,...,m}$ is equal to $min[MIS(i_1), MIS(i_2),...,MIS(i_m)]$. So if all items within an itemset occur frequently then a high *MIS* value will be assigned while if there exists even one 1-itemset that occurs rarely then a low *MIS* value will be assigned so that the rules corresponding to that itemset will be found. Of course assigning every itemset a different *MIS* value means that the downward closure property that prunes itemsets in the single support algorithms no longer holds. This problem is nevertheless solved by introducing and using the sorted closure property, where the 1-items are sorted according to their *MIS* values in ascending order and also all items within every itemset are sorted according to their *MIS* values.

Using Information Retrieval Techniques

Kouris et al. (2005) have proposed a completely different view in the problem of data mining and have followed a novel approach. More specifically, instead of viewing association rules and the database as something static and off-line, a system using IR (information retrieval) techniques acting as a search engine has been proposed. Among the problems solved by this system, was that of scalability (the techniques borrowed from IR were used with great success for many years in much larger and complex collections), that of neglecting the real significance of items and also that of neglecting the number of appearances of the items in every transaction, as well as that arising from shortcomings of the support and confidence measures. The specific system offered a wide variety of services but we will briefly present only the ranked queries scenario as it is used for our purposes too.

The whole procedure is very simple and conceptually could be divided into three subparts. First an index is created with the existing transactions as we would do with a collection of documents, using inverted files. Each transaction t is a set of items. All 1-items are modelled in an m-dimensional Euclidean space where each dimension corresponds to a 1-item. Consequently every transaction is represented as a vector in this space. The coordinate of a transaction t in the direction corresponding to an item i is determined by two quantities, namely the item weight and the intratransaction item frequency. The item weight tries to simulate the importance the data miner gives to an item i and has a similar function as the *IDF* factor in the *TFIDF* scheme (Witten, Moffat, & Bell, 1999). An important item will enjoy a large weight whereas an unimportant one a very small weight. The formula used for determining the item weight is the following:

$$w_i = \ln\left(1.718 + \frac{f_i \cdot PM_i}{\max TP_k} \right)$$

formula (1)

where *maxTPk* is the maximum total profits we have from an item in our database, f_i is the number of appearances of item i, and *PM* is the profit margin of item i. The intratransaction itemset frequency component $itf_{t,i}$ in essence controls how the appearances of the items within the transactions are going to be evaluated. This number has a similar function as the *TF* component of the *TFIDF* scheme (Witten et al., 1999), and is given by the following formula:

$$itf_{t,i} = \ln\left(K + (1-K)\frac{f_{t,i}}{\max_c f_{t,c}} \right)$$

formula (2)

Variable K is a tuning constant that controls the balance between the first and all later appearances of an item in a transaction, $f_{t,i}$ is the number of appearances of term i in transaction t and the factor $maxcf_{t,c}$ is the maximum frequency of any term in transaction *t*. The vector of a transaction *t* in the direction of an item *i* is then calculated as follows:

$$w_{t,i} = itf_{t,i} \cdot w_i$$ formula (3)

After all existing transactions have been indexed then every new transaction a user makes is a ranked query which is transformed to a vector in the same space as the existing transactions and is passed to our system. The vector of a query *q* in the direction of an item *i* is calculated as follows:

$$w_{q,i} = itf_{q,i} \cdot w_i$$ formula (4)

The $itf_{q,i}$ component is given by the same formula as the $itf_{t,i}$ component above. Every time a customer adds a new product to his basket then this forms a new ranked query and is issued again to our system. The final part now is to measure the proximity between the vector $\vec{q}$ of our query and the vectors $\vec{d}$ of all transactions in our index, find the closest ones and return to the user the items he is most probable to buy. In calculating the proximity we use the widely used cosine measure which is given by the following formula:

$$\cos(Q, D_d) = \frac{1}{W_d W_q} \sum_{t \in Q \cap D_d} (1 + \log_e f_{d,t}) \cdot w_{d,t}$$ formula (5)

According to the cosine measure we try to find the cosine of the angle between the query vector $\vec{q}$ and every relevant document vector $\vec{d}$. The larger the cosine value the greater the similarity. Of course unlike the indexes comprising of documents or Web pages where the users issued a query and they would be presented with the most relevant documents or pages to choose from, in our case we are not interested in transactions proposals but rather in items proposals. In practice we might be searching for the most relevant transaction/s but finally we want to propose to the users the items that they are most probable to buy. So two alternative strategies could be followed in this final recommendation phase. Either we look only into the highest ranked transaction and from that propose the most relevant items (after we have also ranked the items according to how important they are based on their weights and their exact number of appearances), or we can look at a number of the subsequent transactions and from each propose some of the first most important items (again after we have ranked the specific items also).

Suppose for example that the system based on the items inside a transaction proposes as most relevant the following transaction (where every tuple contains first the item and then the number of times it appears in the specific transaction): <(A,2), (C,2), (E,7)>. If the weights of the specific items are w_A=0,2, w_C=0,5 and w_E=0,1 then the multiplication of the weight of every item with its number of appearances would rank them as follows: [C, E, A], and this would be the order that they would be presented to the user. In the second strategy the exact same procedure is followed but this time we also rank the items chosen from the subsequent transactions.

Searching for Negative Associations Between Itemsets

The approach presented in this section is based on the classic two stepped model of association rules; that is find all frequent itemsets that satisfy some support threshold and then use these itemsets to generate all association rules that satisfy some confidence threshold. The first issue that has to be addressed is how the data is going to be stored and processed in the database. Consequently, for every item being removed from a basket we do not remove it from the transaction but we mark it in some way (the specific way this marking is performed depends on the system and the application we use). This removed element is depicted by putting a minus sign before it. For example suppose we have transaction A C F V and we decide to remove item F. Then the specific transaction becomes A C V-F (of course if an item is removed, and later comes back into the transaction then we keep only its positive appearance). An item having a minus sign before it in a transaction is considered as being different from the normal item (i.e., item F is different from item -F) and is called a negative item. The number of negative items in a database can be as high as the number of the positive ones. Finally the number of appearances of a positive item is called the positive count whereas that of a negative one the negative count.

In terms of significance and interactions, we view and process the removed items the same way we treat the remaining ones. More specifically in the approaches up to now we treated every item being left inside a transaction as interacting with all the other items inside the same transaction, no matter whether they were bought before or after it. The same is applied for the removed items (i.e., they are negatively correlated with all other items present in the basket).

Finally as far as the final phase of generating the corresponding rules after having found all frequent itemsets is concerned, according to the systems proposed up to now the proposal of an item based on the itemsets already in a shopping basket was dictated based only on pure statistical criteria (i.e., which item appears most with the itemsets inside a shopping basket). In our case though we take into consideration also the fact that the proposal of an itemset can indeed trigger the removal of another one. Hence, in order to minimize the losses incurred by such a case the new item must be at least as significant as the removed one. For the case of a retail firm that we use as a working example throughout this chapter this would simply mean that we have to make sure that the item proposed must present at least the same net profits as the item that might be removed.

Handling Negative and Positive Itemsets as Different Entities

All items, negative and positive are processed as a whole. We make a first pass over the data where we count the number of appearances of all 1-items and we treat the negative itemsets as separate entities. More specifically we view item -i as a completely different item from item +i. Accordingly the data is processed using an algorithm which is a variation of algorithm MSApriori (Liu et al., 1999a), where we do not pre-assign mis values to any of the 1-items before even running our algorithm as it was done with the classic MSApriori, but we wait until we have made one pass over the data. Our algorithm does not need any mis values for the 1-items until the end of the first pass, and so at the end of that pass when we know the counts for all 1-items we assign the corresponding mis values using the following equation:

$$mis(\pm i) = \begin{cases} \min\sup & \forall \pm i, if & count(\pm i) \geq \min\sup \\ \\ \dfrac{count(-i)}{r} & \forall -i, if & count(-i) \leq \min\sup\ and\ count(-i) \geq \dfrac{count(i)}{r} \end{cases}$$

equation (2)

Every negative or positive 1-item that has a count at least equal to the minimum support value takes as *mis* value the minimum support. Every negative 1-item that has a count below the minimum support value but above the ratio of the count of its corresponding positive itemset divided by a constant r takes as mis value its own count divided by the same constant r. That way the mis value and subsequently the significance of a negative item depend directly upon the count of the corresponding positive item. If we would have used a second lower support value for all the negative items then we would have missed the relation between the negative and corresponding positive item. This can be seen better through an example. Suppose we have a database with 1000 transactions and we decided to use two minimum support thresholds one for the positive and one for the negative items instead of equation (2). Suppose we have set the "positive" threshold equal to 10% and the "negative" to 1%. Suppose also we have item A appearing in 600 transactions and its corresponding negative item –A appearing in only 12. Then both items would have been frequent (sup(A)=600>100 and sup(-A)=12>10). Nevertheless the number of appearances of –A compared to that of A (i.e., only 12 as compared to 600) suggest that we should not take it into consideration since they are insignificant. Having used our method with r value set to 10 then item –A must have appeared in at least 60 transactions in order to be considered significant. The choice of the r value is a subjective decision, depending on the needs of the data miner. All other items that satisfy neither of the two conditions are simply infrequent (or practically unimportant) and are thus immediately pruned. Subsequently all 1-items are sorted in ascending order according to their mis values and from that point after our algorithm proceeds exactly like algorithm MSApriori.

This procedure has as an effect the increase of the number of distinct 1-items, which in the worst case can be as high as the number of positive 1-items. Nevertheless in practice the removed 1-items (i.e., the negative) that are finally also interesting (i.e., above a user specified minimum) are extremely few and so the total number of distinct 1-items is not comparably too big.

Generating Rules

After all frequent itemsets have been found the next step is the use of these items for generating the corresponding association rules. In our case though, where we have both positive and negative itemsets things are more complicated.

We will use the property that for a given frequent itemset, if a rule with consequent c holds then so do rules with consequents that are subsets of c. Thus if for example the rule $AB \rightarrow CD$ holds, then the rules $ABC \rightarrow D$ and $ABD \rightarrow C$ must also hold. Using both negative and positive itemsets as input we first generate all rules with one item in the consequent that satisfy the minimum confidence, then all rules with two items in the consequent, three items, and so on. At each step, before going into the next one (i.e., from rules with one item in the consequent to rules with two items in the consequent) we employ an additional pruning procedure for our case, where we prune all "kindred" rules.

Procedure kill_kindred-rules

Kindred rules are those rules that have the same antecedent but their consequent differ in only one item, which is also a negative item. This procedure is applied in order to remove all contradicting rules (e.g., a rule that suggests that the user should choose a specific item and one that suggests exactly the opposite). Hence, for every

Figure 1. Algorithm for generating all association rules

```
1.              Database=set of transactions;
2.              Items=set of items;
3.       forall  frequent k-itemsets l_k, k>=2 do begin
4.              H_1={consequents of rules derived from l_k with one item in the consequent};
5.              call ap-genrules (l_k, H_1);
6.              call minimize-losses
7.       End
8.
9.       Procedure ap-genrules (l_k: frequent k-itemset, H_m: set of m-item consequents)
10.             If (k > m+1) then begin
11.                 H_{m+1}=apriori-gen (H_m);            /* refer to Agrawal & Srikant (1994) */
12.                 forall h_{m+1} ∈ H_{m+1} do begin
13.                     conf = support (l_k)/support (l_k-h_{m+1});
14.                     if (conf ≥ minconf) then
15.                         output the rule (l_k-h_{m+1}) → h_{m+1} with confidence = conf and support =
                    support(l_k);
16.                     Else
17.                         delete h_{m+1} from H_{m+1};
18.                 End
19.             call kill_kindred-rules
20.             call minimize-losses
21.             call ap-genrules(l_k, H_{m+1})
22.       End
```

two such rules we check the support ratio of the positive rule to the negative one. Suppose for example we have the rule AB → F and AB → -F. Both rules have the same antecedent (i.e., AB) but differ in their consequent (i.e., F vs. –F). What we do then is we check the ratio sup(A∪B∪F)/sup(A∪B∪-F). If this ratio is above 1, then we keep the positive rule after we have updated its confidence as follows:

$$P(AB \to F) = \left[\frac{S(A \cup B \cup F) - S(A \cup B \cup -F)}{S(A \cup B)} \right]$$

formula (6)

In other words we remove the negative rule as less powerful but at the same time we take it into consideration by reducing the importance (i.e., the confidence) of the positive one. The opposite procedure is applied when this ratio is below 1, where we keep the negative rule after we have also updated its confidence as follows:

$$P(AB \rightarrow -F) = \left[\frac{S(A \cup B \cup -F) - S(A \cup B \cup F)}{S(A \cup B)} \right]$$

formula (7)

Finally, if the specific ratio is equal to 1 then we remove both rules, since practically, the specific item presents a 50-50% probability to remain or be later removed from the transaction and so we should better propose the next best item. All other rules remain as they are and we move into the next step where we generate all consequents with two itemsets than can appear from the rules of the previous step. Again we perform the same update step and so on until we have generated all possible rules.

Procedure minimize-losses

After we have generated all possible rules and have pruned all the contradicting kindred ones, we employ the next pruning step. According to this step we try to minimize the losses incurred in any possible itemset suggestion. As stated previously (see section *Searching for Negative Associations Between Itemsets*) a new itemset proposed must be at least as significant as the itemsets already in a transaction and that are probable to be removed. It is no use to propose new items all the time (practically, to try to sell more and more items to a customer) if these new items might trigger the removal of the ones already in a transaction. Or, at least, the new items must be as important as the ones that might be removed so that finally we do not incur any losses. So for every rule having in its consequent only positive items, we generate all possible combinations of the antecedent (that is by changing one positive item at a time) with the same consequent and check the support of these items. Suppose we have the rule $AB \rightarrow Z$. What we check is the support of itemset {ABZ} compared to {-ABZ} and also that of {A-BZ} (we do not check also itemset {-A-BZ} because we consider that at any time only one item can change status i.e., only one removal can take place). If its support is larger than the supports of both items then we use this rule. If, on the other hand, the support of {ABZ} is smaller or equal to either {-ABZ} or {A-BZ} then we check the net profits of item Z to that of A and B (in the case we assume we are operating in a retail firm which primary goal are the net profits). If it is at least equal to both of them, then again we keep the rule ABZ whereas in the opposite case we remove it. That way we make sure that even if the item that we propose triggers the removal of one of those already in our basket, we will still gain. Practically we try to make all possible itemsets proposals a win-win situation for the company or the organization using such a system.

Indexing Negative and Positive Items

Kouris et al. (2005) have proposed a system that among other problems also solved those created by having too many distinct items by making use of information retrieval techniques. Following the specific work and in order to be able to include as much information as possible since especially in this case the existence of the negative items in addition to the positive ones can act as a bottleneck to any algorithm or system used, we propose three alternatives all having as their base the specific system. The first two alternatives try to embed the negative items into the indexing process either by modifying properly the weights corresponding to the respective positive items or by treating the negative items as distinct entities (artificial items) that also get indexed; this second alternative thus follows the negative association rules discovery process described previously where the negative items were treated as distinct, autonomous entities.   The third alternative avoids the engagement of negative items into the indexing process, and simply uses the negative items as triggers for proposing to the customers items that may fill their needs; that is, the third alternative does not store any information when items are removed but it is suitably designed so that it can respond to such user operations, by treating them as a negative feedback operation. The first two approaches are presented in the next subsection entitled *Normal Indexing* while the third approach is presented in the section entitled *Immediate Use of Negative Itemsets.*

Normal Indexing

The user is presented with two options regarding the negative and positive items. Either he can embody the negative occurrences of an item into its positive occurrences (for example by maintaining a global counter that is increased whenever a positive occurrence takes place and decreases whenever a negative occurrence takes place), or he can treat the negative and positive occurrences of an item as distinct quantities and index them both. The differences are obvious. In the first case we would create a system with less complexity leading to faster answers but at the cost of being less accurate. Also in its creation (i.e., in creating the index from our database) the time and resources required would be much less. In the second case, since more information is exploited, we could expect that the system will function more accurately requiring however when being maintained and created more time, space, and cpu resources.

Let's consider the first option, that of embodying the negative items into the positive ones. What changes is first of all the first step which consists of assigning every item a weight. The formula used in (Kouris et al., 2005) (see also formula [1]) now becomes:

$$w_i = \ln\left(1.718 + \frac{(f_{+i} - f_{-i}) \cdot PM_i}{\max TP_k}\right)$$

formula (8)

where from the number of appearances of the positive itemset (f_{+i}) we subtract those of the negative one (f_{-i}). For the difference f_{+i}-f_{-i} we use as a lower bound the value 0. The intratransaction itemset frequency formula (see formula [2]) remains exactly the same by supposing that even if an item was removed and later on entered again the transaction or vice versa, we take into consideration and store only its final status. The next steps remain also the same as in Kouris et al. (2005) that is again every transaction is transformed into a ranked query and is issued to our system that matches it against all existing transactions. The similarity measure used is also the cosine measure. In the last and final phase, that of recommending the most important items from the relevant transactions, we have a minor change. Let's consider the case where from the most relevant transaction we rank all items according to how important they are based on their number of appearances and their assigned weights. Suppose that we have already itemsets A, -B, C, and D in our basket. This is issued as a ranked query to our system which based on these items returns the following transaction as most relevant {B, D, E, F}. All items could be just ranked according to how important they are and then presented to the user apart from item B, which appears to have been removed from our current transaction but is among the proposed ones. Subsequently the user could follow two different strategies with such items. The most trivial one would be to exempt it from the final proposals as the user has already removed it in the past. Another strategy, though, would be if we proposed it to the user supposing that he might reconsider his initial decision to remove it. In our opinion, the first strategy is the most logical one since the matching of our transaction to all existing transactions was made based also on the removed items. The fact that the highest ranked transaction/s might also include some removed items as positive items (i.e., not removed) might occur due to other reasons like for example the specific transaction might include too many important positive items. Also, this might result in annoying the user or even evolve into lack of confidence to a system that insists on proposing items that he or she alone previously removed. This procedure is followed also in the case where we use the second strategy for recommending items, which is to check also some of the subsequent transactions returned (see section *Using Information Retrieval Techniques*).

In the second option, now, where the negative and positive itemsets are treated as different entities and are indexed separately, things are a less complicated. Both formulae, that for finding the itemset weight and that for finding the intratransaction itemset frequency remain the same as in Kouris et al. (2005). Also the way the existing transactions as well as the new ones (i.e., the ranked queries) are transformed into corresponding vectors remain also the same. The same holds also for the calculation of the proximity between them since we use again the cosine measure. What changes in this case is only the final recommendation phase. So in this case we can have negative items also among the proposed items, since negative items get also indexed. Suppose we have in our basket items A, -B, C, and D and the most relevant transaction returned contains items -A, B, D, E, and F. All items are handled as in the previous system (that is they are ranked according to their importance apart from item B which is exempted as it had been removed in the past by the user) and the only difference appears with item A which had remained in our current transaction but in the proposed one is being removed. Naturally we simply exempt the specific item also since it does not make any sense to suggest to the user to remove an item he still has in his basket. After all in the end we are trying to sell more items, not to remove the existing ones. The same is applied in the case we look into the subsequent transactions.

Immediate Use of Negative Itemsets

In order to be able to take the existence of negative items into consideration and to present some justifiable suggestions to the users, such data must be readily available. However, as noted in the beginning, no system or company that we are aware of keeps track of this kind of information. Only in very few cases such information could be extracted or inferred from other sources but again the resulting data would be of questionable quality and integrity, leading to dubious results. On the other hand, even if one decided to store that information, he would have to wait for considerable time before gathering the required amount of data in order to get some meaningful conclusions. This time depends on various parameters such as the sector where a company or an organization operates in their sizes as well as on the nature of the application implemented. If we view the negative items as products just entering the market and try to compare their sales to that of products that are years on the market, then we understand that the time required to assembly enough data might be particularly long, forcing all the approaches proposed above to remain in disuse for that period. The heuristic that we propose in this subsection manages to tackle this obstacle in that it allows the user to start taking into consideration the existence of the negative items immediately, by making use of a relevance feedback mechanism into an indexing system. Let's see how.

First of all the database is indexed using the same system as that used in (Kouris et al., 2005). Since we suppose that in the data we have thus far there do not exist any negative items, the index created will consist of only positive items. Suppose now that we follow the ranked queries scenario where every new transaction a customer makes is a ranked query issued to our system which subsequently matches it against the existing transactions and the most relevant ones are returned. Every time a new item is added to a transaction, then this constitutes a new ranked query issued again to our system and so on and so forth. In the case we have only positive itemsets (i.e., we do not have any removals from a transaction) then the procedure followed is that described above. What happens though when one or more items are removed from a transaction? In that case the system considers this action as a negative relevance feedback from the user regarding the specific item, the same way a collaborative filtering system uses an implicit voting system (see Breese, Heckerman, & Kadie, 1998). In an implicit voting system we interpret user-behavior or selections to impute vote or preference by using various types of information access patterns (like for example browsing data). Nevertheless in the case of such a system a completely different procedure and philosophy is followed leading to different suggestions made (practically we try to match user profiles whereas in our case we try to match transactions). Even so the votes like in our case the negative itemsets must be readily available, otherwise the user must again wait for a considerable period of time to gather the required data. So the use of such a system is not feasible for our purposes. On the other hand, relevance feedback has been a very successful technique for refining the results returned to a user's query and adjusting the corresponding ranks to the user's special tastes without the need of previously gathered information. In a relevance feedback system the initial ranked responses are presented together with a rating form (a simple binary useful/useless opinion is all that is asked for), the system reads the responses and feeds it back to the system and the new reformed answers are returned. In such a system the user can express either positive or negative preference.

So in our case we view the removal of an itemset as a "dissatisfaction vote" the same way it was viewed in a collaborative filtering implicit voting system but try to use it through a relevance feedback mechanism. Using a modified version of Rocchio's method (Buckley, Salton, & Allan, 1994; Buckley, Salton, Allan, & Singhal, 1994) for folding in user feedback, the query (i.e., the transaction) is reformulated and fed back to our system according to the following formula:

$$\vec{q}\,' = \alpha\vec{q} - \gamma\sum\vec{d}$$

According to this formula the new query vector $\vec{q}'$ is calculated by subtracting from the original query vector $\vec{q}$ a weighted sum of the vectors corresponding to the removed items. The values for the constants α and γ are usually set equal to 8 and 4 respectively as these values were determined reasonable also in TREC[1] 2. By the time enough data is gathered, the user is free to start using any of the approaches presented above or to keep using the specific approach.

A system like the one in Kouris et al. (2005) would have treated the removal of an item from a transaction as a simple absence, and also no new query would have been issued. That is if for example a user had items A, B, and D in his basket and then decided to remove item B then no new query would have been issued. But even if the system issued a new query it would consist of items A and D. With our approach though apart from trying to match the remaining items as accurately as possible to the existing transactions that contain the same items, we also try to "move away" as far as possible from those transactions that contain the removed items. This has as a result the generation of completely different suggestions.

Experimental Results

This section gives a brief presentation of the experiments made in order to explore and verify the validity of the suggestions made regarding the existence and significance of the negative relations between items, since this was our main concern and not the performance evaluation of the proposed algorithms for addressing it. In most works up to now experiments involving association rules are made using either synthetic data created using the synthetic data generator available from IBM,[2] or by using real data. In this case however both solutions provided no viable way for evaluating the proposed approaches. So we conducted experiments using a set of subjects, using an experimental methodology that was hypothesis driven rather than hypothesis generating.

Volunteers and Experiment Setup

For the qualitative evaluation of the approaches we used a rather reverse approach. Normally in the methods and algorithms proposed in the literature up to now we would process some data, either synthetic or real, accumulated in the past through some system, and try to extract patterns and rules that confirm our suggestions. In our case though first of all there does not exist such data since no system or company that we are aware of keeps track of the information when itemsets leave a transaction. They only keep track of the itemsets that finally remained in a transaction. On the other hand since we expect the removals to be rarer than the final purchases of itemsets but indeed very important, even if we set up a fictitious Web store and try to find such rules we would require immense amounts of data in order to come to a justified conclusion. So we decided to identify and preordain a specific rule and try to prove its validity. In that direction we worked as follows.

First we begun talks with employees from various companies and from various posts (but mainly from the sales department) trying to get their opinion on such rules. Then we begun observing customers in several stores (mostly in those selling electronics) trying to discover a buying pattern that could fit into our hypothesis. Accordingly, we concluded the following observation. Customers that buy a cellular phone, especially those that buy an expensive one, immediately chose also an expensive leather case for their phone. However in their way to the cash register when their eye fell on an offer selling an inexpensive plastic case along with a set of hands-free device most of them would return the expensive leather case and would take instead the offer[3]. When the offer was removed from their immediate eyeshot then they would proceed with their initial choice of products. So we decided to replicate this setting in the artificial environment of a Web store.

Our experiment was carried out as follows. We formed two sets of people, 100 persons each. Both sets of people consisted of people in the age of 18 to 25 years old all studying at the same university and at the same department. All of them were technology savvy quite familiar with the computers and the Internet and had a cell phone and/or have visited a store selling them at a percentage almost 100%. Accordingly, we built a fictitious Web store selling a range of specific expensive cell phones and some accessories. The products, their names and most of the prices used in our Web store were real. The people in both sets were unaware of the purpose of the experiment so that they would make all buys uninfluenced and only knew that they had a specific amount of money to spend. This amount was determined after actually asking all people what they were willing to spent or have spent in the near past on buying such a product and calculating an average.

Consequently the test was implemented as follows. Both sets of people had to choose first a cell phone. Immediately the system recommended them also the expensive leather case. The cost of these two items was chosen so that it was almost equal to the amount of money they had to spend in total. We then had the first set of people not getting any more recommendations while the second one getting as a recommendation an offer including a plastic case along with a hands-free set. The cost of this set was chosen so that it was equal to the cost of the leather case in order to make the choice of either item money-independent. The results were astonishing. First we found that most people from both sets indeed chose the cell phone along with the leather case as their initial purchase (at a percent of 80%). In the first set of people the remaining 20% simply requested some other product. In the second set of customers where our main interest was, we found out that of this 80% only a 10% kept their initial purchases until the check out whereas a 67% replaced the leather case with the offer. The rest 3% for some strange reason decided to request an alternative accessory after having being recommended the offer. So we can safely conclude that our initial hypothesis that the itemsets can be negatively correlated was indeed confirmed. A system not having taken into consideration the existence and significance of negative relations between itemsets would have never identified this relation as well as any similar ones. In a real environment one would have then to decide whether he would chose to propose the plastic case along with the hands-free or not based probably on the net profits either product would produce.

Conclusion and Future Work

We have managed to prove using a rather unorthodox and bizarre setting the existence of the negative itemsets. Unfortunately the nature of the problem as well as the fact that it has not been proposed previously prohibited us from finding and using real data. In a real environment with hundreds of items and most importantly with thousands or even millions of customers and transactions we are confident that there would be uncovered many more such cases with even strangest findings regarding negative relationships between itemsets. Therefore it would be very interesting to attempt to come in contact and convince some company to store such data so that extensive experiments could be performed on a real environment. Of course this will be a very difficult task since even if one got over all the commercial, legal and privacy inhibitions of the companies he would still have to accumulate data corresponding to at least a couple of years of sales in order to come to some meaningful and quantifiable suggestions.

The solution that used relevance feedback methods into an indexing system apart from the fact that managed to give a way of immediately taking into consideration the existence of negative itemsets was also a small step for the work in Kouris et al. (2005). More specifically despite the fact that the use of relevance feedback methods has also been proposed by the specific researches nevertheless they avoided using it for various reasons the most important of which was the weakness to capture the users preferences. As they state it: "Even if the answer returned was no good the users are either too annoyed by it or too anxious to find the right one that again they do not wish to waste any time in providing the system with feedback." With our proposal, the user provides the system with feedback and gets better suggestions without even noticing it. Again, an interesting point would be to experiment with alternative relevance feedback methods in systems gathering negative feedback from the users, and check the results.

The procedure that we propose in section *Generating Rules* for generating all association rules and especially the second pruning step (i.e., the sub procedure minimize-losses), is neither the only nor the optimal one. It constitutes our own proposal in handling these itemsets and one of the many that could be followed depending on the desired output. Nevertheless it is a rather good approach, more oriented towards the practical side of the problem and that efficiently solves many ambiguities. In the future we would like to take (if possible) a more theoretical view of the specific problem and wish to optimize the set of possible rules as it was done previously with rules generated only with positive items (Bayardo & Agrawal, 1999; Liu et al., 1999b).

Finally a very promising open subject in the specific area is the handling and the utilization of transactional data through a spatial, a temporal, or a spatiotemporal prism. In brief transactional data could be viewed as a special form of spatiotemporal data, where apart from the id or the bar code of every product we could introduce and take into consideration also a spatial, a temporal, or a spatiotemporal component depending on the application and our needs. This component is inherent in every transaction, but was left aside by all approaches, mainly due to the weakness of all approaches thus far to efficiently handle it.

References

Adrians, P., & Zantige, D. (1996). *Data mining*. Addison-Wesley.

Agrawal, R., Imielinski, T., & Swami, A. (1993, May). Mining association rules between sets of items in large databases. In *Proceedings of 1993 ACM-SIG-MOD Conference on Management of Data (SIGMOD '93)*, Washington, DC, 207-216.

Agrawal, R., & Shafer, J. C. (1996, December). Parallel mining of association rules: Design, implementation and experience. *IEEE Transactions on Knowledge and Data Engineering (TKDE)*, 8(6), 962-969.

Agrawal, R., & Srikant, R. (1994, September). Fast algorithms for mining generalized association rules. *In Proceedings of 1994 International Conference on Very Large Data Bases (VLDB '94)*, Santiago, Chile (pp. 487-499).

Antonie, M.-L., & Zaiane, O. R. (2004, September 20-24). Mining positive and negative association rules: An approach for confined rules. In *Proceedings of the 8th European Conference on Principles and Practice of Knowledge Discovery in Databases (PKDD '04)* (LNCS 3202, pp. 27-38). Pisa, Italy: Springer Verlag.

Arunasalam, B., Chawla, S., & Sun, P. (2005, May). Striking two birds with one stone: Simultaneous mining of positive and negative spatial patterns. In *Proceedings of the 5th SIAM International Conference on Data Mining (SDM '05)*, Newport Beach, CA (pp.173-183).

Bayardo, R. J., & Agrawal, R. (1999, August). Mining the Most Interesting Rules. *In Proceedings of the 5th ACM SIGKDD International Conference on Knowledge Discovery and Data Mining (KDD '99)*, San Diego, CA (pp. 145-154).

Breese, J., Heckerman, D., & Kadie, C. (1998, July). Empirical analysis of predictive algorithms for collaborative filtering. In *Proceedings of the 14th Conference on Uncertainty in Artificial Intelligence* (pp. 43-52). Madison, WT: Morgan Kaufmann Publisher.

Brin, S., Motwani, R., & Silverstein, C. (1997). Beyond market basket: Generalizing association rules to correlations. In *Proceedings of 1997 ACM-SIGMOD Conference on Management of Data (SIGMOD '97)*, 265-276

Brin, S., Motwani, R., Ullman, J. D., & Tsur, S. (1997, May). Dynamic itemset counting and implication rules for market basket data. In *Proceedings of 1997 ACM-SIGMOD Conference on management of data (SIGMOD '97)*, Tucson, AZ (pp. 255-264).

Buckley, C., Salton, G., & Allan, J. (1994). The effect of adding relevance information in a relevance feedback environment. In *Proceedings of the 17th Annual International ACM SIGIR Conference on Research and Development in Information Retrieval (SIGIR '94)* (pp. 292-300).

Buckley, C., Salton, G., Allan, J., & Singhal, A. (1994). Automatic query expansion using SMART: TREC 3. In *Proceedings of the 3rd Text Retrieval Conference (TREC-3)* (pp. 69-81). NIST Special Publications.

Chen, M. S., Han, J., & Yu, P. S., (1996). Data mining: An overview from a database perspective. *IEEE Transactions on Knowledge and Data Engineering (TKDE)*, 8(6), 866-883.

Cheung, D. W., Han, J., Ng, V., & Wong, C. Y. (1996, February). Maintenance of discovered association rules in large databases: An incremental updating technique. In *Proceedings of the 12th International Conference on Data Engineering (ICDE '96)*, New Orleans, LO (pp. 106-114).

Fayad, U., Piatetsky-Shapiro, G., & Smyth, P. (1996). From data mining to knowledge discovery in databases. *AI Magazine, 17*(3), 37-54.

Han, J., & Fu, Y. (1995). Discovery of multiple-level association rules from large databases. In *Proceedings of 1995 International Conference on Very Large Data Bases (VLDB '95)*, Zurich, Switzerland (pp. 420-431).

Han, J., Pei, J., & Yin, Y. (2000). Mining frequent patterns without candidate generation. In *Proceedings of 2000 ACM-SIGMOD Conference on Management of Data (SIGMOD '00)*, Dallas, TX (pp. 1-12).

Holt, J. D., & Chung, S. M. (2001). Multipass algorithms for mining association rules in text databases. *Knowledge and Information Systems (KAIS), 3*(2), 168-183.

Hussain, F., Liu, H., Suzuki, E., & Lu, H. (2000, April). Exception rule mining with a relative interestingness measure. In *Proceedings of the 3rd Pacific Asia Conference on Knowledge Discovery and Data Mining (PAKDD '00)* (pp. 86-97). Kyoto, Japan: Springer.

Hwang, S., Ho, S. & Tang, J. (1999, April). Mining exception instances to facilitate workflow exception handling. In *Proceedings of the 6th International Conference on Database Systems for Advanced Applications (DASFAA '99)*. IEEE Computer Society, Hsinchu, Taiwan (pp. 45-52).

Kleinberg, J., Papadimitriou, C., & Raghavan, P. (1998). A microeconomic view of data mining. *Data Mining and Knowledge Discovery Journal, 2*(4), 311-324.

Kouris, I. N., Makris C. H., & Tsakalidis, A. K. (2005, March). Using Information Retrieval techniques for supporting data mining. *Data & Knowledge Engineering (DKE)*, *52*(3), 353-383

Lee, C.-H., Lin, C.-R., & Chen, M.-S. (2001, November). Sliding window filtering: An efficient algorithm for incremental mining. In *Proceedings of the ACM 10th International Conference on Information and Knowledge Management (CIKM'01)* (pp. 263-270).

Liu, B., Hsu, W., & Ma, Y. (1999a, August). Mining association rules with multiple minimum supports. In *Proceedings of the 5th ACM SIGKDD International Conference on Knowledge Discovery and Data Mining (KDD'99)*, San Diego, CA (pp. 337-341).

Liu, B., Hsu, W., & Ma, Y. (1999b, August). Pruning and summarizing the discovered associations. In *Proceedings of the 5th ACM SIGKDD International Conference on Knowledge Discovery and Data Mining (KDD'99)*, San Diego, CA (pp. 125-134).

Liu, H., Lu, H., Feng, L., & Hussain, F. (1999, April). Efficient search of reliable exceptions. In *Proceedings of the 3rd Pacific Asia Conference on Knowledge Discovery and Data Mining (PAKDD'99)* (pp. 194-204). Beijing, China: Springer-Verlag.

Mannila, H. (1998). Database methods for data mining. In *Proceedings of the 4th ACM SIGKDD International Conference on Knowledge Discovery and Data Mining (KDD'98)*, tutorial.

Padmanabhan, B., & Tuzhilin, A. (2000). Small is beautiful: discovering the minimal set of unexpected patterns. In *Proceedings of the 6th ACM SIGKDD International Conference on Knowledge Discovery and Data Mining (KDD'00)* (pp. 54-63). Boston: ACM.

Padmanabhan, B. & Tuzhilin, A. (1998). A belief-driven method for discovering unexpected patterns. In *Proceedings of the 4th ACM SIGKDD International Conference on Knowledge Discovery and Data Mining (KDD'98)* (pp. 94-100). Newport Beach, CA: AAAI.

Park, J.-S., Chen, M.-S., & Yu, P. S. (1995a, May). An effective hash based algorithm for mining association rules. In *Proceedings of 1995 ACM-SIGMOD Conference on Management of Data (SIGMOD'95)*, San Jose, CA (pp. 175-186).

Park, J.-S., Chen, M.-S., & Yu, P. S. (1995b, November). Efficient parallel data mining for association rules. In *Proceedings of the ACM 5th International Conference on Information and Knowledge Management (CIKM'95)*, Baltimore (pp. 31-36).

Savasere, A., Omiecinski, E., & Navathe, S. B. (1998). Mining for strong negative associations in a large database of customer transactions. In *Proceedings of 14th International Conference on Data Engineering (ICDE'98)* (pp. 494-502).

Savasere, A. , Omiecinski, E., & Navathe, S. B. (1995). An efficient algorithm for mining association rules in large databases. In *Proceedings of the 21st International Conference on Very Large Data Bases (VLDB '95)*, Zurich, Switzerland (pp. 432-444).

Srikant, R., & Agrawal, R. (1996, June). Mining quantitative association rules in large relational tables. In *Proceedings of 1996 ACM-SIGMOD Conference on Management of Data (SIGMOD '96)*, Montreal, Canada (pp. 1-12).

Srikant, R., & Agrawal, R. (1995, September). Mining generalized association rules. In *Proceedings of 1995 International Conference on Very Large Data Bases (VLDB '95)*, Zurich, Switzerland (pp. 407-419).

Suzuki, E. (1997). Autonomous discovery of reliable exception rules. In *Proceedings of the 3nl ACM SIGKDD International Conference on Knowledge Discovery and Data Mining (KDD '97)* (pp. 259-262). Newport Beach, CA: AAAI.

Suzuki, E., & Shimura, M. (1996). Exceptional knowledge discovery in databases based on information theory. In *Proceedings of the 2nd ACM SIGKDD International Conference on Knowledge Discovery and Data Mining (KDD '96)*. AAAI, Portland, OR (pp. 275-278).

Thiruvady, D., & Webb, G. (2004, May). Mining negative rules using GRD. In *Proceedings of the 8th Pacific Asia Conference on Knowledge Discovery and Data Mining (PAKDD '04)* (pp. 161-165). Sydney, Australia: Springer.

Toivonen, H. (1996, September). Sampling large databases for finding association rules. In *Proceedings of 1996 International Conference on Very Large Data Bases (VLDB '96)*, Mumbay, India (pp. 134-145).

Yuan, X., Buckles, B., Yuan, Z., & Zhang, J. (2002). Mining negative association rules. In *Proceedings of the 7th International Symposium on Computers and Communications (ISCC '02)* (pp. 623-629).

Wang, K., He, Y., & Han, J. (2000, September). Mining frequent itemsets using support constraints. In *Proceedings of 2000 International Conference on Very Large Data Bases (VLDB '00)* (pp. 43-52).

Webb, G. I. (2000). Efficient search for association rules. In *Proceedings of the 6th ACM SIGKDD International Conference on Knowledge Discovery and Data Mining (KDD '00)*, (pp. 99-107). Boston: ACM.

Witten, I., Moffat, A., & Bell, T. (1999). *Managing gigabytes: Compressing and indexing documents and images* (2nd ed.). San Francisco: Morgan Kaufmann.

Wu, X., Zhang, C., & Zhang, S. (2002). Mining both positive and negative association rules. In *Proceedings of the 19th International Conference on Machine Learning (ICML '02)* (pp. 658-665).

Endnotes

[1]   Text Retrieval Conference (http://trec.nist.gov/pubs/trec2/)

[2]   http://www.almaden.ibm.com/cs/quest/syndata.html

[3]   This specific buying behavior could only be explained through other sciences such as customer psychology or marketing management and therefore is out of the scope of this book to further discuss it.

Chapter II

A Disk-Based Algorithm for Fast Outlier Detection in Large Datasets

Faxin Zhao, Northeastern University, and
Tonghua Teachers College, China

Yubin Bao, Northeastern University, China

Huanliang Sun, Northeastern University, China

Ge Yu, Northeastern University, China

Abstract

In data mining fields, outlier detection is an important research issue. The number of cells in the cell-based disk algorithm increases exponentially. The performance of this algorithm will decrease dramatically with the increasing of the number of cells and data points. Through further analysis, we find that there are many empty cells that are useless to outlier detection. So this chapter proposes a novel index structure, called CD-Tree, in which only non-empty cells are stored, and a cluster technique is adopted to store the data objects in the same cell into linked disk pages. Some experiments are made to test the performance of the proposed algorithms.

The experimental results show that the performance of the CD-Tree structure and of the cluster technique based disk algorithm outperforms that of the cell-based disk algorithm, and the dimensionality processed by the proposed algorithm is higher than that of the old one.

Introduction

Outlier detection is an important research issue in data mining. Compared to association rules (Agrawal, Imielinski, & Swami, 1993), classification (Rastogi & Shim, 1998) and clustering (Ng & Han, 1994; Zhang, Ramakrishnan, & Livny, 1996), it aims to discover "Small Pattern" or outliers — the data objects that are dissimilar or inconsistent with the remainder of the data. Hawkins' definition captures the spirit of outlier: "an outlier is an observation that deviates so much from other observations as to arouse suspicious that it was generated by a different mechanism" (Hawkins, 1980). In many applications, exceptional patterns are more significant than general patterns, such as intrusion detection, telecom and credit card fraud detection, loan approval, and weather prediction.

Some researchers have designed many algorithms for outlier detection based on various assumptions of outliers existing. Knorr and Ng (1998, 1999) proposed a cell-based algorithm for outliers detection, which quantizes each of data objects into a k-D (k is equal to the dimensionality of objects in the dataset) space that has been partitioned into cells. Outliers detection is based on these cells, the algorithm has a complexity of $O(c^k + N)$ which is linear wrt N, but exponential wrt k, k being the dimensionality and N being the number of objects in the dataset. The algorithm doesn't work effectively for high dimensionality or fine granularity partition because the number of cells is too many. We find that all cells generated by the algorithm are stored and processed. In fact, there exist plenty of empty cells in the partitions of a dataset, and these empty cells are useless for outlier detection except wasting memory and processing time. So, in this chapter, in order to solve the above problems, we present an efficient index structure named CD-Tree (Cell Dimension Tree), which only stores non-empty cells. Based on the index structure CD-Tree, we propose a disk-based algorithm for fast outlier detection in large datasets, and then a cluster technique is also employed to improve the efficiency of the algorithm further. The experimental results show that the performance of the CD-Tree and cluster technique based disk algorithm outperforms that of the cell-based disk algorithm, and the number of dimensions processed by the proposed algorithms is higher than that of the old one.

The remainder of this chapter is organized as follows: Related work work is discussed. The cell-based disk algorithm for outlier detection (CS-d) is introduced. Structure and related algorithms of CD-Tree are presented. The CD-Tree based disk algorithm for outlier detection (CDT-d) is presented. Also, the cluster technique is presented, and then the CD-Tree and cluster technique based disk algorithm for outlier detection (CCDT-d) is also presented. Last, we compare our algorithm (CDT-d and CCDT-d) with CS-d in (Knorr, 1998) and present conclusions.

Related Work

The problem of outliers detection has been extensively studied in the field of statistics (Hawkins, 1980; Barnett & Lewis, 1994), in the view of statistics, the data objects have to be modeled using a statistical distribution (such as Gaussian distribution), and outliers are the points that deviate away from the model. The shortage of this method is that the distribution of data must obey some standard distribution, but in many cases, users don't know the distribution of data in a dataset and the real-life data also often don't fit any standard mathematical distribution very well. In order to solve this problem, Knorr and Ng (1998) proposed the distance-based algorithms. They defined outlier as follows: "An object O in a dataset D is a DB (δ, d)-outlier if at least a fraction δ of the objects in D lies greater than distance d from O." The authors proposed three efficient algorithms for outlier detection. Except for cell-based algorithm which we have already referred to in the introduction part, one is the nested-loop algorithm (NL) with complexity $O(k*N^2)$, where k is the dimensionality of data, and N is the size of dataset, another one is index-based algorithm with complexity $O(k*N^2)$. The cell-based algorithm in them is the most contributive one.

Ramaswamy, Rastogi, and Shim (2000) proposed another distance-based outlier detection algorithm, which also included the NL algorithm, index-based algorithm, and partition-based algorithm. The complexity of the first two algorithms is $O(k*N^2)$. The third algorithm uses a clustering algorithm to partition the dataset, then calculates the bounds of each partition, selects the candidate partitions containing outliers, and calculates outlier points from the candidate partitions. This algorithm can present the level of outliers, but its efficiency is influenced by clustering algorithms.

Moreover, Ruts and Rousseeuw (1996) proposed a depth-based algorithm, and the complexity of the algorithm is $\Omega(N^{\lceil k/2 \rceil})$; Breunig, Krigegel, Ng, and Sander (2000) utilized a density-based algorithm called OPTICS (Ester, Kriegel, Sander, & Xu, 1996) to detect outliers. They proposed a concept of *local outlier factor* and then proposed a density-based algorithm for outlier detection. Li and Sun (2003) presented a grid-based algorithm called GridOF, which first filters out crowded grids and then finds outliers by computing adjusted mean approximation of the density function. Finally, literature (He, Xu, & Deng, 2003) presented a measure called

CBLOF for identifying the physical significance of an outlier and then applied the measure to discover outliers.

Cell-Based Disk Algorithm
for Outlier Detection (CS-d)

In this section, we discuss the cell-based algorithm for outlier detection and the problems of the algorithm mentioned in (Knorr & Ng, 1998). For simplicity of discussion, the author suppose M be the maximum number of objects within the d-neighborhood of an outlier, in other words, $M = N \times (1-\delta)$. Where the d-neighborhood of an object O is a set of data points that are within distance d from O.

In the algorithm, the partition interval is $d / 2\sqrt{k}$. Each cell has two layers surrounding it. The first layer is one cell thick, while the second is $\lceil 2\sqrt{k} - 1 \rceil$ cells thick. For a given cell w, it accumulates three counts — the number of points in the cell, the number of points in the cell and in the first layer's cells together, and the number of points in the cell and in the cells of the two layers together. Let's refer to these counts as $Count_w$, $Count_{w2}$ and $Count_{w3}$, respectively. The basic idea of the algorithm is as follows:

1. If $Count_w > M$, all the objects in cell w and the first layer neighbors of w are not outliers, then label w red, and label each of the first layer neighbors of w pink, where the neighbors have not already been labeled red.

2. If $Count_w < M$ and $Count_{w2} > M$, none of the objects in cell w is an outlier, then label w pink.

3. If $Count_{w3} \leq M$, every object in cell w is an outlier, then label w yellow.

4. If $Count_{w2} \leq M$ and $Count_{w3} > M$, then it is possible that some of the objects in w may be outliers. To detect these outliers, it is necessary to compare each object O in w with the objects in the second layer. For the objects in w, only those having no more than M points in their d-neighborhood are outliers.

However, the algorithm CS-d in (Knorr & Ng, 1998) designed by the above ideas could be improved further in the following aspects:

1. The number of cells generated by CS-d is exponential wrt dimensionality k. In fact, there exist plenty of empty cells in these cells, which affect the efficiency (memory usage and time complexity) of algorithms because of the

storing and visiting of empty cells. So the dimensionality that this algorithm can process is too low. But in practice, only the non-empty cells are useful to algorithm, and it is impossible that the number of non-empty cells in CS-d increases exponentially. Because the number of non-empty cells can't exceed the total number of data objects in a dataset even in the worst case that each data object is mapped into a separated cell.

2. The number of layer 2 neighbors of a cell increases with dimensionality k in terms of $(2\lceil 2\sqrt{k}\rceil-2)^k$. The time complexity for searching layer 2 neighbors and discriminating empty or non-empty of cells will increasing super-exponential wrt dimensionality. So time complexity for searching layer 2 neighbors will be a bottleneck of algorithm's performance with the increasing of dimensionality even all cells can fit into main memory.

3. In CS-d, it is possible that data objects which is mapped to various color cells exist in the same disk page in dataset. So we need plenty of operations in the algorithm to discriminate and exclude useless data objects. Such operations affect remarkably the efficiency of the algorithm.

CD-Tree Based Disk Algorithm for Outlier Detection

In this section, we present an index structure called CD-Tree and related algorithms for solving the first two problems in *CS-d*, and then design the corresponding algorithm *CDT-d*. Finally, we employ cluster technique for solving the third problem in *CS-d*, and then design the corresponding algorithm *CCDT-d*.

CD-Tree Structure and Related Algorithms

Definition 1. CD-Trees.

The CD-Tree is a balanced tree of a dataset under a partition, and has the following properties:

1. It has a root node and $k+1$ levels, where k is the dimensionality of the dataset.

2. Each dimension of the dataset corresponds to a level of the tree. The $(k+1)$-th level is a special one in which each node records the information of a non-empty cell.

3. The nodes at the *i*-th level except the (*k+1*)-*th* level, that is, all non-leaf nodes, contain internal-nodes with the form (*cNO, pointer*), where *cNO* is a keyword, a distinct interval number of *i-th* dimension corresponding to a cell. The *pointer* of *k-th* level internal-nodes points to a leaf node. The *pointer* of other level internal-node points to a (*i+1*)-*th* node, which contains all the distinct interval numbers of the next dimension corresponding to the non-empty cells based on intervals of the anterior *i* dimensions.

4. A path from the root node to a leaf node corresponds to a cell.

Figure 1a shows the cell structure of a 2-D dataset under a partition, and each dimension is divided into 6 intervals, so interval number of each dimension is from 1 to 6. The black cells denote non-empty cells. The cell (2, 3) denotes one of which interval number is 2, 3 respectively on these two dimensions. 2 presents the 2nd interval on the first dimension X, 3 is the 3rd interval on the second dimension Y. Figure 1b shows the CD-Tree structure corresponding to the cell structure, which only store non-empty cells. The CD-Tree has 3 levels. The first two levels correspond to X dimension and Y dimension of the dataset respectively, and the last one is cells level. The first dimension has six intervals, but only interval 2, 3, 5, and 6 contain data objects, so the root node has 4 internal-nodes. The first internal-node 2 of the root node points to the second level of the CD-Tree, there are two intervals, 2 and 3. A path from the root to a leaf such as (2, 3) corresponds to a cell which stores some information, such as data points falling in this cell, the count of points.

The algorithm of creating CD-Tree is shown in algorithm 1. Its steps are as follows: step 1 initializes root node of CD-Tree; step 2 reads data objects from dataset; step 2 (a) computes coordinates (i.e., the interval number of each dimension) of each data object; step 2 (b) inserts data object into CD-Tree by calling procedure *Map-Point*.

Figure 1. An example of a CD-Tree

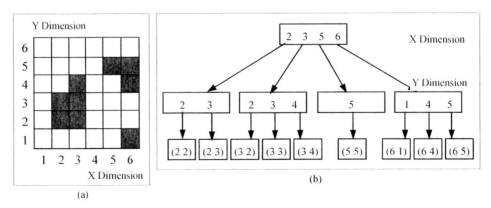

(a)

(b)

Algorithm 1.

```
Algorithm 1. CreateCDTree
Input: Dataset D
Output: CD-Tree
Begin
1.    Root=NULL;
2.    for each data object P in dataset D
            a. map P to CellNO
            b. MapPointTOCell(CellNO, root, NULL,1 )
End

Procedure MapPointTOCell (CellNO, current, currentPre, level )
Begin
1. if level=dim+1 return; //dim is dimensionality
2. if Current=NULL then
            a. Current=new Node; //create a new node
            b. if level=1 then Root=current  //Root points to node of first level
            c. else  CurrentPre=current  // The pointer of previous level points to the new node
3. if CellNO[level] not existing in current node then  //CellNO[level]: a coordinate of current dimension
            a. if level ≠ dim then insert CellNO[level] into current node by ascending order
            b. else create a new cell and insert information of the point into the cell
4. else
    if level=dim then
        update the information of corresponding cell(leaf node)
5. currentPre=current
6. current=current.NextNode; // current point to next level
7. MapPointTOCell (CellNO, current, currentPre, level+1)
End
```

Procedure *MapPoint* starts from first dimension to search coordinate value of a data point in current dimension corresponding to cell in related level of CD-Tree. If all coordinate components of the data object have existed in the CD-Tree, then the information of the data object is stored into the corresponding leaf node of the CD-Tree; if not exist, then create a new node of the next level starting from non-existent level, and create a new leaf node in the final level of the CD-Tree. If current node is NULL, then create a new node (step 2). If a node exists, there are two cases. First, the value of keyword doesn't exist in the node, then the value must be inserted into the node by ascending order (step 3). Second, if it exists, then the algorithm updates the information of corresponding cell (leaf node) (step 4) and call procedure *MapPoint* to process next level (step 5-7).

Based on CD-Tree, neighbor query of current cell can be executed on CD-Tree. Thus it avoids the search and judgment about empty cells during the neighbor search, and improves the search efficiency on non-empty neighbors.

The algorithm for neighbor query on CD-Tree is shown in algorithm 2. The *NeighborQuery* query is different from the general range query. It has one cell as center,

Algorithm 2.

```
Algorithm 2.  NeighborQuery(Current, CellCoo, Radius, Level )
Input:  CD-Tree
            CellCoo// CellCoo is the coordinate of a cell
            Radius //the radius of query
            Level //current level number of CD-Tree, from 1 to k+1
Output: Result // Query result
Begin
1.  DimCoo = CellCoo.CurrentDimensionKeyword;
2.  for each Coordinate Dim in node of current level that abs(Dim-DimCoo)<= Radius;
        a.    if (Level ≠ k) then //there exists next level, continue recursion
                  Current =pointer that Dim corresponded to which points to the node of next dimension level
                       NeighborQuery (Current, CellCoo, Radius, Level+1)
         b.  else
                  Current = pointer that Dim corresponded to which points to a leaf node;
                                              //the leaf node is a neighbor cell in query result
                       Result.Add(Current ); // add query results into a set
End
```

and the several interval lengths as radius. The results of query are the cells and all points in these cells within the interval lengths. The algorithm calls *NeighborQuery* recursively until finding leaf node in step 2 (a) and stores all position information of leaf nodes that satisfied query conditions as the query results in step 2 (b).

The CD-Tree Based Disk Algorithm (CDT-d)

CS-d is used to handle large dataset that can't fit into main memory. The basic idea of the algorithm is as follows: The data objects that are mapped to *white cells* (the cells in which may be existing outliers) and *yellow cells* (the cells in which all the data objects are outliers) are all stored into corresponding cells: other cells which only store disk pages of data objects that are mapped to the corresponding cells. However, the algorithm doesn't work effectively for high dimensionality because the number of cells is too many. So it is only applied to large datasets with lower dimensionality. In this section, we improve the performance of CS-d by applying CD-Tree to the algorithm, in other words, using CD-Tree to store the non-empty cells and implementing *NeighborQuery* operation on it. The process of the algorithm is the same as CS-d, here the detailed presentation of the algorithm are omitted. The experimental results show that the performance of the CD-Tree based disk algorithm (CDT-d) outperforms that of CS-d, and the dimensionality processed by *CDT-d* is also higher than that of *CS-d*.

Figure 2. The clustered storage structure

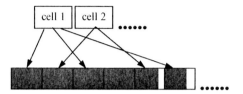

The CD-Tree and Cluster
Technique Based Disk Algorithm (CCDT-d)

It can be seen that although the first two problems existed in *CS-d* have been solved and the performance of *CDT-d* outperforms that of *CS-d*, the third problem in *CS-d* is still unresolved. The following several reasons result in this situation. First, data objects in *white* and *yellow* cells need to be read into main memory, but these data objects generally distribute in different disk pages for their random distribution, and many data objects mapped to the cells with various colors are always included in the same disk page. However, CS-d reads all the data objects in one page once a time, so a large amount of time is consumed in discriminating and excluding useless data objects and disk I/O operations. Secondly, it reads all data objects in *non-white* and *non-yellow* cells which have some *white* cells as their layer 2 neighbors, and then compares with all data objects in their layer 2 neighbors with *white* color. Beside the existing shortages in above, the process must search all layer 2 neighbors with *white* color for every data object that satisfies the condition. So the time consumed on searching increases remarkably with the number of data objects in cells and dimensionality.

To solve the previous problems, we presented several strategies as follows:

1. The data cluster technique: As shown in Figure 2, for each data object in original dataset, it will be saved in a disk page corresponding to the cell while mapping it to the leaf node of the CD-Tree. We can save the data objects in a cell in several disk pages if they can't fit into one disk page, and then connect these disk pages as a link and save the link information in corresponding cell. The size of disk page can be set according to the size of *M*, here we recommend $\lceil M/2 \rceil$ as the size value. Data cluster technique and the method to create linked disk pages are shown in Algorithm 3.

Algorithm 3.

```
Algorithm 3: DataSetCluster(D)
Input: dataset D
Output: dataset CD with cluster
Begin
1. for each data object Q which will map to cell C of CD-Tree
   a. if C not exist then
      1. apply for a new disk page P while create C , save Q in P ;
      2. add page number of P to tail of the disk pages link in C ;
   b. else
      1. if corresponding disk page P of the tail of the link in C is not full then
      save Q in P;
   2. else
      apply for a new disk page Pn, save Q in Pn;
         add page number of Pn to tail of the disk pages link in C ;
End
```

2.   For *non-white* and *non-yellow* cells corresponding to data objects in disk pages, we first search *white* layer 2 neighbors of the cells, and then save the searching results in a pointer link of cells. Therefore, we use the pointer link rather than retrieve again on CD-Tree to search *white* layer 2 neighbors of the remainder data objects in the cells.

Based on CD-Tree and previous strategies, we present a new disk algorithm (CCDT-d) for outlier detection in large dataset. Because of adopting CD-Tree index structure and cluster technique, CCDT-d greatly differs from CS-d (see Algorithm 4). Its steps are as follows. Step 1 maps each data object P of dataset D to corresponding cell in CD-Tree by calling procedure *CreateCDTree*, and save P in another disk page corresponding to the cell. It should be pointed out that CCDT-d no longer saves P in a cell. Step 2 labels all cells in which the number of data objects is greater than M as *red*, and labels layer 1 neighbors of the *red* cells as *pink* which has not already been labeled *red* at the same time. Step 3 labels the cells which domain $count_{w2}$ is greater than M as *pink* and label the cells that satisfy $count_{w3} <= M$ as *yellow*. Step 4 reads all data objects in dataset that are mapped to *white* and *yellow* cells into the corresponding cells. But, because of adopting cluster technique, data objects can be read directly from disk pages corresponding to disk page link in the cell, and large number of operations in CS-d such as reading and discriminating data objects in *non-white* and *non-yellow* cells is not required any more. In step 6, besides adopting the methods of step 4, we also adopt the technique of cell-based rather than data-object-based for searching *white* layer 2 neighbors. Therefore, it further improves the performance of the algorithm.

Algorithm 4.

Algorithm 4 . FindAllOutsCDD
Input: DataSet D, d
Output: OutlierSet
Begin
1. **for** each data object P in D, do
a. map *P* to cell C_q in CD-Tree by calling *CreateCDTree*;
b. save number of data objects and disk pages link corresponding to C_q in C_q;
c. save *P* in another disk page corresponding to C_q;
2. **for** each C_q cell in CD-Tree do
a. **if** *Count$_q$>M* **then** label C_q red;
b. query layer 1 neighbors of C_q by calling NeighborQuery (*Root, Cq, 1, 1*), save results in *Result*;
c. label cells which have not already been labeled *red* in *Result pink*.
3. **for** each white (i.e., uncolored) cell Cw in CD-Tree
a. $count_{w2}=Count_w+\sum_{i\in L1(Cw)}Count_i$
b. **if** $count_{w2}$>*M* **then** label C_w *pink*
c. **else**
1. $count_{w3}=count_{w2}+\sum_{i\in L2}(Cw)Count_i$
2. **if** $count_{w3}$<=*M* **then** label C_w *yellow* // all data objects in C_w are outliers
3. **else** $Sum_w = count_{w2}$
4. **for** each *white* and *yellow* cell C_q in CD-Tree
a. read all data objects *P* in disk page corresponding to C_q;
b. save *P* in C_q,
c. set $Kount_p=Sum_q$.
5. **for** each *white* cell C_w in CD-Tree
a. query layer 2 neighbors of C_w by calling NeighborQuery (*Root, C_w,* $\lceil 2\sqrt{k} \rceil$, 1), save results in Result
b. **for** each data object *P* in C_w
For each *white* or *yellow* cell C_n in *Result*
For each data object *Q* in C_n
if dist(*P,Q*)<=*d* **then**
1. $Count_p=Count_p+1$;
2. **if** $Count_p$>*M* **then** label *P red*, and go to next *P*.
6. **for** each *non-white* and *non-yellow* cell C_r in CD-Tree
// *WhiteLinkL2* is a set of *white* layer 2 neighbors of C_w
a. *WhiteLinkL2*=NeighborQuery (*Root*, C_w, $\lceil 2\sqrt{k} \rceil$, 1)
b. **for** each data object *Q* in C_r //read *Q* from disk page according to disk page link in C_r
For each white cell C_w in *WhiteLinkL2*
For each data object *P* in C_w
if dist(*P,Q*)<=*d* **then**
1. $Count_p=Count_p+1$;
2. if $Count_p$>*M* **then** label *P red*, and go to next *P*.
7. output all outliers. //all the data objects in yellow cells and white data objects in white cells
End

Experimental Results

The following experiments are conducted on Microsoft Windows 2000 Server with 512MB main memory and 2.5GHz CPU. The dataset is produced by image Fourier coefficients. The experimental results are shown in Figure 3 and Figure 4.

Figure 3 shows the results for various algorithms and dataset sizes for 3-D, $\delta=0.999$ and d=0.06, the number of tuples is from 200,000 to 1,000,000. It can be seen that the performance of CD-Tree based disk algorithm CDT-d outperforms that of original

Figure 3. Performance comparison for different dataset size

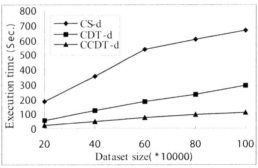

Figure 4. Performance comparison for different dimensionality

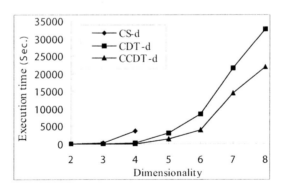

Table 1. The setup of parameter d

Dimensionality	2	3	4	5	6	7	8
d	0.04	0.04	0.1	0.1	0.15	0.15	0.2

disk based algorithm, CS-d, and as well as the efficiency of CD-Tree and cluster technique based CCDT-d to that of CD-Tree based CDT-d.

Figure 4 gives the execution time of the three algorithms as the dimensionality is increased from two to eight, the number of tuples is 200,000 and δ=0.9999. In order to get the same proportion of the points to dataset sizes as outlier, we change the value of parameter d with the increasing of dimensionality as shown in Table 1.

From the experimental results as shown in Figure 4, it is clear that CCDT-d and CDT-d can handle large datasets with higher dimensionality. However, CS-d can't work well on large dataset with over four dimensionalities because the number of cells is up to 455 under current partition when the dimensionality of dataset is five and it is impossible to process all the cells in main memory. But, in fact, the number of non-empty cells is only 106879, just 53.44% of 200,000 (the size of the dataset), less then 0.6‰ of 455 (total number of cells that CS-d generating).

Conclusion and Future Work

CS-d is an effective algorithm with lower dimensionality. But in fact, there exist plenty of empty cells under a given partition of a dataset. Thus, to store and process empty cells remarkably affect the performance of the algorithms for outlier detection. This chapter proposes an efficient index structure, CD-Tree, which only stores the non-empty cells. It is convenient for the algorithm to travel and query neighbors on CD-Tree. The efficiency and dimensionality processed by our algorithm are improved remarkably by applying CD-Tree to cell-based algorithm. Disk-based algorithm is an efficient method to deal with large dataset. However, because data objects randomly distribute in a dataset, we need to process many useless data objects corresponding to the current cells. To solve this problem, we designed a new disk algorithm for outlier detection by adopting the data cluster technique and the strategy of cell-based layer 2 neighbors query. The experimental results show that the performance of our algorithm outperforms that of CS-d.

The best setting of disk page size, which is not discussed in this chapter is a problem needed to be further investigation. It should consider that the proportion of sparse cells (the cells in which the number of data objects is less than the given threshold) as well as dense cells (the cells to which the number of data objects are mapped is more than the threshold). When the former is bigger, inappropriate setting of disk page size may cause the length of cluster file increases severely. On the contrary, when the latter is bigger, it may cause the link of disk page corresponding to cells too long. Both of them affect the performance of the algorithm. So we need investigate how to set the size of disk page according to the distribution of data objects in a dataset and the value of parameter M.

References

Agrawal, R., Imielinski, T., & Swami, A. (1993). Mining association rules between sets of items in large databases. In *Proceedings of the ACM-SIGMOD International Conference on Management of Data (SIGMOD '93)*, Washington, DC (pp. 207-216). New York: ACM Press.

Barnett, V., & Lewis, T. (1994). *Outliers in statistical data*. New York: John Wiley and Sons.

Breunig, M. M., Kriegel, H-P., Ng, R., & Sander, J. (2000). LOF: Identifying Density-Based Local Outliers. In *ACM SIGMOD Conference Proceedings* (pp. 93-104). New York: ACM Press.

Ester, M., Kriegel, H. P., Sander, J., & Xu, X. (1996). A density-based algorithm for discovering clusters in large spatial databases. In *Proceedings of KDD '96*, Portland OR (pp.226-231). Portland, OR: AAAI Press.

Hawkins, D. (1980). *Identification of outliers*. London: Chapman and Hall.

He, Z., Xu, X., & Deng, S. (2003). Discovering cluster based local outliers. *Pattern Recognition Letters, 24*(9-10), 1641-1650.

Knorr, E., & Ng, R. (1998). Algorithms for mining distance-based outliers in large data sets. In *Proceedings of the 24th International Conference on Very Large Data Bases*, New York (pp. 392-403). San Francisco: Morgan Kaufmann.

Knorr, E.,& Ng, R. (1999). Finding international knowledge of distance-based outliers. In *Proceedings of the 25th International Conference on Very Large Data Bases*, Scotland (pp. 211-222). San Francisco: Morgan Kaufmann.

Li, C. H., & Sun, Z. H. (2003). GridOF: An efficient outlier detection algorithm for very large datasets. *Journal of Computer Research and Development, 40*(11), 1586-1592.

Ng, R., & Han, J. W. (1994). Efficient and effective clustering methods for spatial data mining. In *Proceedings of the 20th International Conference on Very Large Data Base Conference*, Santiago, Chile (pp. 144-155). San Francisco: Morgan Kaufmann.

Ramaswamy, S., Rastogi, R., & Shim, K. (2000). Efficient algorithms for mining outliers from large data sets. In *Proceedings of ACM SIGMOD International Conference on Management of Data* (pp. 427-438). New York: ACM Press.

Rastogi, R., & Shim, K. (1998). Public: A decision tree classifier that integrates building and pruning. In *Proceedings of the 23rd International Conference on Very Large Data Bases*, New York (pp. 404-415). San Francisco: Morgan Kaufmann.

Ruts, I., & Rousseeuw, P. (1996). Computing depth contours of bivariate point clouds. *Computational Statistics and Data Analysis, 23*(1), 153-168.

Zhang, T., Ramakrishnan, R., & Livny, M. (1996). Birch: An efficient data clustering method for very large databases. In *Proceedings of the ACM SIGMOD International Conference on Management of Data*, Montreal, Canada (pp. 103-114). New York: ACM Press.

Chapter III

Maintenance of Association Rules Using Pre-Large Itemsets

Tzung-Pei Hong, National University of Kaohsiung, Taiwan

Ching-Yao Wang, National Chiao-Tung University, Taiwan

Abstract

Developing an efficient mining algorithm that can incrementally maintain discovered information as a database grows is quite important in the field of data mining. In the past, we proposed an incremental mining algorithm for maintenance of association rules as new transactions were inserted. Deletion of records in databases is, however, commonly seen in real-world applications. In this chapter, we first review the maintenance of association rules from data insertion and then attempt to extend it to solve the data deletion issue. The concept of pre-large itemsets is used to reduce the need for rescanning the original database and to save maintenance costs. A novel algorithm is proposed to maintain discovered association rules for deletion of records. The proposed algorithm doesn't need to rescan the original database until a number of records have been deleted. If the database is large, then the number of deleted records allowed will be large too. Therefore, as the database grows, our proposed approach becomes increasingly efficient. This characteristic is especially useful for real-world applications.

Introduction

Due to the increasing use of very large databases and data warehouses, mining useful information and helpful knowledge from transactions is evolving into an important research area. In the past, researchers usually assumed databases were static to simplify data-mining problems. Thus, most proposed algorithms focus on batch mining (Agrawal, Imielinksi, & Swami, 1993; Agrawal & Srikant, 1994; Agrawal & Srikant, 1995; Agrawal, Srikant, & Vu, 1997; Han & Fu, 1995; Mannila, Toivonen, & Verkamo, 1994; Park, Chen, & Yu, 1997; Srikant & Agrawal, 1995; Srikant & Agrawal, 1996) and do not utilize previously mined patterns for later maintenance. This may require considerable computation time to obtain the updated set of association rules or patterns (Cheung, Han, Ng, & Wong, 1996).

Researchers have recently developed efficient mining algorithms for maintaining association rules and avoiding the above-mentioned shortcomings when new transactions are inserted. Examples include the FUP algorithm (Cheung et al., 1996), the adaptive algorithm (Sarda & Srinivas, 1998), and the incremental updating technique based on the concept of *negative border* (Feldman, Aumann, Amir, & Mannila, 1997; Thomas, Bodagala, Alsabti, & Ranka, 1997). The common idea among these approaches is that previously mined patterns are stored in advance for later use. When new transactions are inserted, a large part of the final results can be obtained by comparing the patterns mined from the newly inserted transactions with the pre-stored mined knowledge. Only a small portion of the patterns need to be re-processed against the entire database, thus saving much computation time.

Among these approaches, the FUP algorithms (Cheung et al., 1996) store the previously mined large itemsets for later maintenance. Some approaches utilize *negative borders* (Feldman et al., 1997; Thomas et al., 1997) to enlarge the amount of pre-stored mined information, thus improving maintenance performance at the expense of storage space. Furthermore, we proposed an incremental mining algorithm based on the concept of *pre-large itemsets* for data insertion (Hong, Wang, & Tao, 2001). The concept of pre-large itemsets is denoted as the set of itemsets having support between a lower support threshold, which is smaller than the given minimum support, and an upper support threshold, which is equal to the given minimum support. Therefore, using the pre-large itemsets to enlarge the amount of pre-stored mined information can avoid rescanning the original database until the accumulative amount of new transactions exceeds the safety bound at the expense of storage spaces. This is because they act as a buffer to avoid the movements of itemset directly from small to large and vice-versa during the incremental mining process.

In addition to record insertion, record deletion is also commonly seen in real-world applications. For example, the records which were generated some years ago may be moved to a magnetic tape. Developing efficient maintenance algorithms for deletion of records is practical and necessary. In this chapter, we first review the maintenance of association rules from data insertion and then attempt to extend it to solve the data deletion issue. The concept of pre-large itemsets is also used to reduce the need for rescanning the original database and to save maintenance costs. Therefore, the proposed algorithm doesn't need to rescan the original database until a number of records have been deleted. If the database is large, then the number of deleted records allowed will be large too. This characteristic is especially useful for real-world applications.

The remainder of this chapter is organized as follows. Some incremental mining algorithms for record insertion are reviewed in *Related Work*. A maintenance algorithm for record insertion we proposed is reviewed in *Rule Maintenance for Record Insertion*. The problem of rule maintenance for record deletion is described in the section *Rule Maintenance for Record Deletion*. Theoretical foundation is shown in *Theoretical Foundation for Record Deletion*. A novel maintenance algorithm for record deletion is proposed in *The Proposed Maintenance Algorithm for Record Deletion*. Experimental results are described in *Experiments*. The chapter is finalized in the *Discussion and Conclusion* section.

Related Work

In real-world applications, a database grows over time such that existing association rules may become invalid or new implicitly valid rules may appear. In these situations, conventional batch-mining algorithms do not utilize previously mined patterns for later maintenance, and may require considerable computation time to re-process the entire updated database to get all up-to-date association rules. Some approaches have thus been proposed to use previously mined information to improve rule-maintenance performance. The details are illustrated as follows.

Figure 1. Four cases of candidate itemsets to be considered when inserting new transactions to an existing database

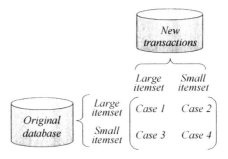

Considering an original database and newly inserted transactions, four cases of candidate itemsets shown in Figure 1 may arise:

- **Case 1:** A candidate itemset is large in both the original database and the new transactions;
- **Case 2:** A candidate itemset is large in the original database but small in the new transactions;
- **Case 3:** A candidate itemset is small in the original database but large in the new transactions; and
- **Case 4:** A candidate itemset is small in both the original database and the new transactions.

Since itemsets in Case 1 are large in both the original database and the new transactions, they are still large after the weighted average of the supports. Similarly, itemsets in Case 4 are still small after the new transactions are inserted. Cases 1 and 4 will not affect the final association rules. However, Case 2 may remove existing association rules, and Case 3 may generate new association rules.

Cheung et al. (1996) proposed an incremental mining algorithm, called FUP (Fast UPdate algorithm), to efficiently cope with these four cases by pre-storing previously mined large itemsets from the original database. The FUP algorithm first calculates the large itemsets in the newly inserted transactions and compares them with the pre-stored large itemsets. According to the comparison results, it can efficiently handle Cases 1, 2, and 4, and then if necessary, re-process only the itemsets without sufficient information in Case 3 against the original database.

The performance of the FUP algorithm will get degraded if a lot of candidate itemsets from the newly inserted transactions belong to Case 3. For example, suppose $\{A\}$, $\{B\}$, and $\{AB\}$ are all the previously mined large itemsets from the original database and $\{C\}$, $\{D\}$, and $\{CD\}$ are the three candidate itemsets from the new transactions; the final results can not be determined without re-processing the original database. As a result, Thomas et al. (1997) and Feldman et al. (1997) utilized the concept of *negative border* (Mannila & Toivonen, 1996) to enlarge the amount of pre-stored mining information in the FUP algorithm to reduce the number of itemsets in Case 3. Let R be a set of items, and L be a subset of the power set of R, which is closed with respect to the set inclusion relation. The *negative border NB* (L) for L is a set that consists of the minimal itemsets $X \subseteq R$ and $X \notin L$. Therefore, the negative border of large itemsets can be formed by excluding the set of large itemsets from the set of candidate itemsets generated level by level. In other words, it consists of the itemsets which are candidates but do not have enough supports. The processing time for Case 3 in the FUP algorithm can be reduced by additionally keeping the negative border of large itemsets.

Rule Maintenance for Record Insertion

We proposed an incremental mining algorithm based on the concept of *pre-large itemsets* to reduce the number of rescans over the original database during the incremental mining process (Hong et al., 2001). In general, the number of newly inserted transactions is much smaller than the number of records in the original database. Only the small itemsets whose supports are a little less than the minimum support in the original database are possible to be large after the database is updated. The concept of pre-large itemsets is denoted as the set of itemsets having support between a lower support threshold, which is smaller than the given minimum support, and an upper support threshold, which is equal to the given minimum support. Therefore, using the pre-large itemsets to enlarge the amount of pre-stored mined information can avoid rescanning the original database at the expense of storage spaces. This is because they act as a buffer to avoid the movements of itemset directly from small to large and vice-versa in the incremental mining process. When few new transactions are inserted, the original small itemsets will at most become pre-large and cannot become large, thus reducing the amount of rescanning necessary. The safety bound of new transactions is derived by the upper and lower support thresholds and the number of records in the original database. This algorithm is described in the following list.

The incremental mining algorithm based on the concept of pre-large itemsets:

- **INPUT:** A lower support threshold, an upper support threshold, a set of previously mined large and pre-large itemsets, and a set of new transactions.
- **OUTPUT:** A set of large itemsets for the updated database.
  - **Step 1:** Generate candidate 1-itemsets with counts from the set of new transactions.
  - **Step 2:** Set $k = 1$, where k records number of items currently being processed.
  - **Step 3:** Partition all candidate k-itemsets into three cases as follows:
    - *Case 1.* A candidate k-itemset is among the previously mined large itemsets.
    - *Case 2.* A candidate k-itemset is among the previously mined pre-large itemsets.
    - *Case 3.* A candidate k-itemset is among the original small itemsets.
  - **Step 4:** Calculate a new support for each itemset in Cases 1 and 2, and remove the ones whose supports smaller than the lower support threshold.
  - **Step 5:** Rescan the original database if the accumulative amount of new transactions exceeds the calculated safety bound.

- ○ **Step 6:** Generate candidate (k+1)-itemsets from updated large and pre-large k-itemsets and go to Step 3 until no candidate itemsets have been generated.

Rule Maintenance for Record Deletion

When records are deleted from databases, the original association rules may also become invalid, or new implicitly valid rules may appear in the resulting updated databases. For example, assume a database has eight records as shown in Table 1 and the minimum support is set at 50%. The mined large 1-itemsets in Table 1 are {A}, {B}, {C}, and {E}, respectively. If two records TID = 200 and TID = 300 are deleted from Table 1, the originally small itemset (D) will become large.

Table 1. An original database

TID	Items
100	*ACD*
200	*BCE*
300	*ABCE*
400	*ABE*
500	*ABE*
600	*ACD*
700	*BCDE*
800	*BCE*

Figure 2. Nine cases of candidate itemsets to be considered when deleting old records from an existing database

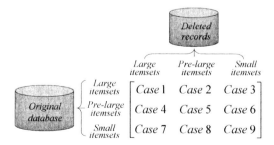

Conventional batch-mining algorithms must re-process the entire updated databases to find final association rules for managing these situations. Considering an original database and deleted records using the concept of pre-large itemsets, the following nine cases of candidate itemsets as shown in Figure 2 may arise:

- **Case 1:** A candidate itemset is large in both the original database and the deleted records;
- **Case 2:** A candidate itemset is large in the original database but pre-large in the deleted records;
- **Case 3:** A candidate itemset is large in the original database but small in the deleted records;
- **Case 4:** A candidate itemset is pre-large in the original database but large in the deleted records;
- **Case 5:** A candidate itemset is pre-large in both the original database and the deleted records;
- **Case 6:** A candidate itemset is pre-large in the original database but small in the deleted records;
- **Case 7:** A candidate itemset is small in the original database but large in the deleted records;
- **Case 8:** A candidate itemset is small in the original database but pre-large in the deleted records; and
- **Case 9:** A candidate itemset is small in both the original database and the deleted records.

Table 2. Nine cases and their results

Cases: Original – Deleted	Results
Case 1: Large – Large	Large or pre-large or small, decided from the existing information
Case 2: Large – Pre-large	Always large
Case 3: Large – Small	Always large
Case 4: Pre-large – Large	Pre-large or small, decided from the existing information
Case 5: Pre-large – Pre-large	Large or Pre-large or small, decided from the existing information
Case 6: Pre-large – Small	Large or pre-large, decided from the existing information
Case 7: Small – Large	Always small
Case 8: Small – Pre-large	Always small
Case 9: Small – Small	Pre-large or small, when the number of deleted records is small

Cases 2, 3, 4, 7, and 8 do not affect the final association rules. Case 1 may remove existing association rules, and cases 5, 6, and 9 may generate new association rules. If we pre-store all large and pre-large itemsets from the original database, then cases 1, 5, and 6 can be handled easily. An itemset in case 9 cannot possibly be large for the entire updated database as long as the number of deleted records is a considerably small proportion of the original database. This point will be proven later. A summary of the nine cases and their results is given in Table 2.

Theoretical Foundation for Record Deletion

The notations used in this chapter are defined in Table 3. Some related theorems are stated as follows:

Theorem 1. Given the S_l, S_u and d, if $t \le \dfrac{(S_u - S_l)d}{S_u}$ then an itemset that is small (neither large nor pre-large) in both D and T is not large for U.

Table 3. Related notations

Parameter	Description
D	The original database
T	The set of deleted records
U	The entire updated database, i.e., $D - T$
d	The number of records in D
t	The number of records in T
S_l	The lower support threshold
S_u	The upper support threshold, $S_u > S_l$
L_k^D	The set of large k-itemsets in D
L_k^U	The set of large k-itemsets in U
P_k^D	The set of pre-large k-itemsets in D
P_k^U	The set of pre-large k-itemsets in U
C_k	The set of all candidate k-itemsets
R_k^T	The set of all k-itemsets in T which exist in $(L_k^D \cup P_k^D)$
$S^D(I)$	The count of an itemset I in D
$S^U(I)$	The count of an itemset I in U

Proof. The following derivation can be obtained from $t \leq \frac{(S_u - S_l)d}{S_u}$:

$$t \leq \frac{(S_u - S_l)d}{S_u}$$
$$\Rightarrow tS_u \leq (S_u - S_l)\, d$$
$$\Rightarrow tS_u \leq dS_u - dS_l$$
$$\Rightarrow dS_l \leq S_u(d - t)$$
$$\Rightarrow \frac{dS_l}{d - t} \leq S_u. \qquad\qquad \text{equation (1)}$$

Besides, if an itemset I is small (neither large nor pre-large) in D, then $S^D(I) < d*S_l$; if I is small in T, then $t*S_l \geq S^T(I) \geq 0$; and thus the new support of I in U, $\frac{S^U(I)}{d - t}$, can be derived as:

$$\frac{S^U(I)}{d - t} = \frac{S^D(I) - S^T(I)}{d - t}$$
$$< \frac{dS_l - S^T(I)}{d - t}$$
$$< \frac{dS_l}{d - t}$$
$$< S_u. \qquad\qquad \text{equation (2)}$$

I is thus not large for U.

$\square$

Example 1. Given $d=100$, $S_l=50\%$ and $S_u=60\%$, the allowed t such that D need not be re-scanned for rule maintenance is:

$$\frac{(S_u - S_l)d}{S_u} = \frac{(0.6 - 0.5)}{0.6} = \frac{1}{6}.$$

Thus, if t is less than or equal to 16, then I is absolutely not large for U.

$\square$

From theorem 1, the allowed number of deleted records for efficiently handling case 9 is determined by S_l, S_u, and d. It can easily be seen from the inequality mentioned in Theorem 1 that if D grows larger, then the allowed number of deleted records will be larger too, and our proposed approach becomes increasingly efficient. This characteristic is especially useful for real-world applications. We can also determine the ratio of t to d as follows:

Corollary 1: Let r denote the ratio of t to d. If $r \leq \dfrac{S_u - S_l}{S_u}$, then an itemset that is small (neither large nor pre-large) in both D and T is not large for U.

Example 2: Given S_l=50% and S_u=60%, the allowed ratio of t to d such that D need not be re-scanned for rule maintenance is:

$$\frac{(S_u - S_l)}{S_u} = \frac{(0.6 - 0.5)}{0.6} = \frac{1}{6}.$$

If the ratio of deletion is equal to or less than 1/6, then I is absolutely not large for U. Note that 1/6 is quite a large ratio for a large database.

$\square$

The Proposed Maintenance Algorithm for Record Deletion

According to the discussion above, an efficient maintenance algorithm can be designed for record deletion in an incremental way. The large and pre-large itemsets with their counts in preceding runs are pre-stored for later rule-maintenance. When some records are deleted, the proposed algorithm first scans them to find the 1-itemsets that exist in the previously retained large or pre-large 1-itemsets, and then recalculate their new supports which are calculated with their new count over the updated number of records. For the small itemsets in the original database, they are absolutely not large for the entire updated database as long as the number of deleted records is less than the safety bound. In this situation, no action is needed. However, when the accumulative number of deleted records exceeds the safety bound, the original database has to be re-scanned for not losing any information. Candidate 2-itemsets are then generated from the final large 1-itemsets and the ones that exist in the previously retained large or pre-large 2-itemsets but not exist in the candidate 2-itemsets are removed (since they are absolutely not large or pre-large in the next run). A similar process is then executed to find the final large 2-itemsets. This procedure is repeated until all large itemsets have been found. A variable, c, is used to record the number of deleted records since the last re-scan of the original database. The details of the proposed maintenance algorithm are shown in the following list.

The proposed maintenance algorithm for record deletion:

- **INPUT:** A lower support threshold S_l, an upper support threshold S_u, a set of pre-stored large and pre-large itemsets in the original database D consisting of $(d - c)$ records, and a set of deleted records T consisting of t records.

- **OUTPUT:** A set of final association rules for the updated database U.

  ○ **Step 1:** Calculate the safety bound of deleted records, f, according to Theorem 1 as follows:

  $$f = \left\lfloor \frac{(S_u - S_l)d}{S_u} \right\rfloor . \qquad\qquad \text{equation (3)}$$

  ○ **Step 2:** Set $k = 1$, where k records the number of items currently being processed.

  ○ **Step 3:** Find all the k-itemsets R_k^T with their counts from T that exist in the pre-stored large k-itemsets L_k^D or in the pre-large k-itemsets P_k^D of D.

  ○ **Step 4:** For each itemset I existing in L_k^D, do the following substeps (for managing Cases 1 to 3):

    ⌐ **Substep 4-1:** If I exists in R_k^T, then set the new count $S^U(I) = S^D(I) - S^T(I)$; otherwise, set $S^U(I) = S^D(I)$.

    ⌐ **Substep 4-2:** If $S^U(I)/(d - c - t) \geq S_u$, assign I as a large itemset, set $S^D(I) = S^U(I)$ and keep I with $S^D(I)$; otherwise, if $S^U(I)/(d - c - t) \geq S_l$, assign I as a pre-large itemset, set $S^D(I) = S^U(I)$ and keep I with $S^D(I)$; otherwise, neglect I.

  ○ **Step 5:** For I existing in P_k^D, do the following substeps (for managing Cases 4 to 6):

    ⌐ **Substep 5-1:** If I exists in R_k^T, then set the new count $S^U(I) = S^D(I) - S^T(I)$; otherwise, set $S^U(I) = S^D(I)$.

    ⌐ **Substep 5-2:** If $S^U(I)/(d - c - t) \geq S_u$, assign I as a large itemset, set $S^D(I) = S^U(I)$ and keep I with $S^D(I)$; otherwise, if $S^U(I)/(d - c - t) \geq$

S_l, assign I as a pre-large itemset, set $S^D(I) = S^U(I)$ and keep I with $S^D(I)$; otherwise, neglect I.

○ **Step 6:** If $(t + c) \leq f$, then do nothing; otherwise, rescan D to determine large or pre-large itemsets (for managing Cases 7 to 9).

○ **Step 7:** Generate candidate $(k + 1)$-itemsets C_{k+1} from ($L_k^U \cup P_k^U$) in a way similar to that in the *apriori* algorithm (Agrawal & Srikant, 1994).

○ **Step 8:** Set $k = k + 1$.

○ **Step 9:** Set $L_k^D = L_k^D \cap C_k$ and $P_k^D = P_k^D \cap C_k$.

○ **Step 10:** Repeat STEPs 3 to 9 until no new large or pre-large itemsets are found.

○ **Step 11:** Derive the association rules from the final large itemsets for U.

○ **Step 12:** If $(t + c) > f$, then set $d = d - c - t$ and set $c = 0$; otherwise, set $c = c + t$.

After Step 12, the final association rules for the updated database can then be found.

Experiments

We implemented all the algorithms for the experiments in C++ on a workstation with dual Pentium-III 800MHz processors and 512MB main memory. A synthetic dataset called *T5I4D200K* and a real dataset called *BMS-POS* were used. The *T5I4D200K* dataset was generated by a generator, considering the parameters listed in Table 4.

Table 4. Parameters considered when generating datasets

Parameter	Description
D	Number of transactions
N	Number of items
L	Number of maximal potentially large itemsets
T	Average size of items in a transaction
I	Average size of items in maximal potentially large itemsets

Figure 3. The relationship between execution times and lower support thresholds on T5I4D200K

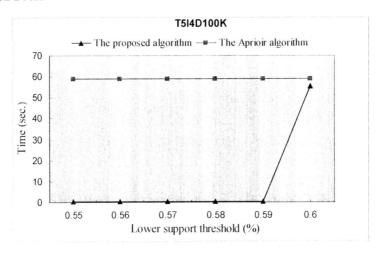

The generator first generated 2000 maximal potentially large itemsets, each with an average of 5 items. The items in the potentially large itemsets were randomly chosen from the total 1000 items according to their actual sizes. The generator then generated 200,000 transactions, each with an average length of 4 items. The items in a transaction were generated according to the 2000 maximal potentially large itemsets in a probabilistic way. The *BMS-POS* dataset (Zheng, Kohavi, & Mason, 2001) contains several years of point-of-sale data from a large electronics retailer. Each transaction in this dataset is a customer purchase transaction consisting of all the product categories purchased at one time. There are 515,597 transactions in the dataset. The number of distinct items is 1,657, the maximal transaction size is 164, and the average transaction size is 6.5. This dataset was also used in the KDDCUP 2000 competition.

We first compare the performance of our proposed algorithm with the most well-known apriori algorithm. Figure 3 shows the relationship between execution times and lower support thresholds on *T5I4D200K*, when the number of deleted records was 100 and the upper support threshold was set at 0.6%. It can be easily seen that the execution times by our proposed approach were much less than those by the apriori approach for the lower support thresholds set to a value below 0.6. When the lower support threshold was set at 0.6, meaning that no pre-large itemsets are generated, the execution time of the proposed approach was nearly the same as that of the apriori approach. In this case, the former was still faster than the latter since the proposed approach reduced some checking time for existing large itemsets.

Figure 4. The relationship between execution times and lower support thresholds on BMS-POS

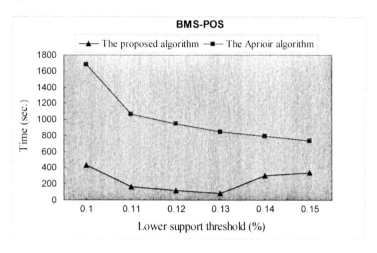

Figure 5. The relationship between numbers of large and pre-large itemsets and lower support thresholds

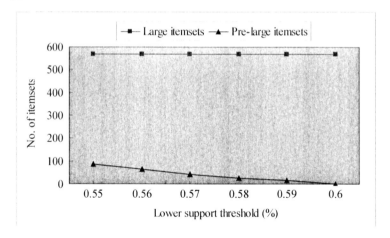

Figure 4 shows the relationship between execution times and lower support thresholds on *BMS-POS*, when the number of deleted records was 100, the upper support threshold was set at 0.15%. The result is quite consistent with the previous discussion.

The relationship between numbers of large and pre-large itemsets and lower support thresholds for *T514D200K* is shown in Figure 5. From Figure 5, it can be easily

Figure 6. The relationship between execution times and numbers of transactions

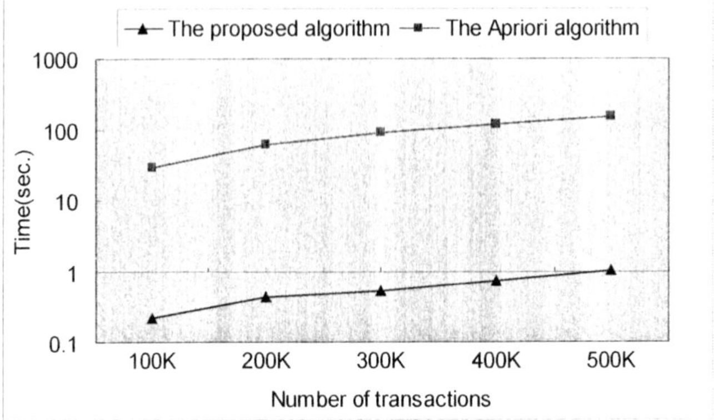

seen that the number of pre-large itemsets decreased as the lower support threshold increased. The number of large itemsets for different lower support thresholds was, however, constant because the upper support threshold was always set at 0.6%. From Figures 3 and 5, the trade-off between decreasing execution time and increasing pre-stored mining information in our proposed approach seems worthy.

The relationship between execution times and numbers of transactions in *T5I4D200K* for a lower support threshold set at 0.59% is shown in Figure 6. It can be easily seen that the execution times by the proposed algorithm were much less than those by the apriori algorithm for different transactions. It can also be observed that the proposed approach become increasingly efficient as the database grows.

Discussion and Conclusion

In this chapter, we have proposed a novel algorithm to maintain discovered as-sociation rules for deletion of records. The concept of pre-large itemsets is used to reduce the need for rescanning the original database and to save maintenance costs. The safety bound for not rescanning the original database is derived and proven. In summary, our proposed algorithm has the following attractive features.

1.   It utilizes previously discovered information in maintenance.
2.   It focuses on deleted records, thus greatly reducing the number of candidate itemsets.

3. It uses a simple check to further filter the candidate itemsets in deleted records.

4. It effectively reduces the number of rescans over the original database until the accumulative number of deleted record exceeds the derived safety bound.

5. If the size of the database grows larger, then the number of deleted records allowed will be larger.

These characteristics are especially useful for real-world applications.

Acknowledgment

This research was supported by the National Science Council of the Republic of China under contract NSC94-2213-E-390 -005.

References

Agrawal, R., Imielinksi, T., & Swami, A. (1993). Mining association rules between sets of items in large database. *ACM SIGMOD Conference*, Washington, DC (pp. 207-216).

Agrawal, R., & Srikant, R. (1994). Fast algorithm for mining association rules. *ACM VLDB Conference* (pp. 487-499).

Agrawal, R., & Srikant, R. (1995). Mining sequential patterns. *IEEE ICDE Conference* (pp. 3-14).

Agrawal, R., Srikant, R., & Vu, Q. (1997). Mining association rules with item constraints. *ACM KDD Conference*, Newport Beach, CA (pp. 67-73).

Cheung, D. W., Han, J., Ng, V. T., & Wong, C. Y. (1996). Maintenance of discovered association rules in large databases: An incremental updating approach. *IEEE ICDE Conference* (pp. 106-114).

Feldman, R., Aumann, Y., Amir, A., & Mannila, H. (1997). Efficient algorithms for discovering frequent sets in incremental databases. *ACM SIGMOD Workshop on DMKD* (pp. 59-66).

Han, J., & Fu, Y. (1995). Discovery of multiple-level association rules from large database. *ACM VLDB Conference*, Zurich, Switzerland (pp. 420-431).

Hong, T. P., Wang, C. Y., & Tao, Y. H. (2001). A new incremental data mining algorithm using pre-large itemsets. *An International Journal: Intelligent Data Analysis, 5*(2), 111-129.

Mannila, H., Toivonen, H., & Verkamo, A. I. (1994). Efficient algorithm for discovering association rules. *AAAI Knowledge Discovery in Databases Workshop* (pp. 181-192).

Mannila, H., & Toivonen, H. (1996). On an algorithm for finding all interesting sentences. *The European Meeting on Cybernetics and Systems Research,* (Vol. 2).

Park, J. S., Chen M. S., & Yu, P. S. (1997). Using a hash-based method with transaction trimming for mining association rules. *IEEE Transactions on Knowledge and Data Engineering, 9*(5), 812-825.

Sarda, N. L., & Srinivas, N. V. (1998). An adaptive algorithm for incremental mining of association rules. *IEEE Database and Expert Systems Workshop* (pp. 240-245).

Srikant, R., & Agrawal, R. (1995). Mining generalized association rules. *ACM VLDB Conference,* Zurich, Switzerland (pp. 407-419).

Srikant, R., & Agrawal, R. (1996). Mining quantitative association rules in large relational tables. *ACM SIGMOD Conference,* Montreal, Canada (pp. 1-12).

Thomas, S., Bodagala, S., Alsabti, K., & Ranka, S. (1997). An efficient algorithm for the incremental update of association rules in large databases. *ACM KDD Conference* (pp. 263-266).

Zheng, Z., Kohavi, R., & Mason, L. (2001). Real world performance of association rule algorithms. *ACM KDD Conference* (pp. 401-406).

Chapter IV

An XML-Based Database for Knowledge Discovery:
Definition and Implementation

Rosa Meo, Università di Torino, Italy

Giuseppe Psaila, Università di Bergamo, Italy

Abstract

Inductive databases have been proposed as general purpose databases to support the KDD process. Unfortunately, the heterogeneity of the discovered patterns and of the different conceptual tools used to extract them from source data make the integration in a unique framework difficult. In this chapter, we explore the feasibility of using XML as the unifying framework for inductive databases, and propose a new model, XML for data mining (XDM). We show the basic features of the model, based on the concepts of data item (source data and patterns) and statement (used to manage data and derive patterns). We make use of XML namespaces (to allow the effective coexistence and extensibility of data mining operators) and of XML-schema, by means of which we can define the schema, the state and the integrity constraints of an inductive database.

Introduction

Data mining applications are called to extract descriptive patterns, typically used for decision making, from the data contained in traditional databases and recently also from other unconventional information systems such as the web.

Examples of these applications are the *market basket analysis*, that extracts patterns such as association rules between purchased items, sequential patterns (that extract temporal descriptions between observed events), classification, clustering and link analysis as in Quinlan (1993) and Agrawal, Imielinski, and Swami (1993) (that provide, in other words, user profiles, text mining, graph mining, and so on). Furthermore, these patterns can be used to give an explanation of the patterns themselves. In this case the data patterns are considered as data to be analysed (and not necessarily with the same analysis tool that was used to obtain them).

Inductive databases have been launched in Imielinski and Mannila (1996) as general-purpose databases in which both the data and the patterns can be represented, retrieved, and manipulated with the goal to assist the deployment of the *knowledge discovery process* (KDD). Thus, KDD becomes a querying sequence in a query language designed for a specific data mining problem (Boulicaut, Klemettinen, & Mannila, 1998). Consequently, an inductive database should integrate several heterogeneous data mining tools that deal with very different heterogeneous and complex data models. For example, source raw data may be represented as flat tables, or, nowadays, by loosely structured documents containing data coming from the Web as well. Also, the conceptual models are different: classification tools usually adopt a data model that is a classification tree, while basket analysis usually represents patterns by means of set enumeration models.

In this chapter, we propose a semi-structured data model specifically designed for inductive databases and, more generally, for *knowledge discovery systems*. This model is called XDM (XML for data mining). It is based on XML and is devised to cope with several distinctive features at the same time (Bray, Paoli, & Sperberg-McQueen, 1997).

- At first, it is semi-structured, in order to be able to represent an a-priori infinite set of data models.

- Second, it is based on two simple and clear concepts, named *Data Item* and *Statement*: a data item is a container of data and/or patterns; a statement is a description of an operator application.

- Third, with XDM the inductive database state is defined as the collection of data items and statements, and the knowledge discovery process is represented as a set of relationships between data items and statements.

- Fourth, it provides a definition of the database schema by means of the set of integrity constraints over inputs and outputs for operators. Moreover, it constitutes the meta-data of the KDD process (i.e., in terms of the kind of data produced by the operators). The database schema was obtained with the aid of XML-schema, which makes possible to define constraints that must hold on some specific data items or operators, thus ensuring a certain level of correctness of data and patterns. XML-schema specifications constrain the structure of XML documents and overcome the limitations of classical XML DTDs, by adding the concept of data type for attributes. Refer to Thompson, Beech, Maloney, and Mendelson (2001) and Biron and Malhotra (2001) for detailed descriptions on XML-schema.

The above discussed features of the model set the foundations to achieve operator interoperability within a unique framework (provided that the various operators' API are XML compliant). Finally, the adoption of XML as syntactic format provides several benefits; in particular, the concept of *namespace* opens the way to the integration of several data formats and operators inside the same framework (Bray, Hollander, & Layman, 1999).

XDM provides several interesting features for inductive databases:

- At first, source raw data and patterns are represented at the same time in the model.
- Second, the pattern derivation process is stored in the database: this is determinant for the phase of pattern interpretation and allows pattern reuse. Patterns may be stored either extensionally, that is materializing patterns in the database, or intentionally, in other words, by storing only the statements that generate the patterns.
- Furthermore, the framework can be easily extended with new data mining operators because each of them brings its own namespace and the namespaces for managed data models.

Thus inductive databases based on XDM really become open systems that are easily customizable according to the kind of patterns in which the user/analyst is interested in. Thanks to the interoperability that operators obtain in the XDM model, inductive databases really become the unifying framework in which the various KDD data transformation phases take place. Finally, the use of XML allows the inclusion and the management of semi-structured data inside inductive databases.

The chapter will point out an important difference of XDM w.r.t. other XML formats for data mining and knowledge discovery, such as in PMML (DMG Group).

For short, PMML is a format to exchange patterns among different systems, thus it is focused on the description of patterns. XDM is not focused on the description of specific patterns; it is a framework for knowledge discovery activities, and the XML structure is the suitable format to host different representations for data and patterns.

Finally, note that the main concepts on which XDM is based are not necessarily tied to XML, but certainly XML provides a flexibility that is difficult to obtain with other formats. Since XDM is independent of the specific format for data and patterns, we might imagine that patterns represented by PMML documents might be stored inside an inductive database based on XDM.

The chapter will be organized as follows. First of all, we will start defining the tree data model at the basis of the XDM model and defining the first fundamental XDM concept of *data item* and related features, such as the possible relationships with other data items. The concept of *schema* for data items is provided as well: it will be useful to check constraints and consistence status of the inductive database.

Second, we will define the second fundamental concept of *statement*. This one specifies the application of an operator (for data manipulation and analysis tasks) whose execution causes the generation of a new, derived data item. The concept of schema is defined for XDM statements as well, and will be used by the inductive database system to verify semantics constraints of data items. We will make a key observation: data items and statements have the same concept of schema. This is important, because it puts in evidence the fact that data items and statements are dual. Thus, data items and statements are the two faces of the same coin (i.e., the knowledge discovery process).

At this point, we will be able to define the concepts of *database schema* and *database state*. The XDM database is both a data item base and a statement base. When a new statement is executed, the new database state is obtained from the former one by adding both the executed statement and the new data item. This structure represents the two-fold nature of the knowledge discovery process: data and patterns are not meaningful if considered in isolation; in contrast, patterns are significant if the overall process is described, because the meaning of data items is clarified by the clauses specified in the data mining operators that generate data items.

We will present the implementation of an inductive database system based on XDM model, discussing the technical solutions and the architectural choices. Then we will extensively discuss how it is possible to deal with multiple data and pattern formats within our framework; this discussion will be based on a detailed example that is reported and fully explained in the Appendix.

Background

Inductive databases, proposed in Imielinski and Mannila (1996), are intended to be general purpose databases in which both source data and mined patterns can be represented, retrieved and manipulated; however, the heterogeneity of models for mined patterns makes difficult to realize them. In Catania, Maddalena, Mazza, Bertino, and Rizzi, (2004) a framework for data mining pattern management is proposed in which an object-oriented methodology is adopted. It allows to represent the pattern type and its hierarchy and the allowed set of operations for pattern generation and manipulation. In Rizzi (2004) UML is used instead. As regards query languages in inductive databases, a survey is provided in Botta, Boulicaut, Masson & Meo (2004).

CRoss-Industry Standard Process for Data Mining (CRISP-DM) has been released to support the user in a (tool neutral) representation of patterns and in the process of their generation. It is an open industry standard that is based on SQL interfaces (ODBC, JDBC) to access data. The model generation is described by JDM (a Java Data Mining API), the SQL/MM package for data mining (part 6 of the SQL3 standard), and OLEDB/DM. OLE DB/DM (Netz, Chaudhuri, Fayyad, & Bernhart, 2001) has been released by Microsoft for Analysis Server to support data mining functionalities with an SQL-like interface for data mining operations (built upon OLEDB/SQL).

Thanks to the flexibility it allows, XML is becoming the universal format for data exchange between applications and the WEB is used as the common location where to publish and access public data. Thus, researchers are now proposing the application of standard data mining techniques to XML documents, such as in Zaki and Aggarwal (2003) and Braga, Campi, Ceri, et al. (2003). Discovered patterns are stored and managed in native XML DBMS such as Tamino or in RDBMS capable to store XML documents, as in Kappel, Kapsammer, Rausch-Schott, and Retschitzegger (2000) and Klettke and Meyer (2000).

Standards such as WSDL (WS 2002) and UDDI (2004) have been proposed as protocols, based on WEB services, which support e-business applications. PMML (DMG Group), and XML for Analysis (XMLA, an open industry standard) are currently being released as standards respectively for the representation of data mining patterns (such as association rules, classification models, etc.) and analytical data discovered by statistical applications in XML documents.

In Abiteboul et al. (2003) and Abiteboul, Benjelloun, and Milo (2004), Active XML documents have been defined with the purpose to manage and keep up-to-date derived data on the basis of the application of sophisticated statistical operations and applications. In this proposal, WEB services have been effectively adopted as the technological solution.

In Meo and Psaila (2002) we explored the feasibility of using XML as the unifying framework for KDD, introducing a first proposal of XML for data mining and its data model.

XDM is suitable to support KDD applications because it integrates source raw data with heterogeneous mined patterns, it allows the application of different statements, designed for data management and pattern generation. The flexibility of the XDM representation allows extensibility to new pattern models and new mining operators: this makes the framework suitable to build an open system, easily customized by the analyst. Similar functionalities are available also in the XML-based framework proposed in Alcamo, Domenichini, & Torlone (2000), with the difference that XDM is designed to be adopted inside the framework of inductive databases.

Main Thrust of the Chapter

The critical issues related to the development of a system supporting the KDD process are the management of several sources of data and of multiple patterns having different heterogeneous format. Also, extensibility towards new applications is an important aspect because new data mining operators and novel user requirements are developed every day. Let us think, for instance, of privacy issues that require new data mining solutions. Also, efficiency and scalability still remain ones of the main concerns. In this way, the user would like to extend the system with new features and the last optimized version of every data mining operator.

The XDM data model, is suitable to support KDD applications because it integrates source raw data with heterogeneous mined patterns. Also, it allows the applications of different statements, designed for data management and pattern generation. XDM allows the management of semi-structured and complex patterns thanks to the semi-structured nature of the data that can be represented by XML. In XDM the pattern definition is represented together with data. This allows the "reuse" of patterns by the inductive database management system and the representation of intentional XML data. In particular, XDM explicitly represents the statements executed in the pattern derivation process. The flexibility of the XDM representation allows to extend the framework with new pattern models and new mining operators: this makes the framework suitable to build an open system, easily customized by the analyst.

XDM Data Items

Tree model. An XML document or fragment is represented as a tree of nodes.

A *StructuralNode* is a generic node in the tree. It can be either an *ElementNode* or a *TextualNode* (with a textual content). An *ElementNode n* has a possibly empty set of *attributes*, in other words, pairs *(Name: String, Value: String)*, denoted as *n.Attributes* which are the attributes defined by the XML syntax within tags). Furthermore, an *ElementNode* has the following properties: the element tag name *n.Name*, the prefix associated to the name space *n.Prefix*, the name space *r.NameSpace* specifying the name space URI (hereafter we will refer to an *ElementNode* with the notation *Prefix:Name*); finally, *ElementNode* has a content *n.Content*, which is a possibly empty sequence of *StructuralNode*.

Definition 1. An *XDM Data Item* is a tree fragment defined as follows:

- The root *r* is an *ElementNode* XDM:DATA-ITEM, belonging to the standard XDM name space whose prefix is XDM. In the content *r.Content*, only XDM:DERIVATION and XDM:CONTENT nodes are allowed (defined hereafter).

- The root node *r* has a set of attributes, *r.Attributes*, denoting the data item features: Name, Date, Version, and Virtual (a boolean denoting whether the data item is virtual or materialized).

□

Definition 2. The XDM:CONTENT node is an *ElementNode* (defined on the standard XDM name space), here denoted as *c*. The XDM:CONTENT node has no attributes, and only one child *ElementNode n* in *c.Content*. The XDM:CONTENT node is not present in a XDM:DATA-ITEM element if its attribute Virtual is set to "yes".

□

Example 1. Consider the following XDM data item:

```
<XDM:DATA-ITEM Name="Purchases" Version="1" Virtual="NO"
      Date="..." xmlns:XDM="http://.../NS/XDM">
  <XDM:CONTENT>
    <TRANSACTIONS>
      <PRODUCT TID="1" CUSTOMER="c1" ITEM="A"  PRICE="25"/>
      <PRODUCT TID="1" CUSTOMER="c1" ITEM="B"  PRICE="12"/>
      <PRODUCT TID="2" CUSTOMER="c3" ITEM="C"  PRICE="30"/>

      . . . .
```

```
      </TRANSACTIONS>
     </XDM:CONTENT>
   </XDM:DATA-ITEM>
```

The start tag XDM:DATA-ITEM defines the attributes for the XDM data item named Purchases. This XDM data item is not virtual (it is materialized): it contains the data from which the analysis process starts.

Notice the namespace definition xmlns:XDM="http://.../NS/XDM", which says that all element nodes prefixed as XDM belong to the namespace identified by the specified URI.

The content of the Purchases data item consists of a set of purchase transactions (introduced here by the tag TRANSACTIONS), where each transaction contains the detail data of a purchased product (specified by tag PRODUCT).

□

Definition 3. The XDM:DERIVATION node is an *ElementNode* (defined on the standard XDM name space), here denoted as *d. d.Content* is empty and *d.Attributes* contains only one mandatory attribute Statement, which contains the identifier of the XDM *statement* that generated the data item (see next sections for a detailed discussion on derivation). If the XDM:DERIVATION node is present in an XDM:DATA-ITEM node, the data item is said *derived*, since it is generated by a statement, otherwise is *not derived*.

□

Note that the *Content* of a data item node *r* does not contain the XDM:CONTENT node if it represents a virtual item, while the XDM:DERIVATION node is required (only derived items can be virtual). On the contrary, a non-derived data item contains the XDM:CONTENT node only.

Figure 1. Sample KDD process within the XDM framework

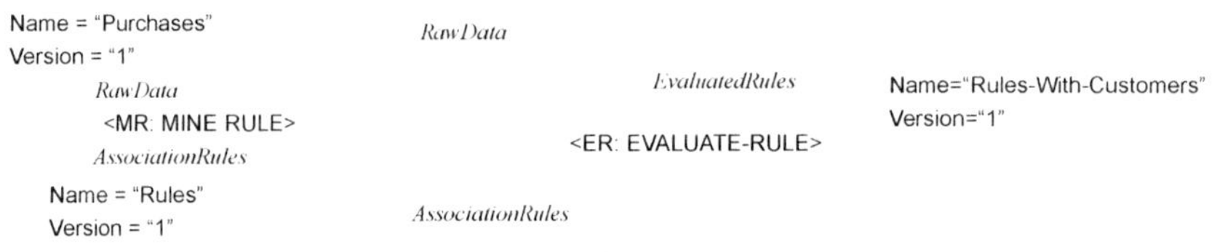

Example 2. We now show a derived XDM data item, named Rules, containing the association rules extracted from the purchase data in the data item named Purchases. These data items are shown in the left hand side of Figure 1 that shows a sample KDD process.

```
<XDM:DATA-ITEM Name="Rules" Version="1" Virtual="NO"
       Date="..." xmlns:XDM="http://.../NS/XDM">
 <XDM:DERIVATION Statement="00128"/>
 <XDM:CONTENT>
   <AR:ASSOCIATION-RULE-SET
       xmlns:AR="http://...NS/DATA/AssRules">
       <AR:RULE>
         <AR:BODY>
           <AR:ELEMENT Name="ITEM"> A </AR:ELEMENT>
           <AR:ELEMENT Name="ITEM"> C </AR:ELEMENT>
         </AR:BODY>
         <AR:HEAD>
           <AR:ELEMENT Name="ITEM"> B </AR:ELEMENT>
         </AR:HEAD>
         <AR:SUPPORT value="0.5"/>
         <AR:CONFIDENCE value="1"/>
       </AR:RULE>
....
   </AR:ASSOCIATION-RULE-SET>
 </XDM:CONTENT>
</XDM:DATA-ITEM>
```

The XDM:DERIVATION element specifies the identifier of the statement which derived (generated) the data item (statements will be described later). In particular, this item is generated by a statement based on the MR:MINE-RULE operator (see later) which extracts association rules from a data item.

The generated set of association rules is included in the XDM:CONTENT section (inside AR:ASSOCIATION-RULE-SET element), which is present since the data item is derived and not virtual. Note that this fragment is based on a specific namespace, (with prefix AR and its own URI http://... NS/DATA/AssRules) defined for association rule sets descriptions. Note that the URI belonging to the standard XDM namespace could be different w.r.t. the URI of the specific data mining operator. Indeed, XDM is independent w.r.t. the operators which can be added to the XDM-based system even in a following time.

In the data item, we report one single rule; notice the semi-structured representation of the association rule:

$\{ A, C \} \Rightarrow \{ B \}$, *support=0.5, confidence=1.0*

The reader can notice that this semi-structured representation is suitable to represent a complex format such as the one of association rules, which are hardly represented in a flat relational manner.

□

Schema for XDM data items. The XML syntactic structure of XDM data items is very rich. However, behind this structure, we can identify the concept of *Schema*. Given an XDM data item *di*, the schema of *di*, denoted as *Schema(di)*, is a four-tuple:

Schema(di) = < NameSpace, Prefix, Root, xsd >

where *NameSpace* is the namespace URI on which the content of the XDM data item is defined, *Prefix* is the namespace prefix associated to the namespace URI, *root* is the root node element of the XML fragment in the data item's XDM:CONTENT element; finally, xsd is the name of the file containing the XML-Schema definition that defines the XML structure for documents belonging to the specified namespace URI. For example, the schema of item in Example 2 is:

```
<"http://...NS/DATA/AssRules","AR",
     "ASSOCIATION-RULE-SET", "ar.xsd">
```

XDM Statements

The XDM model is devised to capture the KDD process and therefore it provides also the concept of *statement*. This one specifies the application of an operator (for data manipulation and analysis tasks) whose execution causes the generation of a new, derived data item.

Definition 4. An XDM statement *s* is specified by a tree fragment, whose structure is the following:

- The root of the fragment is an element node XDM:STATEMENT denoted as *s*. *s* has the attribute ID, which is the statement identifier.

- The *Content* of XDM:STATEMENT is a non-empty list of XDM:SOURCE-ITEM nodes, followed by an XDM:OPERATOR node (describing the application of the operator), followed by a non empty list of XDM:OUTPUT-ITEM nodes.

- A XDM:SOURCE-ITEM node specifies a *source XDM data item*, which constitutes one input for the operator application.

- A XDM:OUTPUT-ITEM node specifies an *output XDM data item*, which constitutes one output of the operator application.

□

Example 3. The following example shows a statement which applies the MR:MINE-RULE operator (see Meo, Psaila, & Ceri, 1998, for a complete description of the operator).

```
<XDM:STATEMENT ID="00128" xmlns:XDM="http://.../NS/XDM">
   <XDM:SOURCE-ITEM Role="RawData"
    Name=" Purchases" Version="1"/>
   <XDM:OPERATOR>
      <MR:MINE-RULE xmlns:MR="http://.../NS/MINE-RULE">
         <MR:GROUPING select="TRANSACTIONS/PRODUCT"
                     common-value="@TID"/>
         <MR:RULE-ELEMENT name="ITEM" select="@ITEM"/>
         <MR:MEASURES>
            <MR:SUPPORT threshold="0.5"/>
            <MR:CONFIDENCE threshold="0.8"/>
         </MR:MEASURES>
      </MR:MINE-RULE>
   </XDM:OPERATOR>
<XDM:OUTPUT-ITEM Name="Rules" Virtual="NO"
    Role="AssociationRules"
    Root="MR:RULE-SET" NS="http://.../NS/DATA/Rules"/>
</XDM:STATEMENT>
```

Notice that the operator and its specific element nodes are defined in the namespace prefix MR, corresponding to the URI "http://.../NS/MINE-RULE", because they are outside the standard XDM namespace. SOURCE-ITEM specifies the input of the operator providing Name and Version number of the XDM data item. OUTPUT-ITEM specifies the output data item: its name is specified by Name, while the fragment in the data item's content is rooted in an element specified by Root, as well as its format is defined in a specific name space (attribute NS). The Role attribute is exploited by the operator to distinguish the role of each data item w.r.t. the operator application.

Consider the data item reported in Example 2. The MINE-RULE operator analyses it looking (see element MR:RULE-ELEMENT) for association rules which associate values of attribute ITEM in elements PRODUCT; these elements are logically grouped (see element MR:GROUPING) by the value of attribute TID, since association rules must denote regularities w.r.t. single transactions (i.e., rules must put in evidence the most common associations of products bought within the same transaction). Finally, rules are extracted if their support (frequency among the data) and confidence (conditional probability) are greater than the respective thresholds specified in the MR:MEASURES element.

□

Example 4. We now show the application of another operator, namely EVALUATE-RULE. This operator has been specifically designed to retrieve the original data (stored in XDM data items) for which already extracted association rules (in other XDM data items) are satisfied. Therefore, this operator computes cross-references between rules and original data. A complete description of this operator, in an SQL version for relational databases, can be found in Psaila (2001).

The application of an EVALUATE-RULE statement is shown in Figure 1. This operator takes two XDM data items as input: with the role of RawData it takes the first version of the data item named Purchases, and with the role of AssociationRules it takes the first version of the data item named Rules. It gives in output a new data item, named Rules-With-Customers containing for each association rule the list of customers for which it holds; this data item has the role EvaluatedRules. The XDM statement is the following:

```
<XDM:STATEMENT ID="00133" xmlns:XDM="http://.../NS/XDM">
    <XDM:SOURCE-ITEM Role="RawData"
     Name="Purchases" Version="1"/>
    <XDM:SOURCE-ITEM Role="AssociationRules"
      Name="Rules" Version="1"/>
    <XDM:OPERATOR>
      <ER:EVALUATE-RULE xmlns:ER="http://.../NS/EVALUATE-RULE">
```

```
      <ER:GROUPING select="TRANSACTIONS/PRODUCT"
         common-value="@TID"/>
      <ER:RULE-ELEMENT name="ITEM" select="@ITEM"/>
      <ER:EVALUATION-FEATURE name="CUSTOMER"
            select="@CUSTOMER"/>
    </ER:EVALUATE-RULE>
  </XDM:OPERATOR>
  <XDM:OUTPUT-ITEM Name="Rules-With-Customers" Version="1"
    Virtual="NO" Role="EvaluatedRules"
    Root="EVALUATED-ASSOCIATION-RULE-SET"
    NS="http://.../NS/DATA/EvAssRules"/>
</XDM:STATEMENT>
```

Notice that the specific element nodes of the operator are defined in the namespace ER, corresponding to the URI "http://.../NS/EVALUATE-RULE", outside the standard XDM namespace.

The first XDM:SOURCE-ITEM node specifies the data item with the role of RawData; it is the data set over which rules are evaluated. The second XDM:SOURCE-ITEM node specifies the data item with the role of Association-Rules, that is, the set of association rules to evaluate.

Within the operator, element ER:GROUPING states that rules express regularities w.r.t. transaction identifiers; element ER:RULE-ELEMENT specifies that rules associate values of attribute ITEM in elements PRODUCT; element ER:EVALUATION-FEATURE says that rules are evaluated w.r.t. customer identifiers. Consequently, the operator produces a new data item, which contains the same rules extended with the list of customers for which each rule holds.

The output data item is specified by the XDM:OUTPUT-ITEM. Evaluated association rules have a specific role (EvaluatedRules) and in the case of this statement will be materialized (attribute Virtual="NO"). The name of the root node in the data item's content is defined by the Root attribute and its namespace (ERD) is defined by a NS specification.

The new data item produced by the previous statement is the following:

```
<XDM:DATA-ITEM Name="Rules-With-Customers"
       Version="1" Virtual="NO"
       Date="..." xmlns:XDM="http://.../NS/XDM">
  <XDM:DERIVATION Statement="00133"/>
  <XDM:CONTENT>
```

```
<EAR:EVALUATED-ASSOCIATION-RULE-SET
  mlns:AR="http://.../NS/DATA/EvAssRules">
   <EAR:RULE>
     <EAR:BODY>
        <EAR:ELEMENT Name="ITEM"> A </EAR:ELEMENT>
      <EAR:ELEMENT Name="ITEM"> C </EAR:ELEMENT>
     </EAR:BODY>
     <EAR:HEAD>
       <EAR:ELEMENT Name="ITEM"> B </EAR:ELEMENT>
     </EAR:HEAD>
     <EAR:SUPPORT value="0.5"/>
     <EAR:CONFIDENCE value="1"/>
     <EAR:EVALUATED-FOR>
        <EAR:ELEMENT Name="CUSTOMER"> c1 </EAR:ELEMENT>
        <EAR:ELEMENT Name="CUSTOMER"> c3 </EAR:ELEMENT>
        <EAR:ELEMENT Name="CUSTOMER"> c4 </EAR:ELEMENT>
     </EAR:EVALUATED-FOR>
   </EAR:RULE>
....
  </EAR:ASSOCIATION-RULE-SET>
 </XDM:CONTENT>
</XDM:DATA-ITEM>
```

Notice that this data item is structurally similar to the one shown in Example 2, named Rules. In particular, it is defined on a different namespace associated with the prefix EAR; furthermore, for each rule an element named EAR:EVALUATED-FOR is added, which contains the set of customers for which the rule holds (notice that each customer is described by an occurrence of element EAR:ELEMENT, whose attribute Name specifies the feature whose value is reported in the content).

□

Schema for XDM statements. Statements as well are based on the XML syntactic structure. Anyway, similarly to XDM data items, it is possible to identify, behind the syntax, the concept of *schema*. Given an XDM statement *s*, the schema of *s*, denoted as *Schema(s)*, is a four-tuple:

Schema(s) = < NameSpace, Prefix, Root, xsd >

where *NameSpace* is the namespace URI on which the operator is defined, *Prefix* is the namespace prefix associated to the namespace URI, *root* is the root element of the XML fragment describing the operator application, *xsd* is the XML-schema definition that defines the XML structure for the operator application belonging to the specified namespace URI. For example, the schema of the MINE-RULE statement of Example 3 is:

<"http://.../NS/MINE-RULE","MR","MINE-RULE","mr.xsd">.

It is important to note that, although the syntactic structure for data items and statements is slightly different, the concept of schema is identical. This is important, because it evidences the fact that data items and statements are dual. Thus, data items and statements are really two faces of the same coin, in other words, the knowledge discovery process.

XDM Database Schema and State

Defined the two basic XDM concepts, we can formally define the concepts of XDM *database schema* and XDM *database state*.

> **Definition 5.** The *schema of an XDM database* is a 4-tuple <*S, I, In, Out*>, where *S* is a set of statement schemas, and *I* is a set of data item schemas.
>
> *In* is a set of tuples <*Operator, InputRole, InputFormat*>, where *Operator* (in the form *prefix:root*) is an operator for which a statement schema is described by a tuple in *S*; *InputRole* is the role expected for the input data by the operator (for instance, the role might be "RawData", for association rule mining); *InputFormat* is a data item content root (in the form *prefix:root*) whose schema is described by a tuple in *I*; if the operator does not require any particular data format for the specified role, *InputFormat* is a *.
>
> *Out* is a set of tuples <*Operator, OutputRole, OutputFormat*> where *Operator* (in the form *prefix:root*) is an operator for which a statement schema is described by a tuple in *S*; *OutputRole* is the role expected for the output data generated by the operator (for instance, the role might be "AssociationRules", for association rule mining); *OutputFormat* (in the form *prefix:root*) is a data item content root, generated by the specified operator, whose schema is described by a tuple in *I*; if the operator does not generate any particular data format, *OutputFormat* is a *.

□

Example 5. With reference to the MINE-RULE and EVALUATE-RULE opera-tors (briefly introduced in previous examples), this is the schema of our database, as far as *In* and *Out* are concerned.

In={<MR:MINE-RULE, RawData,*>,
     <ER:EVALUATE-RULE, RawData,*>,
     <ER:EVALUATE-RULE, AssociationRules, AR:ASSOCIATION-RULE-SET>}
Out={<MR:MINE-RULE, AssociationRules, AR:ASSOCIATION-RULE-SET>,
     <ER:EVALUATE-RULE, EvaluatedRules,
      EAR:EVALUATED-ASSOCIATION-RULE-SET>}

□

Observations. If we reason in terms of schema, in our context the role of the schema is to define the following features: given an operator, which are the expected input formats (if any)? Which are the generated output formats? In other words, this means the introduction of a set of integrity constraints over the input and output data of the operators. Observe that the same questions may be seen from the point of view of data items: given the format for a data item, which are the operators that take it as input format? Which are the operators that generate it? These are meta data on the KDD process that can be exploited by querying the schema of the XDM database in order to check (automatically by the system or explicitly by the user) the consistence among the operations performed over the data.

Definition 6. The state of an XDM database is represented as a pair:

$$< DI: Set\ Of(DataItem),\ ST: Set\ Of(Statement) >,$$

where *DI* is a set of XDM data items, and *ST* is a set of XDM statements. The following constraints hold.

- **Data item identity:** Given a data item d and its mandatory attributes Name, and Version, the pair < Name, Version > uniquely identifies the data item d in the database state.

- **Statement identity:** Given a statement s and its mandatory attribute ID, its value uniquely identifies the statement s in the database state.

- **Relationship between statements and source data items:** Consider an XDM statement s. The attributes Name and Version of each XDM:

SOURCE-ITEM appearing in s must denote a data item in DI.

- **Relationship between derived data items and statements:** Consider a derived XDM data item d. The value specified by the Statement attribute of the XDM:DERIVATION element must identify a statement in ST.

□

Example 6. With reference to the scenario described in Figure 1 the database has moved between three states: state S_0 before the execution of statement 00128 (application of MINE-RULE), state S_1 after MINE-RULE execution and before the execution of statement 00133 (application of EVALUATE-RULE), and finally state S_2 after EVALUATE-RULE execution. More precisely, these states are specified in the following table; for simplicity, for DI we report only the pairs identifying data items (i.e., $<$ *Name, Version* $>$) and for ST we report only statement identifiers.

Sequence of database states.

State	DI	ST
S_0	{<Purchase, 1>}	∅
S_1	{<Purchase, 1>, <Rules, 1>}	{ 00128 }
S_2	{<Purchase, 1>, <Rules, 1>, <Rules-with-customers, 1>}	{ 00128, 00133 }

□

Observations. The XDM database is then both a data item base and a statement base. When a new statement is executed, the new database state is obtained from the former one by adding both the executed statement and the new data item.

This structure represents the two-fold nature of the knowledge discovery process: data and patterns are not meaningful if considered in isolation; in contrast, patterns are significant if the overall process is described, because the meaning of data items is clarified by the clauses specified in the data mining operators that generated data items.

Implementation of a Prototype of the XDM System

We implemented a prototype based on the XDM framework. This prototype is still in its early stage; however, it demonstrated the feasibility of the approach and gave us useful indications to study practical problems related with extensibility issues and performance issues.

Figure 2. The architecture of the XDM system

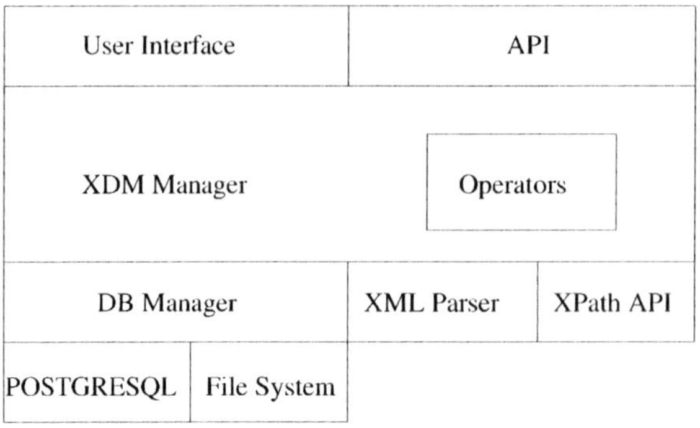

The XDM System is fully realized in Java, and is based on open source components only. Figure 2 shows the general architecture of the XDM System. It is organized in four overlapped layers, such that each of them hides the lower layers to the upper ones.

The *User Interface* and the *XDM API* component constitute the topmost layer, and allow the interaction with the XDM System; in particular, the *XDM API* component is used by applications, while the *User Interface* component is used in an interactive session with the system.

The second layer is constituted by the *XDM Manager*, and by *Operators*, in other words, components which implement data management or data mining operators. *XDM Manager* interprets statements coming from interfaces, activates execution of tools, exploits *DB Manager* to access and store both metadata and data items. *Operators* can interact with the system through an API provided by *XDM Manager* (indeed, from Figure 2 you can notice that *Operators* are confined within the communication channel provided by *XDM Manager*; this means that a tool cannot directly access the database or data items, but can communicate with other system components only through *XDM Manager*). This embedding is beneficial because it provides an inner and immediate compatibility and security check on which operations and accesses are allowed to operators. This is a fundamental feature of an open system since new operators are allowed to be added freely by users at any time, provided that they comply with the allowed operations and methods provided by *XDM Manager* for each data item.

XDM Manager exploits components in the third layer. These components are *DB Manager*, *XML Parser* and *XPath API*; in particular, since both *XML Parser* and *XPath API* might be used by *Operators* for reading data items, *XDM Manager* provides a controlled access to these components (in the sense that these latter components can

Figure 3. Conceptual schema for the database in the XDM system implementation

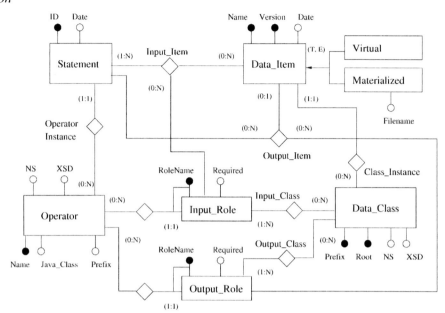

be exploited by various tools in *Operators* only to access input data items). For *XML Parser* we adopted the open source xerces XML Parser developed by the *Apache Software Foundation*. The XPath API has been developed to provide operators with fast access to data items, based on the XPath specification, and without building DOM trees, which are not suitable for dealing with large data sets.

DB Manager encapsulates all data management operations. In particular, it currently exploits POSTGRESQL DBMS to manage the meta-schema of the XDM framework, and the file system to store data items. This latter choice is motivated by efficiency reasons. However, we plan to study the integration of an XML DBMS in *DB Manager*, to study the effectiveness and performance issues of these technical solutions in the case of data mining and knowledge discovery tasks.

The database. As mentioned some lines above, XDM System exploits the POSTGRESQL DBMS to manage the meta-schema of the XDM framework. For the sake of clarity, Figure 3 reports the conceptual schema of this database (we adopt the entity-relationship model with the notation proposed in Atzeni, Ceri, Paraboschi, & Torlone, 1999). The lower side of the conceptual schema in Figure 3 describes the XDM Database Schema. Entity *Data Class* describes classes of data items allowed in the system; entity *Operator* describes operators supported by the system. Entity *Input_Role* is a weak entity of *Operator*: its instances describe input roles of a given operator and are associated to some classes of data items (that, of course, must be allowed in input to the specific operator). Analogous considerations hold for *Output_Role*.

The upper part of the conceptual schema describes data items (i.e., instance of data classes) and statements (i.e., application of operators): notice that relationships *Operator_Instance* and *Class_Instance* associate each statement and data item to the specific operator and data class, respectively. The ternary relationship *Input_Item* denotes, for each statement, the role played by each input data item; the same is for relationship *Output_Item*, except for the fact that the cardinality constraint on the side of *Data_Item* is (0:1) (since an initial data item is not generated by any tool, while a derived data item can be generated by one single statement only).

Notice the hierarchy rooted in entity *Data_Item*: In case of materialized data items, attribute *Filename* denotes the name of the file containing the XML data item. This adoption of the file system as a storage support of the system, useful especially for data items with huge content, was mentioned in the presentation of the system architecture. Note, however, that this reference to the data item filename is not seen at the user level, which is not aware of the implementation details of the system at the lower levels.

Furthermore, notice that the hierarchy is *Total* and *Exclusive* (denoted as (T,E) , since a data item must be either materialized or virtual).

Processing. XDM System allows the easy addition of new operators, provided that they implement a well defined interface. Operator implementation is responsible to implement the actual semantics given to the operator. The XDM Manager provides operators with access services to input data items and gets output data items.

We are well aware that these communication channels are a key factor, in particular in the data mining context, where large data sets might be analyzed. We addressed this problem, by implementing a specific class to access data items without building a main memory representation of the documents; in fact, main memory representations (such as DOM) are not suitable to deal with large XML documents. Anyway, in order to simplify access to data, the class provides an XPath based API, that is exploited by tools to obtain the needed pieces of data. This way, algorithms can be easily adapted and integrated into our framework.

The current solution to the implementation channel is also the basis to investigate the problem of getting data items from different data sources, such as relational databases or native XML database.

Nevertheless, this first version of the XDM System was conceived with the main purpose of demonstrating the feasibility of the XDM approach, in other words, that it is possible to exploit the flexible nature of XML for integrating different kinds of data and patterns. Indeed, with this first version of the XDM System we were able to quickly develop and deploy an open and easily extensible system for data mining and knowledge discovery tasks. Evaluation issues on the obtained system are further discussed in the section *Evaluation and Open Issues*.

Evaluation and Open Issues

Although the system is a preliminary prototype, it is possible to perform some evaluation about the results we obtained; furthermore, based on the experience obtained working on its development, it is also possible to clearly understand which are the open issues that will be addressed in the near future.

Evaluation. First of all, we demonstrated the feasibility of the XDM idea. The software architecture is clean, not complex, and very modular. In particular, we were able to experience modularity, in that we easily introduced the sophisticated *DB Manager* in place of the first early solution of adopting a pure file system-based solution. Modularity has been proved as far as the development of data mining operators is concerned: in fact, we easily developed and quickly integrated a few data mining tools, first of all MINE-RULE and EVALUATE-RULE that allow to extract and evaluate frequent data mining patterns such as itemsets, association rules and elementary sequential patterns (constituted by two ordered itemsets). This fact demonstrated that the XDM framework can be the basis for really open systems.

The main negative drawback we experienced with XDM System is the negative effect of representing data and patterns in XML, if compared to a flat representation of them (which is the representation generally used to evaluate data mining algorithms). To estimate this fact, consider the data item reported in Example 1. Each PRODUCT element represents a row in a table. If we suppose that this table is represented as a flat ASCII file with comma separated fields, the first row may be represented as 1,c1,A,25 which occupies *9* bytes, while the XML representation requires *52* bytes! In contrast, if data were stored by relational databases, usually the difference results not so evident, then our approach is not so disadvantageous. Anyway, we think that the problem of reducing the waste of space in case of large data sets is an open and interesting issue, which could be solved by the new data compressions methods of XML data, that seem to start to be delivered to the market.

Open Issues. In the near future, we plan to address several issues concerning, in particular, performance problems.

Due to the availability of XML document compressors, we plan to experiment with them in the system, to understand which are the drawbacks of this solution when data are accessed (in particular as far as the computation overhead is concerned).

At the moment, we considered only data items stored inside the system: in fact, at the moment, data items must be loaded in the system before exploiting them. We also want to explore the feasibility of linking, and treat external data items as virtual items or relations of a relational database. In this way, several data sources might be connected without moving the data.

Finally, we plan to evolve XDM system into a distributed, grid-like, system, where both distributed data sources and distributed computational sources are connected through the internet to build a unique XDM database.

Dealing with Multiple Formats

The XDM framework is able to deal with multiple formats for representing data and patterns. This is particularly important when the same model can be represented in several distinct formats. This is the case of classification, one of the most popular data mining techniques: the classifier usually produces either a decision tree or a set of classification rules. In the following, through a practical example, we show how it is possible to deal with multiple formats and complex structures (such as trees) within the XDM framework. For the sake of clarity, in this section we discuss the problem, without going in details as far as examples are concerned. In the Appendix, all statements and data items will be described in details.

A classification task is performed in two steps. In the first step, a classification model is built from a data set called *training set*, which is constituted by a set of classified samples; in the second step, the classification model is used to classify new unknown samples. A typical application case is for car insurance: based on previous experience, a company may obtain a model of the risk, so that it can be exploited to better assign a risk class to new applicants.

Suppose we have the following training set:

```
<XDM:DATA-ITEM Name="Training Set" Version="1"
        Date="..." xmlns:XDM="http://.../NS/XDM">
    <XDM:CONTENT>
     <CAR-INSURANCE>
       <PROFILE AGE="17" CAR-TYPE="Sports" RISK="High" />
       <PROFILE AGE="43" CAR-TYPE="Family" RISK="Low" />
       <PROFILE AGE="68" CAR-TYPE="Family" RISK="Low" />
...
     </CAR-INSURANCE>
    </XDM:CONTENT>
</XDM:DATA-ITEM>
```

Each sample of the training set is described by an empty element named PROFILE, whose attributes describe properties (i.e., AGE and CAR-TYPE) that characterize each classified profile and the class to which they have been assigned (Risk Attribute); for simplicity, we consider only two risk classes: low and high.

Observe that this is one possible representation of the training set. A possible alternative representation, allowed by the semi-structured nature of XML, might be the following one (we consider only the first PROFILE element).

```
<PROFILE> <AGE>17</AGE> <CAR-TYPE>Sports</CAR-TYPE>
          <RISK>High</RISK> </PROFILE>
```

Notice that this representation pushes single pieces of data into the content of elements named AGE, CAR-TYPE and RISK contained in each PROFILE element. Although less synthetic, it is equivalent to the former representation.

Building the classification model. The first step for solving a classification problem is to build the classification model based on the training set. Suppose that an operator named MINE-CLASSIFICATION is available; we can then write the following XDM statement.

```
<XDM:STATEMENT ID="00243" xmlns:XDM="http://.../NS/XDM">
    <XDM:SOURCE Role="Training-Set"
     Name="Training Set" Version="1" />
    <XDM:OPERATOR>
     <CLASS:MINE-CLASSIFICATION
        xmlns:CLASS="http://.../NS/CLASS">
        <CLASS:CLASSIFICATION-UNIT
          select="CAR-INSURANCE/PROFILE">
        <CLASS:PARAM name="AGE" select="@AGE" Type="Integer"/>
        <CLASS:PARAM name="CAR-TYPE" select="@CAR-TYPE"
           Type="String"/>
        <CLASS:CLASS-PARAM select="@RISK"/>
      </CLASS:CLASSIFICATION-UNIT>
     </CLASS:MINE-CLASSIFICATION>
    </XDM:OPERATOR>
    <XDM:OUTPUT Name="Risk Classes" Virtual="No"
          Role="Classification-Model"
          Root="CT:CLASSIFICATION-TREE"
          NS="http://.../NS/DARA/CTree"/>
</XDM:STATEMENT>
```

Figure 4. Sample classification tree

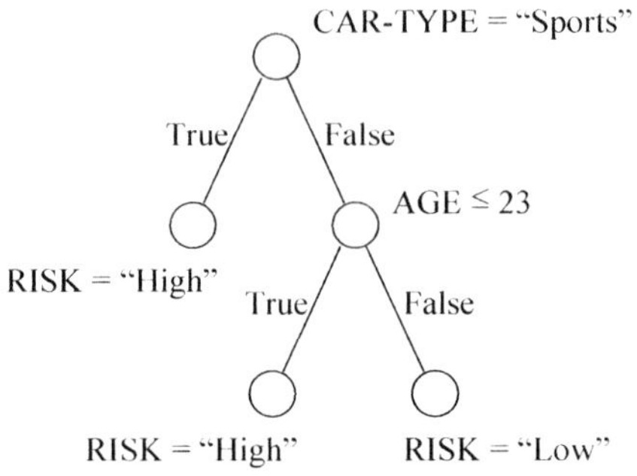

The applied operator is named MINE-CLASSIFICATION, and will be explained in details in the Appendix. Here note that, in the statement, data item "Training set" is the input and plays the role of training set for the operator. Then the statement produces a new data item named "Risk Classes", which is the XML representation of the classification tree in Figure 4 (but if the user chooses a classification rule set, it would be easily represented by a different XML representation).

The Appendix shows that it is possible to write a similar statement for the nested representation of profiles (discussed earlier), since XPath expressions within the operator, easily deal with different formats.

The test phase. Typically, the classification model is used to classify unclassified data. For example, suppose that a new data item, named New Applicants, is loaded into the XDM database, consisting of unclassified applicant profiles. The user wishes to classify each new applicant based on the classification model Risk Classes.

```
<XDM:DATA-ITEM Name="New Applicants" Version="1"
      Date="..." xmlns:XDM="http://.../NS/XDM">
   <XDM:CONTENT>
     <NEW-APPLICANTS>
      <APPLICANT Name="John Smyth" AGE="22" CAR-TYPE="Family"/>
      <APPLICANT Name="Marc Green" AGE="60" CAR-TYPE="Family"/>
      <APPLICANT Name="Laura Fox" AGE="35" CAR-TYPE="Sports"/>
     </NEW-APPLICANTS>
   </XDM:CONTENT>
</XDM:DATA-ITEM>
```

Observe that the root element (NEW-APPLICANTS) and the elements in its content (APPLICANT elements) which describe single profiles of new applicants, are different w.r.t. the corresponding elements of the training set, such as CAR-INSURANCE and PROFILE; in particular, data about applicants also describe applicants' name.

To obtain a classified data item from the previous one, obtained by adding an attribute denoting the risk class to XML elements APPLICANT, we might write a new statement based on a specific operator, named TEST-CLASSIFICATION, specifically developed. It is described in details in Appendix. Here, it is important to note that this statement generates a new data item named "Classified Applicants", containing the classified data; its format is not predefined (as for classification tree) but it is derived from the a priori unknown source data item.

The XDM framework is very suitable to deal with the previous situations, thanks to the concept of XDM database schema. Suppose the following is the schema concerning the classification operators.

```
In={<CLASS:MINE-CLASSIFICATION, Training-Set,*>,
    <CLASS:TEST-CLASSIFICATION, Test-Data,*>,
    <CLASS:TEST-CLASSIFICATION, Classification-Model,
        CT:CLASSIFICATION-TREE>,
    <CLASS:TEST-CLASSIFICATION, Classification-Model,
        CT:CLASSIFICATION-RULES>}
Out={<MR:MINE-CLASSIFICATION, Classification-Model,
        CT:CLASSIFICATION-TREE >,
    <MR:MINE-CLASSIFICATION, Classification-Model,
        CT:CLASSIFICATION- RULES >,
    <CLASS:TEST-CLASSIFICATION, Classified-Data, *>}
```

☐

The star in the input roles means that the operators are able to read any kind of format, as training set and test set; in effect, the operators exploit the XPath syntax to specify the pieces of data of interest. The same is for the output role Classified-Data, because the operator generates a new version of the source test data extended with the classification class.

Furthermore, other roles appear both for input data items and for output data items with more than one data format (in particular, CT:CLASSIFICATION-RULES and CT: CLASSIFICATION-TREE): in effect, the classification operators are able to deal with both rules and trees as classification models.

Consequently, the schema of the database captures this situation and makes the system able to check correctness of statements, based on the constraints w.r.t. data format. As the reader can see, this is not a limitation, since the framework remains able to deal with multiple formats for data items w.r.t. operators.

Future Trends

CRISP-DM, XMLA, PMML, JDM, OLEDB/DM, WSDL, UDDI: a constellation of standards is continuously being developed, as a testimonial of the growing needs of the users and industrial companies towards the development of open systems, suitable to support a wide variety of functionalities for knowledge discovery over the WEB and over multiple sources of structured and semi-structured data. We expect that in the next future one of these standards will effectively emerge over the others and will settle, or some APIs will be developed to translate the calls to the primitives offered by one in the others. At that point the development of open systems for KDD will really be considered as a matter of fact. The development of applications for analytical solutions will result much more easy and fast to develop, to manage and use than today. Applications will also be more powerful since users will be able to install their own preferred operators, peculiar for their specific needs; analysts will also be able to follow the state of the resulting, integrated knowledge base.

Conclusion

In this paper we presented a new, XML-based data model, named XDM. It is designed to be adopted inside the framework of inductive databases.

XDM allows the management of semi-structured and complex patterns thanks to the semi-structured nature of the data that can be represented by XML.

In XDM the pattern definition is represented together with data. This allows the reuse of patterns by the inductive database management system. In particular, XDM explicitly represents the statements that were executed in the derivation process of the pattern. The flexibility of the XDM representation allows extensibility to new pattern models and new mining operators: this makes the framework suitable to build an open system, easily customized by the analyst.

We experimented the XDM idea by means of a first version of a system prototype that resulted to be easily and quickly extendible to new operators.

One drawback of using XML in data mining, however, could be the large volumes reached by the source data represented as XML documents.

References

Abiteboul, S., Baumgarten, J., Bonifati, A., Cobena, G., Cremarenco, C., Dragan, F., et al. (2003). Managing distributed workspaces with active XML. In *Proceedings of the 2003 International Very Large Database Conference*, Berlin, Germany.

Abiteboul, S., Benjelloun, O., & Milo, T. (2004). Active XML and active query answers. In *Proceedings of the 2004 International Conference on Flexible Query Answering Systems*, Lyon, France.

Agrawal, R., Imielinski, T., & Swami, A. (1993). Mining association rules between sets of items in large databases. In *ACM SIGMOD-1993 International Conference on Management of Data* (pp. 207-216).

Alcamo, P., Domenichini, F., & Turini, F. (2000). An XML based environment in support of the overall KDD process. In *Proceedings of the International Conference on Flexible Query Answering Systems*, Warsaw, Poland.

Atzeni, P., Ceri, S., Paraboschi, S., & Torlone, R. (1999). *Database systems.* McGraw-Hill.

Baralis, E., & Psaila, G. (1999). Incremental refinement of mining queries. *First International Conference on Data Warehousing and Knowledge Discovery,* Florence, Italy (pp. 173-182).

Biron, P. V., & Malhotra, A. (2001, May). *XML Schema Part 2: Data Types, REC-xmlschema-2-20010502.* World Wide Web Consortium. Retrieved from http://www.w3.org/TR/2001/REC-xmlschema-2-20010502/

Botta, M., Boulicaut, J.-F., Masson C., & Meo, R. (2004). Query languages supporting descriptive rule mining: A comparative study. In R. Meo, P. Lanzi, & M. Klemettinen, (Eds.), *Database Support for Data Mining Applications* (LNCS 2682, pp. 27-54). Springer-Verlag.

Boulicaut, J.-F., Klemettinen, M., & Mannila, H. (1998). Querying inductive databases: A case study on the MINE RULE operator. In *PKDD-1998 International Conference on Principles of Data Mining and Knowledge Discovery,* Nantes, France (pp. 194-202).

Braga, D., Campi, A., Ceri, S., Klemettinen, M., & Lanzi, P. L. (2003). Discovering interesting information in XML data with association rules. In *Proceedings of ACM Symposium of Applied Computing*, Melbourne, FL.

Bray, Y., Paoli, J., & Sperberg-McQueen, C. M. (1997). Extensible Markup Language (XML). In *PR-xml-971208*. Retrieved from http://www.w3.org/XML

Bray, T., Hollander, D., & Layman, A. (1999). *Namespaces in XML* (Tech. Rep. No. REC-xml-names-19990114). World Wide Web Consortium.

Catania, B., Maddalena, M., Mazza, M., Bertino, E., & Rizzi, S. (2004). A framework for data mining pattern management. In *Proceedings of ECML-PKDD Conference*, Pisa, Italy.

CRISP-DM, CRoss-Industry Standard Process for Data Mining. (n.d.). Retrieved from http://www.crisp-dm.org

DMG Group. (n.d.). *The Predictive Model Mark-up Language* (v. 2.0). Retrieved from http://www.dmg.org/pmml-v2-0.htm.

Imielinski, T. & Mannila, H. (1996). A database perspective on knowledge discovery. *Communications of the ACM, 39*(11), 58–64.

Kappel, G., Kapsammer, E., Rausch-Schott, S., & Retschitzegger, W. (2000). X-Ray — Towards integrating XML and relational database systems. In *Proceedings of the ER '2000 International Conference on the Entity Relationship Approach*, Salt Lake City, UT.

Klettke, M. & Meyer, O. (2000). XML and object-relational database systems — enhancing structural mappings based on statistics. In *Proceedings of the WebDB 2000 International Workshop on Web and Databases*, Dallas, TX.

Meo, R., Psaila, G., & Ceri, S. (1998). An extension to SQL for mining association rules. *Journal of Data Mining and Knowledge Discovery, 2*(2).

Meo, R, & Psaila, G. (2002). Toward XML-based knowledge discovery systems. In *Proceedings of the 2002 IEEE International Conference on Data Mining*, Maebashi, Japan.

Netz, A., Chaudhuri, S., Fayyad, U. M., & Bernhardt, J. (2001). Integrating data mining with SQL databases: OLE DB for data mining. In *Proceedings of IEEE ICDE International Conference on Data Engineering*, Heidelberg, Germany (pp. 379-387).

Psaila G. (2001). Enhancing the KDD process in the relational database mining framework by quantitative evaluation of association rules. In *Knowledge Discovery for Business Information Systems*. Kluwer Academic Publisher.

Quinlan, R. (1993). *C4.5 Programs for machine learning*. Los Altos, CA: Morgan Kauffmann.

Rizzi, S. (2004). UML-based conceptual modeling of pattern-bases. In *Proceedings of the International Workshop on Pattern Representation and Management*, Heraklion, Hellas.

Thompson, H. S., Beech, D., Maloney, M., & Mendelson, N. (2001, May). *XML Schema Part 1: Structures, REC-xmlschema-1-20010502*. Retrieved from http://www.w3.org/TR/2001/REC-xmlschema-1-20010502/

UDDI. (2004, October). *UDDI executive overview: Enabling service-oriented architecture*. Retrieved from http://www.oasis-open.org

WS. (2002). *Web services.* Retrieved from http://www.w3.org/2002/ws

Xpath. (1999). *XML Path Language (XPath)* (Version 1.0). Retrieved from http://
www.w3.org/TR/1999/REC-xpath-19991116.

XMLA, XML for Analysis. (n.d.). Retrieved from http://www.xmla.org/

Zaki, M. J., & Aggarwal, C. C. (2003). An effective structural classifier of XML data.
In *Proceedings of the 2003 ACM SIGKDD Conference*, Washington DC.

Appendix

The section *Dealing with Multiple Formats* is based on a classification example.
For the sake of clarity, in that section we did not report statements and data items.
Here, we report and discuss them in details. This way, the interested reader can
better understand the full potential of XDM.

Building the classification model. First of all, consider the application of the operator named MINE-CLASSIFICATION to data item Training Set; this is statement "00243"
(previously reported).

The applied operator is named MINE-CLASSIFICATION, and is defined with the prefix
CLASS, which denotes the classification operators, whose namespace is identified
by the URI "http://.../NS/CLASS". The statement specifies that data item "Training set"
is the input and plays the role of training set for the operator.

In the operator, the element named CLASSIFICATION-UNIT denotes which elements
inside the selected CAR-INSURANCE element must be considered for building the
classification model; in particular, the select attribute denotes (through an XPath
expression that implicitly operates in the context defined by the XDM:SOURCE element, that is, within the XDM:CONTENT element) the set of elements in the training set
whose properties must be used to build the classification model. In fact, a non empty
set of CLASS:PARAM elements denotes the properties that will be used to build the
classification model (always through XPath expressions). The Type attribute specifies the data type (e.g., integers, real numbers, strings, etc.) that will be used for the
evaluation of the property. Notice that this is necessary to overcome the absence of
data types in XML documents when the XML-Schema specification is not used (as
in the case of the training set). Finally, the CLASS:CLASS-PARAM element specifies
the property inside the classification unit that defines the class (always by means
of an XPath expression denoted by the select attribute).

In our sample case, the elements named PROFILE are the classification units. The
CLASS:PARAM nodes denote that the properties that will be used for the classification model are the attributes AGE and CAR-TYPE (through the XPath expressions @

AGE and @CAR-TYPE) in the context PROFILE nodes. The class label is included in attributes RISK, as specified by the XPath expression @RISK in the CLASS:CLASS-PARAM node.

After the operator, the output data item is specified by means of the XDM:OUTPUT element. Observe that the specified root element must be defined for the chosen role in the database schema; furthermore, we can guess that the operator implementation is able to generate both trees and classification rule sets; it is driven by the Root attribute specified in the XDM:OUTPUT element. In this case, the tree representation has been chosen.

If PROFILE elements were nested, such as:

```
<PROFILE> <AGE>17</AGE> <CAR-TYPE>Sports</CAR-TYPE>
          <RISK>High</RISK> </PROFILE>
```

it would be sufficient to change the Xpath expressions within the statement. For instance, parameter AGE would be specified as follows:

```
<CLASS:PARAM name="AGE" select="AGE/." Type="Integer"/>
```

Notice the different Xpath expression in the select attribute.

The classification model. Statement "00243" produces a new data item containing a classification tree; suppose it is the simplified tree reported in the following data item and shown in Figure 4.

```
<XDM:DATA-ITEM Name="Risk Classes" Version="1"
       Date="..." xmlns:XDM="http://.../NS/XDM">
  <XDM:DERIVATION statement=0243"/>
  <XDM:CONTENT>
  <CT:CLASSIFICATION-TREE
     xmlns:CT="http://.../NS/DARA/CTree">
   <CT:CLASS-PARAM Name="RISK"/>
   <CT:CONDITION>
     <CT:EQ> <CT:PARAM Name="CAR-TYPE"/>
       <CT:VALUE String="Sports"/> </CT:EQ>
   </CT:CONDITION>
   <CT:TRUE-BRANCH>
    <CT:CLASS Value="High"/>
   </CT:TRUE-BRANCH>
   <CT:FALSE-BRANCH>
```

```
  <CT:CONDITION>
    <CT:LEQ> <CT:PARAM Name="AGE"/>
       <CT:VALUE Integer="23"/> </CT:LEQ>
    </CT:CONDITION>
   <CT:TRUE-BRANCH>
    <CT:CLASS Value="High"/>
   </CT:TRUE-BRANCH>
   <CT:FALSE-BRANCH>
    <CT:CLASS Value="Low"/>
   </CT:FALSE-BRANCH>
  </CT:FALSE-BRANCH>
 </CT:CLASSIFICATION-TREE>
 </XDM:CONTENT>
</XDM:DATA-ITEM>
```

Consider the element CT:CLASSIFICATION-TREE. The first child element in the content, named CT:CLASS-PARAM, specifies which parameter constitutes the class (the risk property). Then, a sequence of three elements, named CT:CONDITION, CT:TRUE-BRANCH and CT:FALSE-BRANCH, describes the condition to be applied in the root node, the branch to follow if the condition is evaluated to true, and the branch to follow when it is false, respectively.

Inside a branch, it is possible to find either a class assignment (denoted by element CT:CLASS, which is also a leaf of the tree), or another triple CT:CONDITION, CT:TRUE-BRANCH, and CT:FALSE-BRANCH, and so forth.

As far as conditions are concerned, they are usually based on comparisons between properties and numerical ranges or categorical values; the syntax chosen in our sample classification tree is just an example to show that it is possible to represent decision trees in XML.

The test phase. Given an unclassified set of applicants, represented by data item named New Applicants (shown in the section *Dealing with Multiple Formats*), the following statement generates a new data item named Classified Applicants, that is obtained by extending the previous data item by adding a new attribute named Risk (evaluated by means of the classification tree).

```
<XDM:STATEMENT ID="00245" xmlns:XDM="http://.../NS/XDM">
   <XDM:SOURCE Role="Test-Data"
       Name="New Applicants" Version="1"/>
   <XDM:SOURCE Role="Classification-Model"
       Name="Risk Classes" Version="1"/>
   <XDM:OPERATOR>
```

```
  <CLASS:TEST-CLASSIFICATION
      xmlns:CLASS="http://.../NS/CLASS">
   <CLASS:CLASSIFICATION-UNIT
      select="NEW-APPLICANTS/APPLICANT">
    <CLASS:PARAM name="AGE" select="@AGE"/>
    <CLASS:PARAM name="CAR-TYPE" select="@CAR-TYPE"/>
    </CLASSIFICATION-UNIT>
    <CLASS:EXTEND-WITH-CLASS Name="Risk" Type="Attribute"/>
    </CLASS:TEST-CLASSIFICATION>
  </XDM:OPERATOR>
  <XDM:OUTPUT Name="Classified Applicants" Virtual="No"
      Role="Classified-data"
      Root="*" />
</XDM:STATEMENT>
```

This statement can be read as follows. The first XDM:SOURCE element specifies the data item containing the data to classify, while the second XDM:SOURCE element specifies the data item containing the classification tree.

The TEST-CLASSIFICATION operator is defined on the same namespace of the MINE-CLASSIFICATION operator. Similarly to the MINE-CLASSIFICATION operator, the CLAS-SIFICATION-UNIT element specifies the nodes in the data item that contains the data to classify. In this case, the select attribute says that nodes named APPLICANT contains data to classify (select="NEW-APPLICANTS/APPLICANT"). Inside this element, a set of CLASS:PARAM elements denotes the nodes in the data item that describe the classification model parameters. In this case, the lines:

```
<CLASS:PARAM name="AGE" select="@AGE"/>
<CLASS:PARAM name="CAR-TYPE" select="@CAR-TYPE"/>
```

map attributes AGE and CAR-TYPE (see the XPath expressions in the select attributes) in the APPLICANT nodes to the homonymous parameters in the classification tree.

The next element, named CT:EXTEND-WITH-CLASS, specifies how the data to classify are extended with the class label, when the new data item containing classified data is generated. In particular, in our case:

```
<CLASS:EXTEND-WITH-CLASS Name="RISK" Type="Attribute"/>
```

the element says that a new object is added to the APPLICANT node; this object is called RISK and is an attribute (alternatively, it is possible to add a node/element).

Finally the OUTPUT element denotes the name of the new data item (the TEST-CLAS-SIFICATION operator is polymorphic w.r.t. the structure of classified data, so no output type must be specified). In our case,

```
<XDM:OUTPUT Name="Classified Applicants" Virtual="No"
Role="Classified-data"
Root="*" />
```

says that the new generated data item is called Classified Applicants and is not based on any specific data class or namespace (and it could not be, since it is obtained by extending another data item). This data item is shown next.

```
<XDM:DATA-ITEM Name="Classified Applicants" Version="1"
      Date="..." xmlns:XDM="http://.../NS/XDM">
<XDM:DERIVATION statement="00128"/>
   <XDM:CONTENT>
    <NEW-APPLICANTS>
      <APPLICANT Name="John Smyth" AGE="22" CAR-TYPE="Family"
       RISK="High"/>
      <APPLICANT Name="Marc Green" AGE="60" CAR-TYPE="Family"
       RISK="Low" />
      <APPLICANT Name="Laura Fox" AGE="35" CAR-TYPE="Sports"
       RISK="High"/>
    </NEW-APPLICANTS>
   </XDM:CONTENT>
</XDM:DATA-ITEM>
```

Observe that each APPLICANT element has now a new attribute, named RISK, which describes the class; its value has been determined based on the classification tree. The reader can easily check these values, for example, by using the graphical representation of the classification tree reported in Figure 4.

Chapter V

Enhancing Decision Support Systems with Spatial Capabilities

Marcus Costa Sampaio, Federal University of
Campina Grande, Brazil

Cláudio de Souza Baptista, Federal University of
Campina Grande, Brazil

André Gomes de Sousa, Federal University of
Campina Grande, Brazil

Fabiana Ferreira do Nascimento, Federal University of
Campina Grande, Brazil

Abstract

*This chapter introduces spatial dimensions and measures as a means of enhancing
decision support systems with spatial capabilities. By some way or other, spatial
related data has been used for a long time; however, spatial dimensions have not been
fully exploited. It is presented a data model that tightly integrates data warehouse
and geographical information systems — so characterizing a spatial data warehouse*

(SDW) — ; more precisely, the focus is on a formalization of SDW concepts, on a spatial-aware data cube using object-relational technology, and on issues underlying a SDW — specially regarding spatial data aggregation operations. Finally, the MapWarehouse prototype is presented aiming to validate the ideas proposed. The authors believe that SDW allows for the efficient processing of queries that use, jointly, spatial and numerical temporal data (e.g., temporal series from summarized spatial and numerical measures).

Introduction

Decision support systems aim to identify historical and localizable tendencies, behaviors and information patterns, which help the decision support process. The technologies that underpin this process, using time and space dimensions as decisive factors, are: data warehouse (DW) — with online analytical processing (OLAP) interface — and geographical information systems (GIS). DW/OLAP systems are responsible for both data extraction from several operational sources and data organization according to a historical, thematic and consolidated multi-dimensional model (Malinowski & Zimányi, 2004), composed by facts (numerical measurements related to business processes) and dimensions (descriptive aggregated information, often hierarchically disposed, which is arranged to define the facts). Conceptually, a DW is a multi-dimensional array, or simply a data cube. OLAP queries over a DW provide data exploration and analysis operations by means of aggregate navigation through dimension hierarchies — drill-down, roll-up. Other typical OLAP operations are data cube slicing, dicing and pivoting. Materialized data cubes aim to guarantee high performance of OLAP operations. On the other side, GIS provide manipulation, storage and visualization of spatial data, so that decision-makers may enhance the quality of their analysis using the spatial dimension.

The main objective of this chapter is to present a spatial data warehouse (SDW) (Rivest, Bédard, & Marchand, 2001; Pourabbas, 2003) conceptual model which tightly integrates DW and GIS. Also, we rigorously define a logical model suitable for implementing decision-making processes using spatial data. The other two main contributions of the chapter are: (1) the proposal of a query language for the logical model with query optimization techniques, and (2) the presentation of a prototype developed in order to validate our ideas.

The advantages separately provided by GIS and DW technologies have motivated research on their integration. Existent integration approaches do not fulfill the requirements for a *stricto sensu* integration, which are: (1) to summarize spatial data (e.g., map-overlay, region merge) through spatial dimensions — spatial roll-up and its counterpart, spatial drill-down —, and (2) to synchronize spatial and numerical historical summarized data.

A case study on agricultural crops in Brazil is discussed throughout the chapter. In order to have an efficient seed distribution policy to Brazilian farmers, several issues ought to be taken into account including soil type, rainfall and type of seed. Hence, a SDW may help authorities in finding the best policy for a particular situation, based on dynamic maps, tables, graphics, reports, and so on. As it can be noticed, this application encompasses space, time and analytical dimensions. Query examples exploiting these dimensions in this particular application domain include:

- Which cultivation better adapts to each municipality, region or state following the plantation conditions of last year (semester or month, etc.)?
- What are the favorable pattern conditions to the corn (mango or coffee, etc.) cultivation for a particular geographical region?
- Where is the best place to plant a particular crop?
- When is the best season for planting a given crop?

The remainder of this chapter is organized as follows. A background with discussion of related work is presented in the following section. Then our spatial multidimensional model is addressed, followed by the proposal of an object-relational spatial data cube. Query optimization techniques and a description of a prototype which aims to validate the proposed ideas — the MapWarehouse Project — are presented. Finally, the conclusion and further research to be undertaken are highlighted.

Background

The research on spatial data warehouse is very incipient. Many of the research proposals are based on either federated or integrated architectures. In federated architecture, numerical and spatial data are linked through some common properties without affecting their original sources. Moreover, the responsibility for information capture and translation among different sources is limited to some components. This usually originates lost of transparency and some semantic problems (Kouba et al., 2000; Rivest et al., 2001; Pourabbas, 2003). One of the prominent research project based on this federated architecture is GOLAP (Kouba et al., 2000).

In the GOLAP project, the main component is a mediator — an integration module — which is responsible for the correspondence between a GIS and a DW/OLAP system, by using metadata. Although the system aims to be a generic solution, there is no interaction between the functions of the GIS tool and those of the DW/OLAP. The integration between these systems is restricted to the isolated use of GIS capabilities and related dimensions of the DW. The main drawbacks of this approach are the low performance, as there is no way to perform query optimization jointly on GIS and DW; and the loss of transparency, since for every new GIS and OLAP application, the mediator must be reconfigured.

On the other hand, the integrated architecture uses a singular and adapted environment in which queries involving both spatial and numerical data may be posed. This results in high flexibility and expression power of OLAP operations. Two proposals are highlighted: GeoMiner (Han et al., 1997) and Map Cube (Shekhar et al., 2001).

GeoMiner is a project of spatial data mining that includes three modules for complete numerical-spatial data integration: spatial data cube construction, analytical-spatial query processing, and spatial data mining. To reduce the query processing costs of queries, some algorithms are proposed to selective data materialization, considering the object access frequency. Nevertheless, the Spatial OLAP query module is very incipient: operations like roll-up and drill-down, fundamental in decision support interfaces, are not provided. Hence, GeoMiner cannot be considered a truly SDW.

MapCube is defined by an operator that has a base map parameter, together with data tables and some cartographic preferences, to produce an album of maps, arranged through aggregation hierarchies. It is based on conventional data cube, but it enables the visualization of the results as data tables and maps. Despite of allowing spatial observation (through maps) of summarized data, MapCube does not support spatial roll-up/drill-down OLAP operations. Therefore, MapCube, as GeoMiner, cannot be considered a truly SDW.

As it can be inferred from the previous classification and from the Introduction, our MapWarehouse project is based on an integrated architecture. This architecture is based on well-established standards: Open Geospatial Consortium (OGC, 2005) and Common Warehouse Model (CWM, 2005). The use of such standards aims to achieve interoperability through the integration of heterogeneous data sources.

Heterogeneity in information systems has been classified as semantic, schematic and syntactic (Bishr, 1998). Currently our approach encompasses schematic and syntactic levels. However, as there is a strong interest in semantic heterogeneity, especially with the advent of the semantic Web, SDW may be modeled as ontological commitments which enable interoperability at semantic level. Such ontologies should be used in the extraction, transformation and loading process from heterogeneous spatial and OLAP data sources (Vassiliadis, Simitsis, & Skiadopoulos, 2002). Hence, semantic translations would be employed in order to transform the original data model into OGC and CWM standards used in our approach.

There are several works which address semantic interoperability. Mackey (1999) focuses on the issue of semantic integration of environmental models, in which both GIS and decision support systems play an important role. Fonseca, Davis, and Camara (2003) propose an ontology-driven GIS which aims to integrate heterogeneous GIS without demanding the use of a unique standard. Reitsma and Albrecht

(2005) claim the use of ontologies to model earth systems which may provide interoperability among models and simulators. They argue that in the occurrence of natural disasters, the use of the semantic Web enables the integration of models with spatial decision-support systems, providing quick response to the emergency rescue teams.

Nonetheless, none of these works have addressed the integration of GIS with spatial DW in order to obtain an enhanced decision support system which may provide OLAP and spatial capabilities to better retrieve the underlying information.

A Spatial Multidimensional Model

Our spatial multidimensional conceptual model integrates completely the common warehouse model (CWM) for DW with the OGC geometry object model (OGC, 2005). Moreover, extensions of traditional OLAP operations (especially drill-down, roll-up) to deal with spatial objects are proposed. For spatial queries, the use of spatial operations such as contains, meets, covers, intersection, union, buffer and so on, is considered. Finally, query results may be presented as maps and tables.

A CWM Schema is a logical container of elements of an OLAP model. It consists of Cube classes, which contain Dimension classes. Dimension classes contain Hierarchy classes, which are level-based (LevelBasedHierarchy classes). A Dimension class generalizes specific dimension classes, such as TimeDimension.

In order to support spatial elements, we extended the CWM model with a new dimension class, SpatialDimension, which extends the Dimension class. A spatial dimension may contain SpatialLevel objects inside Hierarchy classes — SpatialHierarchies. A Spatial-Level object can be shared by several spatial hierarchies. Moreover, we introduce a SpatialMeasure class that is part of the Cube class.

The Geometry class from the OGC specification contains a class hierarchy which may represent vector spatial data as points, lines, areas and collections of these elements. The details of that class are outside the scope of the chapter; the interested reader could refer to OGC (OGC, 2005). Concerning our integration model, the OGC Geometry class is part of both the SpatialLevel and SpatialMeasure classes.

Spatial Model Semantics

Now, we discuss in more details the semantics of the following spatial elements of the model: spatial hierarchy, spatial dimension, spatial fact, and spatial cube. In the discussion, dimension classes apart from the SpatialDimension class are sometimes named NonSpatialDimension classes.

Figure 1. A spatial hierarchy

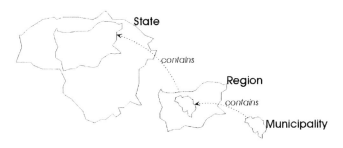

A SpatialLevel class is composed of geometric classes for which the application needs to keep its geometry. SpatialLevel classes can relate to each other through topological relationships such as contains, intersects, overlaps, and so forth. A SpatialHierarchy class contains one or more SpatialLevel classes. Formally:

Definition 1. Spatial hierarchy.

Let $<$ be a symbol for the inside topological relationship between classes. A SpatialHierarchy class SH is a four-tuple (SL, $<_{SL}$, $\top_{SL}$, $\perp_{SL}$), where SL = { SL_j, $j = 1, \ldots, n$} are the SpatialLevel classes of SH with $n \geq 1$, $<_{SL}$ is the inside topological operator on the SL_j's, with $\top_{SL} \in$ SL and $\perp_{SL} \in$ SL being the top and the bottom element of the ordering, respectively.

Figure 1 is an example of a SpatialHierarchy object, composed of three SpatialLevel objects partially related to each other through the contains topological relationship.

A NonSpatialDimension class is an aggregation criterion for NumericalMeasure classes, all along its NonSpatialHierarchy classes. The unique difference between a SpatialDimension class and a NonSpatialDimension one is that the former includes at least a SpatialHierarchy class. Formally:

Definition 2. Spatial dimension.

A SpatialDimension class D is a three-tuple (SH, ~SH, OT), where SH is a set of SpatialHierarchy classes, ~SH is a set of NonSpatialHierarchy classes, and OT is a set of other classes (that is, different from SpatialHierarchy classes and from NonSpatialHierarchy classes).

Figure 2. Spatial measures and their location

Municipality

＊ Bean plantation area

Figure 3. Geometric union of spatial measures

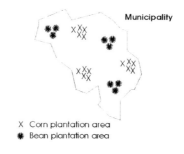

Municipality

X Corn plantation area
＊ Bean plantation area

An example of a SpatialDimension class called Location would be:

SH = {municipality_geometry < microregion_geometry < region_geometry < state_geometry}

~SH = {municipality_name < microregion_name < region_name < state_name}

OT = {municipality_area, estimated_population}

A SpatialMeasure class is composed of a (set of) Geometry class(es), and it can be aggregated according to either SpatialDimension or NonSpatialDimension classes. Figure 2 shows a CropArea — a SpatialMeasure class — object, which is a set of geometric objects (areas) associated with at least a Location — a SpatialDimension class — object, and a Plantation — a NonSpatialDimension class — object (bean). Figure 3 shows the map overlay of two CropArea objects.

A *SpatialMeasure* class can be formalized as follows:

Definition 3. Spatial measure.

Let SpatialDimension classes SD and NonSpatialDimension classes ~SD. A SpatialMeasure class SM is a tuple (G, R), where G is a non-empty set of geometric classes, and R is a geometric-dimension relation $\{(g_i, d_j), i = 1, ...m; j = 1, ..., n\}$, where $g_i \in G$ and $d_j \in (SD \cup \sim SD)$.

A SpatialDataCube class represents an n-dimensional array, in which each cell of the array is either a SpatialMeasure or a NumericalMeasure class, while the dimensions of the array are both SpatialDimension and NonSpatialDimension classes. We may now define formally SpatialDataCube classes.

Definition 4. Spatial data cube.

A SpatialDataCube class SDC is a tuple (SD $\cup$ ~SD, SM $\cup$ NM, GR, ~GR), where SD is a set of SpatialDimension classes, ~SD is a set of NonSpatialDimension classes, SM is a set of SpatialMeasure classes, NM is a set of NumericalMeasure classes, GR is a set of Geometric-Dimension relations and ~GR is a set of NonGeometric-Dimension relations.

In the following section, we precise how one can implement SpatialDataCube classes and their extents.

Towards an Object-Relational Spatial Data Cube

A SpatialDataCube class can be implemented as an object-relational (O-R) type, in the following manner. Each Spatial(NonSpatial)Dimension class is mapped to a distinct O-R type — an O-RDimension type. The set of SpatialMeasure classes, together with the set of NumericalMeasure classes, and together with the set of Geometric(NonGeometric)-Dimension relations are mapped to another O-R type — the O-RFact type. The O-RDimension(Fact) type extents are respectively typed tables. We denote O-R spatial data cube this O-R simulation of a spatial data cube. An O-R spatial data cube is formally defined as follows:

Definition 5. O-R spatial data cube.

An *O-R Spatial Data Cube* is constructed from a SpatialDataCube class SDC as follows:

$\forall$ Spatial(NonSpatial)Dimension class $D_i \in$ SDC,

$f_{\text{D-mapping}}: D_i \to$ O-RD$_i$, where O-RD$_i$ is an O-RDimension type;

$\forall$ SpatialMeasure class SM $\in$ SDC, NumericalMeasure class NM $\in$ SDC, Geometric-Dimension relation GR $\in$ SDC, NonGeometric-Dimension relation ~GR $\in$ SDC

$f_{\text{F-mapping}}:$ (SM $\cup$ NM $\cup$ GR $\cup$ ~GR) $\to$ (O-RSM $\cup$ O-RNM $\cup$ O-RGR $\cup$ O-R~GR) = O-RFact, where O-RFact is an O-R type;

$\forall$ O-RD$_i$, $f_{\text{Dtable-mapping}}:$ O-RD$_i$ $\to$ O-RDTable$_i$, where O-RDTable$_i$ is a typed table of   O-RD$_i$;

For the O-RFact, $f_{\text{Ftable-mapping}}:$ O-RFact $\to$ O-RFactT, where O-RFacT is a typed table of O-RFact.

Figure 4 illustrates an O-R spatial data cube.

We can clearly visualize here something like the Kimball's Relational Star Schema (Kimball & Ross, 2002). That is only similar, not equal. Notice that the AgroDistribution fact table is not in 1ST normal form, because of the non-atomic spatial measure

Figure 4. A spatial data cube example

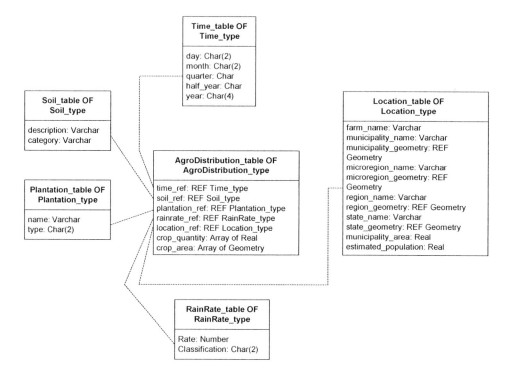

crop_area and the non-atomic non-spatial measure crop-quantity. Shortly, our *O-R Spatial Data Cube Schema* — or *O-R Spatial Star Schema* to pay homage to Kimball — is not 1NF-normalized. Also, we emphasize the REF types in the AgroDistribution table, so eliminating foreign keys, which are truly artificial columns.

As for relational star schemata, by embedding spatial or non-spatial hierarchies, dimension tables may not be 3NF-normalized; for instance, the dimension tables Location and Time in Figure 4 are not 3NF-normalized, in view of their embedded hierarchies.

In order to avoid redundancies of large geometry objects in non-3FN-normalized dimension tables, these objects may be only referenced in the dimension tables (see the Location table, Figure 4) — this elegant solution is not directly supported by relational star schemata.

Like relational star schemata, O-R star schemata obliterate spatial (non-spatial) hierarchies. Observe in table Location, Figure 4, that the spatial hierarchy municipality_geometry ← micro-region_geometry ← region_geometry ← state_geometry, as well as the non-spatial hierarchy farm_name ← municipality_name ← micro-region_name ← region_name ← state_name, are obliterated, due to the still poor semantics of the O-R model, when compared with our conceptual model, in which hierarchies are explicitly defined.

Spatial OLAP Operations

Spatial or geometric aggregate functions for operating through spatial or non-spatial hierarchies are mandatory for O-R spatial star schemata with spatial OLAP interfaces. In particular, we remark the *spatial roll-up* and *drill-down* operations. The action of *spatial roll-up* is straightforward: it creates geometric aggregate values that roll up from the most detailed level to the least detailed level, following a spatial or non-spatial hierarchy. *Spatial drill-down* is the reverse operation of roll-up. Using the UML-Object Constraint Language formalism (Warmer & Kleppe, 1998), we may define these operators as specified in Rule 1.

The formalism for the spatial drill-down operation is similar to the roll-up one as specified in Rule 2.

An example of a *spatial roll-up* operation is given in next section.

Querying the O-R Spatial Star Schema

Although there is no SQL implementation for spatial OLAP, we have proposed an O-R SQL query language suitable for O-R spatial star schemata. In order to show

Rule 1. Spatial roll-up

Parameters:
d   imRLUP: set of dimensions which rolls up n levels according to the set nLevels
n   Levels: bag of integer which indicates how many levels to rollup in the hierarchy
      m: set of measures to be aggregated
a   ggFunc: set of aggregation functions
Returns: a new data cube

context Cube:: spatial_rollup(dimRLUP: Set(Dimension), nLevels:Bag(Integer), m: Set(Measure), aggFunc:
                   Set(String)): Cube
  pre: -- verify whether all rollup dimensions are in the current Cube
           self.containsDimensions-> includeAll(dimRULP) and
           -- verify whether all measures to be aggregated are in the current Cube
           self.containsMeasures-> includeAll(m) and
           -- make sure that all rollup dimensions are not in the last level
           dimRLUP-> forAll(d1 | d1.currentLevel.hierarchyOwn.childOf <> null) and
           -- make sure that exists at least a spatial dimension or spatial measure
           (dimRLUP-> exists(d2 | d2.isSpatial = true) or m-> exists(m1 | m1.isSpatial = true))
  and
           -- verify whether the dimension set size is equals to the levels of rollup set size
           dimRLUP-> size() = nLevels -> size()
           -- verify whether the measure set size is equals to the aggregation function set size
           m-> size() = aggFunc -> size()
  inv: -- update dimension levels
           let dimNewLevels: Set(Dimension) = dimRLUP -> iterate(d:Dimension; resultSetD: Set(Dimension)
                   = Set{} | resultSetD.including(d| upLevel(nLevels -> at (dimRLUP -> indexOf(d)))))
           in createNewCube(m ->iterate(i:Measure; resultSetM: Set(Cube) = Set{} |
           if m.isSpatial then
           resultSetM->including(self.aggregateSpatialFunction(aggFunc->at(m-> indexOf(i), i, dimNewLevels)
                   endif))

  post:
           result.oclNew()

---

the expression power of the language, we give an example that uses a spatial roll-up operation. This query, over the spatial star schema in Figure 4, is "Retrieve the corn crop areas for each micro-region and for each region of the state of Paraíba, during May 2003".

Rule 2. Spatial drill-down

Parameters:
  d imDROWN: set of dimensions which drills down n levels according to the set nLevels
    nLevels: bag of integer which indicates how many levels to drill down in the hierarchy
    m: set of measures to be aggregated
  detFunc: set of detailed functions
Returns: a new data cube

  context Cube:: spatial_drilldown(dimDROWN: Set(Dimension), nLevels:Bag(Integer), m:
Set(Measure),
        detFunc: Set(String)): Cube
p   re: -- verify whether all drilldown dimensions are in the current Cube
        self.containsDimensions-> includeAll(dimDROWN) and
        -- verify whether all measure to be aggregated are in the current Cube
        self.containsMeasures-> includeAll(m) and
        -- make sure that all drill-down dimensions are not in the last level
        dimDOWN-> forAll(d1 | d1.currentLevel.hierarchyOwn.parentOf <> null) and

        -- make sure that exists at least a spatial dimension or spatial measure
        (dimDOWN-> exists(d2 | d2.isSpatial = true) or m-> exists(m1 | m1.isSpatial = true))
and
        -- verify whether the dimension set size is equals to the levels of drill-down set size

        dimDOWN-> size() = nLevels -> size()
        -- verify whether the measure set size is equals to the detailed function set size
        m-> size() = detFunc -> size()
  inv: -- update dimension levels
        let dimNewLevels: Set(Dimension) = dimDOWN -> iterate(d:Dimension;
resultSetD: Set(Dimension)
            = Set() | resultSetD.including(d| downLevel(nLevels -> at (dimDOWN ->
indexOf(d)))))
      in if self.Schema.findCube(dimNewLevels) = null then
            createNewCube(m-> iterate(i:Measure; resultSetM: Set(Cube) = Set{} |
              if m.isSpatial then
                resultsetM -> including(self.detailSpatialFunction(detFunc-> at(m ->
indexOf(i), i,
                        dimNewLevels))
              else   resultSetM -> including(self.detailNumericFunction(detFunc-> at(m->
indexOf(i), i,
                        dimNewLevels))
            endif
          ))
        else
          self.Schema.findCube(dimNewLevels)
        endif

  post: result.oclNew()

Select rl.region_geometry, rl.microregion_geometry, rl.crop_area

From Location_table l, Plantation_table p, Time_table t, AgroDistribution_table a, Roll-up(l.region_geometry, l.microregion_geometry, Geometric_Union(a.crop_area)) rl

Where l.municipality_name = a.location_ref.municipality_name

And t.month = a.time_ref.month And t.year = a.time_ref.year And p.name = a.plantation_ref.name

And t.year = '2003' And t.month = '05' And p.name = 'corn' And l.state_name = 'Paraíba'

The main important new feature of the language is its FROM clause. The new interpretation of this clause is as follows: in it, we define single scan variables, each one associated to its collection — typed table, function returning an object-collection type value, etc. —; more precisely, the state of a scan variable, at any time, is one and only one of the objects of its associated collection. Formally, the FROM clause is a set of pairs <collection> <scan_variable>. In the example-query, l (p) (t) (a) scans Location_table (Plantation_table) (Time_table) (AgroDistribution_table), while rl scans the collection returned by the function roll-up.

The roll-up function arguments are, in this order: (1) the virtual top element in the spatial hierarchy, (2) the virtual bottom element, and (3) the geometric aggregation function. This function returns a collection, more precisely a table from which the columns are respectively <tableScan_variable>.<top_element>, <tableScan_variable>.<bottom_element>, and <tableScan_variable>.<aggregationFunction_argument>. In the query example, the returned table is scanned by the variable rl, and this table is the result of the query itself.

Figures 5 and 6 are the visualization of the query outputs at the micro-region and region levels for the state of Paraíba, respectively. In these figures, crop areas are represented by geometric points, while that micro-regions and regions are repre-

Figure 5. Roll-up operation plantation ← micro-region

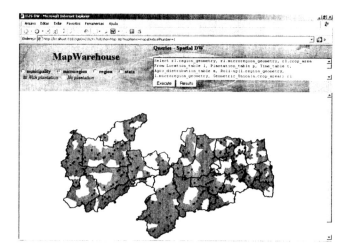

Figure 6. Roll-up operation micro-region ← region

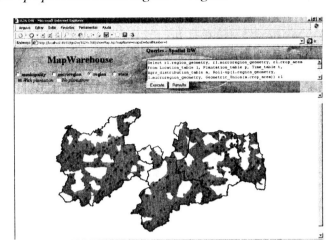

sented by polygons. Gray areas in the maps indicate those municipalities inside their micro-regions (regions) with corn plantations, while that blank areas indicate absence of corn plantations.

Query Optimization

In this section, we consider the problem of guaranteeing the good performance of the OLAP spatial queries submitted to MapWarehouse, through its GUI. First, we characterize what we call *the spatial optimization problem.*

The Spatial Optimization Problem

The spatial optimization problem may so be characterized. Consider, for example, only the geography of Brazilian State of Paraíba. Its political division is depicted in Figure 7.

Suppose that only the base-level data and its dimension data are pre-stored. We have thousands of plantations (corn, bean, rice, etc.). Regarding uniquely the example-query (corn plantations in the state of Paraíba — section *Querying the O-R Spatial Star Schema*), and supposing there exists in average 50 plantations by municipality, this gives approximately 11,150 geometries, so distributed:

Figure 7. Instantiation of the example's spatial hierarchy

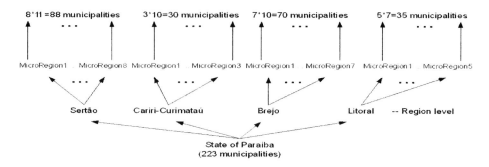

11,150 crop areas;

223 municipality geometries;

23 micro-region geometries;

4 region geometries;

1 state geometry;

Total: 11,401 geometries, approximately.

In addition to this, new maps must be dynamically generated, resulting from unions of crop areas and municipality geometries, from unions of municipality and micro-region geometries, and from micro-region and region geometries. The question that should be answered is: how many spatial union operations are necessary for the query in section *Querying the O-R Spatial Star Schema*? For this, we have:

$223 * 50 = 11{,}150$ union operations crop-municipality;

$8*11 + 3*10 + 7*10 + 5*7 = 223$ union operations (crop-municipality) - micro-region;

$1*8 + 1*3 + 1*7 + 1*5 = 23$ union operations (crop-municipality-micro-region) – region;

Total: 11,396 union operations, approximately.

The next step consists in calculating the cost of these 11,396 union operations.

The spatial optimization problem may be generically stated as follows: *given a spatial query, how many concerned spatial aggregation operations must be previously computed, in order to accomplish the query response time requirement?*

Very importantly, the database administrator (DBA) must assume the query performance control, or the DBA must not fight the DBMS optimizer. These considerations lead to an optimization logical model.

The Spatial Logical Optimization

Our spatial optimization logical model is based on the mechanism of pre-storing spatial aggregates — pre-stored spatial aggregates — an extension of the notion of Kimball's pre-stored summary aggregates (Kimball & Ross, 2002). According to Kimball, an aggregate is a fact table record representing a summarization of base-level fact table records; an aggregate fact table record is always associated with one or more aggregate dimension table records.

The extension of this definition, suitable to the SDW context, is such as: a spatial aggregate is a spatial measure of an object in a base-level typed table representing a summarization of spatial measures of objects of the base-level typed table; a spatial aggregate is always associated with one or more aggregate objects in aggregate dimension typed tables. For example, referring to Figure 4, we can imagine the following spatial aggregates:

- Municipality-level crop area aggregates by plantation by day (a one-way spatial aggregate)
- Micro-region-level crop area aggregates by day (a one-way aggregate)

Figure 8. Spatial hierarchy and pre-stored spatial aggregates

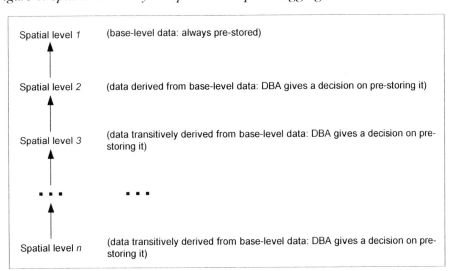

- Region-level crop area aggregates by micro-region (a two-way aggregate)
- Region-level crop area aggregates by micro-region by month (a three-way aggregate)

A pre-stored spatial aggregate is a spatial aggregate computed and stored before query executions which may use it. Pre-stored spatial aggregates are tightly related to spatial hierarchies — Figure 8.

The rationale for our spatial optimization logical model makes the best of a good situation of using pre-stored spatial aggregates in order to ameliorate the performance of the spatial queries; in fact, queries are re-written for accessing the chosen pre-stored spatial aggregates. Once conveniently re-written, queries are still submitted to the specific DBMS's query optimizer — physical optimization — Figure 9.

Returning to our example, the critical factor for the performance of the query in section *Querying the O-R Spatial Star Schema* is the computation of the 11,150 spatial aggregates (here, union operations) at the level 2 — municipality-geometry – of the spatial hierarchy crop_area ← municipality-geometry ← micro-region-geometry ← region-geometry ← state-geometry. Supposing that all corn spatial aggregates at the municipality level — typed table **MunicipalityAgroDistribution_table** (a new fact table) linked to the typed table **Municipality_table** (a new dimension table) and the dimension tables in Figure 4 except Location_table, a one-way spatial aggregate transparent to the user — have been pre-stored, the query is so automatically rewritten:

Select rl.region_geometry, rl.microregion_geometry, rl.crop_area

From Municipality_table l, Plantation_table p, Time_table t, MunicipalityAgroDistribution_table a, Roll-up(l.region_geometry, l.microregion_geometry, Geometric_Union(a.crop_area)) rl

Where l.municipality_name = a.location_ref.municipality_name

And t.month = a.time_ref.month And t.year = a.time_ref.year And p.name = a.plantation_ref.name And t.year = '2003' And t.month = '05' And p.name = 'corn' And

l.state_name = 'Paraíba'

Notice that the two boldface items in the previous query are the items that are different between the base-level query and the municipality-aggregate-level query. Upon close inspection, we see that all the logical optimizer has done is to substitute the Location_table dimension table by the Municipality_table dimension table, and the AgroDistribution_table fact table by the MunicipalityAgroDistribution_table fact table.

Figure 9. Types of optimization supported by MapWarehouse

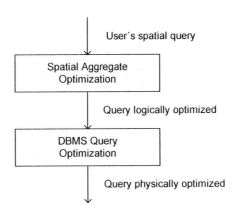

The Map Warehouse Prototype
===

In order to validate the previous ideas we have implemented a prototype called *MapWarehouse,* which implements O-R spatial star schemata in an object-relational DBMS, and with a logical query optimizer according to the discussion in the previous section. Particularly in this prototype, we have chosen the Oracle Object-Relational DBMS due to its support to spatial data, including the OGC Standard and the provision of OLAP infra-structure, by implementing CWM (Oracle, 2005).

The Oracle spatial capabilities are implemented by the Oracle Spatial Cartridge, which uses the MDSYS schema; CWM is implemented via the CWMLITE metadata packages, the OLAPSYS schema and OLAP API.

The MapWarehouse project implements a new Java-based package known as CWM_OLAP_SPATIAL, which extends the CWNLITE package with spatial measures, dimensions, topological operations and spatial roll-up and spatial drill-down. Spatial data is indexed using R-tree.

The MapWarehouse architecture, as shown in Figure 10, is based on three layers:

- **Operational layer:** composed of the conventional and spatial data sources to model the Spatial DW through the extraction, transformation and loading process (ETL)

- **Application layer:** responsible for the Spatial OLAP user request processing. It accesses the CWM/OpenGIS metadata and datasources

- **Display layer:** defines the user interface, according to the previous mentioned requirements

Figure 10. The MapWarehouse architecture

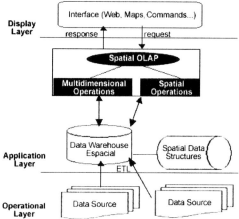

The user interface (GUI) enables to visualize the query results through maps and tables. The maps are rendered using SVG format (SVG, 2005) and they are dynamically produced using the iGIS map server (Baptista, Leite Jr., Silva, & Paiva, 2004). iGIS is a framework for rapid application development of GIS applications on the Web. It may use different datasources, such as Oracle, Postgresql, IBM DB2 and GML. Also, iGIS may use different map rendering including SVG, SGV Tiny and JPEG. User interaction on maps includes zooming, panning, information, and tooltip. This user interface is presented in Figure 11. In this figure, the radio buttons indicate the spatial level (state, region, micro-region or municipality), so that user may execute spatial roll-up or spatial drill-down. In the text box, users may pose their queries using the proposed query language.

The map is presented according to the executed query and a table which contains numeric information about the query is presented. In Figure 11, the user has pointed to the *Sertão* region and the tooltip is activated. Then, the equivalent tabular data is highlighted in the underlying table.

During the experiments, spatial data related to the Brazilian State of Paraiba was used. This state is divided into regions, micro-regions and municipalities. Beside the spatial location, this dataset is temporal, from 2002 to 2003 in which day is the minimum granularity, and it contains plantation type, soil type, and rain rate. The whole size of the database is approximately 250,000 tuples.

The server computer used during the experiments was an Athlon XP 2.5 GHz processor with 1024 MB RAM. The Web browser was the Microsoft Internet Explorer 6.0 with the Adobe SVG Viewer 3.0. The Apache Tomcat/5.0.16 was used as Application Server. We used Java technology (JSP and Servlets) to implement MapWarehouse business logic.

Figure 11. The MapWarehouse GUI

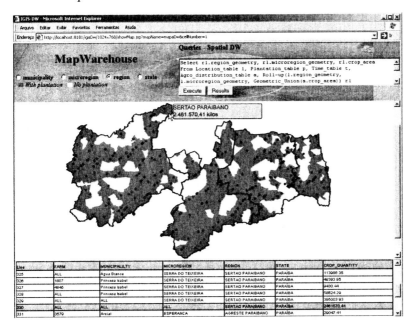

In the experiments we run several queries with and without query optimization. In the following the query: "retrieve the total of all crops (rice, bean, corn, etc) produced in June 2003 by municipality, micro-region, region and state" is detailed. This query can be posed using our extended SQL as:

Select rl.state_geometry, rl.region_geometry, rl.microregion_geometry, rl.municipality_geometry, rl.crop_area

From Location_table l, Plantation_table p, Time_table t, AgroDistribution_table a, Roll-up(l. state_geometry, l.municipality_geometry, Geometric_Union(a.crop_area)) rl

Where l.municipality_name = a.location_ref.municipality_name And t.month = a.time_ref.month

And t.year = a.time_ref.year And t.year = '2003' And t.month = '06' And l.state_name = 'Paraíba'

Table 1 shows the costs of the previous query with and without query optimization. Notice that by using the query optimization the query is re-written according to the technique explained in the section *Query Optimization*.

During the tests, we have noticed that by using query optimization based on pre-stored spatial aggregates the overall response time is reduced in almost 50%. This performance gain is improved for large datasets.

Table 1. Performance evaluation

Costs	Without Query Optimization	With Query Optimization
Cost of pre-storing spatial aggregates	25 sec.	0 sec.
Cost of map generation	25 sec.	25 sec.
Cost of map loading	10 sec.	10 sec.
Total cost	60 sec.	35 sec.

Conclusion

Although data warehouse and geographical information system technologies are very useful in the decision making process, usually they are used separately. Research on integrating these two technologies is in its infancy. This integration coins new terms: spatial datawarehouse (SDW) and spatial OLAP (SOLAP). By using SOLAP, users may enhance their capacity to explore the underlying dataset once spatial methods incorporated into OLAP ones may be used.

In this chapter we have proposed an integrated architecture for a SDW. The main contributions of our proposal include: a formalized data model for SDW; a SQL extension query language which enables spatial roll-up and drill-down; optimization techniques which improve performance of complex spatial queries by pre-storing spatial aggregates; and a prototype, *MapWarehouse*, which validates the ideas proposed.

In order to achieve interoperability, we have chosen to use well-known standards such as OGC for dealing with spatial data and CWM for OLAP. This approach aims to facilitate the integration of *MapWarehouse* with other systems. However, we recognize that the interoperability provided is at schematic and syntactic level. Hence, it is important to mention that a new layer based on semantic Web concepts ought to be developed so that semantic interoperability may be achieved.

As further work, we plan to improve usability as currently user needs to know the query language syntax and the underlying schema in order to pose their queries. We plan to develop a visual query language for SOLAP to facilitate user interaction.

Also, the provision of ad-hoc dimensions, which are defined on-the-fly, is another important issue to be addressed. Nowadays, the spatial interaction is done via pre-defined hierarchies (e.g., State, Region, Micro-region and Municipality); however, sometimes user may choose an arbitrary area via a bounding box and he demands for aggregation on that specific area. In that case, the aggregation is done on-the-fly and new indexing mechanisms need to be investigated.

Finally, another interesting work is to extend the *MapWarehouse* architecture to Web services. Thus, distributed SDW may be provided and SOLAP becomes a service which may be automatically discovered and invoked.

References

Baptista, C. S., Leite Jr., F., Silva, E., & Paiva, A. (2004, August 30-September 3). Using open source GIS in e-government applications. *Proceedings of the 3ʳᵈ International Conference on Electronic Government (EGOV 2004)*, Zaragoza, Spain (LNCS 3183, pp. 418-421). Berlin; Heildelberg, Germany: Springer-Verlag.

Bishr, Y. (1998). Overcoming the semantic and other barriers to GIS interoperability. *International Journal of Geographical Information Science, 12*(4), 299-314.

CWM. (2005). *Data Warehousing, CWM™ and MOF™ Resource Page*. Retrieved from http://www.omg.org/cwm/

Fonseca, F., Davis, C., & Camara, G. (2003). Bridging ontologies and conceptual schemas in geographic information integration. *Geoinformatica, 7*(4), 355-378.

Han, J., Koperski, K., & Stefanovic, N. (1997, May 13-15). GeoMiner: A system prototype for spatial data mining. In *Proceedings of the ACM-SIGMOD International Conference on Management of Data (SIGMOD'97)*, Tucson, AZ (pp. 553-556). ACM Press.

Kimball, R., & Ross, M. (2002). *The data warehouse toolkit: The complete guide to dimensional modeling* (2ⁿᵈ ed.). John Wiley & Sons.

Kouba Z., Matoušek, K., & Mikšovský P. (2000, September 4-8). On data warehouse and GIS integration. In *Proceedings of the 11ᵗʰ International Conference on Database and Expert Systems Applications (DEXA 2000)*, London (LNCS 1873, pp. 604-613). Springer-Verlag.

Mackay, D. S. (1999). Semantic integration of environmental models for application to global information systems and decision-making. *SIGMOD Record, 28*(1), 13-19.

Malinowski, E., & Zimányi, E. (2004, November 12-15). Representing spatiality in a conceptual multidimensional model. In *Proceedings of the ACM Workshop on Geographical Information Systems*, Washington, DC (pp. 12-21). ACM Press.

OGC. (2005). *Open Geospatial Consortium, Inc.* Retrieved from http://www.opengeospatial.org

Oracle. (2005). *Oracle Technology Network.* Retrieved from http://www.oracle.com/

Pourabbas, E. (2003). Cooperation with geographic databases. In M. Rafanelli (Ed.), *Multidimensional databases: Problems and solutions* (pp. 393-432). Hershey, PA: Idea Group.

Reitsma, F., & Albrecht, J. (2005). Modeling with the semantic Web in the geosciences. *IEEE Intelligent Systems, 20*(2), 86-88.

Rivest, S., Bédard, Y., & Marchand, P. (2001). Towards better support for spatial decision-making: Defining the characteristics of spatial on-line analytical processing. *Geomatica, 55*(4), 539-555.

Shekhar, S., Lu, C. T., Tan, X., Chawla, S., & Vatsavai, R. R. (2000). Map cube: A visualization tool for spatial data warehouses. In H. J. Miller & J. Han (Eds.), *Geographic data mining and knowledge discovery* (pp. 74-109). London: Taylor & Francis.

SVG. (2005). *Scalable Vector Graphics, 1.1 Specification.* Retrieved from http://www.w3.org/TR/SVG/

Vassiliadis, P., Simitsis, A., & Skiadopoulos, S. (2002, November 8). Conceptual modeling for ETL processes. In *Proceedings of the 5th ACM International Workshop on Data Warehousing and OLAP*, McLean, VA (pp. 14-21). ACM Press.

Warmer, J., & Kleppe, A. (1998). *The Object Constraint Language: Precise modeling with UML.* Reading, MA: Addison-Wesley Professional.

Chapter VI

Application of Decision Tree as a Data Mining Tool in a Manufacturing System

S. A. Oke, University of Lagos, Nigeria

Abstract

This work demonstrates the application of decision tree, a data mining tool, in the manufacturing system. Data mining has the capability for classification, prediction, estimation, and pattern recognition by using manufacturing databases. Databases of manufacturing systems contain significant information for decision making, which could be properly revealed with the application of appropriate data mining techniques. Decision trees are employed for identifying valuable information in manufacturing databases. Practically, industrial managers would be able to make better use of manufacturing data at little or no extra investment in data manipulation cost. The work shows that it is valuable for managers to mine data for better and more effective decision making. This work is therefore new in that it is the first time that proper documentation would be made in the direction of the current research activity.

Introduction

General Overview

In today's digital economy, knowledge is regarded as an asset, and the implementation of knowledge management supports a company to developing innovative products and making critical management strategic decisions (Su, Chen, & Sha, 2005). This digital economy has caused a tremendous explosion in the amount of data that *manufacturing organizations* generate, collect, and store, in order to maintain a competitive edge in the global business (Sugumaran & Bose, 1999). With global competition, it is crucial for organizations to be able to integrate and employ intelligence knowledge in order to survive under the new *business environment*. This phenomenon has been demonstrated in a number of studies, which include the employment of artificial neural network and decision tree to derive knowledge about the job attitudes of "Generation Xers" (Tung, Huang, Chen, & Shih, 2005). The paper by Tung et al. (2005) exploits the ART2 neural model using the collected data as inputs. Performance classes are formed according to the similarities of a sample frame consisting of 1000 index of Taiwan manufacturing industries and service firms. While there is a plethora of *data mining techniques and tools* available, they present inherent problems for end-users such as complexity, required technical expertise, lack of flexibility, and interoperability, and so on. (Sugumaran & Bose, 1999). Although in the past, most data mining has been performed using symbolic artificial intelligence *data mining algorithms* such as C4.5, C5 (a fast variant of C4.5 with higher predictive accuracy) and CART (Browne, Hudson, Whitley, Ford, & Picton, 2004), the motivation to use *decision tree* in this work comes from the findings of Zhang, Valentine, & Kemp, (2005). The authors claim that *decision tree* has been widely used as a modelling approach and has shown better predictive ability than traditional approaches (e.g., regression). This is consistent with the literature by considering the earlier study by Sorensen and Janssens (2003). The authors conduct an exploratory study that focuses on the automatic interaction detection (AID) — techniques, which belongs to the class of decision tree data mining techniques.

Decision tree is a promising new technology that helps bring *business intelligence* into manufacturing system (Yang et al., 2003; Quinlan, 1987; Li & Shue, 2004). It is a non-parametric modelling approach, which recursively splits the multidimensional space defined by the independent variables into zones that are as homogeneous as possible in terms of response of the dependent variable (Vayssieeres, Plant, Allen-Diaz, 2000). Naturally, *decision tree* has its limitations: it requires a relatively large amount of training data; it cannot express linear relationships in a simple and concise way like regression does; it cannot produce a continuous output due to its binary nature; and it has no unique solution, that is, there is no best solution (Iverson & Prasad, 1998; Scheffer, 2002). Decision trees are *tree-shaped structures* that represent sets of decisions. Specific *decision tree* methods include Classification and Regression Trees (CART) and Chi Square Automatic Interaction Detection (CHAID) (Lee & Siau, 2001).

Figure 1 is a good illustrative example of potential *sources of data for mining* in manufacturing. The diagram shows the various areas of manufacturing where massive data are generated, managed, and used for decision making. Basically, nine aspects of the *manufacturing organization* are discussed: production system, customer relations, employee database, contractor/supplier unit, product distribution, maintenance, transportation, research and development, and raw materials.

The production system is concerned with transformation of raw materials into finished goods. *Daily production* and target figures are used for mining purposes. Trends are interpreted and the future demand of products is simulated based on estimation from historical data. Data on quality that are also mined relate to the number of accepted products, the number of scraps, and reworks, and so forth. The maintenance controller monitors trends and predicts the future *downtime* and *machinery capacity* data. Customer relations department promotes the image of the company through programs. This department also monitors the growth of the company's profit through

Figure 1. Data generated in a modern manufacturing system

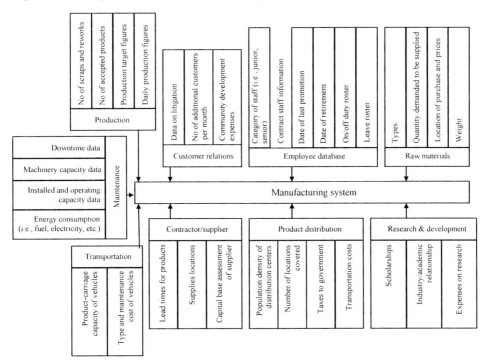

the number of additional customers that patronize the company, and also monitors libel suits against the company in the law courts.

Data are also mined from the *employee database*. Patterns observed in this data-base are used to predict possible employee behaviour, which include possibility of absence from duty. Practical *data mining information* could be obtained from an example of a production supervisor who was last promoted several years ago. If a new employee is engaged and placed higher than him, he may reveal the frustration by handling some of the company's resources and equipment carelessly and with levity. A large amount of data could be obtained from historical facts based on the types and weights of the raw materials usage, quantity or raw materials demanded, location of purchase, prices and the lead-time to supply, and more. Yet another im-portant component of modern manufacturing system is research and development. For product distribution activities, the data miner is interested in the population density of people living in the distribution centers, the number of locations covered by the product distribution, the transportation cost, and so on.

The contractor/supplier unit collects data on the lead-time for product delivery to customers. This information would be useful when considering avoidance of product shortage cost. The transportation unit spends an enormous amount of money on vehicle maintenance. Historical data on this would guide the data mining personnel on providing useful information for the management.

The Information Explosion in Manufacturing

Due to technological development, there is an increase in our capability of both *col-lection and storage of data* (Ananthanarayana, Narasimha, & Subramaman, 2003). This information explosion is largely due to new and improved data processing method, increased security measures and better opportunities for world-wide-Web access via Internet and storage on the World WideWeb (www). The information explosions are also aided by the increasing frequency of partnership/mergers among organizations, new product development activities, and so forth. The availability of the internet and the relatively low cost of access has aided the generation of large amount of data for the manufacturing industries to be utilized for decision making since organizations could post their Web sites on the World Wide Web to be accessed via Internet, access other information relating to the running of business. Improved techniques in various manufacturing processes have led to a high proliferation of data since managers are usually interested in comparing their previous performance with the current performance attained (Berry & Linoff, 1997). Data mined with such improved techniques would assist in making decisions in understanding customers' responses to product purchases, sales figures in various outlets, material sourcing and prices, logistic support activities for company's effective operations, establishment of new project sites, and more (see Lee & Siau, 2001; Darling, 1997; Dunham, 2003; Gargano & Raggad, 1999).

Product development has led to an enormous amount of data generation due to the level of competition among rival companies, which require improved products for the customers. There is also a constant feedback processes for the organizations to identify the needs of their customers and tailor their products to meeting these expectations. *Expansion of projects* is closely related to product development. An expansion program could be for an old project or an entirely new project develop-ment. An organization having the intention to establish a branch or factories in other countries must collect data about the cultural norms of such societies and other information vital to operations in these new places. Such vital information based on data extracted from government agencies, people, market, existing infrastructure, workforce, and so on, are mined before being used for decision making. For new projects, data related to project implementation must be generated, analyzed, and interpreted for successful project implementation. The collected data need to be mined before decisions are made.

Data mining applications (e.g., decision trees used here) encourage adequate and systematic database analysis for correct management decision (Han & Kamber, 2001; Pyle, 1998; Oracle, 2001; Groth, 2000). With today's sophistication in data mining, evaluation and interpretation of relational, transactional or multimedia databases are much easier than before. We can classify, summarize, predict, describe, and contrast data characteristics in a manufacturing milieu to suit our purpose of efficient data management and high productivity (Minaei-Bidgoli & Unch, 2003). This desired level of high operational performance would face a setback in handling the large databases available in industries. Industry professionals ranging from process en-gineers to administrators can effectively manage these unreadily available vast data resources via this application using mining methodologies like pattern evaluation, incorporation of background knowledge, expression and visualization of data mining results, interactive *mining of knowledge* at multiple levels of abstraction, handling noise, and incomplete data. *Data mining* also integrates other disciplines such as statistics, database technology, information science, machine learning, visualization and other disciplines that are industry adaptive (Berson, Smith, & Thearling, 2000; Berson & Smith, 1997; Brown & Kros, 2003; Hanna, M., 2004a, 2004b).

Data mining could be viewed to have five main parameters that make it a popular tool in many fields - classification, forecasting, association, clustering, and sequence or path analyses. Classification refers to a situation where we look for new pat-terns in the data to be analyzed. This may result in a change in the form in which data is organized. Forecasting refers to discovering patterns in data that may lead to reasonable predictions about the future. The parameter "association" looks for patterns where one event is connected to another event. Clustering relates to a situ-ation where we find and visually document groups of facts. Sequence refers to the arrangement of data in a particular fashion.

Background and Relevant Literature

Data mining has been shown capable of providing a significant competitive advantage to an organization by exploiting the potential knowledge of large databases (Bose & Mahapatra, 2001). Recently, a number of *data mining applications* and prototypes have been developed for a variety of domains (Liao, 2003; Mitra & Mitra, 2002) including marketing, finance, banking, manufacturing, and healthcare. There is a large number of broad definitions and discussions on data mining in the data mining literature (Westphal & Blaxton, 1998; Roiger & Geatz, 2003; Adriaans & Zantinge, 1997; Chen, Han, & Yu, 1996; Witten & Frank, 2000). Although not many cases are reported in the manufacturing domain, the common ground of all these definitions is based on the principles and techniques of data mining, which are generally accepted in many fields. With respect to *data mining in manufacturing*, the position taken by Li & Shue (2004) is worthy of note. The authors claim that data mining (also known as knowledge discovery in databases [KDD]) is the process of discovering useful knowledge from large amounts of data stored in databases, data warehouses, or other information repositories (see also Fayyard et al., 1996a,b,c). Data mining seems to be a multi-disciplinary field that integrates technologies of databases, statistics, machine learning, signal processing, and high performance computing. By applying these definitions to the manufacturing domain, customers purchases in different localities or regions could be mined to discover patterns such as comparative purchasing powers of customers in different regions, the tastes of customers with respect to certain items or goods, the most demanded items in all regions, and so forth. Sugumaran and Bose (1999) define data mining from another perspective. These authors view data mining as the process of discovery meaningful correlation, patterns, and trends by sifting through large amounts of data stored in data warehouses and by using pattern recognition technologies as well as statistical and mathematical techniques.

It describes the extraction of information from data in large databases. This previously unknown but potentially useful information must be non-trivial and profoundly implicit. This application leads to pattern evaluation of data revealing new ideas inherent in the available database. A new product can be customized, tailored to meet a specific customer's need by relevant data extraction from large databases. Thus, we also define data mining as the analysis of data in a database using tools, which look for trends or anomalies without knowledge of the meaning of the data. Data mining takes advantage of the huge amount of information gathered by a Web site to look for patterns in user behaviour (Hanna, 2004b). It can also be referred to as sorting through data to identify patterns and establish relationships. Data mining relates to concepts such as knowledge extraction, data/pattern analysis, data archeology, information harvesting, business intelligence, data warehouse, data integration, and more. All these are a body of organized, related information. But what is not data mining? Statistical programs and expert systems cannot be utilized to extract patterns from a database. This is a major difference between mining and similar applications. *Data mining techniques* are applied in such areas as manufacturing, mathematics, cybernetics, genetics, and so on.

Applied to the manufacturing area, the case that relates to the selection of a new supplier of raw materials to a manufacturing company could be considered. Suppose a company X that usually supplies materials to company P winds up due to some uncontrollable factors, and data from prospective suppliers, Y, Z, and more, could be tested against those that company X had been providing before winding up. Statistical analysis could be used for this purpose. In particular, Pearson's correlation coefficient could be used between data from company X and Y, company X and Z, and so on. The time to failure of the products supplied could be noted. Again, values 0.6 and above, 0.50 - 0.59, and 0 - 0.49 could be taken as high, medium, and low respectively. If the correlation coefficient between company X and any of the prospective suppliers is high, accept this supplier. If the value obtained is on the medium scale, additional data needs to be obtained so that the final value would fall either to low or brought up to high. If the result of the correlation test between company X and the other prospective supplier is low, reject the supplier outrightly. This is an example of data mining in manufacturing operations. The next two definitions of data mining relates to Weiss and Indurkhya (1998) and Piatetsky-Shapiro and Frawley (1991). The first two authors define data mining as a search for valuable information in large volumes of data. The last two authors quoted above refers to data mining as the process of non-trivial extraction of implicit, previously unknown and potentially useful information such as knowledge rules, constraints, and regularities from data stored in repositories using pattern recognition technologies as well as statistical and mathematical techniques.

Purpose of Data Mining

The advent of database management systems has provided solution as well as created new challenges to overcome in data processing. Information management systems had created a vast amount of data stored in databases invariably leading to data explosion problems. The complexities of these problems increased in unexpected capacities thus leading to the need for a problem-solving application that can map the database and extract the right data needed. The quick retrieval and evaluation of these data in a flow process is important in arriving at expected composition of mixtures in a paint manufacturing industry for example. Here, a sophisticated mixer equipped with automated devices to measure chemical composition, flow rate, temperature differences, and so forth, can use this application to profoundly locate the exact chemical concentrate needed for production. Various manufacturing processes where data transfer and exchange is required from a large source can, through this application, extract and evaluate useful information from the database thereby reducing operation time of production. It is ironical that despite the extremely large databases at our disposal, we are unsatisfied with the available information and therefore continue to build our data collection with declining knowledge derivation.

An industrialist with a focus on better quality product, faster operation processes, lower product prices, increased customer satisfaction, product innovation, and more, may be whitewashed with data but lacking in some salient knowledge such as flow patterns, constraints, irregularities, and so forth, thus, the advent of this solution application in troubleshooting large database management problems. It is relevant to note the evolution of this application from database creation in the 1960s through relational DBMS in the 1970s to application-oriented DBMS in the 1980s and data mining and data warehousing in the 1990s and recently.

Main Types of Data Required for Mining

Databases are very commonly used in everyday life. Private and governmental organizations are constantly storing information about people, keeping credit and tax records, addresses, phone numbers, and so on. In industry, there exists a colossal amount of data on manpower, materials, economics and technical aspects of varied manufacturing activities, in other words, materials stocked awaiting usage in production, personnel records to be processed by a program such as a payroll application containing age, salary, address, emergency contact of employees, and others. We have some examples of databases as follows: relational, transactional, spatial, multimedia, heterogeneous, legacy, object-oriented, worldwide web, data warehouses, and so forth (Iverson & Prasad, 1998). The relational databases provide a very simple way of looking at data structured into tables. Users can consider the high-level SQL (Structured Query Language) to declaratively specify queries to retrieve information from databases (Lee & Siau, 2001). A manufacturer into various brands of household beverages may want to know such information as the color and weight of a particular product, date of production, number of products sold, distributed product location, names and number of employees in production department at the time, and their salaries. He can retrieve these and many more from his repository of data.

Data Mining Functionality

The evolution of database technology from data collection and creation to present day sophistication in data warehousing, data cleaning, selection, and evaluation has resulted in increased capability of data mining programs to operate as expected during actual service conditions. The functionalities of data mining deploy such techniques as: sequence or path analysis in looking for patterns where one event leads to another event; forecasting, which supports discovering patterns in data that can lead to reasonable predictions about the future. Others include clustering, which coordinates finding and visually documenting groups of facts not previously known: association examines patterns where one event is connected to another event; classification looks for new patterns which may result in a change in the way data is organized.

Furthermore, these techniques can be further exploited using the following functionalities: exploratory data analysis, descriptive Modeling, outlier analysis, trend and evolution analysis, classification and prediction, and other pattern directed or statistical analysis (Iverson & Prasad, 1998). The influence of data mining is remarkably profound in exploratory data analysis. This method is designed to generalize, summarize, and contrast data characteristics such as dry vs. wet regions, imported vs. exported goods, and so forth. Thus, data retrieval and extraction techniques are copiously used to discover hidden facts in compressed composition. In candy manufacturing, the rate of chocolates, bubble gum, and biscuits delivered to different geographical regions can be used to compute these regions' consumption rates, retail promotions required, and so on.

Also, an oil producing company may require the volume of crude oil produced in a flow station within a specific quarter for the last two decades. This analysis can be used to characterize data in this form. Moreover, descriptive modeling is another example of data mining functionality, which examines among other cluster analyses. Here, class label is unknown and we group data to form new classes, otherwise known as cluster vehicles, to find the distribution pattern in a metropolitan area. Also, density estimation could be used in data involving people, houses, vehicles, wild life, production, and more. Furthermore, in outlier analysis of mining functionalities, an irregular data object that does not conform to the distributed data behavior is closely considered especially in fraud detection and rare events analysis. The trend and deviation existing in data and that are comparable to regression analysis are supported under trend and evolution analysis. Other associated areas include sequential pattern mining, periodicity analysis and similarity based analysis. Classification and prediction refer to finding functions that describe and distinguish classes or concepts for future prediction (Iverson & Prasad, 1998). Classification profiles presentation by using decision-tree, and classification rule neural network. Prediction involves some unknown or missing numerical values (Lu, Setiono, & Liu, 1996).

Some Major Issues in Data Mining

Web search and information retrieval programs like data mining and process data, use extraction techniques, which interact with other heterogeneous applications to find patterns and subtle relationships, and also to predict future data results (Simoudis, 1996). Consideration is given here to some salient mining issues such as methodologies and interactions, performance function and scalability, data diversity types, applications, and social impacts. Of special relevance to this topic are mining methodology and user interactions. They define the procedures and algorithms designed to analyze the data in databases. They also examine mining different kinds of knowledge in relational and transactional databases, data warehouses and other information repositories. This new knowledge discovery could describe such application domain as in customer relation management, manufacturing inventories, space science, cellular therapy, credit card usage histories, and so forth. Thus, user interactions with various applications encourage integration in mining methodologies. Also of relevance is the mining of knowledge at multiple levels of abstraction (Iverson & Prasad, 1998). This interactive multimedia interface deploys navigational aids to arrive at a logical conclusion. Moreover, the expression and visualization of hidden facts in *data mining results* establish its application in fraud detection, credit risk analysis and other applications. Also, incorporation of background knowledge, incomplete data handling, query languages are part of this interactive methodologies. Other issues that also need to be addressed include the performance and scalability factor. The efficiency of procedures and algorithms are tested in parallel, distributed, or incremental mining methods to determine the functionality of these programs. Assessment is made of decision making impact through mining applications and protection of data through enactment of privacy laws and also creation of security measures to guide against misappropriation.

The remaining part of the current paper is sectioned into four. In the next section, the financial data that manufacturing organizations are concerned with are discussed. This serves as a springboard on which the methodological frameworks are built. Following the section, the author presents a framework of the decision tree as applied to manufacturing systems. The final section, labeled "conclusion and future directions", concludes the study and proposes areas for future navigation by other research scholars.

Financial Data Collected in Manufacturing Systems

Manufacturing involves effective coordination of technical, financial and material resources to achieve a desired level of production at a profit to the organization. The utilization of data-mining applications in manufacturing has helped in discovery, selection, and development of core knowledge in the management of large databases hitherto unknown. The following are the financial data collected in manufacturing systems.

Cost of Raw Materials Purchased

As material cost adds up to the production cost, raw material cost must be closely monitored due to its variable tendencies. This could be compared with a target monthly performance value with comments made on the relationship between the expected performance and the actual status of performance. Comments could be of three categories: "on target", "below target", or "above target". Based on this, grading of the various performance values could be made in accordance with the sequence of months or their achievement of targets. In the same manner the overall material cost, which is the sum of the various raw materials purchased from different raw materials, is the input needed in the financial analysis of the performance of the organization in a fiscal year. This is also a key factor in the audit of the firm's financial state.

Workers' Salaries/Fringe Benefits/Incentives

Every organization takes a major step to ensuring proper documentation of the amount spent on employees' salaries, allowances and other remuneration. Data representing this sum of money could be mined using any data mining parameters. Also, as organizations undergo expansion and development, their pay roll changes in the number of entries and the amount involved. These provide a variety of data for mining purposes. Such changes in the pay roll could be easily recognized in the historical data of the organization. In some instances, some firms find it burdensome to pay salaries when there are losses incurred in the transactions of the organization. The trends could also be interpreted from the mined data. Thus, data relating to workers' salaries, fringe benefits and incentives is a key financial index that must be known to managers for accountability and planning.

Cost of Maintaining Equipment/Machinery

Assessment must be made about the cost of sustaining production activities through the maintenance functions. Maintenance provides a significant amount of information in a manufacturing organization. This enormous information could be mined in order to provide useful information for decision making in the manufacturing organization. Details of the cost discussed here include cost of replacing worn out or failed parts, lubrication, sub-contracting of jobs, and more. These individuals cost could be mined when collected for a long period of time, particularly for large manufacturing organizations that are engaged in multiple production activities. The mined data would assist organizations that are engaged in multiple production activities to decide on what product gives them the highest level of profit and on what product yields the lowest profit level. In addition to the above data set, manufacturing data must be available during the financial requirement analysis period of the maintenance department. This will lead to the discovery of patterns that would be invaluable for adequate planning and future forecast of requirements.

Total Cost of Fuel for Running Generator, Plant, etc.

Listed in the financial budget is the cost of obtaining fuel to run the various equipment and machineries used in production. These include diesel (to run generators), gas (needed to fire the boiler or welding purposes), and so forth. *Data mining activities* could be performed on the usage of the individual fuel category in relation to supply quantities, the equipment capacity, and the skill level of the operator in handling the equipment. Sometimes the economic effect of fuel cost carries the major part of overhead cost in some firms. Therefore, component analysis of costs may help in the mining activities.

Cost of Electricity Usage

This widely used source of energy is not only relatively cheaper than other energy sources, but also easily obtainable and utilized. Data must be available on this electrical energy cost in order to evaluate the cost of energy consumption not only for production activities, but also energy utilized in the offices, workshop, canteen and all other areas of manufacturing within the firm. Alternative sources of energy must be made available especially in parts of the world where national energy supply is unstable. This increases the cost of electricity significantly and adds to the total cost of operations. All of these data are significant in forming a database that would serve for mining purposes.

Cost of Maintaining Vehicles

From a small or medium sized firm with a few numbers of vehicles to large corporations with fleet of vehicles, the vehicles maintenance cost is usually high on the expenditure list of the companies. Proper monitoring and controlling of these costs could be made using data mining techniques. Thus, better decision could be reached based on informed judgment. Some large firms create workshops that run vehicle maintenance services, which are more profitable to implement in the long run than subcontracting these services. These costs cover purchasing of new motor parts, lubrication, safety and security devices put in place, cost of hired experts, and so on. In addition, the database obtained here is useful for mining purposes.

Methodological Framework

In the data mining literature, decision trees have been widely used in predicting a wide variety of issues. Cases in medicine, agriculture, insurance, banking, and so forth, are worthy of note. A classic reference in this instance is the work of Hanna (2004a) who discussed *decision tree as a data mining method* in Oracle. However, in this section, decision trees are applied to specific financial data in order to demonstrate the feasibility of applying this data mining tools in practice. Decision tree, one of the data mining methods, has been widely used as a modelling approach and has shown better predictive ability than traditional approaches (e.g., regression) (Zhang et al., 2005). However, very little is known from the literature about how decision tree performs in manufacturing data mining activities. In this study, decision tree models were developed to investigate manufacturing data for mining purposes.

In the remaining part of this section, the paper discusses the application of decision trees in understanding the analysis that could be made on cost of fuel and vehicle maintenance cost, cost of raw materials purchased, workers' salaries/fringe benefits/incentives, cost of maintaining equipment/machinery, and so forth. However, the order of treatment shall be in accordance with the listing above.

Costing of Fuel

Figure 2 represents a decision tree that might be created from the data shown in Table 1. For this particular case, the decision tree algorithm is used to determine the most significant attribute that would predict the cost of fuel. In this particular case, it is fuel consumption. As seen in the first split of the decision tree, the decision is made based on fuel consumption.

Table 1. Data set for total cost of fuel

S/No.	Equipment/ Plant Identity	Fuel (demand) consumption	Fuel supply	Fuel availability	Cost of fuel
1.	Perkins (generator)	high	high	high	low
2.	Compressors	low	low	low	high
3.	Boiler	high	low	low	high
4.	Engines (diesel)	high	low	low	high
5.	Engines (petrol)	low	low	high	low
6.	Crane	low	high	high	low
7.	Turbo charger (diesel)	high	high	high	low
8.	Refrigerator	low	low	low	high
9.	Furnace	low	low	low	high
10.	Forklift	high	low	low	high

Figure 2. Analysis of cost of fuel using decision tree

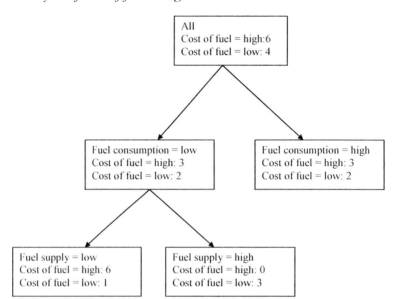

It is obvious that one of the new nodes (i.e., fuel consumption = high) is a leaf node which contains five cases with three cases of high cost of fuel and two cases of low cost fuel. The second node (i.e., fuel consumption = low) has a number of cases with the first node. This predictive model now identifies fuel supply as another important factor in predicting cost of fuel. The two new nodes (divided as a result of the split) show that high fuel supply reduces the cost of fuel, while low supply increases the cost of fuel. Since this model is generated for our purpose, the practical scenario shows that for every equipment, there are lots of factors that determine its cost of fuel more than presently enumerated. Also, in practice, the number of equipment far exceeds the present estimation. Modelling real life cases involves considering extremely large factors in predicting fuel cost. The rules describing this prediction cannot be extracted manually when dealing with practical situations leading to formulating a decision tree.

Data Set for Cost of Raw Materials Purchased

This decision tree (see Figure 3 and Table 2) attempts to predict cost of raw materials purchased in a food and beverage-manufacturing environment. It identifies some determinant factors in this process, such as material consumption, quantity purchased

Table 2. Data set for cost of raw materials purchased (food and beverage Industry)

S/No.	Material Identity	Material consumption	Quantity Purchased	Quality of Material	Cost of raw Material
1.	Flour	High	High	High	Low
2	Beef	Low	Low	High	High
3.	Cooking oil	Low	Low	High	Low
4.	Butter	High	High	High	Low
5.	Cocoa	Low	Low	High	Low
6.	wheat	High	High	High	Low
7.	Sweetner	Low	Low	High	High
8.	Soya beans	Low	Low	High	High
9.	Water	High	High	High	High
10.	Diesel	High	High	High	Low

Figure 3. Analysis of cost of raw materials decision tree

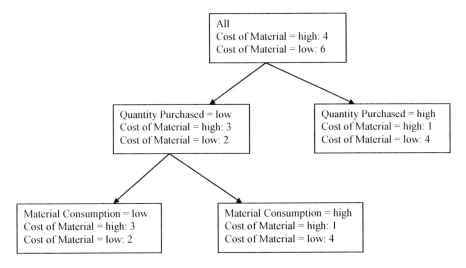

and material quality. From the decision tree, the first split involves quantity purchased separated into leaf nodes (low and high). One leaf part (Quantity purchased = low) shows three cases of high material cost and two cases of low material cost. This implies a low quantity of raw material is purchased when the cost of material is high. The other leaf node (Quantity purchased = high) has four cases of low cost of material and one case of high material cost implying that low material cost is encouraged by high quantity purchase.

Table 3. Dataset for cost of maintaining a clean, safem and beautiful factory premises

S/No.	Factory Area	Level of safety required	Level of beautification	Cost of cleanliness	Cost of keeping facility in acceptable condition
1.	Assembly line	High	Low	High	High
2.	Administrative offices	High	High	High	High
3.	Engineering workshop	High	Low	High	High
4.	Powerhouse	High	Low	Low	High
5.	Kitchen	Low	High	Low	Low
6.	Store	Low	Low	Low	Low
7.	Conference room	Low	High	Low	Low
8.	Guests'/visitors' room	Low	High	Low	Low
9.	Security post	High	Low	Low	Low
10.	Car park	Low	Low	Low	Low
11.	Bathroom/toilet	Low	Low	Low	Low
12.	Refuse dump	High	Low	High	Low
13.	Open space	Low	Low	Low	Low

Figure 4. Decision tree for cost of maintaining factory premises

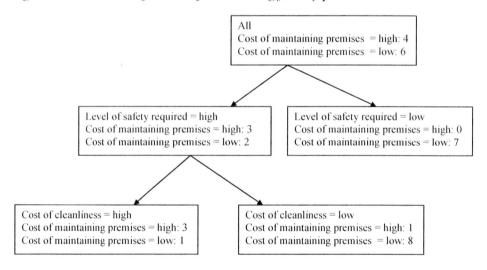

Another important predictor of cost of raw materials is the material consumption. The leaf nodes indicate low cost of material catalyzes high material consumption. Practically, there are much more attributes for each material identified and these material quantities are large. It is then not pragmatic to manually utilize the rules in locating high and low cost of materials. This algorithm we are considering can involve hundreds of attributes and far more number of records in forming a decision tree that models and predicts cost of raw materials.

A similar analysis to previous section could be carried out with the data in the following Table 3. The results are further analyzed in Figure 4.

Conclusion and Future Directions

Decision tree is an important data mining tool, which has been applied in areas such as military operations, medical science, business, insurance, banking, space exploration, and more. There is a current need for an application of decision trees as a data mining tool in manufacturing systems since many articles have largely ignored this application tool in manufacturing to date. After an exposition on the sources of data in manufacturing system, the paper discusses the application of decision tree to manufacturing decision making in order to improve productivity and the quality of decision made. Since manufacturing accounts for an integral part of the world economy, the application of decision tree in manufacturing sector of the economy is a new dimension to research. It is therefore a new contribution to knowledge in the area. Future investigators could integrate tools from statistics and other techniques for mining such as transactional/relational database, artificial intelligence techniques, visualization, genetic algorithms, and so on, into the existing framework of decision tree in order to enhance its functionality more fully. Although decision tree is very useful in manufacturing data mining activities, it has limitations. One limitation of using decision tree to predict the performance of manufacturing systems is that it could not generate a continuous prediction. Therefore, it may not be able to detect the influence of small changes in manufacturing data variables on performance of the organization.

References

Adriaans, P., & Zantinge, D. (1997). *Data mining*. New York: Addison-Wesley.

Ananthanarayana, V. S., Narasimha, M. M., Subramaman, D. K. (2003). Tree structure for efficient data mining using rough sets, pattern recognition letter (Vol. 24, pp. 851-862).

Berry, M., & Linoff, G. (1997). *Data mining techniques*. New York: Wiley.

Berson, A., Smith, S. & Thearling, K. (2000). *Building data mining applications for CRM*. New York: McGraw-Hill.

Berson, A., & Smith, S. J. (1997). Data warehousing, data mining and OLAP. New York: McGraw-Hill.

Brown, L. M., & Kros, J. F. (2003). Data mining and the impact of missing data. *Industrial Management and Data Systems, 103*(8), 611-621.

Bose, I., & Mahapatra, R. K. (2001). Business data mining — a machine learning perspective. *Information and Management, 39*(3), 211-225.

Browne, A., Hudson, B. D., Whitley, D. C., Ford, M. G., & Picton, P. (2004). Biological data mining with neural networks: Implementation and application of a flexible decision tree extraction algorithm to genomic problem domains. *Neurocomputing, 57*, 275-293.

Chen, M. S., Han, J., & Yu, P. (1996). Data mining: An overview from a database perspective. *IEEE Transactions on Knowledge and Data Engineering, 8*(6), 866-83.

Darling, C. B. (1997). Data mining for the masses. *Datamation, 52*, 5.

Dunham, M. H. (2003). Data mining: Introductory and advanced topics. Upper Saddle River, NJ: Pearson Education/Prentice-Hall.

Fayyad, U. M., Piatetsky-Shapiro, G., & Smyth, P. (1996a). The KDD process for extracting useful knowledge from volumes of data. *Communications of the ACM, 39*(11), 27-34.

Fayyad, U., Piatetsky-Shapiro, G., Smyth, P., & Uthurusamy, R. (Eds.) (1996b). *Advances in knowledge discovery and data mining*. Menlo Park, CA: AAAI Press.

Fayyard, U., Piatetsky-Shapiro, G., & Smyth, P. (1996c). From data mining to knowledge discovery: An overview. In U. Fayyad, G. Piatestsky-Shapiro, P. Smyth, & R. Uthurusamy (Eds.), *Advances in knowledge discovery and data mining*. Cambridge, MA: MIT Press.

Gargano, L. M., & Raggad, B. G. (1999). Data mining — A powerful information creating tool. *OCLC Systems and Services, 15*(2), 81-90.

Groth, R. (2000). *Data mining: Building competitive advantage*. Upper Saddle River, NJ: Prentice-Hall.

Hanna, M. (2004a). Data-mining algorithms in Oracle9i and Microsoft sql server. *Campus-Wide Information Systems, 21*(3), 132-138.

Hanna, M. (2004b). Data mining in the e-learning domain. *Campus-Wide Information, 21*(1), 29-34.

Han, J., & Kamber, M. (2001). Data mining: Concepts and techniques. San Francisco, CA: Morgan Kaufmann.

Iverson, L. R., & Prasad, A. M. (1998). Predicting abundance of 80 tree species following climate changes in eastern United States. *Ecological Monograph, 68,* 465-485.

Lee, J. S. & Siau, K. (2001). A review of data mining techniques. *Industrial Management and Data Systems, 101*(1), 41-46.

Li, S., & Shue, L. (2004). *Data mining to aid policy making in air pollution management,* (vol. 27), (pp. 331-340).

Li, S. B., Sweigart, J., Teng, J., Donohue, J., & Thombs, L. (2001). A dynamic programming based pruning method for decision trees. *Journal on Computing, 13*(4), 332-344.

Liao, S.-H. (2003). Knowledge management technologies and applications: Literature review from 1995-2002. *Expert Systems with Applications, 25*(2), 155-164.

Lu, H., Setiono, R., & Liu, H. (1996). Effective data mining using neural networks. *IEEE Transactions on Knowledge and Data Engineering, 8*(6), 957-61.

Minaei-bidgoli, B. & Unch, W. F. III (2003). Using generic algorithms for data mining optimization in an educational web-based system. In *GECCO 2003* (pp. 2252-63). Retrieved from http://www.ion-capa.org

Mitra, S., Pal, S. K., & Mitra, P. (2002). Data mining in soft computing framework: A survey. *IEEE Transactions on Neural Networks, 13*(1), 3-14.

Oracle. (2001). *Oracle 9i data mining, data sheet.* Retrieved from http://oracle.com/products

Pyle, D. (1998). Putting data mining in its place. *Database Programming and Design, 11*(3), 32-6.

Piatetsky-Shapiro, G. & Frawley W. J. (1991). *Knowledge discovery in database.* AAAI/MIT Press.

Quinlan, J. R. (1987). Simplifying decision trees. *International Journal of Man-machine Studies, 27(*3), 221-234.

Roiger, R. J., & Geatz, M. W. (2003). *Data mining: A tutorial-based primer.* Boston: Addison-Wesely/Pearson Education, Inc.

Scheffer, J. (2002). Data mining in the survey setting: Why do children go off the rails? *Res. Lett. Inform. Math. Sci., 3,* 161-189.

Sorensen, K., & Janssens, G. K. (2003). Data mining with genetic algorithms on binary trees, *European Journal of Operational Research, 151,* 253-264.

Simoudis, E. (1996). Reality check for data mining. *IEEE Intelligent Systems and their Applications,* 11(5), 26-33.

Su, C.-T., Chen, Y.-H., & Sha, D. Y. (2005). Linking innovative product development with customer knowledge: A data mining approach. *Technovation, 10*(10), 1-12

Sugumaran, V., & Bose, R. (1999). Data analysis and mining environment: a distributed intelligent agent technology application. *Industrial Management and Data Systems, 99*(2), 71-80.

Tung, K.-Y., Huang, I.-C., Chen, S.-L., & Shih, C.-T. (2005). Mining the Generation Xers' job attitudes by artificial neural network and decision tree: Empirical evidence in Taiwan. *Expert Systems with Applications, 10*(20), 1-12.

Vayssieeres, M. P., Plant, R. E., & Allen-diaz, B. H. (2000). Classification trees: An alternative non-parametric approach for predicting species distribution. *Journal of Veg. Sci., 11*, 679-694.

Weiss, S. H. & Indurkhya, N. (1998). *Predictive data mining: A practical guide.* San Fransisco, CA: Morgan Kaufmann Publishers.

Westphal, C. & Blaxton, T. (1998). *Data mining solutions.* New York: Wiley.

Witten, I. & Frank, E. (2000). *Data mining.* San Francisco: Academic Press.

Yang, C. C., Prasher, S. O., Enright, P., Madramootoo, C., Burgess, M., Goel, P. K., et al. (2003). Application of decision tree technology for image classification using remote sensing data. *Agric. Syst., 76*, 1101-1117.

Zhang, B., Valentine, I., & Kemp, P. (2005). Modelling the productivity of naturalized pasture in the North Island, New Zealand: A decision tree approach. *Ecological Modelling, 186*, 299-311.

Chapter VII

An Implemented Representation and Reasoning System for Creating and Exploiting Large Knowledge Bases of "Narrative" Information

Gian Piero Zarri, University Paris 4/Sorbonne, France

Abstract

In this chapter, we evoke first the ubiquity and the importance of the so-called 'narrative' information, showing that the usual ontological tools are unable to offer complete and reliable solutions for representing and exploiting this type of information. We then supply some details about NKRL (Narrative Knowledge Representation Language), a fully implemented knowledge representation and inferencing environment especially created for an 'intelligent' exploitation of narrative knowledge. The main innovation of NKRL consists in associating with the traditional ontologies of concepts an 'ontology of events', in other words, a new sort of hierarchical organization where the nodes correspond to n-ary structures representing formally generic classes of elementary events like 'move a physical object', 'be present in a place', or 'send/receive a message'. More complex, second order tools based on the 'reification' principle allow one to encode the 'connectivity phenomena' like causality, goal, indirect speech, coordination, and subordination that, in narrative information, link together 'elementary events'. The chapter includes a description of the inference techniques proper to NKRL, and some information about the last developments of this language.

Introduction

A big amount of important, 'economically relevant' information, is hidden within the huge mass of multimedia documents that correspond to some form of 'narrative' description. Examples of narrative documents are many of the 'corporate knowledge' documents (memos, policy statements, reports, minutes, etc.), the news stories, the normative and legal texts, the medical records, many intelligence messages, as well as, in general, a huge fraction of the documents stored on the Web. In these narrative documents, or 'narratives', the main part of the information content consists in the description of temporally and spatially bounded 'events' that relate the behaviour or the condition of some 'actors' (characters, personages, etc.). They try to attain a specific result, experience particular situations, manipulate some (concrete or abstract) materials, send or receive messages, buy, sell, deliver, and so forth. For simplicity's sake, the term 'event' is taken here in its most general meaning, covering also strictly related notions like fact, action, state, situation, episode, activity, and so on. All these notions, both the 'stative' and the 'eventive', have been sometimes grouped under the generic label of 'eventualities' (see Bach, 1981), which is, however, less evocative in our opinion than the standard term 'event'. Note that, in the events evoked by the narrative documents, the actors or personages are not necessarily human beings; we can have narrative documents concerning, for example, the vicissitudes in the journey of a nuclear submarine (the 'actor', 'subject' or 'personage') or the various avatars in the life of a commercial product. Note also that, even if a large amount of narrative documents concerns Natural Language (NL) texts, this is not necessarily true. A photo representing a situation that, verbalized, could be expressed as "Three nice girls are lying on the beach" is not of course an NL text, yet it is still a narrative document.

Because of the ubiquity of these 'narrative' resources, being able to represent in a general, accurate, and effective way their semantic content — in other words, their key meaning — is then both conceptually relevant and economically important.

In this chapter, we will present the main properties of NKRL (Narrative Knowledge Representation Language), a language expressly designed for representing, in a standardized way, the 'meaning' of complex multimedia narrative documents. NKRL has been used as 'the' modelling knowledge representation language for narratives in European projects like Nomos (Esprit P5330), Cobalt (LRE P61011), Concerto (Esprit P29159), Euforbia (IAP P26505) and Parmenides (IST P2001-39023). Many of the examples used in this chapter to illustrate the NKRL's characteristics have been developed in a Parmenides context during an in-depth application of NKRL techniques on data concerning the 'terrorism in the Philippines'; these data have been supplied by the Greek Ministry of Defense (MoD), one of the Parmenides partners, see (Zarri & Bernard, 2004a). The main references for NKRL are (Zarri, 1997; 1998; 2003a); with respect to these last papers, the present chapter is more oriented towards a general discussion about the desirable characteristics of a formal language for dealing with narratives.

In the next section, *Background*, we will examine previous and current solutions proposed for the representation and processing of narratives, their strengths, and weaknesses. The following section, *The NKRL Approach*, will represent the main thrust of the chapter and will include, among other things, a relative in-depth description of the inference techniques proper to NKRL. After a section on the future developments, a short *Conclusion* will end the chapter.

Background

The "Standard" Ontology Approach and The "*n*-ary" Problem

Usual ontologies — both in their 'traditional', see Noy, Fergerson, and Musen (2000), and 'semantic Web' (W3C) versions, see McGuinness and van Harmelen (2004) — are not very suitable for dealing with narratives. Basically, ontologies organize the 'concepts' — that we can identify here with the important notions to be represented in a given application domain — into a hierarchical structure, able to supply an elementary form of definition of these concepts through their mutual generic/specific relationships ('IsA' links). A more precise definition is obtained by associating with them a set of *binary relationships* of the property/value type (e.g., a frame). Semantic Web languages like RDF and OWL, see Zarri (2005a) for an overview — and the great majority of the languages/environments for setting up 'ontologies' — are then denoted as '*binary*'. The combination of these two representational principles is largely sufficient to provide a *static, a priori* definition of the concepts and of their properties.

Unfortunately, this is not true when we consider the *dynamic behavior* of the concepts, in other words, we want to describe their *mutual relationships* when they take part in some concrete action, situation, and so forth ('events'), see the very simple narrative "John has given a book to Mary". In this example, "give" is now an *n-ary (ternary) relationship* that, to be represented in a *complete and unambiguous way*, asks for some form of complex syntax where the arguments of the predicate, in other words, "John", "book", and "Mary", are introduced by some sorts of *'conceptual roles'* such as, "agent of give", "object of give" and "beneficiary of give" respectively. For representing the 'meaning' of narrative documents, the notion of *'role'* must then be necessarily added to the traditional 'generic/specific' and 'property/value' representational principles in order to specify the *exact function* of the different components of an event within the *formal description* of this event. Moreover, in a narrative context, there exists — beyond the simple 'elementary event' level — a 'higher level' that refers to a more complex 'story level' or 'plot'. This must take care of those *'connectivity phenomena'* like causality, goal, indirect speech, co-ordination and subordination and so forth, that link together the basic 'elementary events'. It is very likely, in fact, that, dealing with the sale of a company, the global information to represent is something like: "Company X has sold its subsidiary Y to Z *because* the profits of Y have fallen dangerously these last years *due to* a lack of investments" or, returning to our previous example, that "John gave a book to Mary yesterday *as a* present for her birthday" or that, dealing with the relationships between companies in the biotechnology domain, "X made a milestone payment to Y *because* they decided to pursue an in vivo evaluation of the candidate compound identified by X", and so forth. In Computational Linguistics terms, we are here in the domain of the 'Discourse Analysis' which deals, in short, with the two following problems: (1) determining the nature of the information that, in a sequence of statements, goes beyond the simple addition of the information conveyed by a single statement; (2) determining the influence of the context in which a statement is used on the meaning of this individual statement, or part of it. It is now easy to imagine the awkward proliferation of binary relationships that, sticking to the traditional ontological paradigm, it would be necessary to introduce to approximate high-level notions like those of 'role' and 'connectivity phenomena'. The traditional, 'binary' approach to the set up of ontologies is then insufficient to deal exhaustively with narrative documents.

Note that a common misunderstanding consists in saying that the definition of specific *n*-ary languages for managing narratives is not at all necessary given that any *n*-ary relationship, with $n > 2$, can be reduced in a very simple way to a set of binary relationships. More formally — and leaving aside, for simplicity's sake, problems like those introduced by temporal information — we can say that an *n*-ary relation $R(t_1, \ldots, t_n)$ can normally be represented, with the aid of the existential quantifier, as: (exists e) ($R(e)$ & $Rb_1(e, t_1)$ & $Rb_2(e, t_2)$ & ... & $Rb_n(e, t_n)$). In this last expression, e must be understood as an event or situation of type R; in a triadic situation involving a predicate like "give", we have then GIVE(e). Rb_1, Rb_2 ... Rb_n is some fixed set of binary relations, corresponding to "agent of give" and so forth in the previous example. This sort of decomposition is not only formally interesting, but also important for many practical problems, for example, for storing efficiently n-ary relationships into standard databases.

However, the decomposition *does not eliminate* the need for argument e, which is still necessary to link all the binary relationships together. In a relational databases context, this is equivalent to say that — after having decomposed a relationship in the GIVE style into three 2-column tables named "agent", "object" and "beneficiary" where the first column is reserved to the predicate — to recover the *global information* it is now necessary to '*join*' again the three 2-column tables on the column that represents the predicate (GIVE). This implies also that, if we want to execute some 'reasoning' about "John gave a book to Mary yesterday" by respecting the true 'meaning' of this event, recognizing the existence of binary relationships between a given book or a human being and this event is not really useful without (1) 'returning' to the original, ternary meaning of GIVE, and (2) taking into account that the relationships among GIVE and its three 'arguments', "John", "book", and "Mary" are labelled in different ways, as "agent", "object", and "beneficiary". Now, with respect to the current vogue of 'translating' pre-existing high-level (n-ary) knowledge representation languages into the (more fashionable) W3C (binary) languages, an important point to emphasize here is that, notwithstanding the formal transformation, *the n-ary languages are still n-ary after that the 'translation' has been realized*, like the GIVE relationship above is still ternary even if formally reduced to a set of binary relationships. This means that, to exploit in full the representational power of n-ary languages like NKRL, Conceptual Graphs (Sowa, 1999) or CycL (Witbrock et al., 2004) — for example, for executing complex inference operations — the original n-ary inferencing tools of those languages must be used. As a consequence, these languages — after a possible conversion into binary format — must in fact be 'translated back' into the original format n-ary to get the best of their characteristics and to avoid the usual 'binary' limitations.

The discussion above should have demonstrated the need of disposing of 'true' n-ary language to deal adequately with narrative documents. Unfortunately, suggestions in this context are quite scarce in a Semantic Web (W3C) context — W3C languages like RDF and OWL represent actually the most popular paradigm in the knowledge representation domain. The most recent one consists in a working paper from the W3C Semantic Web Best Practices and Deployment Working Group (SWBPD WG) about "Defining N-ary Relations on the Semantic Web", see Noy and Rector (2005). That paper proposes some extensions to the binary paradigm to allow the correct representation of narratives like: "Christine has breast tumour with high probability", "Steve has temperature, which is high, but failing", "John buys a "Lenny the Lion" book from books.Example.com for $15 as a birthday gift" or "United Airlines flight 3177 visits the following airports: LAX, DFW, and JFK"

— this last example has be added to the previous three in the more recent versions of the document. The mentioned working paper has aroused many criticisms. Leaving aside the fact that only four, very particular 'narratives' are examined, without any convincing justification for that choice, the criticisms have focused mainly on the arbitrary introduction, through reification processes, of fictitious (and inevitably *ad hoc*) 'individuals' to represent the *n*-ary relations — note that this one is the usual (*ad hoc*) solution used by the builders of 'classical' binary ontology to simulate some simple *n*-ary situations. More specific and 'technical' remarks have been also formulated, about, in other words, the use in the proposed *n*-ary solutions of 'infamous' W3C constructs like the RDF 'blank nodes', aka 'anonymous resources'. We can also note, eventually, that the paper says nothing about the way of dealing, in concrete situations, with those 'connectivity phenomena' evoked previously.

Previous '*n*-ary' Solutions and Related Problems

A well-formed and complete solution to the *n*-ary problem has been long known: it is based on the notions of 'conceptual predicate' and, as already stated, of 'conceptual role'. Returning then to the "John gave a book…" example above, a complete representation that captures all the 'meaning' of this elementary narrative amounts to:

- Defining john_, mary_, book_1 and yesterday_ as 'individuals', instances of general 'concepts' like *human_being*, *information_support* and *calendar_day* or of more specific concepts. Concepts and instances (individuals) are, as usual, collected into a 'binary' ontology (built up using a tool like, e.g., Protégé).

- Defining an *n*-ary structure (a sort of generalized frame) structured around a conceptual predicate like, for example, PHYSICAL_TRANSFER, and associating the above individuals (the arguments) to the predicate through the use of conceptual roles that specify their 'function' within the global narrative. john_ will then be introduced by an AGENT (or SUBJECT) role, book_1 by an OBJECT (or PATIENT) role, mary_ by a BENEFICIARY_ role, yesterday_ by a TEMPORAL_ANCHOR role.

Formally, an *n*-ary structure defined according the above guidelines can be described as:

$$(L_i (P_j (R_1 \ a_1) (R_2 \ a_2) \ldots (R_n \ a_n))) \qquad \qquad \text{equation (1)}$$

where L_i is the symbolic label identifying the particular *n*-ary structure (e.g., that corresponding to the "John gave a book…" example), P_j is the conceptual predicate,

R_k is the generic role and a_k the corresponding argument (the individuals john_, mary_ etc.). Note that if, in the binary decomposition $Rb_i(e, Arg_i)$ introduced above, we equate: e with P_j, Rb_i with R_k, and Arg_i with a_k, we obtain a set of binary relationships that coincide with the $(R_i\, a_i)$ cells of (1) taken *individually*. As already stated, the main point here is that the whole conceptual structure represented by (1) must be considered *globally*.

Many solutions that can be reduced formally to (1) have been suggested in the last 60 years. To limit ourselves to some 'Knowledge Representation-oriented' examples, we can mention here Silvio Ceccato's 'correlators' (a sort of roles) used, in the context of his experiments of mechanical translation, to represent narratives as a network of triadic structures, see (Ceccato, 1967). Other examples concern the conceptual dependency theory of Schank (Schank, 1973), which makes use of conceptual predicates under the form of the well-known 'primitive actions' like INGEST and MOVE associated with seven role relationships, Schubert's propositional notation (Schubert, 1976), Sowa's conceptual graphs (Sowa, 1984; 1999), NKRL, and so forth. Linguistic theories that make use of notions similar to that of "role" are Case Grammars (Fillmore, 1966), Jackendoff's thematic roles (Jackendoff, 1990), Kamp's Discourse Representation Structures (Kamp & Reyle, 1993), and so forth. Always in a 'linguistic' context, a recent trend concerns the fact of dealing with 'events' like 'grammatical objects', see Tenny and Pustejovsky (2000), in the sense that the semantics of events can be seen to depend from verbs' syntactic structures. The 'story trees' of Mani and Pustejovsky, (see Mani & Pustejovsky, 2004), introduced from a computational linguistics and text summarization perspective have, moreover, strong similarities with the 'binding structures' of NKRL used to deal with the already mentioned 'connectivity phenomena'. Eventually, in a description logics context, a language called DLR that supports *n*-ary relations has also been mentioned (see Berardi, Calvanese, & De Giacomo 2001), along with details about its use for reasoning on Unified Modeling Language (UML) class diagrams. The basic conceptual elements of DLR are 'concepts' and '*n*-ary relations'.

We can then wonder why we are today obliged to re-discuss again the *n*-ary problem. The answer lies mainly in the *combinatorial explosion* linked with all the possible associations among predicates, roles and arguments that arise when passing from binary expressions in the $Rb_i(e, Arg_i)$ style to *n*-ary expressions like equation (1). The situation gets also worse when we consider that:

- No universal agreement exists on the list of roles.
- Predicates are primitives in Schank's conceptual dependency and NKRL, then lowering the number of possible combinations, but totally free in, for example, Schubert, Sowa or in the linguistic theories.
- The arguments a_k in equation (1) can be represented, in turn, by complex structures introducing new conceptual operators and new conceptual argu-

ments. If the above example becomes, for example, "John gave a book and some flowers to Mary yesterday", a correct representation of the argument introduced by the OBJECT/PATIENT role must in fact (1) include an operator in the COORDINATION style, and (2) ways of SPECIFYING 'flowers' (a plural...) as 'some' — see, in the next sections, the 'binding operators' and the 'expansions' in NKRL.

When we add also the problem of taking into account the story structures and the 'connectivity phenomena' evoked above, it is easy to understand why, for example, solutions *à la* Schank are under specified (no complete description of his system have ever been supplied) and other solutions, like in Sowa for example, are largely theoretical — in Sowa's case, some complete, even formalized, upper level descriptions of possible concrete systems exist, but no practical indications on how to choose and combine the P_j, R_k and a_k terms in equation (1) have ever been given.

The need for producing an *operational, standardized, theoretical, and practical solution* to *n*-ary relationships problems still exists.

The NKRL Approach

Generalities

NKRL innovates with respect to the current ontological paradigms by adding to the usual ontologies of concepts an 'ontology of events', that is to say, a new sort of hierarchical organization where the nodes correspond to *n*-ary structures called 'templates'. In the NKRL environment, the 'ontology of concepts' is called HClass (hierarchy of classes): HClass is not fundamentally different from one of the 'traditional' ontologies that can be built up by using tools in the Protégé style. The 'ontology of events' — HTemp, hierarchy of templates — is, on the contrary, basically different from classical ontologies; as it will become evident in the following, the two hierarchies operate in a strictly integrated way in an NKRL context.

A partial representation of HClass is given in Figure 1; a full description is given in Zarri (2003b); see Zarri (1997) for a discussion about concepts like non_sortal_concept (the specializations of this concept, that is, its subsumed concepts, cannot be endowed with direct instances), sortal_concept or substance_. Figure 2 reproduces the 'symbolic labels' (symbolic names) of part of the templates included in the Produce: branch of HTemp. Both HClass and HTemp are the 'pragmatic' result of many years of successful experiments in dealing with complex narrative information by using high-level conceptual tools.

Figure 1. Partial representation of HClass, the "traditional" ontology of concepts

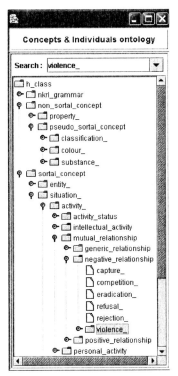

Instead of using the traditional *object (class, concept) — attribute — value* organization, templates are generated from the association of *quadruples* that follow the general schema (1) supplied above. Predicates pertain to the set {BEHAVE, EXIST, EXPERIENCE, MOVE, OWN, PRODUCE, RECEIVE}, and roles to the set {SUBJ(ect), OBJ(ect), SOURCE, BEN(e)F(iciary), MODAL(ity), TOPIC, CONTEXT}; predicates and roles are then 'primitives'. An argument a_k of the predicate, see (1), denotes indirectly through a 'variable' either a simple 'concept' (according to the traditional, 'ontological' meaning of this word) or a structured association ('expansion') of several concepts. In both cases, the concepts can only be chosen among those included in the HClass hierarchy; this fact, linked with the 'primitive' character of predicates and roles, allows to reduce considerably the potential combinatorial explosion associated with formulas like equation (1).

Templates formally represent generic classes of elementary events like "move a physical object", "be present in a place", "produce a service", "send/receive a message", "build up an Internet site", and so forth — for additional details and a full

Figure 2. Partial representation of the PRODUCE branch of HTemp, the "ontology of events".

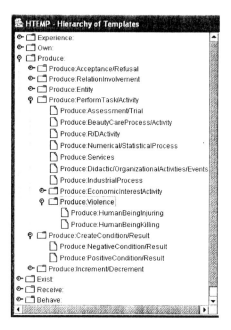

description of HTemp, see again Zarri (2003b). When a particular event pertaining to one of these general classes must be represented, the corresponding template is 'instantiated' to produce what, in the NKRL's jargon, is called a 'predicative occurrence'. To represent a simple narrative — extracted from one of the new stories of the MoD original corpus — like: "On November 20, 1999, in an unspecified village, an armed group of people has kidnapped Robustiniano Hablo", we must then select firstly in the HTemp hierarchy the template corresponding to "execution of violent actions", see Figure 2 and Table 1a. This template is a specialization (see the 'father' code in Table 1a) of the particular PRODUCE template corresponding to "perform some task or activity".

As it appears from Table 1a, the arguments of the predicate (the a_k terms in equation [1]) are represented in practice by variables with associated constraints — which are expressed as HClass concepts or combinations of HClass concepts. When deriving a predicative occurrence (an instance of a template) like mod3.c5 in Table 1b, the role fillers in this occurrence must conform to the constraints of the father-template. For example, in this occurrence, ROBUSTINIANO_HABLO (the 'BEN(e)F(iciary)' of the action of kidnapping) and INDIVIDUAL_PERSON_20 (the unknown 'SUBJECT', actor, initiator etc., of this action) are both 'individuals', instances of the HClass concept individual_person: this last is, in turn, a specialization of human_being_or_social_body,

Table 1. Building up and querying predicative occurrences

(a)

name: Produce:Violence
father: Produce:PerformTask/Activity
position: 6.35
NL description: 'Execution of Violent Actions on the Filler of the BEN(e)F(iciary) Role'

```
PRODUCE  SUBJ      var1: [(var2)]
         OBJ       var3
         [SOURCE   var4: [(var5)]]
         BENF      var6: [(var7)]
         [MODAL    var8]
         [TOPIC    var9]
         [CONTEXT  var10]
         {[modulators], ≠abs}
```

var1 = *<human_being_or_social_body>*
var3 = *<violence_ >*
var4 = *<human_being_or_social_body>*
var6 = *<human_being_or_social_body>*
var8 = *<criminality/violence_related_tool>* | *<general_characterising_property>* | *<machine_tool>* |
         <small_portable_equipment> | *<violence_ >* | *<weapon_>*
var9 = *<h_class>*
var10 = *<situation_ >* | *<spatio/temporal_relationship>* | *<symbolic_label>*
var2, var5, var7 = *<geographical_location>*

(b)

```
mod3.c5)   PRODUCE   SUBJ      (SPECIF INDIVIDUAL_PERSON_20 weapon_wearing
                                  (SPECIF cardinality_ several_)): (VILLAGE_1)
                     OBJ       kidnapping_
                     BENF      ROBUSTINIANO_HABLO
                     CONTEXT   #mod3.c6
                     date-1:   20/11/1999
                     date-2:
```

Produce:Violence (6.35)

*On November 20, 1999, in an unspecified village (*VILLAGE_1*), an armed group of people has kidnapped Robustiniano Hablo.*

(c)

PRODUCE
SUBJ : human_being :
OBJ :   violence_
BENF : human_being :
⫫
date1 : 1/1/1999
date2 : 31/12/1999

Is there any information in the system concerning violence activities during 1999?

---

see, in Table 1a, the constraint on the variables var1 and var6. kidnapping_ is a concept, specialization of violence_, see var3, and so forth. Throughout this chapter, we will use small letters to represent a concept_, capital letters to represent an INDIVIDUAL_.

The constituents (as SOURCE in Table 1a) included in square brackets are optional. A 'conceptual label' like mod3.c5 is the symbolic name used to identify the NKRL code corresponding to a specific predicative occurrence (see Zarri & Bernard, 2004b:

Appendix B) for details about the representation of NKRL data structures onto ORACLE databases. The first component of this 'pointed' notation identifies the original document represented into NKRL format, in this case, the third news story of the MoD corpus. The second half, c5, tells us that the corresponding (predicative) occurrence is the fifth within the set of predicative and 'binding' (see the following) occurrences that represent together the NKRL 'image' of the semantic content of the original document. This complete image is called a 'conceptual annotation' of the document in the NKRL's jargon.

The 'attributive operator', SPECIF(ication), is one of the four operators that make up the AECS sub-language, used for the set up of 'structured arguments' ('expansions'). Apart from SPECIF(ication) = S, AECS includes also the disjunctive operator, ALTERN(ative) = A, the distributive operator, ENUM(eration) = E, and the collective operator, COORD(ination) = C. The interweaving of the four operators within an expansion is controlled by the so-called 'precedence rule', see Zarri (1997; 1998) for the details.

In particular, the SPECIF lists, with syntax (SPECIF e_i p_1 ... p_n), are used to represent the properties or attributes which can be asserted about the first element e_i, concept or individual, of the list — for example, in the SUBJ filler of mod3.c5, Table 1b, the attributes weapon_wearing and (SPECIF cardinality_ several_) are both associated with INDIVIDUAL_PERSON_20. weapon_wearing is a specialization of the dressing_attribute concept of HClass; this means that, via the generalizations dressing_attribute and physical_aspect_attribute, it is also a specialization of animate_entity_property. (SPECIF cardinality_ several_), which is in turn a SPECIF lists, is the standard way of representing the 'generic plurality' in NKRL (see Zarri, 1997). several_ — a concept of the logical_quantifier branch of HClass — 'gives details' about cardinality_, that is a specialisation of quantifying_property, and so on.

The 'location attributes', represented in the predicative occurrences as lists, are linked with the predicate arguments by using the colon operator, ':', see the individual VILLAGE_1 in Table 1b. In the occurrences, the two operators date-1, date-2 materialize the temporal interval normally associated with narrative events, see again Table 1b; a detailed description of the methodology for representing temporal data in NKRL can be found in Zarri (1998).

Until now, we have evoked the NKRL solutions to the problem of representing *elementary (simple) events*. To deal now with the 'story structures', that is, with those '*connectivity phenomena*' that arise when several elementary events are connected through causality, goal, indirect speech, co-ordination and subordination links (and others), the basic NKRL knowledge representation tools have been complemented by more complex mechanisms that make use of second order structures created through *reification* of the conceptual labels of the predicative occurrences. A simple example concerns the filler of the CONTEXT role in the occurrence mod3.c5 of Table 1b: in this case ('completive construction'), the 'context' of the kidnapping is supplied by a whole predicative occurrence, mod3.c6, telling us that the kidnapping happened when Robustiniano Hablo was on his way home with his father. The code '#' indicates to the NKRL interpreter that the associated item is a conceptual label and not a concept or individual.

More complex examples of second order constructions introduced to take the connectivity phenomena into account are the 'binding occurrences'. *Binding occurrences* are NKRL structures consisting of lists of symbolic labels (coll$_i$c$_j$) of *predicative occurrences*; the lists are differentiated making use of specific binding operators like GOAL, COND(ition) and CAUSE. Let us suppose we would now state that: "…an armed group of people has kidnapped Robustiniano Hablo *in order to* ask his family for a ransom", where the new elementary event: "the unknown individuals will ask for a ransom" corresponds to a new predicative occurrence: mod3.c7. To represent this situation completely (see Table 2), we must add to the usual predicative occurrences that make up the conceptual annotation for the Robustiniano Hablo's story a *binding occurrence*, for example, mod3.c8, to link together the conceptual labels mod3.c5 (corresponding to the kidnapping predicative occurrence, see also Table 1b) and mod3.c7 (corresponding to the new predicative occurrence that describes the intended result). mod3.c8 will have then the form: "mod3.c8) (GOAL mod3.c5 mod3.c7)", see Table 2. The meaning of mod3.c8 can be paraphrased as: "the activity described in mod3.c5 is focalized towards (GOAL) the realization of mod3.c7". We can note that — see again Zarri (1998) for more details:

- The second predicative occurrence mentioned in a GOAL binding structure (the second argument of a GOAL operator, i.e., the intended result), which corresponds to an elementary events that will happen '*in the future*' with respect to the event described by the first predicative occurrence (the first argument of GOAL, i.e., the precondition), is systematically marked as '*hypothetical*' by the presence of an uncertainty validity attribute, code "*", see occurrence mod3.c7 in Table 2.

- The (unknown) date of the (possible) ransom request is simulated by a "fork" in the first date field (date-1) of mod3.c7, where the first term of the fork is the kidnapping date, and the second (reconstructed, i.e., not specifically attested in the original documents, see the 'parenthesis' codes) corresponds to a month after. The meaning of the global date-1 filler amounts then to say that the request will be (possibly) made at an unknown date included within this interval. Note that the insertion of (20/12/1999) in the second date field (date-2) of mod3.c7 would have led to this interpretation of mod3.c7, see Zarri (1998): the (possible) action of sending the ransom's request to the Robustiniano Hablo's family will take a full month.

Table 2. Predicative and binding occurrences

```
mod3.c8)      (GOAL  mod3.c5  mod3.c7)
```

The information conveyed by mod3.c8 *says that the aim of the 'behaviour' related in* mod3.c5 *is to arrive at the situation described in* mod3.c7.

```
mod3.c5)   PRODUCE    SUBJ     (SPECIF INDIVIDUAL_PERSON_20 weapon_wearing
                                   (SPECIF cardinality_ several_)): (VILLAGE_1)
                      OBJ      kidnapping_
                      BENF     ROBUSTINIANO_HABLO
                      CONTEXT  #mod3.c6
                      date-1:  20/11/1999
                      date-2:
```

Produce:Violence (6.35)

*On November 20, 1999, in an unspecified village (*VILLAGE_1*), an armed group of people has kidnapped Robustiniano Hablo.*

```
*mod3.c7)   MOVE     SUBJ     (SPECIF INDIVIDUAL_PERSON_20 (SPECIF cardinality_ several_))
                     OBJ      RANSOM_DEMAND_1
                     BENF     (SPECIF family_ ROBUSTINIANO_HABLO)
                     TOPIC    (SPECIF hostage_release ROBUSTINIANO_HABLO)
                     date-1:  20/11/1999, (20/12/1999)
                     date-2:
```

Move:GenericInformation (4.41)

The kidnappers will (possibly) send a ransom demand to the family of Robustiniano Hablo about his release.

"Search Patterns" and the First Level of Inference Procedures

The *basic building block* for all the NKRL querying and inference procedures is the Fum, Filtering Unification Module (see also Zarri & Bernard, 2004b). It takes as input specific NKRL data structures called 'search patterns'.

Search patterns can be considered as the NKRL counterparts of natural language queries; they offer then the possibility of querying *directly* an NKRL knowledge base of conceptual annotations. Formally, these patterns correspond to *specialized/partially instantiated templates* pertaining to the HTemp hierarchy, where the '*explicit variables*' that characterize the templates (var_i, see Table 1a) *have been replaced by concepts/individuals compatible with the constraints imposed on these variables in the original templates*. In a search pattern, the concepts are used then as '*implicit variables*'. When trying to unify a search pattern with the predicative occurrences of the knowledge base, a concept can *match* (1) the individuals representing its own instances, and (2) all its subsumed concepts in HClass with their own instances. The set of predicative occurrences unified by a given search pattern constitutes the *answer* to the query represented by the pattern.

A simple example of search pattern, translating the query: "Is there any information in the system about violence events occurred during the year 1999?" is reproduced in Table 1c, producing the occurrence mod3.c5 (Table 1b) as one of the possible answers. Note that the search pattern of Table 1c — as, by the way, the answer mod3.c5 of Table 1b — derives from the template Produce:Violence (6.35) of Table 1a where all the explicit variables var$_i$ have been replaced by HClass concepts (implicit variables) corresponding to some of the original constraints. The two timestamps, date1 and date2 associated with the pattern constitute now the 'search interval' used to limit the search for unification to the slice of time that it is considered appropriate to explore.

The unification/filtering operations executed by Fum are 'oriented', which means that *all the terms* used to build up a search pattern must be *explicitly found* in the matched occurrences, either in an identical form (e.g., predicate and roles), or as subsumed concepts or instances of the implicit variables. For example, both INDIVIDUAL_PERSON_20 and ROBUSTINIANO_HABLO of mod3.c5 have been registered in HClass as instances of individual_person — specific term of human_being, the 'implicit variable' that appears in the SUBJ(ect) and BEN(e)F(iciary) roles of the pattern in Table 1c — at the moment of the coding in NKRL terms of the Robustiniano Hablo news story. kidnapping_ in 1b is a subsumed concepts of the implicit variable violence_ in 1c. Additional terms — roles, fillers and part of fillers — with respect to those explicitly declared in the pattern can be freely found in the occurrences, see terms like weapon_wearing or VILLAGE_1 in Table 1b. Moreover, the unification of complex fillers (expansions) built up making use of the AECS operators, see the previous section, must take into account the NKRL criteria for the creation of well-formed expansions. This implies that, during the unification, the complex fillers of both the search pattern and the occurrences must be *decomposed into tree structures* labelled with the four operators, and that the unification of these tree structures must follow the constraints defined by the 'priority rule' already mentioned, see Zarri (1997; 2003a). The algorithmic structure of Fum is, eventually, quite complex, but this complexity is totally transparent for the user, who is only required to specify in the search pattern the *essential elements* he wants to retrieve in the occurrences, without being bothered, as in OWL-QL for example, see Fikes, Hayes, and Horrocks (2004), by the need of declaring "Must-Bind Variables", "May-Bind Variables", "Don't-Bind Variables", "Answer Patterns", among others.

Because of all the (semantic/conceptual) 'expansion operations' undergone by the search patterns during the match operations, we can define the process of search patterns unification as a *first level of inferencing* of NKRL.

High Level Inference Procedures, 'Hypotheses' and 'Transformations'

The *high-level inferencing operations* of NKRL correspond mainly to the use of two complementary classes of inference rules, hypotheses and transformations — other sorts of rules, such as, 'filtering' rules, have been employed for particular applications of NKRL, see Bertino, Ferrari, Perego, and Zarri (2005) for some information in this context. Execution of both hypotheses and transformations require the use of a real InferenceEngine, having Fum as its core mechanism. To describe the functioning of InferenceEngine in a 'hypothesis' environment we will make use of a 'standard', very simple example that implies only two steps of reasoning and can then be described relatively in-depth and in a concise way.

Let us then suppose we have directly retrieved, thanks to an appropriate search pattern, the occurrence conc2.c34, see Table 3a, which corresponds to the information: "Pharmacopeia, an USA biotechnology company, has received 64,000,000 USA dollars from the German company Schering in connection with a R&D activity". We will suppose, moreover, that this occurrence is not *explicitly* related with other occurrences in the base by second order elements, see above. Under these conditions, we can activate the InferenceEngine module of NKRL, asking it to try to *link up automatically* the information found by the search pattern (making use of Fum) with other information present in the base. If this is possible, this last information will represent, in a way, a sort of 'causal explanation' of the information originally retrieved — in other words, in our example, an 'explanation' of the money paid to Pharmacopeia by Schering. A possible hypothesis rule that could fit our case is hypothesis h1 reproduced in Table 3b.

From an algorithmic point of view, InferenceEngine works according to a standard backward chaining approach with chronological backtracking, see Clocksin and Mellish (1981). The differences with respect to other examples of use of this approach (Mycin, PROLOG …) are mainly linked with the complexity of the NKRL data structures that implies, after a deadlock, the execution of difficult operations of restoration of the program environment to return to the previous choice point. Four *'environment variables'* are used:

- VALAFF (*valeurs affectables* in French), holds the values provisionally assigned to the variables var_i of the three schemata of Table 3 (premise, cond1 and cond2) that implement the reasoning steps of the hypothesis: these values can be deleted after a backtracking operation;

- DESVAR holds the final values associated with the variables var_i when the successful processing of one of the reasoning schemata has been completed;

Table 3. An example of hypothesis rule

```
(a)
conc2.c34)  RECEIVE  SUBJ     (SPECIF PHARMACOPEIA_ (SPECIF biotechnology_company USA_))
                     OBJ      (SPECIF money_ usa_dollar (SPECIF amount_ 64,000,000))
                     SOURCE   (SPECIF SCHERING_ (SPECIF pharmaceutical_company
                                                                        GERMANY_))

                     TOPIC    r_and_d_activity
                     date1 :
                     date2 :


(b)
HYPOTHESIS h1

premise :

RECEIVE  SUBJ     var1
         OBJ      money_
         SOURCE   var2

var1 = company_
var2 = human_being, company_

A company has received some money from another company or a physical person.

first condition schema (cond1) :

PRODUCE  SUBJ   (COORD var1 var2)
         OBJ    var3
         BENF   (COORD var1 var2)
         TOPIC  (SPECIF process_ var4)

var3 = mutual_relationship, business_agreement
var4 = artefact_

The two parties mentioned in the premise have concluded an agreement about the creation of a some sort of 'product'.

second condition schema (cond2) :

PRODUCE  SUBJ     var1
         OBJ      var4
         MODAL    var5
         CONTEXT  var3

var5 = industrial_process, technological_process

The company that received the money has actually created the product mentioned in the first condition schema.
```

- RESTRICT holds all the constraints (HClass terms) associated with the variables var_i of the different reasoning schemata: these constraints will be used to build up systematically *all* the search patterns that can be derived from these schemata, see the proceeding;

- OCCUR holds the list of the symbolic names of all the occurrences retrieved by the search patterns derived from the reasoning schemata: the values bound to var_i that have been retrieved in these occurrences are used to build up the VALAFF lists.

The first set of operations corresponds to the execution of the Exeprem sub-module of InferenceEngine, and consists in trying to unify, *using* Fum, the premise of the hypothesis, see Table 3b, and the event (the payment in our case, see conc2.c34) to be 'explained' — more exactly, in trying to unify (using Fum) *the event and the different search patterns derived from the premise by systematically substituting to the variables* var1 *and* var2, *see Table 3b, the associated constraints.* As already stated, search pattern processed by Fum can only include implicit variables (concepts). This first step allows then (1) to verify that the hypothesis tested is, in principle, suitable to 'explain' the particular event at hand, and (2) to obtain from the external environment (the event, i.e., conc2.c34) some values for the premise variables var1, var2. In our case, the premise variable var1 can only be substituted by the constraint company_; on the contrary, two substitutions, var2 = human_being and var2 = company_ are possible for the variable var2. A first search pattern will be then built up by substituting human_being for var2 (a value human_being is provisionally associated with var2 in VALAFF), that is to say a first unification with the event to explain will be tried by using a search pattern corresponding to a payment done by an *individual person* instead of a *company*. This unification obviously fails.

The engine then 'backtracks' making use of a second sub-module of InferenceEngine, Reexec: Reexec is systematically used during the execution of a hypothesis rule (1) to backtrack when a deadlock occurs, and (2) to reconstruct, making use of the environment variables, the data structures (environment) proper to the previous choice point. The association var2 = human_being is removed and, using the constraint values stored in RESTRICT, the engine builds up a new pattern making use now of the value var2 = company_, that will unify the value SCHERING_ in conc2.c34. The engine can then continue the processing of the hypothesis h1; the two values var1 = PHARMACOPEIA_ and var2 = SCHERING_ will then be stored in DESVAR and passed to the first condition schema (cond1), see Table 2b. The search patterns derived from this condition schema — by taking into account the values already bound in DESVAR to var1 and var2 and by replacing systematically, as usual, all the other variables with the associated constraints — will be tested by a third sub-module of InferenceEngine, Execond. This last is called *whenever there exist conditions favourable for advancing in the hypothesis*, in other words, for being able to process a new condition schema. Exeprem and Execond perform then the forward traversal of the choice tree, with Reexec being systematically called whenever the conditions for a backtracking exist. The difference between Exeprem and Execond consists mainly in the fact that, in an Execond context, the unification of the search patterns derived from the condition schemata is tested *against the general knowledge base of predicative occurrences to (try to) find possible unifications with these occurrences* while, in an Exeprem context, the unification concerns only the search patterns derived from the premise and the (unique) starting occurrence.

As usual, many deadlocks are generated in the course of the Execond operations. Some are due, as in the premise case, to the *chronological utilization* of the constraints.

For example, when trying to make use of a pattern derived from cond1 where the variable var3 has been substituted by its first constraint mutual_relationship, see Table 3b (and Figure 1), a failure will be generated and Reexec will be invoked again. The occurrences we must retrieve in the knowledge base about the relationships between Pharmacopeia and Schering concern, in fact, possible sorts of *commercial* agreements between Pharmacopeia and Schering — such as r_and_d_agreement and sale_agreement, see the following, both specific terms in HClass of business_agreement (the second constraint on var3) — and not a *private* arrangement like mutual_relationship. We will, eventually, find in the base an instantiation of cond1 corresponding to an event of the form: "Pharmacopeia and Schering have signed two agreements concerning the production by Pharmacopeia of a new compound, COMPOUND_1". The values associated with the variables var3 (r_and_d_agreement and sale_agreement) and var4 (COMPOUND_1) in cond1 will then be used to create the search patterns derived from cond2. It will then be possible to retrieve an occurrence corresponding to the information: "In the framework of an R&D agreement, Pharmacopeia has actually produced the new compound", see Zarri (2003a) for more details. The global information retrieved through the execution of the hypothesis, see Table 4, can then

Table 4. Final results for hypothesis h1

```
                          The start occurrence :

conc2.c34)  RECEIVE   SUBJ     (SPECIF PHARMACOPEIA_ (SPECIF biotechnology_company USA_))
                      OBJ      (SPECIF money_ usa_dollar (SPECIF amount_ 64,000,000))
                      SOURCE   (SPECIF SCHERING_ (SPECIF pharmaceutical_company
                                                                    GERMANY_))

                      TOPIC    r_and_d_activity
                      date1 :
                      date2 :
```

Pharmacopeia, a USA biotechnology company, has received 64,000,000 dollars by Schering, a German pharmaceutical company, in relation to R&D activities.

```
                          The result for level 1 :

conc13.c3)  PRODUCE   SUBJ     (COORD PHARMACOPEIA_ SCHERING_)
                      OBJ      (COORD r_and_d_agreement sale_agreement)
                      BENF     (COORD PHARMACOPEIA_ SCHERING_)
                      TOPIC    (SPECIF synthesis_ (SPECIF COMPOUND_1 new_))
                      date1 :
                      date2 :
```

Pharmacopeia and Schering have signed two agreements (have produced two agreements having themselves as beneficiaries) concerning the production of a new compound .

```
                          The result for level 2 :

conc13.c7)  PRODUCE   SUBJ     PHARMACOPEIA_
                      OBJ      COMPOUND_1
                      MODAL    biotechnology_process
                      CONTEXT  r_and_d_agreement
                      date1 :
                      date2 :
```

In the framework of an R&D agreement, Pharmacopeia has actually produced the new compound .

supply a sort of 'plausible explanation' of the Schering's payment: Pharmacopiea and Schering have concluded some agreements for the production of a given compound, and this compound has been actually produced by Pharmacopeia.

The second class of inference rules considered here, the 'transformation rules', are used to obtain a *plausible answer* from a repository of predicative occurrences also in the absence of the explicitly requested information (i.e., when a direct query formulated in Fum terms fails), by searching *semantic affinities* between what is requested and what is really present in the repository. The principle employed consists in using these rules to automatically 'transform' the original query (i.e., the original search pattern) into one or more different queries (search patterns) that *are not strictly 'equivalent' but only 'semantically close' to the original one.*

As a first informal example, let us suppose that working in the context of a hypothetical knowledge base of NKRL occurrences about university professors, we want to ask a query like: "Who has lived in the United States", even without an explicit representation of this fact in the base. If this last contains some information about the degrees obtained by the professors, we can tell the user that, although we do not explicitly know who lived in the States, we can nevertheless look for people having an American degree. This last piece of information, obtained by transformation of the original query, would indeed normally imply that some time was spent by the professors in the country, the United States, which issued their degree. To pass now to a Parmenides (MoD) example, suppose we ask: "Search for the existence of some links between ObL (a well known international 'terrorist') and Abubakar Abdurajak Janjalani, the leader of the Abu Sayyaf group" — the Abu Sayyaf group is one of the Muslim independence movements in Southern Philippines. In the absence of a direct answer, the corresponding search pattern can be transformed into: "Search for the attestation of the transfer of economic/financial items between the two", which could lead to retrieve this information: "During 1998/1999, Abubakar Abdurajak Janjalani has received an undetermined amount of money from ObL through an intermediate agent".

From a formal point of view, transformation rules are made up of a left-hand side, the '*antecedent*' — the formulation, in search pattern format, of the 'query' to be transformed — and one or more right-hand sides, the '*consequent(s)*' — the NKRL representation(s) of one or more queries (search patterns) that must be substituted for the given one. A transformation rule can, therefore, be expressed as: A (antecedent, left-hand side) $\Rightarrow B$ (consequent(s), right-hand side). The 'transformation arrow', '$\Rightarrow$', has a double meaning:

- Operationally speaking, the arrow indicates the *direction* of the transformation: the left-hand side A (the original search pattern) is removed and replaced by the right-hand side B (one or more new search patterns).

- The 'semantic' meaning of the arrow is that the information obtained through *B implies* (in a weak meaning) the information we should have obtained from *A*.

Some formal details can be found in Zarri (2003a). A representation of the Parmenides 'economic/financial transfer' transformation introduced informally before is given in Table 5. Note that the left-hand side (antecedent) of this transformation corresponds to a partial instantiation of the template (1.3112) Behave:FavourableConcreteMutual that is routinely used to represent into NKRL format a (positive) mutual behaviour among two or more entities.

Now, with respect to the implementation details, the InferenceEngine version used for transformations is quite identical to that used for executing the hypothesis rules. The sub-module Antexec (execution of the antecedent) corresponds, in fact, to the Exeprem sub-module; Consexec (execution of the consequent(s)) corresponds to Execond. Reexec is the same in the two versions. Note that many of the transformation rules used in NKRL are characterized by the very simply format of Table 5 implying only one 'consequent' schema. An example of 'multi-consequent' transformation is given by this specific Parmenides (MoD) rule: "In a context of ransom kidnapping, the certification that a given character is wealthy or has a professional role can be substituted by the certification that (1) this character has a tight kinship link with another person (first consequent schema, conseq1), and (2) this second person is a wealthy person or a professional people (second consequent schema, conseq2)". Let us suppose that, during the search for all the possible information items linked with the Robustiniano Hablo's kidnapping, see occurrence mod3.c5 in Table 1b, we ask to the system whether Robustiano Hablo is wealthy. In the absence of a direct answer, the system will automatically 'transform' the original query making use of the previous

Table 5. A simple example of 'transformation' rule

'economic/financial transfer' transformation :

T1)	BEHAVE	SUBJ	(COORD1 var1 var2)	$\Rightarrow$	RECEIVE	SUBJ	var2
		OBJ	(COORD1 var1 var2)			OBJ	var4
		MODAL	var3			SOURCE	var1

var1	=	human_being_or_social_body
var2	=	human_being_or_social_body
var3	=	business_agreement, mutual_relationship
var4	=	economic/financial_entity

To verify the existence of a relationship or of a business agreement between two (or more) persons, try to verify if one of these persons has received a 'financial entity' (e.g., money) from the other.

Figure 3. Application of the "kinship" transformation to the query about Robustiniano Hablo's status

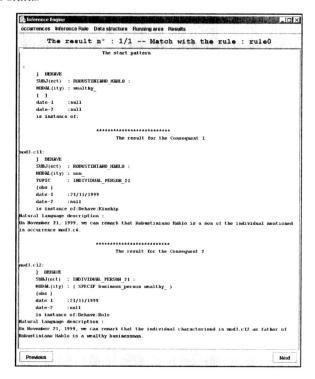

'kinship' rule. The result is reproduced in Figure 3; we do not know if Robustiano Hablo is wealthy, but we can say that his father is a wealthy businessperson.

Recent Developments

In the context of the already mentioned MoD/Parmenides application on terrorism in Philippines, it has been decided to integrate the two main modalities of inferencing of NKRL, 'hypotheses' and 'transformations', in order to get the best from the high-level modelling capabilities of the language. Integrating the two inferencing modes corresponds to:

- From a practical point of view, transformations can now be used to try to find successful unifications with information in the knowledge base when the search patterns *derived directly* from the condition schemata of a hypothesis fail. A hypothesis deemed then to fall short can continue successfully until its normal end.

- From a more general point of view, transformations can be used to modify in an (at least partially) *unpredictable way* the reasoning steps (condition schemata) to be executed within a 'hypothesis' context, independently from the fact that these steps have been successful or not. This is equivalent to 'break' the *strictly predefined scenarios* proper to the hypothesis rules, and to augment then the possibility of discovering 'implicit information' within the knowledge base.

Table 6. Inference steps for the h2 *hypothesis*

> - (Cond1) The kidnappers are part of a separatist movement or of a terrorist organization.
> - (Cond2) This separatist movement or terrorist organization currently practices ransom kidnapping of particular categories of people.
> - (Cond3) In particular, executives or assimilated categories are concerned (other rules deal with civil servants, servicemen, members of the clergy etc.).
> - (Cond4) It can be proved that the kidnapped is really a businessperson or assimilated.

Table 7. Rule h2 *in the presence of transformations concerning the intermediary inference steps*

> - (Cond1) The kidnappers are part of a separatist movement or of a terrorist organization.
>   - **(Rule T3, Consequent1)** *Try to verify whether a given separatist movement or terrorist organization is in strict control of a specific sub-group and, in this case,*
>   - **(Rule T3, Consequent2)** *check if the kidnappers are members of this sub-group. We will then assimilate the kidnappers to 'members' of the movement or organization.*
> - (Cond2) This movement or organization practices ransom kidnapping of given categories of people.
>   - **(Rule T2, Consequent)** *The family of the kidnapped has received a ransom request from the separatist movement or terrorist organization.*
>   - **(Rule T4, Consequent1)** *The family of the kidnapped has received a ransom request from a group or an individual person, and*
>   - **(Rule T4, Consequent2)** *this second group or individual person is part of the separatist movement or terrorist organization.*
>   - **(Rule T5, Consequent1)** *Try to verify if a particular sub-group of the separatist movement or terrorist organization exists, and*
>   - **(Rule T5, Consequent2)** *check whether this particular sub-group practices ransom kidnapping of particular categories of people.*
>   - ...
> - (Cond3) In particular, executives or assimilated categories are concerned.
>   - **(Rule T0, Consequent1)** *In a 'ransom kidnapping' context, we can check whether the kidnapped person has a strict kinship relationship with a second person, and*
>   - **(Rule T0, Consequent2)** *(in the same context) check if this second person is a businessperson or assimilated.*
> - (Cond4) It can be proved that the kidnapped person is really an executive or assimilated.
>   - **(Rule T6, Consequent)** *In a 'ransom kidnapping' context, 'personalities' like consultants, physicians, journalists, artists etc. can be assimilated to businesspersons.*

A complete description on the integration procedures can be found in Zarri and Bernard (2004a); a recent, detailed paper on this topic is also Zarri (2005b). We will limit ourselves to supply here some general information about the integration and an example.

Let us suppose that, as one of the possible answers to a question concerning the kidnapping events in Southern Philippine during 1999, we have retrieved the information: "Lieven de la Marche and Eric Brake have been kidnapped by a group of people on June 13, 1999". Making use of a hypothesis rule like that of Table 6 to 'explain' the kidnapping will give rise to a failure because of the impossibility of satisfying directly the 'intermediate' steps Cond1, Cond2 and Cond3 of h2, that is, of founding *direct matches* of the search patterns derived from these condition schemata with information in the knowledge base.

If we allow now the use of transformations in a hypothesis context, this means to make use of a hypothesis h2 having a format *potentially equivalent* to that of Table 7. For example, the proof that the kidnappers are part of a terrorist group or separatist organization can be now obtained *indirectly*, transformation T3, by checking

Figure 4. Application of the transformation rule about the 'renegades'

```
********* the result for condition 1  ****************
******************************************************************************
***Entering an internal transformation module : internal level 1 ******************
******************************************************************************
***                    The model to transform
***
***:
***      ] BEHAVE
***      SUBJ(ect)  : INDIVIDUAL_PERSON_68 :
***      MODAL(ity) : part_of
***      TOPIC      : separatist_movement
***      ()
***      date-1     :null
***      date-2     :null
***      is instance of:
***
***          ********* the result for consequent 1  ****************
***mod57.c17:
***      ] OWN
***      SUBJ(ect)  : MORO_ISLAMIC_LIBERATION_FRONT :
***      OBJ(ect)   : control_ :
***      TOPIC      : MORO_ISLAMIC_RENEGADE
***      (poss )
***      date-1     :24/3/1999
***      date-2     :null
***      is instance of:Own:Control
***Natural language description :
***On March 24, 1999, it is possible that the MILF is still in control of its renegades.
***
***          ********* the result for consequent 2  ****************
***mod33.c10:
***      ] BEHAVE
***      SUBJ(ect)  : ( SPECIF INDIVIDUAL_PERSON_68 ( SPECIF cardinality_ several_ ) ) :
***      MODAL(ity) : part_of
***      TOPIC      : MORO_ISLAMIC_RENEGADE
***      (obs )
***      date-1     :13/6/1999
***      date-2     :null
***      is instance of:Behave:Member
***Natural language description :
***The kidnappers are member of a group of renegades of the Moro Islamic Liberation Front
```

whether they are members of a specific subset of this group or organization. We can see, in particular, that there is a whole family of transformations corresponding to the condition schemata Cond2 of h2. They represent variants of this general scheme: the separatist movement or of a terrorist organization, or some group or single persons affiliated with them, have requested/received money for the ransom of the kidnapped. Note that, in this family of transformations, transformation T2 implies only one 'consequent' schema, whereas all the residual transformations are 'multi-consequent'.

Figure 4 illustrates the use of rule T5 to satisfy the requirements of the condition schema Cond1 of hypothesis h2: it is impossible to demonstrate that the kidnappers are part of a separatist movement, but we can show that they are part of the renegades of the Moro Islamic Liberation Front and that, at the moment of the kidnapping, the Moro Islamic (MILF) was still in control of its renegades.

Figure 5 refers to the application of transformation T4 to satisfy the condition schema Cond2 (the ransom kidnapping activity of the Moro National Liberation Front is proved by the fact that some of its members have required a ransom to the family of Wilmarie Ira Furigay); and so forth.

Figure 5. People related to MILF ask for ransom

```
         ********* the result for condition 2    *****************
************************************************************************
***Entering an internal transformation module : internal level 1 ************************
************************************************************************
***                     The model to transform
***
***:
***      ] PRODUCE
***      SUBJ(ect)  : MORO_ISLAMIC_LIBERATION_FRONT :
***      OBJ(ect)   : ransom_kidnapping :
***      BENF       : human_being :
***      ()
***      date-1     :null
***      date-2     :null
***      is instance of:
***
***          ********* the result for consequent 1    *****************
***mod18.c10:
***      ] PRODUCE
***      SUBJ(ect)  : ( SPECIF INDIVIDUAL_PERSON_67 ( SPECIF cardinality_ several_ ) ) :
***      OBJ(ect)   : RANSOM_DEMAND_1 :
***      BENF       : ( SPECIF family_ WILMARIE_IRA_FURIGAY ) :
***      TOPIC      : ( SPECIF hostage_release WILMARIE_IRA_FURIGAY )
***      ( )
***      date-1     :11/8/1999 28/8/1999
***      date-2     :null
***      is instance of:Produce:PerformTask/Activity
***Natural language description :
***In a period included between August 11, 1999, the date of the kidnapping, and August 28, 1999, the
date of the news, the kidnappers have sent a ransom demand to the family of Wilmarie Ira Furigay.
***
***          ********* the result for consequent 2    *****************
***mod18.c7:
***      ] BEHAVE
***      SUBJ(ect)  : ( SPECIF INDIVIDUAL_PERSON_67 ( SPECIF cardinality_ several_ ) ) :
***      MODAL(ity) : part_of
***      TOPIC      : MORO_ISLAMIC_LIBERATION_FRONT
***      (obs )
***      date-1     :11/8/1999
***      date-2     :null
***      is instance of:Behave:Member
***Natural language description :
***The kidnappers were members of the Moro Islamic Liberation Front.
************************************************************************
```

Future Trends

NKRL is a fully implemented language/environment. The software exists in two versions, an ORACLE-supported and a file-oriented one. The reasons that justify the existence of a file-oriented version are mainly the following:

- The possibility of running a quite-complete version of the NKRL software on machines unable to support a full-fledged version of ORACLE, for example, low-range portable computers.

- Several procedures — the most complex inferencing operations involving a co-ordinated running of 'hypotheses' and 'transformations' — are considerably accelerated in the file version. Note that a certain 'sluggishness' of the inferencing procedures in the standard ORACLE version is not a default in itself, given that these rules must be conceived more as a powerful tool for discovering all the possible *implicit relationships among the data* than as a standard question-answering system. However, there are situations — such as demos — where an immediate answer can be valuable.

Now, with respect to the possible improvements, some of them are mainly of a 'cosmetic' nature. For example, many of the visualization features (including the visualization of the results of the inference rules, see Figures 3, 4, and 5) are inherited from 'old' software developed in early European projects: they are somewhat 'ugly' and do not do justice to the complexity and interest of the results. More substantial improvements will concern mainly:

- The addition of features that allow querying the system in Natural Language. Very encouraging experimental results have already been obtained in this context thanks to the use of simple techniques that implement the 'translation' of NL queries into search pattern using shallow parsing techniques — like the AGFL grammar and lexicon, see Koster (2004) — and the standard NKRL inference capabilities.

- On a more ambitious basis, the introduction of some features for the semi-automatic construction of the knowledge base of annotation/occurrences making use of full NL techniques. Some preliminary work in this context has been realised in a Parmenides framework making use of the syntactic/semantic Cafetière tools provided by the University of Manchester Institute of Science and Technology (UMIST), see Black et al. (2004). Similar work is actually in progress in collaboration with the Friedrich-Alexander-Universität in Erlangen-Nürnberg, Germany.

- The introduction of optimisation techniques for the (basic) chronological back-tracking of the NKRL InferenceEngine, in the style of the well-known techniques developed in a logic programming context see Clark and Tärnlund (1982). This should allow us, among other things, to align the processing time of the inference rules in the ORACLE version with that of the file-oriented version of the software, which goes actually from few seconds to a maximum of one or two minutes even in the presence of complex (integrated) rules and of an extended knowledge base.

Even in its present format, NKRL has however been able to deal successfully, in a 'intelligent information retrieval' mode, with the most different 'narrative' domains — from history of France to terrorism, from Falkland War to the corporate domain, from the legal field to the beauty care domain or the analysis of customers' motivations, and so forth, see the bibliography. This means that the fundamental 'architectural' choices of the language — the dichotomy HClass/HTemp, or the use of a relatively limited number of 'narrative' templates (very easy indeed to customize) — are not totally unfounded.

Conclusion

In this chapter, we have first shown that the usual ontological tools, both the 'traditional' (frame-based) ones and the new ones proposed in a semantic Web context, are unable to offer complete and reliable solutions to the problem of a non-trivial representation and exploitation of that economically important and ubiquitous type of multimedia information corresponding to the 'narratives'. After having recalled the existence of early proposals in this field, we have supplied some details about NKRL (Narrative Knowledge Representation Language), a fully implemented, up-to-date knowledge representation and inferencing system especially created for an 'intelligent' exploitation of narrative knowledge. The main innovation of NKRL consists in associating with the traditional ontologies of concepts an 'ontology of events', that is, a new sort of hierarchical organization where the nodes correspond to n-ary structures called 'templates'. Templates — 150 at present, but new templates can be easily created on the model of the existing ones — represent formally generic classes of elementary events like "move a physical object", "be present in a place", "produce a service", "send/receive a message", "build up an Internet site", and so on. More complex, second order tools based on the 'reification' principle allow us to encode narratives characterized by the presence of elementary events linked by relationships like causality, goal, indirect speech, coordination and subordination, and so forth. After having discussed in some depth the query/answering and inferencing tools presently associated with NKRL, the chapter ends by mentioning recent work in the inferencing domain and some improvements that could be introduced in the NKRL software.

References

Bach, E. (1981). On time, tense, and aspect: An essay in English metaphysics. In P. Cole (Ed.), *Radical Pragmatic*. New York: Academic Press.

Berardi, D., Calvanese, D., & De Giacomo, G. (2001). Reasoning on UML class diagrams using description logic based systems. In *Proceedings of the 2001 Workshop on Applications of Description Logics (ADL-2001)* (CEUR vol. 44). Aachen: CEUR Publications. Retrieved from http://sunsite.informatik. rwth-aachen.de/Publications/CEUR-WS//Vol-44/

Bertino, E., Ferrari, E., Perego, A., & Zarri, G. P. (2005). A multi-strategy approach to rating and filtering online resources. In *Proceedings of the 16th International Workshop on Database and Expert Systems Applications (DEXA 2005)*. Los Alamitos, CA: IEEE Computer Society Press.

Black, W. J., Jowett, S., Mavroudakis, T., McNaught, J., Theodoulidis, B., Vasila-kopoulos, A., et al. (2004). Ontology-enablement of a system for semantic an-notation of digital documents. In *Proceedings of the 4th International Workshop on Knowledge Markup and Semantic Annotation (SEMANNOT 2004) — 3rd International Semantic Web Conference*. Hiroshima, Japan: W3C.

Ceccato, S. (1967). Correlational analysis and mechanical translation. In A. D. Booth (Ed.), *Machine Translation*. Amsterdam: North-Holland.

Clark, K. L., & Tärnlund, S.-A. (Eds.) (1982). *Logic programming*. London: Aca-demic Press.

Clocksin, W. F., & Mellish, C. S. (1981). *Programming in PROLOG*. Berlin: Springer-Verlag.

Fikes, R., Hayes, P., & Horrocks, I. (2004). OWL-QL — A language for deductive query answering on the semantic Web. *Web semantics: Science, services and agents on the World Wide Web, 2*, 19-29.

Fillmore, C. J. (1966). Toward a modern theory of case. In D. A. Reibel, & S. A. Schane (Eds.), *Modern studies of English: Readings in transformational gram-mar*. Englewood Cliffs, NJ: Prentice Hall.

Jackendoff, R. (1990). *Semantic structures*. Cambridge, MA: The MIT Press.

Kamp, H., & Reyle, U. (1993). *From discourse to logic*. Dordrecht: Kluwer.

Koster, C. H. A. (2004). Head/modifier frames for information retrieval. In *Computational Linguistics and Intelligent Text Processing: Proceedings of the 5th International Conference (CICLing 2004)*. Berlin: Springer-Verlag.

Mani, I. & Pustejovsky, J. (2004). Temporal discourse models for narrative structure. In *Proceedings of the ACL Workshop on Discourse Annotation*. East Stroudsburg, PA: Association for Computational Linguistics.

McGuinness, D. L. & van Harmelen, F. (2004, February 10). *OWL WEB Ontology Language Overview — W3C Recommendation*. Retrieved from http://www.w3.org/TR/owl-features/

Noy, F. N., Fergerson, R. W. & Musen, M. A. (2000). The knowledge model of Protégé-2000: Combining interoperability and flexibility. In *Knowledge Acquisition, Modeling, and Management — Proceedings of the 12th European Knowledge Acquisition Conference (EKAW 2000)*. Berlin: Springer-Verlag.

Noy, N. & Rector, A. (Eds.) (2005, September 7). *Defining N-ary relations on the semantic Web — W3C Editor's Draft*. Retrieved from http://smi-web.stanford.edu/people/noy/nAryRelations/n-aryRelations-2nd-WD.html

Schank, R. C. (1973). Identification of conceptualisations underlying natural language. In R. C. Schank, & K. M. Colby (Eds.), *Computer models of thought and language*. San Francisco: Freeman and Co.

Schubert, L. K. (1976). Extending the expressive power of semantic networks. *Artificial Intelligence, 7*, 163-198.

Sowa, J. F. (1984). *Conceptual structures: Information processing in mind and machine*. Reading, MA: Addison-Wesley.

Sowa, J. F. (1999). *Knowledge representation: Logical, philosophical, and computational foundations*. Pacific Grove, CA: Brooks Cole Publishing Co.

Tenny, C. L. & Pustejovsky, J. (Eds.) (2000). *Events as grammatical objects: The converging perspectives of lexical semantics, logical semantics and syntax*. Stanford: CSLI Publications.

Witbrock, M., Panton, K., Reed, S. L., Schneider, D., Aldag, B., Reimers, M., et al. (2004). Automated OWL annotation assisted by a large knowledge base. In *Proceedings of the 4th International Workshop on Knowledge Markup and Semantic Annotation (SEMANNOT 2004) — 3rd International Semantic Web Conference*. Hiroshima, Japan: W3C.

Zarri, G. P. (1997). NKRL, a knowledge representation tool for encoding the "meaning" of complex narrative texts. *Natural Language Engineering: Special issue on knowledge representation for natural language processing in implemented systems, 3*, 231-253.

Zarri, G. P. (1998). Representation of temporal knowledge in events: The formalism, and its potential for legal narratives. *Information & Communications Technology Law: Special issue on models of time, action, and situations, 7*, 213-241.

Zarri, G. P. (2003a). A conceptual model for representing narratives. In R. Jain, A. Abraham, C. Faucher, & van der Zwaag (Eds.), *Innovations in knowledge engineering*. Adelaide: Advanced Knowledge International.

Zarri, G. P. (2003b). *NKRL manual, Part II — Description of the ontologies* (Parmenides Technical Report). Paris: University of Paris IV/Sorbonne.

Zarri, G. P. (2005a). RDF and OWL for knowledge management. In D. Schwartz (Ed.), *Encyclopaedia of knowledge management*. Hershey, PA: Idea Group Inc.

Zarri, G. P. (2005b). Integrating the two main inference modes of NKRL, transformations and hypotheses. *Journal on Data Semantics (JoDS), 4*, 304-340.

Zarri, G. P., & Bernard, L. (2004a). *Using NKRL inference techniques to deal with MoD "terrorism" information* (Parmenides IST Report). Paris: University of Paris IV/Sorbonne.

Zarri, G. P., & Bernard, L. (2004b). *NKRL manual, Part III — The NKRL software* (Parmenides IST Report). Paris: University of Paris IV/Sorbonne.

Chapter VIII

A Literature Overview of Fuzzy Database Modeling

Z. M. Ma, Northeastern University, China

Abstract

Fuzzy set theory has been extensively applied to extend various data models and resulted in numerous contributions, mainly with respect to the popular relational model or to some related form of it. To satisfy the need of modeling complex objects with imprecision and uncertainty, recently many researches have been concentrated on fuzzy semantic (conceptual) and object-oriented data models. This chapter reviews fuzzy database modeling technologies, including fuzzy conceptual data models and database models. Concerning fuzzy database models, fuzzy relational databases, fuzzy nested relational databases, and fuzzy object-oriented databases are discussed, respectively.

Introduction

A major goal for database research has been the incorporation of additional semantics into the data model. Classical data models often suffer from their incapability of representing and manipulating imprecise and uncertain information that may occur in many real-world applications. Since the early 1980s, Zadeh's fuzzy logic (Zadeh,

1965) has been used to extend various data models. The purpose of introducing fuzzy logic in databases is to enhance the classical models such that uncertain and imprecise information can be represented and manipulated. This resulted in numerous contributions, mainly with respect to the popular relational model or to some related form of it.

Also rapid advances in computing power have brought opportunities for databases in emerging applications in CAD/CAM, multimedia and geographic information systems (GIS). These applications characteristically require the modeling and manipulation of complex objects and semantic relationships. It has been proved that the object-oriented paradigm lends itself extremely well to the requirements. Since classical relational database model and its extension of fuzziness do not satisfy the need of modeling complex objects with imprecision and uncertainty, currently many researches have been concentrated on fuzzy object-oriented database models in order to deal with complex objects and uncertain data together.

Database modeling can be carried out at two different levels: conceptual data modeling and database modeling. Therefore, we have conceptual data models (e.g., ER/EER and UML) and logical database models (relational databases, nested relational databases, and object-oriented databases). Logical database models are often created through mapping conceptual data models into logical database models. This conversion is called conceptual design of databases. Since fuzzy database approaches were first created in the late 1970s by several research groups, a significant body of research in the area of fuzzy database modeling has been developed over the past 30 years. Although there have been a lot of fuzzy database papers, ones only find few comprehensive review papers of fuzzy database modeling (Yazici, Buckles, & Petry, 1992; Kerre & Chen, 1995). It has been nearly 10 years since a latest comprehensive overview paper has appeared in this area (Kerre & Chen, 1995). This chapter aims to provide a literature overview of fuzzy database modeling to satisfy the obvious need for an updating. The topics of the literature referred in the chapter include fuzzy logical database modeling, fuzzy conceptual data modeling, and design and implementation of fuzzy databases. It should be noticed that, however, it does not means that this chapter covers all publications in the research area and gives complete descriptions.

The remainder of this chapter is organized as follows. The second section gives the basic knowledge about imperfect information and fuzzy sets theory. Issues about fuzzy logical (relational, nested relational, object-oriented, and object-relational) database models are described in the third section. The fourth section investigates issues about fuzzy conceptual data (ER/EER, IFO, and UML) models. The fifth section discusses issues about design and implementation of fuzzy databases, including the conceptual design, indexing techniques, and prototypes. The last section concludes this chapter.

Imperfect Information and Fuzzy Sets Theory

Inconsistency, imprecision, vagueness, uncertainty, and ambiguity are five basic kinds of imperfect information in database systems in (Bosc & Prade, 1993). Inconsistency is a kind of semantic conflict, meaning the same aspect of the real world is irreconcilably represented more than once in a database or in several different databases. Information inconsistency usually comes from information integration. Intuitively, the imprecision and vagueness are relevant to the content of an attribute value, and it means that a choice must be made from a given range (interval or set) of values but we do not know exactly which one to choose at present. In general, vague information is represented by linguistic values. The uncertainty is related to the degree of truth of its attribute value, and it means that we can apportion some, but not all, of our belief to a given value or a group of values. The random uncertainty, described using probability theory, is not considered in the paper. The ambiguity means that some elements of the model lack complete semantics leading to several possible interpretations. Generally, several different kinds of imperfection can co-exist with respect to the same piece of information. Imprecision, uncertainty, and vagueness are three major types of imperfect information. Vagueness and uncertainty can be modeled with possibility theory (Zadeh, 1978). Many of the existing approaches dealing with imprecision and uncertainty are based on the theory of fuzzy sets (Zadeh, 1965).

Smets (1997) presents some aspects of imperfection, in which *imprecision, inconsistency,* and *uncertainty* are the major groups. Imprecision and inconsistency are properties related to the content of the statement: either more than one world or no world is compatible with the available information, respectively. Uncertainty is a property that results from a lack of information about the world for deciding if the statement is true or false. Imprecision and inconsistency are essentially properties of the information itself whereas uncertainty is a property of the relation between the information and our knowledge about the world. To model imprecision and uncertainty, the various approaches are presented in (Smets, 1997). These models are grouped into two large categories, namely, the symbolic and the quantitative models. Fuzzy sets introduced by Zadeh (1965) have been widely used for the quantification of imprecision.

Fuzzy data was originally described as a fuzzy set by Zadeh (1965). Let U be a universe of discourse. A fuzzy value on U is characterized by a fuzzy set F in U. A membership function:

$$\mu_F: U \to [0, 1]$$

is defined for the fuzzy set F, where $\mu_F(u)$, for each $u \in U$, denotes the degree of membership of u in the fuzzy set F. Thus the fuzzy set F is described as follows:

$$F = \{\mu_F(u_1)/u_1, \mu_F(u_2)/u_2, ..., \mu_F(u_n)/u_n\}$$

When U is an infinite set, then the fuzzy set F can be represented by:

$$F = \int_{u \in U} \mu_F(u)/u$$

When the membership function $\mu_F(u)$ above is explained to be a measure of the possibility that a variable X has the value u, where X takes values in U, a fuzzy value is described by a possibility distribution π_X (Zadeh, 1978).

$$\pi_X = \{\pi_X(u_1)/u_1, \pi_X(u_2)/u_2, ..., \pi_X(u_n)/u_n\}$$

Here, $\pi_X(u_i)$, $u_i \in U$ denotes the possibility that u_i is true. Let π_X and F be the possibility distribution representation and the fuzzy set representation for a fuzzy value, respectively.

Let A and B be fuzzy sets in the same universe of discourse U with the membership functions μ_A and μ_B, respectively. Then we have the following:

- **Union:** The union of fuzzy sets A and B, denoted $A \cup B$, is a fuzzy set on U with the membership function $\mu_{A \cup B}: U \to [0, 1]$, where:

  $$\forall u \in U, \mu_{A \cup B}(u) = \max(\mu_A(u), \mu_B(u)).$$

- **Intersection:** The intersection of fuzzy sets A and B, denoted $A \cap B$, is a fuzzy set on U with the membership function $\mu_{A \cap B}: U \to [0, 1]$, where:

  $$\forall u \in U, \mu_{A \cap B}(u) = \min(\mu_A(u), \mu_B(u)).$$

- **Complementation:** The complementation of fuzzy set $\bar{A}$, denoted by $\bar{A}$, is a fuzzy set on U with the membership function $\mu_{\bar{A}}: U \to [0, 1]$, where:

  $$\forall u \in U, \mu_{\bar{A}}(u) = 1 - \mu_A(u).$$

Definition. A fuzzy set F of the universe of discourse U is convex if and only if for all u_1, u_2 in U:

$$\mu_F (\lambda u_1 + (1 - \lambda) u_2) \geq \min (\mu_F (u_1), \mu_F (u_1))$$

where $\lambda \in [0, 1]$.

Definition. A fuzzy set F of the universe of discourse U is called a normal fuzzy set if $\exists u \in U, \mu_F (u) = 1$.

Definition. A fuzzy number is a fuzzy subset in the universe of discourse U that is both convex and normal.

Now several notions related to fuzzy numbers are discussed. Let U be a universe of discourse and F a fuzzy number in U with the membership function $\mu_F: U \rightarrow [0, 1]$. We have then the following notions:

- **Support:** The set of elements that have non-zero degrees of membership in F is called the support of F, denoted by:

  $$\text{supp} (F) = \{u| u \in U \text{ and } \mu_F (u) > 0\}.$$

- **Kernel:** The set of elements that completely belong to F is called the kernel of F, denoted by:

  $$\text{ker} (F) = \{u| u \in U \text{ and } \mu_F (u) = 1\}.$$

- **α-cut:** The set of elements whose degrees of membership in F are greater than (greater than or equal to) α, where $0 \leq \alpha < 1$ ($0 < \alpha \leq 1$), is called the strong (weak) α-cut of F, respectively denoted by:

  $$F_{\alpha+} = \{u| u \in U \text{ and } \mu_F (u) > \alpha\} \text{ and } F_\alpha = \{u| u \in U \text{ and } \mu_F (u) \geq \alpha\}.$$

It is clear that the α-cut of a fuzzy number corresponds to an interval. Let A and B be the fuzzy numbers of the universe of discourse U and let A_α and B_α be the α-cuts of the fuzzy numbers A and B, respectively, where:

$A_\alpha = [x_1, y_1]$ and $B_\alpha = [x_2, y_2]$.

Then we have:

$(A \cup B)_\alpha = A_\alpha \underline{\cup} B_\alpha$ and $(A \cap B)_\alpha = A_\alpha \underline{\cap} B_\alpha$,

where $\underline{\cup}$ and $\underline{\cap}$ denote the union operator and intersection operator between two intervals, respectively. The $A_\alpha \underline{\cup} B_\alpha$ and $A_\alpha \underline{\cap} B_\alpha$ are defined as follows:

$$A_\alpha \underline{\cup} B_\alpha = \begin{cases} [x_1, y_1] \, or \, [x_2, y_2], if A_\alpha \cap B_\alpha = \Phi \\ [\min(x_1, x_2), \max(y_1, y_2)], if A_\alpha \cap B_\alpha \neq \Phi \end{cases}$$

$$A_\alpha \underline{\cap} B_\alpha = \begin{cases} \Phi, if A_\alpha \cap B_\alpha = \Phi \\ [\max(x_1, x_2), \min(y_1, y_2)], if A_\alpha \cap B_\alpha \neq \Phi \end{cases}$$

Fuzzy Logical Database Models

Many database researchers have aimed their effort to extend different database models for the purpose of dealing with fuzzy data, and fuzzy database models have appeared as a result. Two major fuzzy logical database models can be found in literature, which are fuzzy relational databases and fuzzy object-oriented databases. In addition, few studies have been done in fuzzy nested relational databases and fuzzy object-relational databases.

Fuzzy Relational Databases

Fuzzy information has been extensively investigated in the context of the relational databases. For a comprehensive review of what has been done in the development of the fuzzy relational databases, please refer to Petry (1996); Chen (1999); Yazici and George (1999); Ma (2005a); and Yazici, Buckles, and Petry (1992). The following are some major issues in current studies of fuzzy relational databases.

Representations and Models

Several approaches have been taken to incorporate fuzzy data into relational database model. One of the fuzzy relational data models is based on similarity relation (Buckles & Petry, 1982), or proximity relation (Shenoi & Melton, 1989), or resemblance (Rundensteiner, Hawkes, & Bandler, 1989). The other one is based on possibility distribution (Prade & Testemale, 1984; Raju & Majumdar, 1988), which can further be classified into two categories: tuples associated with possibilities and attribute values represented by possibility distributions (Raju & Majumdar, 1988).

The form of an n-tuple in each of the above-mentioned fuzzy relational models can be expressed, respectively, as:

$$t = <p_1, p_2, \ldots, p_i, \ldots, p_n>, t = <a_1, a_2, \ldots, a_i, \ldots, a_n, d> \text{ and } t = <\pi_{A1}, \pi_{A2}, \ldots, \pi_{Ai}, \ldots, \pi_{An}>,$$

where $p_i \subseteq D_i$ with D_i being the domain of attribute A_i, $a_i \in D_i$, $d \in (0, 1]$, π_{Ai} is the possibility distribution of attribute A_i on its domain D_i, and $\pi_{Ai}(x)$, $x \in D_i$, denotes the possibility that x is the actual value of $t[A_i]$.

Based on the above-mentioned basic fuzzy relational models, there are several extended fuzzy relational database models. It is clear that one can combine two kinds of fuzziness in possibility-based fuzzy relational databases, where attribute values may be possibility distributions and tuples are connected with membership degrees. Such fuzzy relational databases are called *possibility-distribution-fuzzy relational models* in (Umano & Fukami, 1994). Another possible extension is to combine possibility distribution and similarity (proximity or resemblance) relation, and the *extended possibility-based fuzzy relational databases* are hereby proposed in (Chen, Vandenbulcke, & Kerre, 1992; Ma, Zhang, & Ma, 2000; Rundensteiner, Hawkes, & Bandler, 1989), where possibility distribution and resemblance relation arise in a relational database simultaneously.

- **Definition.** A fuzzy relation r on a relational schema $R (A_1, A_2, ..., A_n)$ is a subset of the Cartesian product of Dom $(A_1) \times$ Dom $(A_2) \times ... \times$ Dom (A_n), where Dom (A_i) may be a fuzzy subset or even a set of fuzzy subset and there is the resemblance relation on the Dom (A_i). A resemblance relation *Res* on Dom (A_i) is a mapping: Dom $(A_i) \times$ Dom $(A_i) \to [0, 1]$ such that:

    (1) for all x in Dom (A_i), *Res* $(x, x) = 1$ (reflexivity)
    (2) for all x, y in Dom (A_i), *Res* $(x, y) = Res (y, x)$ (symmetry)

Semantic Measures and Data Redundancies

To measure the semantic relationship between fuzzy data, some investigation results for assessing data redundancy can be found in literature.

a.   Rundensteiner, Hawkes, and Bandler in 1989 proposed the notion of nearness measure. Two fuzzy data π_A and π_B were considered α-β redundant if and only if the following inequality equations hold true:

$$\min_{x,\,y\,\in\,\text{supp}\,(?A)\,\cup\,\text{supp}\,(?B)} (\text{Res }(x,y)) \geq \alpha \text{ and } \min_{z\,\in\,U} (1 - |?_A\,(z) - ?_B\,(z)|) \geq \beta,$$

where α and β are the given thresholds, $Res\ (x, y)$ denotes the resemblance relation on the attribute domain, and supp (π_A) denotes the support of π_A. It is clear that a twofold condition is applied in their study.

b.   For two data π_A and π_B, Chen, Vandenbulcke and Kerre (1992) define the following approach to assess the possibility and impossibility that $\pi_A = \pi_B$.

$$E_c\,(\pi_A, \pi_B)\,(T) = \text{supp}_{x,\,y\,\in\,U,\,c\,(x,y)\,\geq\,\alpha} (\min\,(\pi_A\,(x),\,\pi_B\,(y)))\text{ and}$$

$$E_c\,(\pi_A, \pi_B)\,(F) = \text{supp}_{x,\,y\,\in\,U,\,c\,(x,y)\,<\,\alpha} (\min\,(\pi_A\,(x),\,\pi_B\,(y)))$$

Here $c\ (x, y)$ denotes a closeness relation (being the same as the resemblance relation).

c.   In Cubero and Vila (1994), the notions of weak resemblance and strong resemblance are proposed for representing the possibility and the necessity that two fuzzy values π_A and π_B are approximately equal, respectively. Weak resemblance and strong resemblance can be expressed as follows:

$$\Pi\,(\pi_A \approx \pi_B) = \text{supp}_{x,\,y\,\in\,U} (\min\,(\text{Res }(x,y),\,\pi_A\,(x),\,\pi_B\,(y)))\text{ and}$$

$$N\,(\pi_A \approx \pi_B) = \inf_{x,\,y\,\in\,U} (\max\,(\text{Res }(x,y),\,1 - \pi_A\,(x),\,1 - \pi_B\,(y)))$$

The semantic measures were employed as a basis for a new definition of fuzzy functional dependencies in Cubero and Vila (1994).

d.   Bosc and Pivert (1997) give the following function to measure the interchangeability that fuzzy value π_A can be replaced with another fuzzy data π_B, that is, the possibility that π_A is close to π_B from the left-hand side:

$$\mu_{\text{repl}}\,(\pi_A, \pi_B) = \inf_{x\,\in\,\text{supp}\,(?A)} (\max\,(1 - \pi_A\,(x),\,\mu_S\,(\pi_A, \pi_B)\,(x))),$$

where $\mu_S\,(\pi_A, \pi_B)\,(x)$ is defined as:

$$\mu_S (\pi_A, \pi_B) (x) = \sup_{y \in \text{supp } (?B)} (\min (\text{Res } (x, y), 1 - |\pi_A (x) - \pi_B (y)|)).$$

It has been shown that counterintuitive results are produced with the treatment of (a) due to the fact that two criteria are set separately for redundancy evaluation (Chen, Vandenbulcke, & Kerre, 1992; Bosc & Pivert, 1997). Therefore the approaches of (b) and (d) tried to set two criteria together for the redundancy evaluation. But for the approach in (b), there also exist some inconsistencies for assessing the redundancy of fuzzy data represented possibility distribution (Ma, Zhang, & Ma, 1999). The approach in (d) is actually an extension of the approach of (a) and the counterintuitive problem in (a) still exists in the approach in (d), which has been demonstrated in (Ma, Zhang, & Ma, 2000). As to the approach in (c), the weak resemblance, however, appears to be too "optimistic" and strong resemblance is too severe for the semantic assessment of fuzzy data (Bosc & Pivert, 1997). So in Ma, Zhang, and Ma (2000), the notions of semantic inclusion degree and semantic equivalence degree are proposed.

For two fuzzy data π_A and π_B, semantic inclusion degree SID (π_A, π_B) denotes the degree that π_A semantically includes π_B and semantic equivalence degree SED (π_A, π_B) denote the degree that π_A and π_B are equivalent to each other. Based on possibility distribution and resemblance relation, the definitions of calculating the semantic inclusion degree and the semantic equivalence degree of two fuzzy data are given as follows:

$$\text{SID}_\alpha (\pi_A, \pi_B) = \sum_{i=1 \; u_i, u_j \in U \text{ and } \text{Res}_U (u_i, u_j) \geq \alpha}^{n} \min \quad (\pi_B (u_i), \pi_A (u_j)) / \sum_{i=1}^{n} \pi_B (u_i) \text{ and}$$

$$\text{SED}_\alpha (\pi_A, \pi_B) = \min (\text{SID}_\alpha (\pi_A, \pi_B), \text{SID}_\alpha (\pi_B, \pi_A))$$

The notion of the semantic inclusion (or equivalence) degree of attribute values can be extended to the semantic equivalence degree of tuples. Let $t_i = <a_{i1}, a_{i2}, \dots, a_{in}>$ and $t_j = <a_{j1}, a_{j2}, \dots, a_{jn}>$ be two tuples in fuzzy relational instance r over schema R $(A_1, A_2, \dots, A_n)$. The semantic inclusion degree of tuples t_i and t_j is denoted:

$$\text{SID}_\alpha (t_i, t_j) = \min \{\text{SID}_\alpha (t_i [A_1], t_j [A_1]), \text{SID}_\alpha (t_i [A_2], t_j [A_2]), \dots, \text{SID}_\alpha (t_i [A_n], t_j [A_n])\}.$$

The semantic equivalence degree of tuples t_i and t_j is denoted:

$$\text{SED}_\alpha (t_i, t_j) = \min \{\text{SED}_\alpha (t_i [A_1], t_j [A_1]), \text{SED}_\alpha (t_i [A_2], t_j [A_2]), \dots, \text{SED}_\alpha (t_i [A_n], t_j [A_n])\}.$$

Two types of fuzzy data redundancies: *inclusion redundancy* and *equivalence redundancy* can be classified and evaluated in fuzzy relational databases. Being different from the classical set theory, the condition $A = B$ is essentially the particular case of fuzzy data equivalence redundancy and the condition $A \supseteq B$ or $A \subseteq B$ is essentially the particular case of fuzzy data inclusion redundancy due to the data fuzziness. Here A and B are fuzzy sets. In general, the threshold should be considered when evaluating the semantic relationship between two fuzzy data.

Let π_A and π_B as well as α be the same as the above. Let β be a threshold. If SID_α $(\pi_A, \pi_B) \geq \beta$, it is said that π_B is *inclusively* redundant to π_A. If SED_α $(\pi_A, \pi_B) \geq \beta$, it is said that π_A and π_B are *equivalently* redundant to each other. It is clear that equivalence redundancy of fuzzy data is a particular case of inclusion redundancy of fuzzy data. Considering the effect of resemblance relation in evaluation of semantic inclusion degree and equivalence degree, two fuzzy data π_A and π_B are considered equivalently α-β-redundant if and only if SED_α $(\pi_A, \pi_B) \geq \beta$. If SID_α $(\pi_A, \pi_B) \geq \beta$ and SID_α $(\pi_B, \pi_A) < \beta$, π_B is inclusively α-β-redundant to π_A.

The processing of fuzzy value redundancy can be extended to that of fuzzy tuple redundancy. In a similar way, fuzzy tuple redundancy can be classified into *inclusion redundancy* and *equivalence redundancy* of tuples. Let r be a fuzzy relation on the relational schema R $(A_1, A_2, ..., A_n)$. Let $t = (\pi_{A1}, \pi_{A2}, ..., \pi_{An})$ and $t' = (\pi'_{A1}, \pi'_{A2}, ..., \pi'_{An})$ be two tuples in r. Let $\alpha \in [0, 1]$ and $\beta \in [0, 1]$ be two thresholds. The tuple t' is inclusively α-β-redundant to t if and only if $\min (SID_\alpha$ $(\pi_{Ai}, \pi'_{Ai})) \geq \beta$ holds true $(1 \leq i \leq n)$. The tuples t and t' are equivalently α-β-redundant if and only if $\min (SED_\alpha$ $(\pi_{Ai}, \pi'_{Ai})) \geq \beta$ holds $(1 \leq i \leq n)$.

Query and Data Processing

Classical relational databases suffer from a lack of flexibility in query. The given selection condition and the contents of the relation are all crisp. A query is flexible if the following conditions can be satisfied (Bosc & Pivert, 1992):

- A qualitative distinction between the selected tuples is allowed.

- Imprecise conditions inside queries are introduced when the user cannot define his/her needs in a definite way, or when a prespecified number of responses are desired and therefore a margin is allowed to interpret the query.

Here, typically, the former case occurs when the queried relational databases contain incomplete information and the query conditions are crisp and the later case occurs when the query conditions are imprecise even if the queried relational databases do not contain incomplete information.

In Zemankova and Kandel (1985), the fuzzy relational data base (FRDB) model architecture and query language are presented and the possible applications of the FRDB in imprecise information processing were discussed. In Kacprzyk, Zadrozny, and Ziokkowski (1987), a "human-consistent" database querying system based on fuzzy logic with linguistic quantifiers is presented. Using clustering techniques, Kamel, Hadfield, and Ismail (1990) present a fuzzy query processing method. Takahashi presents a fuzzy query language for relational databases (Takahashi, 1991) and discusses the theoretical foundation of query languages to fuzzy databases in (Takahashi, 1993). Two fuzzy database query languages are proposed, which are a fuzzy calculus query language and a fuzzy algebra query language. In Bosc and Lietard (1996), the concepts of fuzzy integrals and database flexible querying are presented. In Bosc and Pivert (1995), a relational database language called SQLf for fuzzy querying is presented. Selection, join, and projection operations are extended to cope with fuzzy conditions. Also fuzzy query translation techniques for relational database systems and techniques of fuzzy query processing for fuzzy database systems are presented in (Chen & Jong, 1997) and (Chen & Chen, 2000), respectively. In addition, based on matching strengths of answers in fuzzy relational databases, Chiang, Lin, and Shis (1998) present a method for fuzzy query processing. Yang et al. (2001) focus on nested fuzzy SQL queries in a fuzzy relational database. In addition, fuzzy logic techniques have been used in multimedia database querying (Dubois, Prade, & Sedes, 2001).

In addition to query processing in fuzzy relational databases, there are also few studies focusing on the operations of relational algebra in fuzzy relational databases (Umano & Fukami, 1994; Ma & Mili, 2002a). In Zhang and Wang (2000), a type of fuzzy equi-join is defined using fuzzy equality indicators.

Data Dependencies and Normalizations

Integrity constraints play a critical role in a logical database design. Among these constraints, data dependencies are of more interest. Based on various fuzzy relational database models, some attempts have been taken to express the data dependencies, mainly including fuzzy functional dependency (*FFD*) and fuzzy multivalued dependency (*FMVD*).

There are some papers that focus on *FFD*, where we can classify two kinds of papers: the first one has a focus on the axiomatization of *FFD* (Chen, Kerre, & Vandenbulcke, 1994; Cubero & Vila, 1994; Chen, Kerre, & Vandenbulcke, 1995; Saxena & Tyagi, 1995; Liao, Wang, & Liu, 1999; Liu, 1992, 1993a, 1993b) and the second has a focus on the lossless join and decomposition (Raju & Majumdar, 1988; Bhuniya & Niyogi, 1993; Bosc & Pivert, 2003). The later is the basis to implement the normalization of fuzzy relational databases (Chen, Kerre, & Vandenbulcke, 1996). Also there are some papers that focus on *FMVD* (Tripathy & Sakena, 1990; Jyothi

& Babu, 1997; Bhattacharjee & Mazumdar, 1998). Finally some papers focus both on *FFD* and *FMVD* and present the axiomatization of *FFD* and *FMVD* (Liu, 1997; Yazici & Sozat, 1998; Sözat & Yazici, 2001; Ma, Zhang, Ma, & Mili, 2002).

To solve the problems of update anomalies and data redundancies that may exist in the fuzzy relational databases, the normalization theory of the classical relational database model must be extended so as to provide theoretical guideline for fuzzy relational database design. Based on the notion of fuzzy functional dependency, some notions such as relation keys and normal forms are generalized in Chen, Kerre, and Vandenbulcke (1996). As a result, q-keys, fuzzy first normal form (F1NF), q-fuzzy second normal form (q-F2NF), q-fuzzy third normal form (q-F3NF), and q-fuzzy boyce-codd normal form (q-FBCNF) are formulated. Also dependency-preserving and lossless join decompositions into q-F3NFs are discussed. Within the framework of the similarity-based fuzzy data representation, in Bahar and Yazici (2004), similarity, conformance of tuples, the concept of fuzzy functional dependencies, and partial fuzzy functional dependencies are discussed. On the basis, the fuzzy key notion, transitive closures, and the fuzzy normal forms are defined for similarity-based fuzzy relational databases and the algorithms for dependency preserving and lossless join decompositions of fuzzy relations are given. Also it is shown how normalization, dependency preserving, and lossless join decomposition based on the fuzzy functional dependencies of fuzzy relation are done and applied to some real-life applications. By employing equivalence classes from domain partitions, the functional dependencies and normal forms for the fuzzy relational model are defined in Shenoi and Melton (1992) and then the associated normalization issues are discussed.

It should be noticed that the fuzzy data dependencies can be applied in data handling. In Bosc, Dubois, and Prade (1998), *FFD* is used for redundancy elimination. In Intan and Mukaidono (2000), *FFD* is used for approximate data querying. In Chang and Chen (1998); Liao, Wang, and Liu (1999); Ma, Zhang, and Mili (2002), *FFD* is used for fuzzy data compression.

Fuzzy Nested Relational Databases

In Yazici, Buckles, and Petry (1999), an extended nested relational data model (also known as an NF^2 data model) is introduced for representing and manipulating complex and uncertain data in databases and the extended algebra and the extended SQL-like query language are hereby defined. Also physical data representation of the model and the core operations that the model provides are also introduced. In Ma and Mili (2002b), based possibility distribution rather than the similarity relations in Yazici, Buckles, and Petry (1999), an extended possibility-based fuzzy nested relational database model is introduced and its algebra is hereby developed.

It should be pointed out that NF^2 data model is able to handle complex-valued attributes and may be better suited to some complex applications such as office automation systems, information retrieval systems and expert database systems. But it is difficult for NF^2 data model to represent complex relationships among objects and attributes. Some advanced abstracts in data modeling (e.g., class hierarchy, inheritance, superclass/subclass, and encapsulation) are not supported by NF^2 data model, which are needed by many real applications. Therefore, in order to model uncertain data and complex-valued attributes as well as complex relationships among objects, current efforts have being focused on conceptual data models and object-oriented databases (OODB) with imprecise and uncertain information.

Fuzzy Object-Oriented Databases

The incorporation of imprecise and uncertain information in object-oriented databases has increasingly received the attentions, where fuzziness is witnessed at the levels of object instances and class hierarchies. Umano, Imada, Hatono, and Tamura (1998) define a fuzzy object-oriented database model that uses fuzzy attribute values with a certain factor and an SQL type data manipulation language. An uncertainty and fuzziness in an object-oriented (UFO) databases model is proposed in van Gyseghem and de Caluwe (1998) to model fuzziness and uncertainty by means of conjunctive fuzzy sets and generalized fuzzy sets, respectively. That the behavior and structure of the object are incompletely defined results in a gradual nature for the instantiation of an object. The partial inheritance, conditional inheritance, and multiple inheritances are permitted in fuzzy hierarchies. Based on two different strategies, fuzzy types are added into fuzzy object-oriented databases to manage vague structures in Marín, Vila, and Pons (2000); Marín, Pons, and Vila (2001). And it is also presented how the typical classes of an OODB can be used to represent a fuzzy type and how the mechanisms of instantiation and inheritance can be modeled using this kind of new type on an OODB. In Marín, Medina, Pons, Sánchez, and Vila (2003), complex object comparison in a fuzzy context is developed. In Cross (2001, 2003), fuzzy relationships in object models were investigated.

Based on the extension of a graphs-based model object model, a fuzzy object-oriented data model is defined in Bordogna, Pasi, and Lucarella (1999). The notion of strength expressed by linguistic qualifiers was proposed, which can be associated with the instance relationship as well as an object with a class. Fuzzy classes and fuzzy class hierarchies are thus modeled in the OODB. The definition of graph-based operations to select and browse such a fuzzy object oriented database that manages both crisp and fuzzy information is proposed in Bordogna and Pasi (2001).

Based on similarity relationship, in George, Srikanth, Petry, and Buckles (1996), the range of attribute values is used to represent the set of allowed values for an attribute of a given class. Depending on the inclusion of the actual attribute values of the given object into the range of the attributes for the class, the membership degrees of an object to a class can be calculated. The weak and strong class hierarchies were defined based on monotone increase or decrease of the membership of a subclass in its superclass.

Based on possibility theory, vagueness and uncertainty are represented in class hierarchies in Dubois, Prade, and Rossazza (1991), where the fuzzy ranges of the subclass attributes defined restrictions on that of the superclass attributes and then the degree of inclusion of a subclass in the superclass was dependent on the inclusion between the fuzzy ranges of their attributes. Also based possibility distribution theory, in Ma, Zhang, and Ma (2004), some major notions in object-oriented databases such as objects, classes, objects — classes relationships, subclass/superclass, and multiple inheritances are extended under fuzzy information environment. A generic model for fuzzy object-oriented databases and some operations are hereby developed.

Some efforts have been paid on the establishment of consistent framework for a fuzzy object-oriented model based on the standard for the Object Data Management Group (ODMG) object data model (Cross, Caluwe, & van Gyseghem, 1997). In de Tré and de Caluwe (2003), an object-oriented database modeling technique is presented based on the concept "level-2 fuzzy set" to deals with a uniform and advantageous representation of both perfect and imperfect "real world" information. Also it was illustrated and discussed how the ODMG data model can be generalized to handle "real world" data in a more advantageous way.

In Ndouse (1997), a fuzzy intelligent architecture based on the uncertain object-oriented data model, which is initially introduced by Dubois, Prade, and Rossazza (1991), is proposed. The classes include fuzzy IF-THEN rules to define knowledge and the possibility theory is used for representations of vagueness and uncertainty. In Lee, Xue, Hsu, and Yang (1999), an approach to OO modeling based on fuzzy logic is proposed to formulate imprecise requirements along four dimensions: fuzzy class, fuzzy rules, fuzzy class relationships, and fuzzy associations between classes. The fuzzy rules, in other words, the rules with linguistic terms are used to describe the relationships between attributes.

Some special fuzzy object-oriented databases, for example, fuzzy deductive object-oriented databases (Yazici & Koyuncu, 1997; Koyuncu & Yazici, 2003; Koyuncu and Yazici, 2003), fuzzy and probabilistic object bases (Cao & Rossiter, 2003), and so forth, have been developed. In addition, fuzzy object-oriented database have been applied in some areas such as geographical information systems (Cross & Firat, 2000) and multimedia (Candan & Li, 2001; Majumdar, Bhattacharya, & Saha, 2002). Concerning most recent research and application issues about fuzzy object-oriented databases, ones can refer to (Ma, 2004a).

Fuzzy Object-Relational Databases

Object-relational database systems allow database designers to take advantage of both the powerful object-oriented modeling capability and the robustness of the relational data model. Compared with the fuzzy relational databases and the fuzzy object-oriented databases, few studies have been done in fuzzy object-relational databases. Combining object-relational features and fuzzy theory, Cubero et al. (2004) develop a fuzzy object-relational database framework to permit the representation of complex imperfect information based on fuzzy relational and object-oriented databases.

Fuzzy Conceptual Data Models

Conceptual (semantic) data models for conceptual data modeling provide the designers with powerful mechanisms in generating the most complete specification from the real world. The conceptual data models, in other words, ER/EER and UML, represent both complex structures of entities and complex relationships among entities as well as their attributes. So the conceptual data models play an important role in conceptual data modeling and database conceptual design. In order to deal with complex objects and imprecise and uncertain information in conceptual data modeling, one needs fuzzy extension to conceptual data models, which allow imprecise and uncertain information to be represented and manipulated at a conceptual level. While fuzzy databases have been extensively studied in last two decades in the context of the relational database model and current efforts have been concentrated on the fuzzy object-oriented databases, less research has been done in the fuzzy conceptual data modeling.

Fuzzy ER/EER Models

The fuzzy set theory was first applied to some of the basic ER concepts in Zvieli and Chen (1986). Fuzzy entity sets, fuzzy relationship sets and fuzzy attribute sets were introduced in addition to fuzziness in entity and relationship occurrences and in attribute values. Consequently, fuzzy extension to the ER algebra (Chen, 1976) has been sketched. The three levels of fuzziness in the *ER* model can be found.

- At the first level, entity sets, relationships and attributes may be fuzzy. In other words, they may have a membership degree to the ER model.

- The second level is related to the fuzzy occurrences of entities and relationships.

- The third level concerns the fuzzy values of attributes of special entities and relationships.

Formally, let E, R, and A be the fuzzy entity type set, fuzzy relationship type set, and fuzzy attribute set of the fuzzy ER model, respectively, and μ_E, μ_R, and μ_A be their membership functions. Then:

- for an entity type, say E_i, we have $\mu_E(E_i)/E_i$, where $\mu_E(E_i)$ is the degree of E_i belonging to E and $0 \le \mu_E(E_i) \le 1$,

- for a relationship type, say R_i, we have $\mu_R(R_i)/R_i$, where $\mu_R(R_i)$ is the degree of R_i belonging to R and $0 \le \mu_R(R_i) \le 1$, and

- for an attribute of entity type or relationship type, say A_i, we have $\mu_A(A_i)/A_i$, where $\mu_A(A_i)$ is the degree of Ai belonging to A and $0 \le \mu_A(A_i) \le 1$.

Other efforts to extend the ER model can be found in Ruspini (1986; Vandenberghe (1991); and Vert, Morris, Stock, and Jankowski (2000). In Ruspini (1986), an extension of the ER model with fuzzy values in the attributes was proposed and a truth value can be associated with each relationship instance. In addition, some special relationships such as *same-object* and *subset-of*, member-of were also introduced. Vandenberghe (1991) applied Zadeh's extension principle to calculate the truth value of propositions. For each proposition, a possibility distribution was defined on the doubleton true, false of the classical truth values. The proposal of Vert, Morris, Stock, and Jankowski (2000) was based on the notation used by Oracle and used the fuzzy sets theory to treat data sets as a collection of fuzzy objects, applying the result to the area of geospatial information systems (GISs).

Without including graphical representations, the fuzzy extensions of several major EER concepts, including superclass/subclass, generalization/specialization, category and the subclass with multiple superclasses, were introduced in Chen and Kerre (1998). More recently, Galindo et al. (2004) extended the EER models by relaxing some constraints with fuzzy quantifiers.

Fuzzy IFO Model

In addition to the *ER/EER* model, *IFO* data model (Abiteboul & Hull, 1987) is a mathematically defined conceptual data model that incorporates the fundamental principles of semantic database modeling within a graph-based representational framework. The extensions of *IFO* to deal with fuzzy information were proposed in

Vila, Cubero, Medina, and Pons (1996); Yazici, Buckles, and Petry (1999). In Vila et al. (1996), several types of imprecision and uncertainty such as the values without semantic representation, the values with semantic representation and disjunctive meaning, the values with semantic representation and conjunctive meaning, and the representation of uncertain information were incorporated into the attribute domain of the object-based data model. In addition to the attribute-level uncertainty, the uncertainty was also considered to be at the object and class level.

Based on similarity relations (Buckles & Petry, 1982), the IFO model is extended to the ExIFO (extended IFO) model to represent uncertainties at the levels of the attribute, the object, and class in (Yazici, Buckles, and Petry, 1999). Three kinds of attributes are used, which are fuzzy-valued attributes, incomplete-valued attributes and null-valued attributes and three cases are distinguished: in the first case, the true data value may belong to a specific set or subset of values; in the second case, the true data value is not known; in the third case, the true data value is available but is not expressed precisely. For each of these attribute types, there is a formal definition and graphical representation. In addition, a high-level primitives is introduced to model fuzzy entity type whose semantics are related to each other with logic operators OR, XOR, or AND. Using possibility theory, the IFO model is extended to the IF_2O (fuzzy IFO) model to represent fuzziness at the levels of the attribute, the object, and class in (Ma, 2005; Ma & Shen, 2006).

Fuzzy UML Model

UML provides a collection of models to capture the many aspects of a software system (Booch, Rumbaugh, & Jacobson, 1998). Notice that while the UML reflects some of the best OO modeling experiences available, it suffers from some lacks of necessary semantics. One of the lacks can be generalized as the need to handle imprecise and uncertain information although such information exist in knowledge engineering and databases and have extensively being studied (Parsons, 1996). In Sicilia, Garcia, and Gutierrez (2002); Sicilia, Garcia, Diaz, and Aedo (2002), a practical approach and implementation for a fuzzy-UML storage version is described. With including graphical representations, the fuzzy extension of several major UML concepts (class, generalization, aggregation, association, and dependency) is introduced in Ma (2004b).

Design and Implementation of Fuzzy Databases

The need for handling imprecision and uncertainty in database management systems (DBMSs) has already been recognized earlier and a lot of important work has been done on the fuzzy logical database models. However, in order to gain acceptance in practice, these fuzzy logical database models should be implemented in actual DBMSs where they could prove their superior performance.

Conceptual Design of Fuzzy Databases

Traditional databases are generally designed from conceptual data models. By mapping, conceptual data models are converted into database models. It is shown above that less research has been done in modeling fuzzy information in the conceptual data model. It is particularly true in developing design methodologies for implementing fuzzy databases.

Conceptual Design of Fuzzy Relational Databases

Chaudhry, Moyne, and Rundensteiner (1999) propose a method for designing fuzzy relational databases (FRDBs) following the extension of the ER model of Zvieli and Chen (1986), taking special interest in converting crisp databases into fuzzy ones. Their ER model includes fuzzy relationships as relationships with at least one attribute, namely, the membership grade. They propose FERM, a design methodology for mapping a fuzzy ER data model to a crisp relational database in four steps: constructing a fuzzy ER data model, transforming it into relational tables, normalization and ensuring a correct interpretation of the fuzzy relational operators.

The *IFO* model introduced in Abiteboul and Hull (1987) is extended into the fuzzy *IFO* model based on fuzzy set and possibility distribution theory in (Ma, 2005b). An approach to mapping a fuzzy *IFO* model to a fuzzy relational database schema is described.

Conceptual Design of Fuzzy Nested Relational Databases

The *ExIFO* (extended *IFO*) model proposed in Yazici, Buckles, and Petry (1999) is an extended version of the *IFO* model introduced in Abiteboul and Hull (1987), which can represent uncertainties at the levels of the attribute, the object, and class. Using the *ExIFO* model as the semantic data model to represent the database universe at conceptual design level, in Yazici, Buckles, and Petry (1999), a mapping process to transform the *ExIFO* model into the fuzzy extended NF^2 relations including uncertain properties that are represented in both the *ExIFO* model and the NF^2 database model is described.

Conceptual Design of Fuzzy Object-Oriented Databases

Ma, Zhang, Ma, and Chen (2001) work with the three levels of Zvieli and Chen (1986) and they introduce a fuzzy extended entity-relationship (FEER) model to cope with imperfect as well as complex objects in the real world at a conceptual level. They provided an approach to mapping a FEER model to a fuzzy object-oriented database schema. Ma and Shen (2006) present a conceptual and logical data model, namely, the IF_2O model and the fuzzy object-oriented database model. A formal approach to mapping a fuzzy IFO (IF_2O) model to a fuzzy object-oriented database schema is developed.

Index of Fuzzy Databases

High performance is a necessary precondition for the acceptance of the fuzzy databases by end users. One important step in improving the efficiency of a database system is the introduction of powerful index structures. It should be noticed, however, that performance issues have been quite neglected in research on fuzzy DBMS so far. Indexing in fuzzy databases has not received much attention yet and publications on indexing in fuzzy databases are few. Boss and Helmer (1999) propose index structures for fuzzy DBMS based on well-known techniques of superimposed coding together with detailed cost models. In Helmer (2003), several techniques for indexing fuzzy set in databases are proposed to improve the query evaluation performance. The presented access methods are based on superimposed coding or rely on inverted files.

Although there are many indexing techniques for object-oriented data models, there are only a few indexing techniques for fuzzy object-oriented databases. The access structure proposed in Bosc and Pivert (1992a) uses one index per fuzzy predicate tied to an attribute. The objective is to associate each grade of a fuzzy predicate with the list of tuples that satisfy that predicate. This method only deals with homogeneous domains and assumes that the underlying relations are crisp. Another study included in Yazici and Cibiceli (1999) introduces a fuzzy access structure along with a record and a file organization schema for fuzzy relational databases. In this access structure, MLGF structure is extended to index both the crisp and fuzzy attribute values together. In Yazici, Ince, and Koyuncu, (2004), a multi-dimensional indexing technique (the FOOD Index) is proposed to deal with different kinds of fuzziness in similarity-based fuzzy object-oriented databases. It is shown how the FOOD Index supports various types of flexible queries and evaluates performance results of crisp, range, and fuzzy queries using the FOOD index. A comprehensive overview of indexing techniques suitable for fuzzy object-oriented databases is given in Helmer (2004). Four typical query patterns used in fuzzy object-oriented databases are identified, which are *single-valued*, *set-valued*, *navigational*, and *type hierarch access.* For each query pattern index structure are presented that support the efficient evaluation of these queries, ranging from standard index structures (like B-tree) to very sophisticated access methods (like Join Index Hierarchies).

Prototype of Fuzzy Databases

The problem of the implementation of a fuzzy relational database management system (FRDBMS) has been treated in the literature basically following two basic lines (Medina, Vila, Cubero, & Pons, 1995):

- Starting from a RDBMS with precise information, to develop a syntax that allows formulate imprecise queries.
- To build a FRDBMS prototype which implements a concrete fuzzy relational database model.

The proposal in Medina, Vila, Cubero and Pons (1995) is inside the first line, but including the capability of representing and handling fuzzy information in a classical RDBMS. Introducing some criteria for representation and handling of imprecise information, they show a series of mechanisms to implement imprecise information in a classical RDBMS. To design programming interfaces, Sicilia, Garcia, Diaz, and Aedo (2002) describe a software framework called fJDBC that extends the *Java Database Connectivity API* by enabling fuzzy queries on existing relational databases, using externally-stored metadata.

Design and implementation issues in the similarity-based fuzzy object-oriented databases are presented in Yazici, George, and Aksoy (1998). A software architecture for the implementation of the model is described and the details of prototype implemented using the EXODUS storage manager (ESM) are discussed. Also Berzal, Marin, Pons, and Vila (2004) propose a framework and an architecture which can be used to develop fuzzy object-oriented capabilities using the conventional features of the object-oriented data paradigm. Sicilia, Barriocanal, and Gutierrez (2004) try to provide some criteria to select the fuzzy extensions that more seamlessly integrate in the current object storage paradigm known as orthogonal persistence, in which programming-language object models are directly stored, so that database design becomes mainly a matter of object design.

Conclusion

Incorporation of fuzzy information in database model has been an important topic of database research because such information extensively exists in data and knowledge intensive applications such as natural language processing, artificial intelligence, and CAD/CAM, among others, where fuzzy data play an import role in nature. Therefore, research has been conducted into various approaches to represent and deal with fuzzy data. Some of these techniques, developed at a conceptual level, describe the meaning associated with fuzzy data in a database, which are called fuzzy conceptual data modeling, and others, developed at a logical level, concentrate on processing the fuzzy data, which are called fuzzy logical database modeling.

This chapter elaborates on the issue of fuzziness management in the conceptual data models and the logical database models. Three different approaches to the conceptual data modeling are examined, which are the fuzzy ER/EER model, the fuzzy IFO model, and the fuzzy UML model. These models can represent complex objects with fuzziness in the attribute values and even objects with their powerful abstraction mechanism. In the logical database models, the fuzzy relational databases, the fuzzy nested relational databases, the fuzzy object-oriented databases, and the fuzzy object-relational databases are discussed, respectively. The fuzzy relational database model has been the subject of more thorough data presentation and models, query and data processing, and data dependencies and formalization. Finally the question of designing and implementing the fuzzy databases is considered.

Acknowledgment

Work is supported by the *Program for New Century Excellent Talents in University* (NCET-05-0288) and the *MOE Funds for Doctoral Programs* (20050145024).

References

Abiteboul, S. & Hull, R. (1987). IFO: A formal semantic database model. *ACM Transactions on Database Systems, 12*(4), 525-565.

Bahar, O. K., & Yazici, A. (2004). Normalization and lossless join decomposition of similarity-based fuzzy relational databases. *International Journal of Intelligent Systems, 19*, 885-917.

Berzal, F., Marin, N., Pons, O., & Vila, M. A. (2004). A framework to build fuzzy object-oriented capabilities over an existing database system. In *Advances in fuzzy object-oriented databases: Modeling and applications* (pp. 177-205). Hershey, PA: Idea Group Publishing.

Bhattacharjee, T. K., & Mazumdar, A. K. (1998). Axiomatisation of fuzzy multivalued dependencies in a fuzzy relational data model. *Fuzzy Sets and Systems, 96*(3), 343-352.

Bhuniya, B., & Niyogi, P. (1993). Lossless join property in fuzzy relational databases. *Data and Knowledge Engineering, 11*(2), 109-124.

Booch, G., Rumbaugh, J., & Jacobson, I. (1998). *The unified modeling language user guide.* Addison-Welsley Longman, Inc.

Bordogna, G., & Pasi, G.. (2001). Graph-based interaction in a fuzzy object oriented database. *International Journal of Intelligent Systems, 16*(7), 821-841.

Bordogna, G., Pasi, G., & Lucarella, D. (1999). A fuzzy object-oriented data model for managing vague and uncertain information. *International Journal of Intelligent Systems, 14*, 623-651.

Bosc, P., Dubois, D., & Prade, H. (1998). Fuzzy functional dependencies and redundancy elimination, *Journal of the American Society for Information Science, 49*(3), 217-235.

Bosc, P., & Lietard, L. (1996). Fuzzy integrals and database flexible querying. In *Proceedings of the 5ʰ IEEE International Conference on Fuzzy Systems* (pp. 100-106).

Bosc, P., & Pivert, O. (1992a). Fuzzy querying in conventional databases. In *Fuzzy logic for management of uncertainty* (pp. 645-671). John Wiley and Sons Inc.

Bosc, P., & Pivert, O. (1992b). Some approaches for relational databases flexible querying. *Journal of Intelligent Information Systems, 1*, 323-354.

Bosc, P., & Pivert, O. (1995). SQLf: A relational database language for fuzzy querying. *IEEE Transactions on Fuzzy Systems, 3*, 1-17.

Bosc, P., & Pivert, O. (2003). On the impact of regular functional dependencies when moving to a possibilistic database framework. *Fuzzy Sets and Systems, 140*(1), 207-227.

Boss, B., & Helmer, S. (1999). Index structures for efficiently accessing fuzzy data including cost models and measures. *Fuzzy Sets and Systems, 108*, 11-37.

Buckles, B. P., & Petry, F. E. (1982). A fuzzy representation of data for relational database. *Fuzzy Sets and Systems, 7*(3), 213-226.

Candan, K. S., & Li, W. (2001). On similarity measures for multimedia database applications. *Knowledge and Information Systems, 3*, 30-51.

Cao, T. H., & Rossiter, J. M. (2003). A deductive probabilistic and fuzzy object-oriented database language. *Fuzzy Sets and Systems, 140*, 129-150.

Chang, C. S., & Chen, A. L. P. (1998). Efficient refinement of uncertain data by fuzzy integrity constraints. *Information Sciences, 104*(3-4), 191-211.

Chaudhry, N. A., Moyne, J. R., & Rundensteiner, E. A. (1999). An extended database design methodology for uncertain data management. *Information Sciences, 121*(1-2), 83-112.

Chen, G. Q. (1999). *Fuzzy logic in data modeling; Semantics, constraints, and database design.* Kluwer Academic Publisher.

Chen G. Q., Kerre, E. E., & Vandenbulcke, J. (1995). The dependency-preserving decomposition and a testing algorithm in a fuzzy relational data model. *Fuzzy Sets and Systems, 72*(1), 27-37.

Chen, G. Q., & Kerre, E. E. (1998). Extending ER/EER concepts towards fuzzy conceptual data modeling. In *Proceedings of the 1998 IEEE International Conference on Fuzzy Systems* (Vol. 2, pp. 1320-1325).

Chen, G. Q., Kerre, E. E., & Vandenbulcke, J. (1994). A computational algorithm for the FFD closure and a complete axiomatization of fuzzy functional dependency (FFD). *International Journal of Intelligent Systems, 9*, 421-439.

Chen, G. Q., Kerre, E. E., & Vandenbulcke, J. (1996). Normalization based on functional dependency in a fuzzy relational data model. *Information Systems, 21*(3), 299-310.

Chen, G. Q., Vandenbulcke, J., & Kerre, E. E. (1992). A general treatment of data redundancy in a fuzzy relational data model. *Journal of the American Society of Information Science, 43*(4), 304-311.

Chen, P. P. (1976). The entity-relationship model: Toward a unified view of data. *ACM Transactions on Database Systems, 1*(1), 9-36.

Chen, S. M., & Jong, W. T. (1997). Fuzzy query translation for relational database systems. *IEEE Transactions on Systems, Man, and Cybernetics, 27*, 714-721.

Chen, Y. C., & Chen, S. M. (2000). Techniques of fuzzy query processing for fuzzy database systems. In *Proceedings of the 5th Conference on Artificial Intelligence and Applications* (pp. 361-368).

Chiang, D. A., Lin, N. P., & Shis, C. C. (1998). Matching strengths of answers in fuzzy relational databases. *IEEE Transactions on Systems, Man, and Cybernetics-Part C: Applications and Reviews, 28*, 476-481.

Cross, V. (2001). Fuzzy extensions for relationships in a generalized object model. *International Journal of Intelligent Systems, 16*(7), 843-861.

Cross, V. (2003). Defining fuzzy relationships in object models: Abstraction and interpretation. *Fuzzy Sets and Systems, 140*, 5-27.

Cross, V., Caluwe, R., & Van Gyseghem, N. (1997). A perspective from the fuzzy object data management group (FODMG). In *Proceedings of the 1997 IEEE International Conference on Fuzzy Systems* (Vol. 2, pp. 721-728).

Cross, V., & Firat, A. (2000). Fuzzy objects for geographical information systems. *Fuzzy Sets and Systems, 113*, 19-36.

Cubero, J. C., & Vila, M. A. (1994). A new definition of fuzzy functional dependency in fuzzy relational databases. *International Journal of Intelligent Systems, 9*(5), 441-448.

Cubero, J. C., et al. (2004). Fuzzy object management in an object-relational framework. In *Proceedings of the 2004 International Conference on Information Processing and Management of Uncertainty in Knowledge-Based Systems* (pp. 1767-1774).

de Tré, G., & de Caluwe, R. (2003). Level-2 fuzzy sets and their usefulness in object-oriented database modelling. *Fuzzy Sets and Systems, 140*(1), 29-49.

Dubois, D., Prade, H., & Rossazza, J. P. (1991). Vagueness, typicality, and uncertainty in class hierarchies. *International Journal of Intelligent Systems, 6*, 167-183.

Dubois, D., Prade, H., & Sedes, F. (2001). Fuzzy logic techniques in multimedia database querying: A preliminary investigation of the potentials. *IEEE transactions on Knowledge and Data Engineering, 13*, 383-392.

George, R., Srikanth, R., Petry, F. E., & Buckles, B. P. (1996). Uncertainty management issues in the object-oriented data model. *IEEE Transactions on Fuzzy Systems, 4*(2), 179-192.

Helmer, S. (2003). Evaluating different approaches for indexing fuzzy sets. *Fuzzy Sets and Systems, 140*, 167-182.

Helmer, S. (2004). Index structures for fuzzy object-oriented database systems. In Z. Ma (Ed.), *Advances in Fuzzy Object-Oriented Databases: Modeling and Applications* (pp. 206-240). Hershey, PA: Idea Group Publishing.

Intan, R. & Mukaidono, M. (2000). Fuzzy functional dependency and its application to approximate data querying. In *Proceedings of the 2000 International Database Engineering and Applications Symposium* (pp. 47-54).

Jyothi, S., & Babu, M. S. (1997). Multivalued dependencies in fuzzy relational databases and lossless join decomposition. *Fuzzy Sets and Systems, 88*(3), 315-332.

Kacprzyk, J., Zadrozny, S., & Ziokkowski, A. (1987). FQUERY III+: A "human-consistent" database querying system based on fuzzy logic with linguistic quantifiers. In *Proceedings of the 2nd International Fuzzy Systems Association Congress* (pp. 443-453).

Kamel, M., Hadfield, B., & Ismail, M. (1990). Fuzzy query processing using clustering techniques. *Information Processing and Management, 26*, 279-293.

Kerre, E. E., & Chen, G. Q. (1995). An overview of fuzzy data modeling. In *Fuzziness in Database Management Systems* (pp. 23-41). Physica-Verlag.

Koyuncu, M. & Yazici, A. (2003). IFOOD: An intelligent fuzzy object-oriented database architecture. *IEEE Transactions on Knowledge and Data Engineering, 15*(5), 1137-1154.

Koyuncu, M., & Yazici, A. (2005). A fuzzy knowledge-based system for intelligent retrieval. *IEEE Transactions on Fuzzy Sets and Systems, 13*(3), 317-330.

Lee, J., Xue, N. L., Hsu, K. H., & Yang, S. J. H. (1999). Modeling imprecise requirements with fuzzy objects. *Information Sciences, 118*(1-4), 101-119.

Liao, S. Y., Wang, H. Q., & Liu, W. Y. (1999). Functional dependencies with null values, fuzzy values, and crisp values. *IEEE Transactions on Fuzzy Systems, 7*(1), 97-103.

Liu, W. Y. (1992). The reduction of the fuzzy data domain and fuzzy consistent join. *Fuzzy Sets and Systems, 51*(1), 89-96.

Liu, W. Y. (1993a). Extending the relational model to deal with fuzzy values. *Fuzzy Sets and Systems, 60*(2), 207-212.

Liu, W. Y. (1993b). The fuzzy functional dependency on the basis of the semantic distance. *Fuzzy Sets and Systems, 59*, 173-179.

Liu, W. Y. (1997). Fuzzy data dependencies and implication of fuzzy data dependencies. *Fuzzy Sets and Systems, 92*(3), 341-348.

Ma, Z. M. (2004a). *Advances in fuzzy object-oriented databases: Modeling and applications.* Hershey, PA: Idea Group Publishing.

Ma, Z. M. (2004b). Fuzzy information modeling with the UML. In *Advances in Fuzzy Object-Oriented Databases: Modeling and Applications* (pp. 163-176). Hershey, PA: Idea Group Publishing.

Ma, Z. M. (2005a). *Fuzzy database modeling with XML.* Springer.

Ma, Z. M. (2005b). A conceptual design methodology for fuzzy relational databases. *Journal of Database Management, 16*(2), 66-83.

Ma, Z. M., & Mili, F. (2002a). Handling fuzzy information in extended possibility-based fuzzy relational databases. *International Journal of Intelligent Systems, 17*(10), 925-942.

Ma, Z. M., & Mili, F. (2002b). An extended possibility-based fuzzy nested relational database model and algebra. In *IFIP International Federation for Information Processing* (Vol. 221, pp. 285-288). Kluwer Academic Publishers.

Ma, Z. M., & Shen, D. R. (2006). Modeling fuzzy information in the IF_2O and object-oriented data models. *Journal of Intelligent and Fuzzy Systems* (*accepted*).

Ma, Z. M., Zhang, W. J., & Ma, W. Y. (2000). Semantic measure of fuzzy data in extended possibility-based fuzzy relational databases. *International Journal of Intelligent Systems, 15*(8), 705-716.

Ma, Z. M., Zhang, W. J., & Ma, W. Y. (2004). Extending object-oriented databases for fuzzy information modeling. *Information Systems, 29*(5), 421-435.

Ma, Z. M., Zhang, W. J., Ma, W. Y., & Chen, G. Q. (2001). Conceptual design of fuzzy object-oriented databases utilizing extended entity-relationship model. *International Journal of Intelligent Systems, 16*(6), 697-711.

Ma, Z. M., Zhang, W. J., Ma, W. Y., & Mili, F. (2002). Data dependencies in extended possibility-based fuzzy relational databases. *International Journal of Intelligent Systems, 17*(3), 321-332.

Ma, Z. M., Zhang, W. J., & Mili, F. (2002). Fuzzy data compression based on data dependencies. *International Journal of Intelligent Systems, 17*(4), 409-426.

Majumdar, A. K., Bhattacharya, I., & Saha, A. K. (2002). An object-oriented fuzzy data model for similarity detection in image databases. *IEEE Transactions on Knowledge and Data Engineering, 14*(5), 1186-1189.

Marín, N., Medina, J. M., Pons, O., Sánchez, D., & Vila, M. A. (2003). Complex object comparison in a fuzzy context. *Information and Software Technology, 45*(7), 431-444.

Marín, N., Pons, O., & Vila, M. A. (2001). A strategy for adding fuzzy types to an object-oriented database system. *International Journal of Intelligent Systems, 16*(7), 863-880.

Marín, N., Vila, M. A., & Pons, O. (2000). Fuzzy types: A new concept of type for managing vague structures. *International Journal of Intelligent Systems, 15*, 1061-1085.

Medina, J. M., Pons, O., Cubero, J. C., & Vila, M. A. (1997). FREDDI: A fuzzy relational deductive database interface. *International Journal of Intelligent Systems, 12*(8), 597-613.

Medina, J. M., Vila, M. A., Cubero, J. C., & Pons, O. (1995). Towards the implementation of a generalized fuzzy relational database model. *Fuzzy Sets and Systems, 75*, 273-289.

Ndouse, T. D. (1997). Intelligent systems modeling with reusable fuzzy objects. *International Journal of Intelligent Systems, 12*, 137-152.

Parsons, S. (1996). Current approaches to handling imperfect information in data and knowledge bases. *IEEE Transactions on Knowledge and Data Engineering, 8*(2), 353-372.

Petry, F. E. (1996). *Fuzzy databases: Principles and applications.* Kluwer Academic Publisher.

Prade, H. & Testemale, C. (1984). Generalizing database relational algebra for the treatment of incomplete or uncertain information. *Information Sciences, 34,* 115-143.

Raju, K. V. S. V. N., & Majumdar, A. K. (1988). Fuzzy functional dependencies and lossless join decomposition of fuzzy relational database systems. *ACM Transactions on Database Systems, 13*(2), 129-166.

Rundensteiner, E. A., Hawkes, L. W., & Bandler, W. (1989). On nearness measures in fuzzy relational data models. *International Journal of Approximate Reasoning, 3,* 267-98.

Ruspini, E. (1986). Imprecision and uncertainty in the entity-relationship model. In *Fuzzy logic in knowledge engineering* (pp. 18-22). Verlag TUV Rheinland.

Saxena, P. C., & Tyagi, B. K. (1995). Fuzzy functional dependencies and independencies in extended fuzzy relational database models. *Fuzzy Sets and Systems, 69,* 65-89.

Shenoi, S., & Melton, A. (1989). Proximity relations in the fuzzy relational databases. *Fuzzy Sets and Systems, 31*(3), 285-296.

Shenoi, S., & Melton, A. (1992). Functional dependencies and normal forms in the fuzzy relational database model. *Information Sciences, 60,* 1-28.

Sicilia, M. A., Barriocanal, E. D., & Gutierrez, J. A. (2004). Introducing fuzziness in existing orthogonal persistence interfaces and systems. In *Advances in fuzzy object-oriented databases: Modeling and applications* (pp. 241-268). Hershey, PA: Idea Group Publishing.

Sicilia, M. A., Garcia, E., Diaz, P., & Aedo, I. (2002). *Extending relational data access programming libraries for fuzziness: The fJDBC framework* (LNCS 2522, pp. 314-328).

Sicilia, M. A., Garcia, E., & Gutierrez, J. A. (2002). Integrating fuzziness in object oriented modeling language: Towards a fuzzy-UML. In *Proceedings of the 2002 International Conference on Fuzzy Sets Theory and Its Applications* (pp. 66-67).

Smets, P. (1997). Imperfect information: Imprecision-uncertainty. In *Uncertainty management in information systems: From needs to solutions* (pp. 225-254). Kluwer Academic Publishers.

Sözat, M. I., & Yazici, A. (2001). A complete axiomatization for fuzzy functional and multivalued dependencies in fuzzy database relations. *Fuzzy Sets and Systems, 117*(2), 161-181.

Takahashi, Y. (1991). A fuzzy query language for relational databases. *IEEE Transactions on Systems, Man and Cybernetics, 21*(6), 1576-1579.

Takahashi, Y. (1993). Fuzzy database query languages and their relational completeness theorem. *IEEE Transactions on Knowledge and Data Engineering, 5*(1), 122-125.

Tripathy, R. C., & Sakena, P. C. (1990). Multivalued dependencies in fuzzy relational databases. *Fuzzy Sets and Systems, 38*(3), 267-279.

Umano, M., & Fukami, S. (1994). Fuzzy relational algebra for possibility-distribution-fuzzy-relational model of fuzzy data. *Journal of Intelligent Information Systems, 3*, 7-27.

Umano, M., Imada, T., Hatono, I., & Tamura, H. (1998). Fuzzy object-oriented databases and implementation of its SQL-type data manipulation language. In *Proceedings of the 1998 IEEE International Conference on Fuzzy Systems* (Vol. 2, pp. 1344-1349).

van Gyseghem, N. V., & de Caluwe, R. (1998). Imprecision and uncertainty in UFO database model. *Journal of the American Society for Information Science, 49*(3), 236-252.

Vandenberghe, R. M. (1991). An extended entity-relationship model for fuzzy databases based on fuzzy truth values. In *Proceedings of the 4th International Fuzzy Systems Association World Congress* (pp. 280-283).

Vert, G., Morris, A., Stock, M., & Jankowski, P. (2000). Extending entity-relationship modeling notation to manage fuzzy datasets. In *Proceedings of the 8th International Conference on Information Processing and Management of Uncertainty in Knowledge-Based Systems* (pp. 1131-1138).

Vila, M. A., Cubero, J. C., Medina, J. M., & Pons, O. (1996). A conceptual approach for deal with imprecision and uncertainty in object-based data models. *International Journal of Intelligent Systems, 11*, 791-806.

Yang, Q., Zhang, W. N., Liu, C. W., Wu, J., Yu, C. T., Nakajima, H., & Rishe, N. (2001). Efficient processing of nested fuzzy SQL queries in a fuzzy database. *IEEE Transactions on Knowledge and Data Engineering, 13*(6), 884-901.

Yazici, A., & Cibiceli, D. (1999). An access structure for similarity-based databases. *Information Sciences, 115*(1-4), 137-163.

Yazici, A., & George, R. (1999). *Fuzzy database modeling.* Physica-Verlag.

Yazici, A., & Koyuncu, M. (1997). Fuzzy object-oriented database modeling coupled with fuzzy logic. *Fuzzy Sets and Systems, 89*(1), 1-26.

Yazici, A., & Sozat, M. I. (1998). The integrity constraints for similarity-based fuzzy relational databases. *International Journal of Intelligent Systems, 13*(7), 641-660.

Yazici, A., Buckles, B. P., & Petry, F. E. (1992). A survey of conceptual and logical data models for uncertainty management. In *Fuzzy logic for management of uncertainty* (pp. 607-644). John Wiley and Sons Inc.

Yazici, A., Buckles, B. P., & Petry, F. E. (1999). Handling complex and uncertain information in the ExIFO and NF2 data models. *IEEE Transactions on Fuzzy Systems, 7*(6), 659-676.

Yazici, A., George, R., & Aksoy, D. (1998). Design and implementation issues in the fuzzy object-oriented data model. *Information Sciences, 108*(1-4), 241-260.

Yazici, A., Ince, C., & Koyuncu, M. (2004). *An indexing technique for similarity-based fuzzy object-oriented data model* (LNAI 3055, pp. 334-347).

Yazici, A., Soysal, A., Buckles, B. P., & Petry, F. E. (1999). Uncertainty in a nested relational database model. *Data & Knowledge Engineering, 30*(3), 275-301.

Zadeh, L. A. (1965). Fuzzy sets. *Information and Control, 8*(3), 338-353.

Zadeh, L. A. (1978). Fuzzy sets as a basis for a theory of possibility. *Fuzzy Sets and Systems, 1*(1), 3-28.

Zhang, W. N., & Wang, K. (2000). An efficient evaluation of a fuzzy equi-join using fuzzy equality indicators. *IEEE Transactions on Knowledge and Data Engineering, 12*(2), 225-237.

Zvieli, A., & Chen, P. P. (1986). Entity-relationship modeling and fuzzy databases. In *Proceedings of the 1986 IEEE International Conference on Data Engineering* (pp. 320-327).

Section II:

Intelligent Aspects of Database Systems

Chapter IX

Aspects of Intelligence in an "SP" Database System

J. Gerard Wolff, CognitionResearch.org.uk, UK

Abstract

This chapter describes some of the kinds of "intelligence" that may be exhibited by an intelligent database system based on the SP theory of computing and cognition. The chapter complements an earlier paper on the SP theory as the basis for an intelligent database system (Wolff, forthcoming b) but it does not depend on a reading of that earlier paper. The chapter introduces the SP theory and its main attractions as the basis for an intelligent database system: that it uses a simple but versatile format for diverse kinds of knowledge, that it integrates and simplifies a range of AI functions, and that it supports established database models when that is required. Then with examples and discussion, the chapter illustrates aspects of "intelligence" in the system: pattern recognition and information retrieval, several forms of probabilistic reasoning, the analysis and production of natural language, and the unsupervised learning of new knowledge.

Introduction

Ordinary database management systems are not very "intelligent" but they are good at storing large amounts of data and they normally provide such things as concurrency control, error recovery, distributed processing, and security. By contrast, AI systems exhibit one or more features of human-like intelligence but often lack the ability to handle large amounts of data or other features needed for large-scale applications. Development of an intelligent database system means the integration of these two types of system, preserving the best features of both (Bertino, Catania, & Zarri, 2001).

It is, of course, possible to achieve a certain kind of integration by taking an established database management system and bolting an AI system on top of it. This kind of hybrid system may provide a short-term solution for some kinds of problem but it is not likely to be satisfactory in the long term because of underlying differences in the way data is stored or knowledge is represented, with a consequent need for translations across the divide and the likelihood that there will be residual incompatibilities that limit the overall effectiveness of the hybrid system.

To move beyond that kind of short-term integration, we need to look at both kinds of systems to see what they may have in common and whether it may be possible to develop a unified model that accommodates them both.

This is precisely the same logic that was applied when database management systems were first developed: early databases were each hard coded from scratch but it was soon clear that, since all databases need a system for storing and retrieving knowledge and they all need a user interface, a lot of effort could be saved by providing those facilities within a generalized database management system and loading that system with different kinds of data according to need. In a similar way, early hard-coded expert systems gave way to expert system "shells", each providing a means of storing if-then rules, generalized inference mechanisms and a user interface. This kind of expert-system shell can receive various sets of rules, depending on the area of application.

The purpose of this chapter is to introduce a unified model that may pave the way towards that "deeper" kind of integration between database management systems and AI systems that we may hope to see in an intelligent database management system. The unified model that is the main focus of this chapter is the SP theory of computing and cognition, which has been under development since 1987, and which aims to unify a range of concepts in computing, especially AI, and a range of observations and concepts in human perception and cognition. The theory is outlined later in this chapter but readers wishing to know more will find a relatively short overview of the theory in Wolff (2003a), an extended exposition of the theory and its range of potential applications in Wolff (2006), and further information in earlier papers cited in those two sources.

In the present context, the main attraction of the SP system is that it uses a simple but versatile format for diverse kinds of knowledge, it integrates and simplifies a range of AI functions, and it supports established database models when that is required. An earlier paper (Wolff, forthcoming b) describes with examples how the SP system can imitate established database models (the relational model, the network and hierarchical models, and the object-oriented model), and it briefly reviews the kinds of intelligence that the system can demonstrate. This chapter complements that earlier paper by describing with examples some aspects of intelligence in the system including pattern recognition, information retrieval, several forms of probabilistic reasoning, the analysis and production of natural language, and the unsupervised learning of new knowledge.

The main focus in this chapter and the earlier paper is on the way diverse kinds of knowledge may be represented and integrated within the system and the way one relatively simple model supports several aspects of human-like intelligence. Despite the wide scope of the theory, it does not yet aspire to say anything sensible about things like those mentioned earlier: concurrency control, error recovery, distributed processing, and security.

Outline of the SP Theory

The SP theory of computing and cognition is a theory of information processing in *any* kind of system, either natural or artificial. It is founded on principles of *minimum length encoding* pioneered by Solomonoff (1964) and others (see Li & Vitányi, 1997).[1]

The key idea in the SP theory is that all kinds of "computing", "information retrieval", "calculation", "deduction", "inference" or other forms of information processing may be understood as compression of information by processes of searching for patterns that match each other and the merging or "unifying" of patterns that are the same.

The overriding goal of the research has been to develop a single relatively simple model that would integrate and simplify a range of concepts in human cognition and artificial computing, especially such AI functions as fuzzy pattern recognition, recognition at multiple levels of abstraction, best-match information retrieval, semantic forms of information retrieval, planning, problem solving, unsupervised learning, and various kinds of reasoning including classical deduction, probabilistic deduction, abduction, nonmonotonic reasoning and chains of reasoning.

Why is the theory called "SP"? The name derives from the idea that compression of information means *Simplifying* a body of information by removing redundancy within the information whilst retaining as much as possible of its non-redundant descriptive *Power*.

The Abstract Model

The theory is conceived as an abstract model or system that receives "New" information from its environment and transfers it to a repository of "Old" information. At the same time, it tries to compress the information as much as possible by searching for patterns that match each other and merging or "unifying" patterns that are the same. An important part of this process is the building of *multiple alignments*, similar to multiple alignments in bioinformatics but with important differences. Examples will be seen shortly.

In broad-brush terms, the process of adding compressed information to the repository of Old information achieves the effect of unsupervised learning, while the processes of matching patterns and building multiple alignments achieves computational effects such as "information retrieval", "abduction", "deduction", "calculation", and so on.

Computer Models

Two main computer models of the SP system have been created:

- **SP62:** This is a variant of SP61 described in some detail in Wolff (2000) and Wolff (2006, Chapter 3). It is a partial model of the SP system that builds multiple alignments from New information and a body of Old information that must be supplied by the user. It does not add anything to its repository of Old information. This model is relatively robust and mature and provides all the examples in this chapter.

- **SP70:** This model, described in Wolff (2006, Chapter 9) and Wolff (2003b), contains all the main elements of the SP system, including the addition of compressed information to the repository of Old information and including the main components of the SP62 model. This model achieves unsupervised learning of simple grammars but has some weaknesses as it stands now and needs some reorganisation and further development.

Representation of Knowledge and the Building of Multiple Alignments

In the SP system *all* kinds of knowledge are represented as arrays of *symbols* in one or two dimensions called *patterns*. In work to date, the focus has been almost exclusively on one-dimensional patterns but it is envisaged that, in the future, the conceptual framework will be generalised to accommodate patterns in two dimensions.

In this scheme, a *symbol* is a string of non-space characters bounded by spaces or end-of-pattern markers. In itself, a symbol has no meaning such as "go right" for the symbol "→" on a road sign, "U.S. dollar" for the symbol "$" in ordinary text or "end of file" for the symbol "EOF" in computer applications. It is merely a "mark" that can be compared with any other symbol to determine whether it is "the same" or "different". However, by association within a given set of patterns, any symbol or combination of symbols may serve to represent the "meaning" of any other symbol or combination of symbols.

As in bioinformatics, a *multiple alignment* in the SP system is an arrangement of two or more patterns so that, by judicious stretching of zero or more patterns, symbols that match each other are brought into alignment. Any multiple alignment may be evaluated formally in terms of principles of minimum length encoding as described in the sources cited previously. What this means in practice is that "good" multiple alignments are ones with a relatively large numbers of matching symbols.

Multiple alignments in the SP scheme differ from multiple alignments in bioinformatics in the following ways:

- One or more of the patterns in the alignment are designated "New" and the rest are "Old". The evaluation measure for each alignment — its *compression score* — is the amount of compression of the New information in the alignment that can be achieved by encoding it in terms of the Old information in the alignment (as described in the sources cited previously and outlined in the section about processing natural language).

- Any one Old pattern may appear one *or more* times in any alignment. As explained elsewhere, two or more *appearances* of a pattern in an alignment is *not* the same as two or more *copies* of the pattern in the given alignment.

Superficially, it does not look plausible that all kinds of knowledge might be represented with simple "flat" patterns in one or two dimensions. However, the way these patterns are processed by the building of multiple alignments means that SP patterns can be used to represent a wide variety of established formats including tables in a relational database, networks and trees, class hierarchies, part-whole hierarchies, and their integration (see Wolff, forthcoming b), rules in context-free and context-sensitive grammars (see Wolff, 2000, 2006), and discrimination networks and if-then rules in expert systems (see, Wolff, 1999, 2006). It is anticipated that patterns in two-dimensions will provide a natural vehicle for representing such things as pictures, maps, and diagrams.

A potential advantage of using a simple, uniform format for all kinds of knowledge is that it should facilitate the seamless integration of diverse kinds of knowledge and it should help to overcome the awkward incompatibilities between different formats for knowledge that feature so often in conventional applications.

Information Compression and Probabilities

There is a very intimate connection between information compression and concepts of probability (see Wolff, 2006, Chapter 2). Since information compression lies at the heart of the SP system, the system is fundamentally probabilistic. However, as we shall see in the section on reasoning, which will be seen later, it is possible to apply certain kinds of constraints in the operation of the system so that it can emulate the "exact" kinds of processing that are so prominent in logic and mathematics.

Integration, Rationalisation, and Simplification

It is perhaps worth emphasizing again that the overriding goal of the SP program of research is to develop a model that *integrates* a range of concepts in computing (especially artificial intelligence) and cognitive science and to achieve a *rationalization* and overall *simplification* of those concepts within a single, relatively simple model. If it can be achieved, the practical benefits of this enterprise should be an overall simplification of computing systems (with corresponding gains in quality and reductions in cost) and the provision of a range of AI functions within one system without the need for awkward hybrids between two or more different kinds of AI system (see Wolff, 2006, Chapter 4).

When the SP system is fully mature, it should be a match for any AI system dedicated to a single function. However, development of the SP theory and system is still work in progress and any system that is dedicated to a single function may well perform better within the area that it is designed to serve.

Pattern Recognition

This section and the ones that follow provide examples of intelligence in the SP system. Each section represents a large subject that could be expanded to fill a whole chapter or more. The examples shown are intended to indicate the potential of the SP system to support various kinds of intelligence. They are by no means exhaustive treatments of each topic.

All the examples in this chapter are relatively simple, mainly so that they will be easy to understand and also to avoid creating multiple alignments that are too big to fit on the page. However, the simplicity of these examples does not signify the limits of what the system can do. The computational complexity of the SP models is polynomial and they can cope with much more complex examples than what are shown here.

In this section, the focus is on how the system may perform the kind of "fuzzy" pattern recognition which is such a prominent feature of perception in humans and other animals: the ability to recognize things despite errors of omission, addition, and substitution.

Consider the set of patterns shown in Figure 1 (with the conventions described in the caption). The first pattern, "`<flowering_plant> roots stem leaves ...  </flowering_plant>`" expresses the idea that all flowering plants have roots, stem and leaves (and other features not shown in the pattern).

The pattern begins with the symbol "`<flowering_plant>`" and ends with the symbol "`</flowering_plant>`", in the style of start and end markers for elements in XML (Bray, Paoli, Sperberg-McQueen, Maler, & Yergeau, 2004). As we shall see, symbols like these at the start and end of each pattern serve to ensure that the given pattern is properly aligned with other patterns when multiple alignments are created. But the choice of XML-style symbols to mark the start and end of each pattern is purely cosmetic and not a formal part of the SP system: any other convenient style may be used. Indeed, there is no formal requirement to use start and end symbols at all. In many applications, some or all of the patterns do not contain any symbols of that kind.

At the end of each pattern is a number — like "1000" at the end of the first pattern in Figure 1— that represents the relative frequency of the pattern in some domain. These figures have a role in calculating compression scores for each alignment and they are also used in calculating the absolute and relative probability of each alignment and thence the probabilities of inferences that may be drawn from each alignment.

The second and third patterns in Figure 1 describe dicotyledonous plants (with two embryo leaves in each seed) and monocotyledonous plants (with one embryo leaf

Figure 1. A set of SP patterns describing a selection of families of flowering plants and their botanical classification

```
(<flowering_plant> roots stem leaves ... </flowering_plant>)*1000

(<magnoliopsida> <flowering_plant> </flowering_plant>
      <name> dicotyledon </name> two_embryo_leaves ...
</magnoliopsida>)*450

(<liliopsida> <flowering_plant> </flowering_plant>
      <name> monocotyledon </name> one_embryo_leaf ...
</liliopsida>)*550

(<cactaceae> <magnoliopsida> </magnoliopsida>
      <name> cactus </name> succulent fleshy_habit spiny ...
</cactaceae>)*150

(<ranunculaceae> <magnoliopsida> </magnoliopsida>
      <name> buttercup </name> sheathing_leaf_bases numerous_stamens ...
</ranunculaceae>)*200

(<ericaceae> <magnoliopsida> </magnoliopsida>
      <name> heather </name>
      woody leaves_alternate <flowers> </flowers>
      stamens_distinct ...
</ericaceae>)*100

(<arecaceae> <liliopsida> </liliopsida>
      <name> palm tree </name>
      large_fanshaped_leaves leaf_bases_sheathing
      panicular_inflorescence ...
</arecaceae>)*300

(<juncaceae> <liliopsida> </liliopsida>
      <name> rush </name>
      tufted_herb 6_stamens fruit_is_capsule ...
</juncaceae>)*250

(<ericaceae> <flowers> urceolate </flowers> </ericaceae>)*60
(<ericaceae> <flowers> campanulate </flowers> </ericaceae>)*40
```

"..."represents information that would be supplied in a more comprehensive description of each type of flowering plant. Round brackets ("(" and ")") mark the beginning and end of each pattern but are not part of the pattern. The number following "" at the end of each pattern represents the relative frequency of that pattern in some domain.*

in each seed) respectively. Then follows five patterns, each one describing one of the families of cactuses, buttercups, heathers, palm trees and rushes.

Readers will notice that within each of the last five patterns mentioned and the two previous patterns, the second and third symbols in the pattern correspond to the start and end symbols of one of the earlier patterns. Thus, for example, the pat-

tern "`<magnoliopsida> <flowering_plant> </flowering_plant> <name>`
`dicotyledon </name> two_embryo_leaves ... </magnoliopsida>`"
contains the pair of symbols "`<flowering_plant> </flowering_plant>`". In
effect, this says that dicotyledonous plants belong in the super ordinate grouping
of flowering plants. In a similar way, the pair of symbols "`<magnoliopsida> </`
`magnoliopsida>`" within the pattern "`<ranunculaceae> <magnoliopsida>`
`</magnoliopsida> <name> buttercup </name> sheathing_leaf_bases`
`numerous_stamens ... </ranunculaceae>`" says, in effect, that the buttercup
family belongs in the Magnoliopsida group (dicotyledonous plants). As we shall see
in our first example of a multiple alignment, these pairs of symbols have much the
same function as "isa" links in a conventional object-oriented system.

A last point to mention in connection with the patterns shown in Figure 1 is that:

- Some symbols like "`woody`" in the pattern "`<ericaceae> <magnoliopsida>`
  `</magnoliopsida> <name> heather </name> woody leaves_alter-`
  `nate <flowers> </flowers> stamens_distinct ... </ericaceae>`"
  represent simple atomic features of the family of heathers.

- Other symbols, like the pair of symbols "`<flowers> </flowers>`" in the pattern that describes heathers behave like an empty variable in a conventional
  system and, in effect, represent the set of alternative values which is the type
  definition for that variable as described next.

The alternative values for "`<flowers> </flowers>`" — the "type definition" for
that "variable"—is shown by the two patterns at the bottom of Figure 1. The first
of these shows that heather flowers may be "`urceolate`" (urn shaped) while the
second shows that heather flowers may be "`campanulate`" (bell shaped), and the
relative frequencies of these two types are 60 and 40, respectively. Although these
two types of flowers may be found in a variety of other flowering plants, we can
tell that, in this case, the distinction and the relative frequencies apply only to the
Ericaceae. This is because each of the two patterns at the bottom of Figure 1 begins
with "`<ericaceae>`" and ends with "`</ericaceae>`".

Pattern Recognition and the Building of
Multiple Alignments

When we run the SP62 model, we need to provide it with a set of Old patterns representing stored knowledge and at least one New pattern representing information that
is coming in from the environment. Then the program builds a variety of multiple
alignments, each one representing one possible way in which the Old patterns may

Figure 2. The best multiple alignment created by SP62 with the pattern `roots woody xxxxx campanulate stamens_distinct` *in New and the patterns shown in Figure 1 in Old*

```
0                 1              2           3                    4

                  <ericaceae> ------ <ericaceae>
                  <magnoliopsida> --------------- <magnoliopsida>
                                                 <flowering_plant> -- <flowering_plant>
                                                                      <name>
                                                                      flowering
                                                                      plant
                                                                      </name>
roots ----------------------------------------------------------------- roots
                                                                      stem
                                                                      leaves
                                                                      ...
                                                 </flowering_plant> - </flowering_plant>
                                                 <name>
                                                 dicotyledon
                                                 </name>
                                                 two_embryo_leaves
                                                 ...
                  </magnoliopsida> --------------- </magnoliopsida>
                  <name>
                  heather
                  </name>
woody ----------- woody
xxxxx             leaves_alternate
                  <flowers> -------- <flowers>
campanulate ---------------------- campanulate
                  </flowers> ------- </flowers>
stamens_distinct - stamens_distinct
                  ...
                  </ericaceae> ----- </ericaceae>

0                 1              2           3                    4
```

be matched to the New pattern or patterns and each one with a compression score showing how well the New pattern(s) may be encoded in terms of the Old patterns. Normally the focus is on the multiple alignment with the highest compression score or the best two or three multiple alignments.

When we run SP62 with the patterns in Figure 1 loaded into the repository of Old patterns and the pattern "`roots woody xxxxx campanulate stamens_dis-tinct`" provided as the New pattern, the best multiple alignment created by the program is the alignment shown in Figure 2.

By convention, the New pattern (or patterns) is always shown in column 0 of any multiple alignment while the Old patterns are shown in the remaining columns, one pattern per column. Apart from the fact that all the New patterns are shown in column 0, the order of the patterns across the other columns is entirely arbitrary and with no special significance.

The most natural way to interpret a multiple alignment like the one shown in Figure 2 is that it is the result of a process of pattern recognition — with the New pattern representing some unknown entity that needs to be recognized and the alignment showing the category or categories to which it has been assigned.

In this case, the unknown entity represented by the features "roots woody xxxxx campanulate stamens_distinct" has been recognized as a member of the family of heathers (column 1). At the same time, it has been recognized as a member of the group of flowering plants (column 4) and, within that group, it has been recognized as a dicotyledonous plant (column 3). Thus the example illustrates one useful feature of the SP system: that it can model the recognition of an unknown entity *at multiple levels of abstraction*, not merely a single level as in simpler kinds of system for pattern recognition.

Another useful feature of the system is that, as indicated earlier, it does not depend on an exact match between the thing to be recognized and any stored pattern but it can cope quite easily with errors of omission, commission, and substitution. In the example shown in Figure 2, the symbol "xxxxx" in the New pattern is not matched to any of the symbols in any of the Old patterns. It represents "noise" in the sensory input that has not prevented successful recognition of the unknown entity as being a heather. The example also shows how recognition has been achieved despite the fact that many of the symbols in the Old patterns — such as "stem" in column 4, "two_embryo_leaves" in column 3, and "leaves_alternate" in column 1 — are not matched to any of the New symbols.

There are, of course, many potential applications for systems with the kinds of capabilities just described. One application that may not immediately spring to mind is the process of diagnosing diseases in people, animals, or plants when that process is viewed as a process of pattern recognition.[2] The way in which the SP system may be applied to medical diagnosis, viewed as a problem of pattern recognition, is discussed quite fully in Wolff (forthcoming a).

Information Retrieval

Pattern recognition is closely related to information retrieval: when we recognize some unknown entity, we are, in effect, retrieving the stored patterns that describe that entity. In the example described in the previous section, the pattern "roots woody xxxxx campanulate stamens_distinct" retrieves the Old patterns shown in Figure 2.

Consider the two SP patterns shown in Figure 3. Each one describes the kind of information that one might find in one row of a table about cars in a relational database. From the first and last symbol in each pattern one can see that the pattern describes a car. Then between those two symbols are "fields" for the registration number of the car, the type of fuel (gasoline or diesel), the engine size, the year of registration, and the number of seats. A "field" in this context is not a formal SP construct, it is simply a pair of symbols like "<reg_no>" and "</reg_no>"

Figure 3. Two SP patterns representing two rows of a table about cars in a relational database

```
(<car> 0 <reg_no> AAA 111 </reg_no>
          <fuel> diesel </fuel>
          <engine_size> 2000 cc </engine_size>
          <year> 2005 </year>
          <seats> 4 </seats>
</car>)

(<car> 1 <reg_no> BBB 222 </reg_no>
          <fuel> gasoline </fuel>
          <engine_size> 4000 cc </engine_size>
          <year> 1999 </year>
          <seats> 6 </seats>
</car>)
```

Figure 4. The two best alignments created by SP62 with the set of patterns {"<year> 2002 </year>", "<seats> 5 </seats>", "<fuel> gasoline </fuel>"} in New and, in the repository of Old patterns, eight patterns like the two shown in Figure 3, each one describing one car

```
0            1                        0            1

             <car>                                 <car>
             5                                     3
             <reg_no>                              <reg_no>
             FFF                                   DDD
             666                                   444
             </reg_no>                             </reg_no>
<fuel> --- <fuel>               <fuel> --- <fuel>
gasoline - gasoline                 gasoline - gasoline
</fuel> -- </fuel>              </fuel> -- </fuel>
             <engine_size>                         <engine_size>
             4000                                  6000
             cc                                    cc
             </engine_size>                        </engine_size>
<year> --- <year>               <year> --- <year>
2002 ----- 2002                     2002 ----- 2002
</year> -- </year>              </year> -- </year>
<seats> -- <seats>             <seats> -- <seats>
5 -------- 5                         5 -------- 5
</seats> - </seats>            </seats> - </seats>
             </car>                                </car>

0            1                        0            1

(a)                                  (b)
```

that may be seen to represent a "variable" (like "`<flowers> </flowers>`" in the example that we saw earlier), with one or more symbols in between that may be seen as a "value" assigned to the variable. In terms of relational database concepts, each field corresponds to one column in a table and each value corresponds to a value in one row of the table.[3]

Given a set of patterns like the two shown in Figure 3, SP62 may extract information from the set in a manner that is similar to "query by example" in an ordinary relational database. If we run the program with the set of three New patterns {"`<year> 2002 </year>`", "`<seats> 5 </seats>`", "`<fuel> diesel </fuel>`"} and eight Old patterns like the two shown in Figure 3, the two best multiple alignments created by the program are the two shown in Figure 4. These are the only two alignments in which there is a match for all the symbols in the set of New patterns.

In this example, the set of New patterns may be regarded as a database "query" ("Find all the cars from the year 2002 with 5 seats that run on gasoline fuel.") and the Old patterns in the two alignments may be regarded as an answer to the query ("The cars in the database with the features specified in the query are the two with registration numbers '`FFF 666`' and '`DDD 444`'.").

Notice that the order of the three New patterns in the "query" is different from their order as they appear in column 0 of the two alignments in Figure 4. SP62 treats a set of two or more New patterns as being an unordered set but, within each pattern of two or more symbols, the order of the symbols must be honored in the building of multiple alignments.[4]

As in the pattern recognition example described in the previous section, the SP62 model matches patterns in a "fuzzy" manner without requiring exact matches between one pattern and another. In this example, there are many symbols in the Old patterns that are not matched to any New symbol. Although the example does not illustrate this point, the system is quite capable of forming alignments where one or more of the New symbols are not matched to any Old symbol.

Before we leave this simple example of how the SP system may model information retrieval in the manner of query by example, there are two further points to be made:

- In an ordinary relational database, it is quite usual for two or more tables to be involved in answering a query. We might, for example, want to identify all the cars with six seats that are owned by people living in Washington DC. To answer this query, we need to make a "join" between the table representing cars and another table representing people. How this can be done in the SP framework is described in Wolff (forthcoming b).
- In the example shown, all the numbers in the Old patterns (such as the number of seats in any one car or the size of its engine) do not have their normal

numerical meaning: they are nothing more than symbols that can be matched in an all-or-nothing manner with other symbols. With this example, it would not be possible to ask the system to "Show all the cars with more than 4 seats" or "Show all the cars with an engine size that is less than 6000 cc".

However, there are reasons for believing that the rules of arithmetic (and other aspects of mathematics and logic) can, in principle, be modelled within the SP system by the provision of appropriate patterns within its repository of Old patterns. Relevant examples and discussion may be found in Wolff (2006, Chapter 10). Thus it should be possible, in principle, to provide the system with knowledge of the rules of arithmetic and knowledge of such concepts as "more than" and "less than" so that it can answer queries like the examples most previously given. That said, the details of how this may done have not yet been worked out.

"Semantic" Retrieval of Information

In the simple example of database retrieval previously given, it is necessary to use the word "gasoline" if we wish to retrieve patterns describing cars that run on gasoline fuel. But in the UK people normally use the word "petrol" to mean exactly the same thing as "gasoline". In a similar way, in other contexts, "concurrency" means the same as "parallel processing", "sidewalk" means the same as "pavement", the "trunk" of a car is the same as the "boot" of a car, "IBM" is short for "International Business Machines", "EU" means "European Union", and so on — not to mention all the many alternative names for things across the world's many different languages.

Any database system that provides for the "semantic" retrieval of information by allowing alternative names to be used for the retrieval of any one concept is clearly more useful and user-friendly than a database system that lacks this flexibility. An attractive feature of the SP system is that it can provide semantic retrieval of information without any modification of the core system. All that is necessary is to supply the system with one or more patterns that show associations between words that have meanings that are the same or very similar.

We may, for example, add the pattern "`<fuel> gasoline petrol </fuel>`" to the set of Old patterns used in the previous example. This tells the system that "`gasoline`" and "`petrol`" are equivalent. Then if we run SP62 again with this slightly augmented set of Old patterns and with the set of New patterns {"`<year> 2002 </year>`", "`<seats> 5 </seats>`", "`<fuel> petrol </fuel>`"}, the two best alignments created by the system are the ones shown in Figure 5.

Figure 5. The two best alignments created by SP62 with the set of New patterns {*"*`<year> 2002 </year>`*"*, *"*`<seats> 5 </seats>`*"*, *"*`<fuel> petrol </fuel>`*"*} *and the same Old patterns as were used for the example shown in Figure 4 but with the addition of the pattern* *"*`<fuel> gasoline petrol </fuel>`*"*

```
0           1              2            0           1              2

            <car>                                   <car>
            5                                       3
            <reg_no>                                <reg_no>
            FFF                                     DDD
            666                                     444
            </reg_no>                               </reg_no>
<fuel> --- <fuel> --------- <fuel>      <fuel> --- <fuel> --------- <fuel>
            gasoline ------- gasoline               gasoline ------- gasoline
petrol ------------------- petrol       petrol ------------------- petrol
</fuel> -- </fuel> -------- </fuel>     </fuel> -- </fuel> -------- </fuel>
            <engine_size>                           <engine_size>
            4000                                    6000
            cc                                      cc
            </engine_size>                          </engine_size>
<year> --- <year>                       <year> --- <year>
2002 ----- 2002                         2002 ----- 2002
</year> -- </year>                      </year> -- </year>
<seats> -- <seats>                      <seats> -- <seats>
5 -------- 5                            5 -------- 5
</seats> - </seats>                     </seats> - </seats>
            </car>                                  </car>

0           1              2            0           1              2

(a)                                     (b)
```

As before, the system has, in effect, retrieved the patterns for the cars registered as "`FFF 666`" and "`DDD 444`". This has been achieved despite the fact that in each of those two patterns the fuel is described as "gasoline" but the word "petrol" has been used in the New patterns that serve as a query. The "translation" between these two terms has been achieved by the recently-added pattern showing their association, which appears in column 2 of alignments (a) and (b) in Figure 5.

Reasoning

The key to reasoning in the SP system is the observation that, within any one multiple alignment, any Old symbol that is *not* matched with a New symbol represents an inference that may be drawn from the given multiple alignment. Thus, for example, we can infer from the multiple alignment shown in Figure 2 that the unknown entity represented by the New pattern in column 0:

- has a stem and leaves (column 4) …
- belongs in the group of dicotyledonous plants (column 3), and …
- has leaves that are "alternate" (alternating from one side of the stem to the other along the length of the stem).

This principle applies to all multiple alignments regardless of their size or complexity.

Exact and Probabilistic Kinds of Deduction

Although the SP system is fundamentally probabilistic, deduction in the narrow sense of "material implication" may be modelled in the SP system as follows. Consider the truth table shown here:

p	q	$p \supset q$
T	T	T
T	F	F
F	T	T
F	F	T

The body of this table may be represented by a set of SP patterns like these:

```
(<mi> 0 T T <r> T </r> </mi>)
(<mi> 1 T F <r> F </r> </mi>)
(<mi> 2 F T <r> T </r> </mi>)
(<mi> 3 F F <r> T </r> </mi>) .
```

Here, the symbols "<mi>" and "</mi>" serve to mark the patterns as part of the definition of material implication, the symbols "0", "1", "2" and "3" are used in the scoring of multiple alignments, and the symbols "<r>" and "</r>" serve to mark the position of the "result" of any computation with this function.

Figure 6. A set of SP patterns representing, in highly simplified form, different kinds of rich people and four individual people

```
(<person> 0 aristocrat <name> </name>
     lives_in_castle rich
</person>)*100

(<person> 1 film_star <name> </name>
     lives_in_Hollywood rich
</person>)*500

(<person> 2 entrepreneur <name> </name>
     drives_fast_car rich
</person>)*200

(<person> <name> Peter </name> </person>)

(<person> <name> Sally </name> </person>)

(<person> <name> David </name> </person>)

(<person> <name> Mary </name> </person>)
```

Figure 7. The best multiple alignment created by SP62 with the patterns shown in Figure 6 as Old patterns and the pattern "film_star David" as a New pattern. This is the only multiple alignment that matches all the New symbols.

```
0               1                       2

                <person> ----------- <person>
                1
film_star -  film_star
                <name> ------------- <name>
David -----------------------------  David
                </name> ----------- </name>
                lives_in_Hollywood
                rich
                </person> ---------- </person>

0               1                       2
```

If SP62 is run with these patterns in its repository of Old patterns and with the New pattern "<mi> F T <r> </r> </mi>", the best alignment found by the program is the one shown here:[5]

```
0 <mi>    F T <r>    </r> </mi> 0
  |       | | |       |     |
1 <mi> 2 F T <r> T </r> </mi> 1
```

In this example, the New pattern is, in effect, a query on the truth table meaning "What is the material implication of the truth values "F" and "T" (in that order)?" The multiple alignment delivers the answer, "T", between the columns containing the symbols "<r>" and "</r>" as previously indicated.

In this example, the SP system is able to deliver an all-or-nothing "exact" result by simply discarding all the multiple alignments created by the system except the best one. With suitable refinement of the patterns that define simple functions like these, it is possible to apply a combination of functions so that the "output" of one becomes the "input" to another in a sequence of two or more functions. This is explained and discussed in Wolff (2006, Chapter 10).

For an example that is a little closer to real life, consider the set of patterns shown in Figure 6. These represent, in a very simplified form, different kinds of wealthy people and related information such as names for people. If we run SP62 with these patterns as Old patterns and the pattern "film_star David" as a New pattern (expressing the idea that someone called David is a film star), the best multiple alignment created by the program and the only one that has a match for all the New symbols is the multiple alignment shown in Figure 7.

In accordance with the rule that any Old symbol that is not matched to a New symbol represents an inference that may be drawn from a multiple alignment, we may infer from Figure 7 that, as a film star, the person called David is rich. We may also infer that he lives in Hollywood. In the world as we know it, both these inferences are naively simplistic but, with the limited knowledge supplied to the system, this is best that the SP62 program can do. As we shall see, it can make more realistic inferences when it has better knowledge.

As noted earlier, SP62 can calculate absolute and relative probabilities for multiple alignments and for the inferences drawn from multiple alignments. Normally, the absolute probabilities are rather small and not of much practical interest. But for any given set of alternative alignments, their relative probabilities and the relative probabilities of associated inferences are much more useful. In this case, there is only one multiple alignment that forms a match with all the New symbols so the relative probability of the alignment and of associated inferences is 1.0. In other words, the system infers that David, as a film star, is certainly rich.

Abduction

The example just considered is a simple "deduction" in the manner of syllogistic reasoning ("All film stars are rich. David is a film star. Therefore, David is rich."). Here, quote marks have been put around the word "deduction" because the inference that has been drawn by the system is probabilistic, notwithstanding the fact that, in this case, the calculated probability leaves no room for doubt.

Figure 8. The three best alignments created by SP62 (the ones that form a match with all the New symbols) with the New pattern "David rich" and the patterns shown in Figure 7 in the repository of Old patterns

```
0          1                    2
           <person> ----------- <person>
           1
           film_star
           <name> ------------- <name>
David ---------------------- David
           </name> ----------- </name>
           lives_in_Hollywood
rich -- rich
           </person> --------- </person>

0          1                    2

(a)
```

```
0          1                    2
           <person> -------- <person>
           2
           entrepreneur
           <name> ---------- <name>
David ------------------- David
           </name> -------- </name>
           drives_fast_car
rich -- rich
           </person> ------- </person>

0          1                    2

(b)
```

```
0          1                    2
           <person> -------- <person>
           0
           aristocrat
           <name> ---------- <name>
David ------------------- David
           </name> -------- </name>
           lives_in_castle
rich -- rich
           </person> ------- </person>

0          1                    2

(c)
```

An attractive feature of the SP system is that it can work just as easily in a "backwards" abductive style as in the "forwards" deductive style just considered. If we run SP62 again with the same Old patterns as before but with the New pattern "David rich" (meaning that David is rich), the best multiple alignments formed by the program — the ones that match all the New symbols — are shown in Figure 8.

Now we see that, in accordance with commonsense, the fact that David is rich does not guarantee that he is a film star living in Hollywood. He might be an aristocrat living in a castle or he might be an entrepreneur and drive a fast car. The relative probabilities for these three possibilities that are calculated by SP62 — using the rather inaccurate frequency values that have been assigned to the SP patterns — are 0.625 (film star), 0.25 (entrepreneur), and 0.125 (aristocrat).

Nonmonotonic Reasoning and Default Values in Reasoning

Classical logic is "monotonic", meaning that after a deduction has been made it remains valid regardless of any new knowledge that may come later. This is different from "nonmonotonic" reasoning — much closer in spirit to how people reason in everyday life — where new knowledge may indeed lead to a revision of earlier inferences. The much-quoted example is that we may initially learn that "Tweety" is a bird and infer from that knowledge that Tweety can probably fly (although it is possible that Tweety is a penguin or an ostrich or other flightless bird). If we learn later that Tweety is a penguin then we revise our original inference and we conclude that Tweety cannot fly.

Our example of film stars, aristocrats and entrepreneurs may be revised to support this style of reasoning if we can show that being rich is something we may naturally assume about film stars (or aristocrats or entrepreneurs) but there is always the possibility that any one such person might never have acquired any money or, if they did, they might have chosen to spend it all or give it away. In other words, being rich is a default value that we may assume about film stars (etc.) when there is no reason to think otherwise but that default value may be overridden in particular cases when we have more information.

Figure 9 shows an augmented and revised version of the patterns shown in Figure 6:

- The first pattern describes the class "person" in general terms with empty fields for "name", "profession", "description", among others, and literal values for "head", "body", and "legs".

- The second pattern records the association between giving all one's money away and the condition of being poor.

- The next three patterns are simple-minded definitions of what it means to be a "film star", "aristocrat", and "entrepreneur".

- The next pattern shows an association between being a film star, living in Hollywood and being rich. As we shall see, the symbol "a2" provides the connection between this pattern and the pattern that defines the concept of film star.

- The last three patterns record three different names for people.

- Symbols like "0" in the first pattern, "d1" in the third pattern, and "2", "3", and "4" in the last three patterns are "identification" symbols used in the scoring of multiple alignments, as will be described next.

- As in earlier examples, the number at the end of each pattern represents the relative frequency of the corresponding class or entity in some domain. As before, the default value is 1 for any pattern without an explicit number.

Figure 9. A set of patterns describing classes of "person" with associated informa-tion to illustrate nonmonotonic reasoning as described in the text

```
(<person> 0
     <name> </name>
     <profession> </profession>
     <description> </description>
     <location> </location>
     <wealth> </wealth>
     <likes> </likes>
     <history> </history>
     head body legs ...
</person>)*10000

(<person>
     <wealth> a1 poor </wealth>
     <history> gave_it_away </history>
</person>)*200

(<person>
     <profession> a2 d1 film_star
</profession>
     <description>
          acts_in_films
          is_famous
     </description>
</person>)*550

(<person>
     <profession> d2 aristocrat
</profession>
     <description> is_high_born
</description>
</person>)*300

(<person>
     <profession> d3 entrepreneur
</profession>
     <description> buys_and_sells
</description>
</person>)*600

(<person>
     <profession> 1 a2 </profession>
     <location> Hollywood </location>
     <wealth> rich </wealth>
</person>)*450

(<name> 2 David </name>)*1000

(<name> 3 Susan </name>)*1500

(<name> 4 Mary </name>)*2000
```

Figure 10. The best alignment (out of three that match all the New symbols) that has been created by SP62 with the New pattern "`David film_star`*" and the Old patterns shown in Figure 9*

```
0              1                     2                    3

              <person> ------- <person>
                               0
                               <name> --------- <name>
                                                2
David -------------------------------------------- David
                               </name> -------- </name>
              <profession> --- <profession>
              a2
              d1
film_star - film_star
              </profession> -- </profession>
              <description> -- <description>
              acts_in_films
              is_famous
              </description> - </description>
                               <location>
                               </location>
                               <wealth>
                               </wealth>
                               <likes>
                               </likes>
                               <history>
                               </history>
                               head
                               body
                               legs
                               ...
              </person> ------ </person>

0              1                     2                    3
```

If SP62 is run with the New pattern "`David film_star`" and the patterns in Figure 9 as the Old patterns, the best multiple alignment found by the program is the multiple alignment shown in Figure 10, the second best is shown in Figure 11 and the third best is shown in Figure 12. These are the only alignments that match all the New symbols.

The multiple alignment in Figure 10 merely connects "`David`" and "`film_star`" via appropriate patterns from Figure 9. Much as we would expect, David is recognized as both a film star (column 1) and a person (column 2) and he inherits appropriate attributes in both cases: head, body, and legs, and so forth, from the pattern describing a person and that he acts in films and is famous from the pattern describing a film star.

Figure 11. The second best alignment (out of three that match all the New symbols) that has been created by SP62 with the New pattern "David film_star" *and the Old patterns shown in Figure 9*

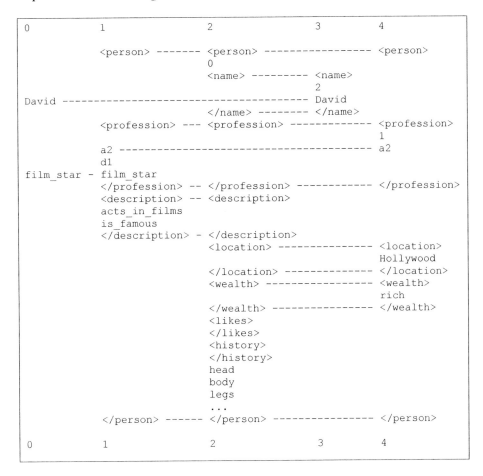

The multiple alignment in Figure 11 is the same as the alignment in Figure 10 except that in column 4 it includes the pattern recording the association between being a film star, living in Hollywood and being rich. The connection between the definition of the concept of a film star (in column 1) and the association just mentioned (in column 4) is provided by the symbol "a2". This multiple alignment says, in effect, that, since David is a film star, it is likely that he lives in Hollywood and that he is rich.

The multiple alignment in Figure 12 is the same as the alignment in Figure 10 except that in column 4 it contains the pattern recording the association between giving

Figure 12. The third best alignment (out of three that match all the New symbols) that has been created by SP62 with the New pattern "`David film_star`" *and the Old patterns shown in Figure 9*

```
0               1                  2                    3          4

                <person> ------- <person> ---------------- <person>
                                 0
                                 <name> --------- <name>
                                                 2
David --------------------------------------------- David
                                 </name> -------- </name>
                <profession> --- <profession>
                a2
                d1
film_star -  film_star
                </profession> -- </profession>
                <description> -- <description>
                acts_in_films
                is_famous
                </description> - </description>
                                 <location>
                                 </location>
                                 <wealth> ----------------- <wealth>
                                                            a1
                                                            poor
                                 </wealth> ---------------- </wealth>
                                 <likes>
                                 </likes>
                                 <history> ---------------- <history>
                                                            gave_it_away
                                 </history> --------------- </history>
                                 head
                                 body
                                 legs
                                 ...
                </person> ------ </person> --------------- </person>

0               1                  2                    3          4
```

all one's money away and the state of being poor. In effect, the multiple alignment says that, since David is a person, it is possible that he has become poor by giving all his money away.

Given the relative frequency values shown in Figure 9, SP62 calculates relative probabilities as follows:

- The probability that David is a film star is calculated as 1.0, reflecting the assertion in the New pattern that David is indeed a film star and the fact that all

Figure 13. The best alignment that has been created by SP62 with the New pattern "David film_star gave_it_away" *and the Old patterns shown in Figure 9. This is the only multiple alignment that matches all the New symbols.*

```
0                    1                    2                    3            4

                     <person> -------     <person> ----------------- <person>
                                          0
                                          <name> --------- <name>
                                                           2
David ------------------------------------------------     David
                                          </name> -------- </name>
                     <profession> --- <profession>
                     a2
                     d1
film_star ----       film_star
                     </profession> -- </profession>
                     <description> -- <description>
                     acts_in_films
                     is_famous
                     </description> - </description>
                                          <location>
                                          </location>
                                          <wealth> ----------------- <wealth>
                                                                     a1
                                                                     poor
                                          </wealth> ---------------- </wealth>
                                          <likes>
                                          </likes>
                                          <history> ---------------- <history>
gave_it_away ---------------------------------------------           gave_it_away
                                          </history> -------------- </history>
                                          head
                                          body
                                          legs
                                          ...
                     </person> ------     </person> ---------------- </person>

0                    1                    2                    3            4
```

three of the multiple alignments shown in Figures 10, 11, and 12 contain the pattern that defines what it is to be a film star (in column 1 in all three cases). The system has no concept of deliberate deception or accidental errors in the information supplied to it so it has no reason to suppose that David might not be a film star.

• The probability that David, as a film star, lives in Hollywood and is rich is calculated to be 0.69.

• The probability that David, as a person, has given all his money away and is poor is calculated as 0.31.

Notice that the second and third probabilities sum to 1.0. They are *relative* probabilities amongst the alternative inferences represented by the multiple alignments created by the program. In a more realistic example, the number of alternative inferences would be much larger than two.

Now if we run SP62 again with the same Old patterns as before (those shown in Figure 9) but with the New pattern "`David film_star gave_it_away`" (instead of "`David film_star`"), the best multiple alignment formed by the program, and the only one to match all the New symbols, is the one shown in Figure 13.

From this alignment we can infer that, notwithstanding the fact that David is a film star and that most film stars are rich, the fact that David has chosen to give all his money away means that he is poor. In accordance with principles of nonmonotonic reasoning, the provision of new knowledge (that David has given all his money away) has caused the earlier inferences to be replaced with the inference that David is certainly poor. The relative probability of this new inference is 1.0 because there is no other alignment that matches all the New symbols.

Analysis and Production of Natural Language

A sentence like *The winds from the West are strong* may be analyzed syntactically as follows:

- A noun phrase (*The winds from the West*) is followed by a verb (*are*) which is followed by an adjective (*strong*). In some analyses, *are strong* would be identified as a "verb phrase".

- The noun phrase may itself be analyzed into the main part (*The winds*) followed by a qualifying phrase (*from the West*). The qualifying phrase may itself be divided into a preposition (*from*) followed by a noun phrase (*the West*).

- The plural form of the main part of the noun phrase (*The winds*) has a number "agreement" with the plural form of the verb (*are*). This agreement bridges the qualifying phrase (*from the West*) and is independent of whether the subordinate noun phrase (*the West*) is singular or plural. The subordinate phrase could, for example be a plural form like *all directions* (in the sentence *The winds from all directions are strong*) and the original number agreement would remain as before.

The elements of this analysis can be described using a set of SP patterns, as shown in Figure 14. Many of these patterns are like rules in an ordinary context-free phrase-structure grammar. For example, the pattern "`<S> <Num> </Num> <NPb> </NPb>`

Figure 14. A fragment of the syntax of English represented with SP patterns

```
(<S> <Num> </Num> <NPb> </NPb> <V> </V> <A> </A> </S>)
(<NPa> <D> </D> <N> </N> </NPa>)
(<NPb> <NPa> </NPa> <Q> </Q> </NPb>)
(<Q> <PP> </PP> <NPa> </NPa> </Q>)
(<D> 0 the </D>)
(<D> 1 a </D>)
(<N> SNG wind </N>)
(<N> PL winds </N>)
(<N> SNG west </N>)
(<V> SNG is </V>)
(<V> PL are </V>)
(<A> 2 strong </A>)
(<A> 3 weak </A>)
(<PP> 4 to </PP>)
(<PP> 5 from </PP>)
(<Num> PL </Num> <N> PL </N> <Q> </Q> <V> PL </V>)
(<Num> SNG </Num> <N> SNG </N> <Q> </Q> <V> SNG </V>)
```

`<V> </V> <A> </A> </S>`" is like the re-write rule "S → NPb V A", meaning that a sentence is composed of a noun-phrase (of type "b") followed by a verb followed by an adjective. Here, the SP pattern contains the pair of symbols "`<Num> </Num>`" that is not in the re-write rule, the pattern lacks the arrow that is present in the re-write rule, pairs of symbols like "`<V> </V>`" are shown as a single symbol "V" in the re-write rule, and the SP pattern has the terminating symbol "`</S>`".

In a similar way, the SP pattern "`<NPa> <D> </D> <N> </N> </NPa>`" is like the re-write rule "NPa → D N", meaning that a noun-phrase (of type "a") is composed of a determiner (words like "the" or "a") followed by a noun.

The last two patterns in Figure 14 are different. The first one, "`<Num> PL </Num> <N> PL </N> <Q> </Q> <V> PL </V>`", expresses the idea that a plural noun ("`<N> PL </N>`") is followed by a plural verb ("`<V> PL </V>`") with a qualifying phrase ("`<Q> </Q>`") in between. The second pattern expresses the same relationship for singular nouns and verbs. Both patterns make the simplifying assumption — not correct for English syntax — that there is always a qualifying phrase in this position. Each pattern starts with the pair of symbols "`<Num> </Num>`" with "PL" or "SNG" in between, showing that the "number" of the given pattern is plural or singular.

These patterns are different from ordinary re-write rules because they represent discontinuous dependencies in sentences rather than simple sequences of structures. As we shall see, they have a role in the building of multiple alignments and in the economical encoding of the sentence. The use of patterns like these to represent discontinuous dependencies in syntactic structure is different from and arguably

Figure 15. The best multiple alignment found by SP62 with the sentence "the winds from the west are strong" *as a New pattern and the patterns shown in Figure 14 as the Old patterns*

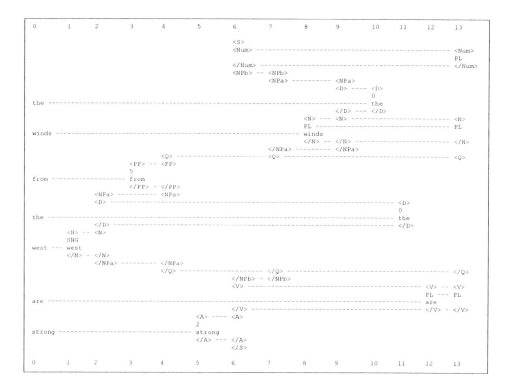

simpler than the methods that are used in other systems for representing syntactic structure (see, for example, Gazdar & Mellish, 1989; Pereira & Warren, 1980).

Parsing a Sentence by the Building of Multiple Alignments

If we run SP62 with the sentence "the winds from the West are strong" as a New pattern and the patterns shown in Figure 14 as Old patterns, the best multiple alignment created by the program is shown in Figure 15.

The multiple alignment shown in this figure is like a syntactic analysis or "parsing" of the sentence into its constituent parts. For example, we can see from the alignment that the first word in the sentence ("the") has been aligned with the same word within the pattern "<D> 0 the </D>" in column 10. This alignment identifies the word as a member of the class of "determiners" represented by the symbols "`<D>`" and "`</D>`" in the pattern. In a similar way, the second word in the sentence ("`winds`") has been aligned with the matching word within the pattern "`<N> PL winds </N>`" in column 8 and is thus identified as a noun ("`<N>`" and "`</N>`") and, more specifically, as a plural noun ("`PL`"). The two patterns mentioned are themselves aligned with the pattern "`<NPa> <D> </D> <N> </N> </NPa>`" in column 7 — which means that the sequence "`the winds`" has been identified as a noun phrase of type "`a`".

In a similar way, all the other constituents of the sentence, at varying levels of abstraction, are marked by the multiple alignment shown in Figure 15. In addition, we can see from the pattern in column 13 that the "number" of the sentence has been recognized as "plural" and that the plural noun in the initial noun phrase ("`winds`") has been linked by this pattern to the plural verb later in the sentence ("`are`") with the qualifying phrase ("`from the west`") in between.

Economical Encoding of the Sentence

As was noted earlier, the SP system aims to create one or more multiple alignments from each of which one can derive an economical encoding of the New pattern (or patterns) in the alignment in terms of the one or more Old patterns in the alignment.

The method for deriving an encoding from a multiple alignment depends on the idea that each SP pattern should contain one or more symbols that are marked as "identification" symbols. Given that certain symbols in each pattern have been marked in this way, an encoding can be derived from any multiple alignment by scanning the alignment from one end to the other and recording any identification symbols that are not matched with any other symbol. The sequence of such unmatched identification symbols constitutes an encoding of the New pattern(s) in the alignment in terms of the Old pattern or patterns in the alignment.

If we apply this procedure to the multiple alignment shown in Figure 15, the encoding that we derive is "`<S> PL 0 5 0 SNG 2 </S>`". The eight symbols in this encoding is actually larger than the seven symbols in the original sentence, but if we take account of the number of bits used to represent each symbol — as described in Wolff (2006, Chapter 3) — the encoding is substantially smaller than the sentence.

A point to notice about the encoding just shown is that it contains only one copy of the symbol "`PL`". This identifies the sentence as one with a plural subject and a plural main verb and so it avoids the need to include one plural symbol for the subject and a second plural symbol for the main verb. This economy in the number of symbols in the encoding of the sentence is possible because the grammar shown in Figure 14 contains the two patterns for discontinuous dependencies, described earlier, that are shown at the bottom of the figure.

*Figure 16. The best multiple alignment found by SP62 with the code sequence "<S>
PL 0 5 0 SNG 2 </S>" as a New pattern and the patterns shown in Figure 14
as the Old patterns*

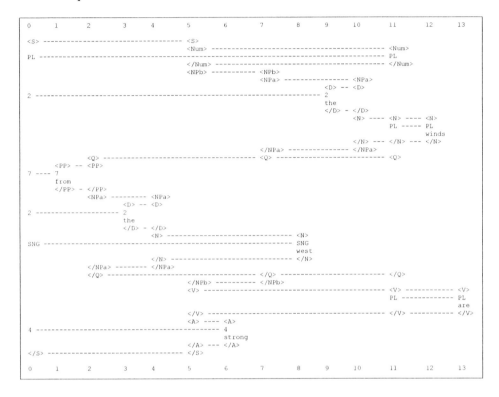

The Production of a Sentence
by Building Multiple Alignments

A neat feature of the SP system is that processing can be reversed, somewhat in the
same way that a suitably-designed Prolog program can derive "data" from "results"
just as easily as it can derive "results" from "data".

If SP62 is run again with the encoding described in the previous subsection ("<S>
PL 0 5 0 SNG 2 </S>") as its New pattern and the same Old patterns as before
(the patterns shown in Figure 14), the best multiple alignment created by the program
is the one shown in Figure 16.

If we scan this multiple alignment from top to bottom and select the symbols in the
rows containing only one symbol (not matched to any other symbol), we obtain
the sequence "the winds from the West are strong", which is, of course,
the original sentence.

This example shows how the SP system can derive a sentence from an encoded form of the sentence using exactly the same mechanisms as were used to derive the code from the sentence in the first place.

Syntax, Semantics and Natural Language Front Ends for Intelligent Databases

If the SP system is viewed as an abstract model of human cognition, what is missing from the examples of natural language processing is any mention of meanings (semantics). When we listen to someone speaking or if we read some printed or hand-written text, we are normally seeking to find the meaning behind the words, not create a meaningless encoding as described previously.

Given the versatility of SP patterns within the SP framework to represent diverse kinds of knowledge, it seems reasonable to assume as a working hypothesis that they may be used to represent "meanings" as well as syntactic forms. This working hypothesis has the attraction of theoretical parsimony:

- We need only postulate one format for syntax and semantics and that format is exceptionally simple.
- Using one format for both syntax and semantics promises an overall simplification of knowledge structures in the brain and the seamless integration of natural language syntax with the meanings derived from syntactic forms.

With regard to intelligent databases — the main focus of this chapter — the use of one simple format for the representation of syntax and semantics should facilitate the creation of natural language user interfaces for SP intelligent databases with seamless integration of the surface forms of language and corresponding meanings. In this case, the "semantic" constructs (that need to be integrated with appropriate syntax of one or more natural languages) are the non-syntactic forms of knowledge in the database, represented using SP patterns and exploiting some or all of the versatility of that format within the SP framework to emulate such things as class hierarchies, part-whole hierarchies, discrimination networks, if-then rules, relational tuples, and more.

Should we therefore conclude that deriving codes from syntax, as described in the previous subsection, is a redherring with no relevance to the ways in which an SP intelligent database might be used in practice? The tentative suggestion here is that adding meanings to the kinds of examples shown earlier is largely a matter of introducing an intermediate stage between the analysis of a sentence and the production of a corresponding code (or the conversion of a code into the corresponding sentence). In this case, the codes that would be derived from spoken or written language would be codes for *meanings*, not codes for the specific words that express the meanings.

Preliminary examples showing how syntax and semantics may be integrated, how an encoding of meanings may be derived from a sentence, and how a natural language sentence may be derived from an encoding of meanings are presented in Wolff (2006, Chapter 5).

Unsupervised Learning

As was outlined earlier, the SP system receives New information from its environment, tries to compress it as much as possible by finding matching patterns and unifying them, and then transfers the compressed information to its repository of Old information. This high-level organisation of the SP system is itself a framework for the acquisition and organisation of knowledge — what we normally call "learning".

This kind of learning is "unsupervised" because it is carried out autonomously without any help from a human or non-human "teacher", without any help from examples that are marked as "wrong", and without the kind of assistance that may accrue from having the information presented in a graded sequence from simple to complex (Gold, 1967).

The process described in the last paragraph but one is a good abstract description of the Lempel-Ziv algorithm for information compression (see, for example, Storer, 1988; Cover & Thomas, 1991) or compression programs that use this algorithm such as WinZip or PKZIP. However, the LZ algorithm lacks much of the character of human learning because it produces structures that are normally rather different from the kinds of structures that people would judge to be "natural" or "correct". This is almost certainly because the algorithm is designed to be "quick and dirty", aiming for speed of processing on an ordinary computer even if that means achieving less compression than would be possible with a more thorough search for matching patterns.

There is good evidence that, if more computational resources are devoted to the task of finding matching patterns and unifying them, the kinds of structures that are identified by this processing are similar to those that people judge to be the natural structure of the original data. For example, a sample of natural language text may first be prepared by removing all spaces, punctuation and capitalization so that there is nothing to mark the boundaries between successive words. This stream of letters may then be processed by a program that is designed to compress the sample as much as possible by the matching and unification of patterns without any prior knowledge of words or other kinds of structure in the given language. In several variations of this idea (see, for example, Wolff, 1977, 1980, 1988; Nevill-Manning & Witten, 1997; Brent, 1999), the structures that are isolated by the program are remarkably similar to the words or phrases that we would naturally recognize in the sample.

SP70

The kinds of study just described were made with programs dedicated to just one facet of intelligence: the ability to learn. By contrast, the SP program of research has aimed to develop a single model to integrate several different aspects of intelligence, as described in the outline of the theory. This difference in orientation has meant that the SP computer models that have been developed differ quite radically from any of the models dedicated purely to learning. Chief amongst the distinctive features of the SP models are the use of "flat" patterns to represent all kinds of knowledge and the concept of multiple alignment as if has been developed in this program of research.

As was indicated earlier, the SP70 model encompasses all the main elements of the SP framework, including those that are realized in the SP62 model. Like the SP62 model, SP70 receives New information and creates multiple alignments to encode the New information economically in terms of whatever Old information it may have stored. Unlike the SP62 model (which must be supplied at the beginning with a set of user-defined Old patterns and does not add anything to that store), SP70 may start without any Old patterns and it may build its store of Old patterns by compressing all the New information that it receives and adding that compressed information to its store.

SP70 operates in two main phases:

1. Create a set of patterns that may be used to encode the New patterns in an economical manner.
2. From the patterns created in Phase 1, compile one or more alternative grammars for the patterns in New in accordance with principles of minimum length encoding. Each grammar comprises a selection of the Old patterns created during Phase 1.

It is envisaged that, in future versions of the model, New information will be received in a succession of batches, that the two phases will operate on each batch and that, at the end of phase two for each batch, all the Old patterns that are *not* contained in the one or two best grammars will be discarded. In this way, the system should gradually build a store of patterns that have proved useful for the economical encoding of the incoming information.

To illustrate processing in Phase 1, consider what happens right at the beginning when SP70's store of Old patterns is empty and it receives a pattern like "t h e w h i t e r a b b i t". In this case, it cannot encode the pattern economically in terms of any stored Old patterns because the store of Old patterns is empty. So the program simply adds some brackets and an identification symbol to the New pattern — which converts it into something like "< %1 t h e w h i t e r a b b i t >" — and then it adds the modified pattern to its store of Old patterns.

At a later stage, the program may receive another New pattern like "t h e j a c k r a b b i t". Now, it is able to form a multiple alignment like this:

```
0       t h e j a c k     r a b b i t     0
        | | |             | | | | | |
1 < %1 t h e w h i t e r a b b i t > 1
```

And this multiple alignment is processed to make a copy of each coherent sequence of matched symbols in row 0 and each coherent sequence of unmatched symbols in row 0 and in row 1. Each such copy is given one or two identification symbols and brackets at each end. In addition, the program creates an "abstract" pattern as described as follows. The result of this processing is a set of patterns like these:

```
< %2 t h e >
< %3 r a b b i t >
< %4 0 j a c k >
< %4 1 w h i t e >
< %5 < %2 > < %4 > < %3 > >
```

and these patterns are added to the repository of Old patterns.

Notice how, in this example, the first four patterns that are isolated are words (in English) and how the fifth pattern records the sequence of matched and unmatched patterns by means of their identification symbols, "%2", "%4" and "%3". Notice also how "< %4 0 j a c k >" and "< %4 1 w h i t e >" both contain the identification symbol "%4" which means that they are alternatives within the larger context represented by the fifth pattern. The identification symbols "0" and "1" in those two patterns provide the means of distinguishing between them.

This simple example gives the flavour of how, in the tradition of structuralist linguistics (see, for example, Harris, 1951; Fries, 1952), the SP70 model is able to isolate significant structures such as words in natural language and distributionally-equivalent classes of words such as the nascent category of "adjective" represented by the symbol "%4".

But Phase 1 of processing by SP70 is not sufficient in itself to isolate things like words and word classes in a tidy manner. A large proportion of the patterns that are generated by the system in this phase of processing are very clearly "wrong". There is a large amount of rubbish mixed up with the patterns that we would naturally regard as the "correct" way to describe the raw data.

It is Phase 2 of SP70 that sorts the wheat from the chaff, extracting those patterns that are useful for the economical encoding of the original New patterns and discarding the rest. The process is a fairly straightforward application of the principle of "hill climbing", building a set of one or more alternative grammars in stages and using the principles of minimum length encoding to evaluate alternative grammars at each stage so that "good" ones are retained and "bad" ones are discarded.

Given a set of simple sentences, SP70 is able to create alternative grammars for the sentences and the best of these grammars (in terms of minimum length encoding) are also grammars that appear subjectively to be "plausible" or "correct", both in terms of the words that are isolated and in terms of the classes of distributionally-equivalent words that are identified.

These results are an encouraging sign that the concepts are developing along the right lines but the program is less successful with examples that are more complex. In particular, while the program is able to isolate low-level structures like words and abstract patterns that describe the overall structure of a sentence, it is not able to isolate intermediate levels of structure such as phrases or clauses. More work will be needed to overcome this problem and other weaknesses in the model as it stands now.

Minimum Length Encoding

With regard to principles of minimum length encoding, the program demonstrates clearly how, in Phase 2, it achieves levels of compression that increase progressively as it searches for grammars that provide the best overall description of the New patterns. This can be seen in Figure 17 which shows measurements made by SP70 when it successfully discovered a plausible grammar for eight simple sentences that were presented to the program as eight New patterns. The X axis shows the succession of New patterns that are processed in Phase 2, and the Y scale on the left shows cumulative sizes (in 10,000 of bits) of the New patterns in their raw state ("O"), the size of the best grammar found at each stage ("G"), the size of the raw data after it has been encoded in terms of the best grammar ("E"), and the sum of G and E at each stage, represented as "T". The plot marked T/O is a measure of the compression achieved at each stage (on the right Y scale), showing how, in accordance with

Figure 17. Measurements made by SP70 (described in the text) as the program derives a plausible grammar from eight sentences presented to the program as eight New patterns.

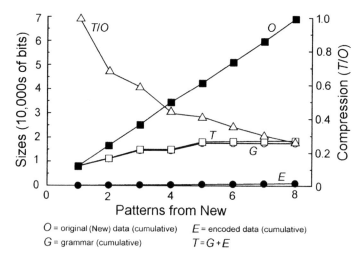

O = original (New) data (cumulative)   E = encoded data (cumulative)
G = grammar (cumulative)   T = G + E

* This figure is reproduced from Wolff (2006, p. 286), with permission

principles of minimum length encoding, $(G + E)$ decreases progressively relative to the size of the raw data.

Learning in an SP Intelligent Database

Ordinary database management systems do not learn as that term is normally understood. They are simply supplied with knowledge by manual input or, sometimes, by the automatic collection of data from some source. Although acquisition of knowledge is one of the elements of learning, and adding knowledge to a database may be seen as a primitive form of learning, something more is expected from an intelligent database if it is to learn in the "intelligent" manner that we associate with human learning.

The key ingredient that is missing from ordinary databases is the ability to organise knowledge in ways that are "meaningful" or "useful". It should, for example, be possible to supply the database with the kind of data that might be gathered by a botanist or zoologist on some field trip or expedition and then the database would organise that knowledge automatically into a taxonomy of classes and subclasses, with associated hierarchies of parts and subparts. It should be possible to analyze the kind of raw data that a company might have stored about its customers and derive rules that may be useful in marketing, such as associations between particular post codes and high-spending customers.

Of course, taxonomies can be derived by the many versions of cluster analysis, and the derivation of rules from raw data has been the subject of intensive investigation in the field of "data mining". But, as indicated, the SP program of research differs from research that is dedicated purely to one facet of intelligence because it aims to develop a framework that *integrates* learning with several other aspects of intelligence.

We have seen how the unsupervised learning of a grammar for a sample of natural language may be achieved within the SP framework but this is not exactly the same as learning class hierarchies, part-whole hierarchies or rules in an intelligent database. However, there are close parallels amongst these forms of learning:

- Part of the process of developing a class hierarchy or a set of rules is the process of identifying the elements of those structures. This similar to the way in which a grammar-induction program must abstract words, phrases and other elements of grammatical structure.

- Likewise, there is a need in all these kinds of learning to identify hierarchies of parts and sub-parts.

- And the learning of a hierarchy of classes and sub-classes is very similar to the learning of grammatical rules at varying levels of abstraction from kinds of "sentence" at the highest level to words, morphemes, phonemes, or allophones at the lower levels of grammatical structure.

In the development of the SP70 model, it is anticipated that if or when the system can be developed to a stage where it has a robust capability for the unsupervised learning of realistic grammars, it may then be applied with little or no modification to the learning of class hierarchies, part-whole hierarchies, and associations and rules of the kind used in expert systems.

With these kinds of capabilities, a mature version of the SP system should be able to automate such processes such as organising raw data into meaningful structures, reorganizing badly-structured data into well-structured knowledge and discovering associations and rules that may later be applied in probabilistic reasoning about the stored knowledge.

Since class-hierarchies and part-whole hierarchies are center-stage in object-oriented software design, object-oriented databases, and in the entity-relationship approach to software engineering, it is anticipated that the mature SP system will provide for the automation or semi-automation of these kinds of application.

Conclusion

The SP system is still being developed and there are still issues to be resolved. However, current models demonstrate clearly that there is a good prospect of achieving the overall goal of this research program — to develop a single, relatively simple framework for a range of different aspects of intelligence.

In this chapter, we have reviewed with examples, some aspects of intelligence that may be provided by an intelligent database founded on the SP concepts. We have seen how the system supports the kind of "fuzzy" pattern recognition that is so prominent in human perception (including pattern recognition through multiple levels of abstraction and the ability to recognize things despite errors of omission, commission, and substitution), how it supports best-match retrieval of information and "semantic" forms of information retrieval, how the system may perform various kinds of reasoning, both classical and probabilistic (including probabilistic deduction, abduction, and nonmonotonic reasoning), how the SP system can support the analysis and production of natural language (so that it may facilitate the provision of a natural language front end to an intelligent database) and how, with some further development, the system is likely to support the kind of unsupervised learning that one might hope to see in any database system that aspires to be intelligent.

What has been described in this chapter is an introduction to the SP system and what it can do. A wider coverage, with more detail, may be found in Wolff (2006). I hope that readers will explore the concepts in more depth and contribute their own research and thinking to the further development of these ideas.

References

Bertino, E., Catania, B., & Zarri, G. P. (2001). *Intelligent database systems*. Harlow: Addison-Wesley.

Brent, M. R. (1999). An efficient, probabilistically sound algorithm for segmentation and word discovery. *Machine Learning*, 34, 1-3.

Cover, T. M., & Thomas, J. A. (1991). *Elements of information theory*. New York: John Wiley.

Bray, T., Paoli, J., Sperberg-McQueen, C. M., Maler, E., & Yergeau, F. (2004). *Extensible Markup Language ({XML}) 1.0* (3rd ed.). World Wide Web Consortium. Retrieved from http://www.w3.org/TR/2004/REC-xml-20040204/

Fries, C. C. (1952). *The structure of English*. New York: Harcourt, Brace & World.

Gazdar, G., & Mellish, C. (1989). *Natural language processing in Prolog*. Wokingham: Addison-Wesley.

Gold, M. (1967). Language identification in the limit. *Information & Control*, 10, 447-474.

Harris, Z. S. (1951). *Methods in structural linguistics*. Chicago: University of Chicago Press.

Li, M. & Vitányi, P. (1997). *An introduction to Kolmogorov complexity and its applications*. New York: Springer-Verlag.

Nevill-Manning, C. G., & Witten, I. H. (1997). Compression and explanation using hierarchical grammars. *Computer Journal*, *40* (2/3), 103-116.

Pereira, F. C. N., & Warren, D. H. D. (1980). Definite clause grammars for language analysis — A survey of the formalism and a comparison with augmented transition networks. *Artificial Intelligence*, 13, 231-278.

Solomonoff, R. J. (1964). A formal theory of inductive inference. Parts I and II. *Information and Control*, 7, 1-22; 224-254.

Solomonoff, R. J. (1997). The discovery of algorithmic probability. *Journal of Computer and System Sciences*, *55*(1), 73-88.

Storer, J. A. (1988). *Data compression: Methods and theory*. Rockville, MD: Computer Science Press.

Wolff, J. G. (1977). The discovery of segments in natural language. *British Journal of Psychology*, 68, 97-106. Retrieved from www.cognitionresearch.org. uk/lang_learn.html#wolff_1977

Wolff, J. G. (1980). Language acquisition and the discovery of phrase structure. *Language & Speech*, 23, 255-269. Retrieved from www.cognitionresearch. org.uk/lang_learn.html#wolff_1980

Wolff, J. G. (1988). Learning syntax and meanings through optimization and distributional analysis. In Y. Levy, I. M. Schlesinger, & M. D. S. Braine (Eds.), *Categories and processes in language acquisition*, (pp. 179-215). Hillsdale, NJ: Lawrence Erlbaum. Retrieved from www.cognitionresearch.org.uk/lang_learn. html#wolff_1988

Wolff, J. G. (1999). Probabilistic reasoning as information compression by multiple alignment, unification and search: An introduction and overview. *Journal of Universal Computer Science*, *5*(7), 418-462. Retrieved from http://arxiv. org/abs/cs.AI/0307010

Wolff, J. G. (2000). Syntax, parsing and production of natural language in a framework of information compression by multiple alignment, unification and search. *Journal of Universal Computer Science*, *6*(8), 781-829. Retrieved from http://arxiv.org/abs/cs.AI/0307014

Wolff, J. G. (2003a). Information compression by multiple alignment, unification and search as a unifying principle in computing and cognition. *Artificial Intelligence Review, 19*(3), 193-230. Retrieved from http://arxiv.org/abs/cs.AI/0307025

Wolff, J. G. (2003b). Unsupervised grammar induction in a framework of information compression by multiple alignment, unification and search. In C. de la Higuera, P. Adriaans, M. van Zaanen, & J. Oncina (Eds.), *Proceedings of the Workshop and Tutorial on Learning Context-Free Grammars* (pp. 113-124). Retrieved from http://arxiv.org/abs/cs.AI/0311045

Wolff, J. G. (2006). *Unifying computing and compression: The SP theory and its applications* (Ebook ed.). Menai Bridge: CognitionResearch.org.uk. Retrieved from http://www.cognitionresearch.org.uk/sp.htm#BOOK

Wolff, J. G. (forthcoming a). Medical diagnosis as pattern recognition in a framework of information compression by multiple alignment, unification and search. To appear in *Decision Support Systems*. Available online from May 17, 2005. Retrieved from http://www.cognitionresearch.org.uk/papers/applications/medical/medical_applications.htm

Wolff, J. G. (forthcoming b). Towards an intelligent database system founded on the SP theory of computing and cognition. To appear in *Data & Knowledge Engineering*. Retrieved from http://www.cognitionresearch.org.uk/papers/dbir/dbir.htm

Endnotes

[1]   The phrase *minimum length encoding* is an umbrella term for the closely-related concepts of "minimum message length" encoding and "minimum description length" encoding. These terms relate to the process of creating or discovering a grammar or other form of knowledge that will describe a given body of raw data. Solomonoff (1964, 1997) realized that there is an infinite range of alternative grammars that may describe any given body of raw data. He proposed that, to discriminate amongst these alternatives, one should try to minimise $(G + E)$, where G is the size of the grammar (in bits of information) and E is the size of the body of raw data (in bits) when it has been encoded in terms of the grammar. Minimising $(G + E)$ is equivalent to compressing the raw data as much as possible, where the compressed representation includes both the code system that is used and the encoding of the raw data. These principles may be applied to any kind of knowledge, not just "grammars" in a narrow sense of that term.

2   It is clear that, when diagnosis is done by a doctor, vet, or plant specialist, causal reasoning also has an important role. Nevertheless, much can be achieved by viewing the diagnostic process purely as a form of pattern recognition.

3   In the absence of any number at the end of each pattern representing the relative frequency of the pattern, SP62 assumes a default value of 1.

4   The main difference between SP62 and SP61 is that the former allows the use of one, two, or more new patterns (treated as an unordered set as described in the text) whereas the latter allows the use of only one new pattern.

5   Compared with multiple alignments shown earlier, this one has been rotated by 90°, simply because it takes up less space on the page. When multiple alignments are shown in this way, the new pattern (or patterns) are always in row 0 and the old patterns appear in the other rows, one pattern per row. The order of the old patterns across the rows is entirely arbitrary, without special significance.

Chapter X

Integrity Checking and Maintenance in Relational and Deductive Databases and Beyond

Davide Martinenghi, Roskilde University, Denmark

Henning Christiansen, Roskilde University, Denmark

Hendrik Decker, Instituto Tecnológico de Informática, Spain

Abstract

Integrity constraints are a key tool for characterizing the well-formedness and semantics of the information contained in databases. In this regard, it is essential that intelligent database management systems provide their users with automatic support to effectively and efficiently maintain the semantic correctness of data with respect to the given integrity constraints. This chapter gives an overview of the field of efficient integrity checking and maintenance for relational as well as deductive databases. It covers both theoretical and practical aspects of integrity control, including integrity maintenance via active rules. New lines of research are outlined, particularly with regard to two topics where a strong impact for future develop-ments can be expected: integrity in XML document collections and in distributed databases. Both pose a number of new and highly relevant research challenges to the database community.

Introduction

Semantic information in databases is typically represented under the form of integrity constraints. Integrity constraints are properties that must always be satisfied for the data to be considered *consistent*. Besides simple forms of constraints such as primary and foreign keys, real-world applications may involve nontrivial integrity requirements that capture complex data dependencies and "business logic". In this regard, the task of an intelligent database management system is to provide means to automatically verify, in an *optimized* way, that database updates do not introduce any violation of integrity. Maintaining compliance of data with respect to integrity constraints is a crucial database issue, since, if some data lack integrity, then answers to queries cannot be trusted. Furthermore, once semantic properties of the data are known to hold, they can be exploited to improve performance of query answering by means of so-called semantic query optimization. Databases, however, usually contain very large collections of data that quickly evolve over time, which makes unabridged checking at each update too time consuming a task to be feasible. In response to this, the database as well as the logic programming and artificial intelligence communities have developed a number of techniques for optimization of integrity checking.

In this chapter we present the main notions involved in this process and briefly give an overview of the most common languages used for the specification of integrity constraints, such as Datalog, relational algebra and calculus, and standard SQL's data definition language statements (e.g., CHECK constraints and ASSERTIONs).

We survey and categorize the main approaches to simplified integrity checking that have been proposed since the early 1980s. These include extensions of the SLD(NF) proof procedure, methods based on induced and potential updates, weakest preconditions *à la* Hoare logic, partial evaluation, update propagation, and incremental view maintenance.

We also outline the main strategies for integrity *maintenance* as opposed to checking. Some approaches pursue complete prevention of inconsistent states by checking, at an early stage and in a possibly simplified way, whether the update will violate integrity. In others, offensive transactions are executed anyhow, and then integrity is restored via corrective actions, such as rollbacks or repairs. As repair actions are, in general, not uniquely determined, this process is necessarily semi-automatic or needs to be extended with user-defined preference criteria.

From a theoretical point of view, we indicate how constraint simplification is strictly related to query containment, and we comment on decidability issues and unavoidable limitations that are intrinsic in any approach.

Orthogonally, we shall discuss the different contexts of applicability of these methods: relational, deductive, and active databases. For relatively recent paradigms, such as semi-structured data, we provide a road map of the solutions proposed so far, both for the specification of constraints and the incremental verification of their satisfaction, and point out the present lines of research. We shall also consider integrity checking in the presence of data that are scattered over different sources, in data integration systems, and distributed databases.

We emphasize the benefits of automated approaches with respect to current techniques based on *ad-hoc* solutions, such as hand-coding of triggers, stored procedures, or code at the application level.

Background

In this section we briefly introduce the basic concepts related to deductive databases. We refer the reader to standard texts in logic, logic programming, and databases such as Ullman (1988), Ceri, Gottlob, and Tanca (1990), and Nilsson and Małuzińsky (1995) for an in-depth treatment of these topics.

We adopt the syntax and terminology of Datalog (Ullman, 1988), which is a uniform language for data description and querying that has evolved from the field of logic programming. Datalog is similar to Prolog. Among the features of Datalog that distinguish it from Prolog, we mention *set-at-a-time* processing (as opposed to Prolog's *tuple-at-a-time*) and pure *declarativity* (as opposed to some procedural constructs in Prolog). Moreover, most authors in the literature also assume an absence of *function symbols* in Datalog (while such symbols do occur in Prolog). These aspects, together with its syntactic simplicity, make Datalog a suitable choice as a database language, which is further motivated by the direct applicability of straightforward proof techniques.

As a notational convention, lowercase letters are used to denote Datalog *predicates* (p, q, ...) and *constants* (a, b, ...), and uppercase letters (X, Y, ...) denote *variables*. Predicates can be divided into three categories: *extensional* predicates (or *relations*), *intensional* predicates (or *views*), and *built-in* predicates (such as equality and comparators $>$, $\geq$, ...). Extensional predicates and intensional predicates are collectively called *database predicates*. A *term* is either a variable or a constant. An *atom* is an expression of the form $p(t_1, ..., t_n)$, where p is a predicate and $t_1, ..., t_n$ are terms. A *literal* is either an atom or an atom preceded by a negation sign (~). According to their predicate, literals are also classified as database or built-in literals.

A distinctive feature of deductive database is the ability of expressing implicit information in terms of deductive units called clauses. A *clause* is an expression of the form:

$$H \leftarrow L_1, ..., L_n$$

where H (the *head*) is an atom, and $L_1, ..., L_n$ (the *body*, n≥0) are literals. Intuitively, a clause indicates that if some premises (the body) hold, then a consequent (the head) also holds. A *rule* (or *view definition*) is a clause whose predicate in the head is intensional, and a *fact* is a clause whose predicate in the head is extensional and variable-free and whose body is empty (understood as *true*). The head atom is said to *depend on* the literals in the body. Besides facts and rules, deductive databases also involve integrity constraints. *Integrity constraints* represent requirements on the consistency of the information stored in the database. They are specified in the database schema and are interpreted as yes/no conditions that must be satisfied in each state of the database. A convenient way to represent integrity constraints is the denial form of clauses. A *denial* is a clause whose head is empty. The intuition behind a denial is that its body indicates a condition that must not hold; or, if it does, then integrity is violated.

The logical understanding of Datalog can be based on the notion of (Herbrand) *models* (Lloyd, 1987). Intuitively, a model is a set of variable-free atoms whose truth implies the truth of all the facts and rules in the database.

Consider, for example, a deductive database D_1 consisting of the following clauses:

R_1:   parent(X,Y) ← father(X,Y)
F_1:   father(john,bob)

Clearly, the set M_1 = { father(john,bob), parent(john,bob) } is a model of D_1, because both the rule and the fact in D_1 are true. In particular, M_1 is the *least* such model of D_1, because any other model of D_1 is a superset of M_1. We note that, in general, a database does not necessarily have a least model, but, under certain conditions, the existence of an *intended* model can be guaranteed. This is the case for the important class of *stratified databases*, that is, those whose recursive rules are not defined through negation; the intended model of a stratified database is called the *standard model* (Apt, Blair, & Walker, 1988). In the following we will focus on stratified databases. We write D(F) = *true* (resp. *false*) to indicate that a formula F holds (resp.

does not hold) in the standard model of stratified database D. In particular, if F is an integrity constraint, D(F) = *true* (resp. *false*) indicates that D is *consistent* (resp. *inconsistent*) with F; then F is said to be *satisfied* (resp. *violated*) in D. Similarly, if F is a set of constraints, D(F) = *true* (resp. *false*) indicates that D is *consistent* with all (resp. *inconsistent* with some) of the constraints in F; then F is said to be *satisfied* (resp. *violated*) in D.

Classification of Integrity Constraints

In the relational setting, it is common to classify constraints according to the entities that they involve. At the most specific level are found *tuple constraints*, that impose restrictions on the combinations of elements in a tuple. Among these, *domain constraints* indicate the possible values that an attribute of a tuple can take.

Constraints that refer to the tuples of a single relation are referred to as *intra-relation constraints* and include different kinds of data dependencies that constrain equalities or inequalities between values of attributes of a relation. Among these, *functional dependencies* (Codd, 1972) and *multi-valued dependencies* (Fagin, 1977) are the most common ones. *Key dependencies* are functional dependencies that impose a *key*, in other words, a subset of attributes of a relation that uniquely identify a tuple in that relation.

Constraints involving two or more relations are known as *inter-relation constraints*. Among these are *inclusion dependencies* (also known as *referential constraints*), that involve two relations and constrain the set of values assumed by some attributes on the first relation to be a subset of the values assumed by the same attributes on the second relation. In particular, when these attributes are a key for the second relation, the constraint is called a *foreign key constraint*.

A more complex, and yet very common kind of constraints is that of *aggregate constraints*, that involve several (possibly all) tuples of a relation simultaneously. For example, constraints on the number of occurrences of certain tuples in a relation or the average of values assumed by certain attributes belong to this category.

In this chapter we only consider the so-called *static* integrity constraints, which indicate properties that must be met by the data in each database state. A disjoint class is that of the so-called *dynamic* constraints, that are used to explicitly impose restrictions on the way the database states can evolve over time. A typical example of dynamic constraint is "the marital status of a person cannot change from *single* to *divorced*". This condition is not static in that it does not refer to a single state, but rather to an *old* and a *new* state at the same time. More complex conditions involving (possibly infinite) sets of states may be expressed by resorting to temporal logics that have constructs such as *since, until, before*, and so on. Dynamic constraints have been considered, such as, in Chomicki (1995) and Cowley and Plexousakis (2000).

Another important distinction can be made between *hard* constraints and *soft* constraints. The former ones are used to model necessary requirements of the world that the database represents. For example, the fact that "every person must be either married or unmarried" can be reasonably considered an intrinsic truth of the world represented, such as, by a database containing information on the personnel of a company. Soft constraints govern what *should* be complied with by the data, although they are not strict requirements. For instance, the fact that "every ordered item should be in the stock" certainly characterizes the good running of an organization but may not be a strict necessity; however, if the company adheres to a policy that guarantees that ordered items will always be available, then this might be considered a hard constraint. In this chapter we concentrate on hard constraints; soft constraints have been considered, for example, in Godfrey, Gryz, and Zuzarte (2001) and in Carmo, Demolombe, and Jones (2001).

More detailed classifications of integrity constraints for deductive databases have been attempted, such as, in Grefen and Apers (1993).

Constraint Specification Languages

Different languages for expressing integrity constraints exist. Common paradigms are, in other words, relational algebra and relational calculus; these (or proper extensions thereof) are known to have exactly the same expressive power as Datalog with negation (Abiteboul, Hull, & Vianu, 1995) (in particular, the algebra plus the while-statement, the calculus plus fixpoint and Datalog with negation are all equivalent).

The techniques presented in this chapter can also be adapted to the context of SQL. For integrity constraints, a mapping between Datalog and SQL, has been described, for example, in Decker (2002). Behrend, Manthey, and Pieper (2001) survey the different forms of integrity constraints that are allowed by the SQL language and compares integrity checking in SQL with checking in deductive databases.

SQL provides built-in constructs for specifying integrity constraints, such as PRIMARY KEY, FOREIGN KEY and UNIQUE. These can be checked and maintained very efficiently by relational database management systems. The SQL2 standard (1992) introduced the CHECK option and the ASSERTION construct as the most general means to express arbitrary integrity constraints declaratively in SQL. However, the verification of CHECK and ASSERTION constraints tends to be extremely expensive unless tackled by an incremental approach. No such approach, however, has been adopted by any database vendors. Most commonly, assertions are not supported at all, and, even when they are, as in the Ocelot SQL DBMS, their use is not encouraged.

Integrity Control

Integrity control addresses the problem of possible integrity violations upon modifications of the database state determined by updates. An *update* U can be viewed as a mapping $U:\mathbf{D}\rightarrow\mathbf{D}$, where $\mathbf{D}$ is the set of all database states. For convenience, for any database state D, we indicate the state arising after update U as D^U.

Given a database state D, a set of integrity constraints F such that $D(F) = true$, and an update U, the constraint checking problem asks whether $D^U(F) = true$ holds too.

However, checking whether $D^U(F) = true$ holds may be too costly, so a suitable reformulation of the problem is called for. One may, for example, wonder whether there exists another set of integrity constraints G (referred to as a *post-test*) such that $D^U(F) = D^U(G)$, and G is somehow "simpler" to evaluate than F. Alternatively, one may try to identify a set of integrity constraints H (referred to as a *pre-test*), also easier to evaluate than F, that can be checked in the state before the update to predict whether the updated state will be consistent, in other words, such that $D^U(F) = D(H)$.

As a matter of fact, the "simpler" constraints (G or H) we are looking for can be determined by exploiting available information, such as the database schema, the given update, the consistency of the database in the old state and, perhaps, the database state. In the literature, it is customary to refer to such G and H as *simplifications* of the original constraints with respect to the update.

Previous Surveys

Mayol and Teniente (1999) compares several methods for integrity checking developed during the nineties and classifies them according to different criteria. In particular, with regard to expressiveness, the authors report whether the surveyed methods allow view definitions and what kind of updates are possible (insertions, deletions, changes, and transactions). As for applicability, they distinguish between methods for integrity *checking*, integrity *maintenance* and *view updating*. Whereas checking amounts to detecting possible inconsistencies introduced by an update, maintenance also tries to restore consistency by performing further actions on the database, such as additional updates or a rollback. View updating, in other words, the problem of translating an update regarding a view to updates for base relations, is strictly related to integrity checking, since integrity constraints may also be regarded as views whose extension must be empty for the database to be consistent.

In this respect, the book by Gupta and Mumick (1999) provides a comprehensive survey of methods and techniques for view materialization.

Besides view updating, other possible applications of integrity constraints are described in Godfrey, Grant, Gryz, and Minker (1998). It is emphasized that, once integrity constraints are known to hold, they can be used for *semantic query optimization*, such as, to make query evaluation more efficient by possibly eliminating or reducing redundant table scans and joins. Knowledge of the integrity constraints can also be used to provide explanations for answers to queries, which is the object of study of *cooperative query answering*. Finally, the authors describe the main approaches for *combining* different databases and resolving possible inconsistencies that may arise after the data have been merged.

Compared to existing surveys, this chapter distinguishes itself by incorporating a wider spectrum of subtopics and describing a broader range of applications of integrity checking techniques, yet without sacrificing generality. Furthermore, it clearly indicates present lines of research and the most likely future directions by pointing to currently open issues, surveying work in progress, and charting out the main areas of interest.

Methods for Incremental Integrity Checking

In the previous section we introduced the term "simplification", which is a central notion in incremental integrity checking. The simplification process was first introduced in Nicolas (1982) and, independently, in Bernstein and Blaustein (1982), for relational databases. We describe here the main approaches to simplification that have been developed for deductive databases.

Update Propagation and Incremental View Maintenance

Update propagation techniques are used to study the effects of an update on integrity constraints or views. In the presence of rules, any database update requested by a user or an application program (from now on also called an *explicit* update) may implicitly cause changes in the extensions of views, the definition of which recurs on updated relations. Such implicit updates are also called *induced updates*. Intuitively, we have an induced insertion if a new instance of the atom in the head of a rule is implied after the update, in other words, because the update was an insertion in a relation in the body of that rule. Similarly, we have an induced deletion if, in a rule, an instance of the head atom cannot be derived after the update, while it was derivable before the update. An update is called *effective* if it is an (induced or explicit) insertion that did not hold in the state before the update or if it is an (induced or explicit) deletion that does no longer hold in the updated state.

Consider rule R_1 and fact F_1 given in the previous section and the following rule:

R_2:   is_parent(X) ← parent(X,Y)

and assume that the insertion of father(john,mary) is executed. It is easy to see that parent(john, mary) is an effective induced update, whereas is_parent(john) is not an effective induced update, since it was possible to derive it already before the update.

Integrity checking can benefit from the computation of induced updates, since the only integrity constraints that need to be checked are to those for which there is a *relevant* induced update, such as, one that matches a literal in the constraint. It can also benefit from distinguishing effective from non-effective induced updates since the latter may not cause any violation of integrity and therefore can be ignored. Constraints for which a relevant effective update exists are also called *relevant*. From the relevant constraints, one can remove the matched literal, which is known to hold in the updated state, thus obtaining an *induced instance*. Integrity checking methods based on induced updates typically consist of the following phases:

1. The *generation* of the effective induced updates
2. The *selection* of the relevant constraints with respect to the effective induced updates
3. The *evaluation* of the induced instances

For example, consider rules R_1 and R_2, fact F_1 and the following integrity constraint:

I_1:   ← is_parent(X), is_baby(X)

that requires that no parent is also a baby. The insertion of father(craig, john) generates several induced updates, among which is_parent(craig) is the only relevant induced update for I_1, whose induced instance is:

II_1:   ← is_baby(craig)

The evaluation of II_1 shows that there is no violation of integrity, since is_baby(craig) is false.

The method of Decker (1987) is based on the computation of effective induced updates and generalizes the method of Nicolas (1982) to the deductive case. After the computation of an effective induced update, the relevant integrity constraints are evaluated.

The common drawback in methods based on induced updates is that many irrelevant induced updates may be generated. Furthermore, the computation of induced updates requires accessing the facts of the database.

An alternative way to identify which views are updated is that of computing the *potential updates*. We have a *potential insertion* of an atom if it matches a head atom that depends on a literal that matches an (explicit or potential) insertion or on a literal whose negation matches an (explicit or potential) deletion; symmetrically for *potential deletions*.

Consider the following rule together with rule R_1 and fact F_1:

R_3:   grandparent(X,Y) ← parent(X,Z), parent(Z,Y)

The insertion of father(craig, john) generates the potential updates: parent(craig, john), grandparent(craig, Y) and grandparent(X, john). Note that the induced update grandparent(craig, bob) is an instance of grandparent(craig, Y), whereas there is no induced update that instantiates grandparent(X, john).

As was the case for induced updates, potential updates can also be exploited for integrity checking with three similar phases. First, potential updates are generated; then, the relevant constraints are selected; finally, they are specialized with respect to the relevant potential updates, thus generating a *potential instance*. Consider, rules R_1, R_3 and the following integrity constraint:

I_2:   ← grandparent(X,Y), is_baby(X)

Upon the insertion of father(craig, john), the only relevant potential updates are grandparent(craig, Y) and grandparent(X, john) and the corresponding potential instances are:

PI_1:   ← grandparent(craig,Y), is_baby(craig)
PI_2:   ← grandparent(X, john), is_baby(X)

Potential instances PI_1 and PI_2 are generated without accessing the database facts and clearly restrict the search space with respect to I_2 because of the presence of specific constants.

The method presented in Lloyd, Sonenberg, and Topor (1987) requires the calculation of two sets, P and N, that represent, respectively, the potential insertions and deletions generated by a given update on the database. A set Θ is then computed, which contains all the most general unifiers of the atoms in P and N with the atoms of corresponding sign in the integrity constraints. The updated database is consistent iff every instance of the integrity constraints with respect to the unifiers in Θ holds in it.

In Bry, Decker, and Manthey (1988), a slightly different strategy is presented. Instead of evaluating the potential instances of the constraints directly, first the potential update is evaluated in order to see if it has an instance which is an effective induced update. For each of those induced updates, the instantiated remainder of the constraint is evaluated.

Recently, renewed attention arose in the field of update propagation building on previous investigations in the area of view maintenance (Gupta & Mumick, 1999). Continuing the work of Griefahn (1997), the author of Behrend (2004) regards integrity checking as an instance of update propagation. In the proposed method, integrity constraints are expressed as propositional predicates that must always be derivable. For example, integrity constraint I_1 would be expressed by the following clauses:

$$ok \leftarrow \sim i_1$$
$$i_1 \leftarrow is\_parent(X), is\_baby(X)$$

where *ok* is a propositional atom that is derivable iff the database satisfies integrity. The database schema is then augmented with new rules that express the incremental evaluation of the new state with respect to a given update, which closely correspond to potential updates. The incrementality of the rules is maximized by rewriting them according to *magic sets* (Bancilhon, 1986) techniques. After the rewriting, however, an originally stratified database may become non-stratified. A reference model (the so-called *well-founded model*, in Van Gelder, Ross, & Schlipf, 1988) for these databases exists, but its computation may be very complex. To this end, a *soft consequence operator* (Behrend, 2003) is then introduced to compute the model of this augmented database. Instead of a symbolic simplification of the original constraints, as, for example, in the method of Nicolas (1982), this method rather provides an efficient way for evaluating the new state of the database. As such, it can be used for an efficient evaluation of constraints that have been simplified by some other method.

Extending Resolution-Based Proof
Procedures for Integrity Checking

All methods and approaches to integrity checking proposed ahead of the publication of Sadri and Kowalski (1988) (and many methods thereafter as well) were
specified, at least in part, by semi-formal descriptions in natural language. Perhaps
the most innovative aspect of the method in Sadri and Kowalski has been that each
step is formalized as an inference step of a resolution procedure. Apart from the
already known backward-oriented reasoning steps in SLD and SLDNF resolution,
Sadri and Kowalski also includes forward reasoning steps, and admits new kinds
of candidate input clauses. Apart from the facts and rules in the database, the Sadri
and Kowalski procedure also considers integrity constraints in denial form as well
as negated facts representing deletions as input.

As suggested in Sadri and Kowalski (1988), and as already mentioned earlier, it is
very convenient to represent integrity constraints in denial form, in other words, as
negations of properties or conditions that should never hold. Now, it is interesting
to note that also Datalog queries are usually represented in denial form. Thus, integrity constraints in denial form can be interpreted as queries whose answer must
be empty. As such, they can be checked against the database by evaluating them as
queries, using a standard query answering procedure such as SLDNF. On the other
hand, unsimplified integrity constraints, when interpreted as queries, usually are
more general and much more complex than ordinary database queries, typically
involving full table scans, potentially huge joins of several tables, nested subqueries,
nested negation and the like. Thus, their evaluation easily becomes prohibitively
expensive, in terms of computation time, storage and CPU resources needed by
standard query evaluation procedures.

Instead of an overly laborious evaluation of integrity constraints in denial form by
backward reasoning from constraints posed as queries, Sadri and Kowalski (1988)
propose to reason forward from given updates through database rules (i.e., clausal
view definitions) towards the bodies of integrity constraints in denial form.

As we have seen already, several other methods also involve forward reasoning for
identifying and simplifying relevant constraints that are potentially violated. For
instance, the method of Lloyd et al. (1987) has such a (semi-formal) forward reasoning phase, which applies the update and its consequences to potentially violated
integrity constraints. A major conceptual difference between the methods in Lloyd
et al. and Sadri & Kowalski (1988) is that, loosely speaking, simplification in the
former consists in applying the update and its consequences only to the constraints.
In the latter, the update and its consequences also are applied to the database. That
way, the search space for evaluating the simplified constraint also shrinks. A simple
example may illustrate this. Let $s(X) \leftarrow q(X)$ be a database rule, "insert q(a)" an
update and $\leftarrow p(X), s(X)$ an integrity constraint which says that the join of the re-

lations p and s must be empty. Forward reasoning according to Lloyd et al. yields the simplified integrity constraint ← p(a), s(a). Forward reasoning with Sadri and Kowalski yields ← p(a). Clearly, the search space for evaluating the latter formula is properly contained in the one for the former, which could in fact be considerably larger, for example, if the s relation is defined not only by the one rule mentioned above, but by several more clauses. They all could take part in the evaluation of the subquery ← s(a), which is not considered at all in the method of Sadri and Kowalski, since it has eliminated this subquery in a single forward reasoning step.

Similarly, the method in Decker (1996) also has a forward reasoning phase which applies the update to the database. An essential difference between the methods of Decker (1996) and Sadri and Kowalski (1988) is that the latter uses a resolution-based proof procedure for each reasoning step, while the former (and also the method in Lloyd et al., 1987) implements the procedural logic of its steps in a way which is not as easily interpreted declaratively, and not as straightforwardly implemented, as in Sadri and Kowalski.

For incorporating each and every step into the resolution procedure, the procedure in Sadri and Kowalski (1988) needed to appeal to meta-logic reasoning for certain steps involving deletions or negative literals in the body of clauses. The rough edges introduced by these meta-reasoning steps have been polished off in a refinement of the procedure in Sadri and Kowalski in Decker and Celma (1994). Essentially, it relies on the use of clauses of the form $\sim A \leftarrow \sim A$ for facts A that are possibly deleted as a consequence of an update. The declarative interpretation of such formulas is tautological: A is not true if A is not true. Their procedural interpretation is: Infer that A has been deleted if all attempts of proving A have finitely failed.

Partial Evaluation

Simplification of integrity constraints with respect to given update patterns resembles *program specialization* by *partial evaluation*, which is the process of creating a specialized version of a given program with respect to partially known input data.

Consider a program P(x,y), where x and y represent the input arguments to P. Partial evaluation of P with respect to a known input value x_0 for x, consists of producing a specialized program $P_{x=x0}(y)$ such that $P(x_0,y_0)$ gives the same result as $P_{x=x0}(y_0)$ for any y_0. A trivial, specialized version may be obtained by inserting $x := x_0$ in front of the code of P, but to produce interesting results in the form of more efficient programs, the knowledge $x=x_0$ must be propagated and employed in the details of P, enabling various semantics preserving transformations. During the last three decades, very sophisticated techniques for partial evaluation have been developed for a variety of programming languages; see Jones, Gomard, and Sestoft (1993) and Jones (1996) for overview.

The analogy to incremental integrity checking is obvious. Assume P is a program that checks consistency of a given database, and assume that the database is specified as D^U, for some database D and update U, plus a Boolean parameter C stating whether the given D is supposed to be consistent; P can thus be written as P(D,U,C). Partial evaluation of P with respect to a specific update $U=U_0$ and C=true, may yield a simplified test for consistency of D^U for any database D. The result obtained in this formulation is a pre-test, but it may alternatively be formulated as post-test.

Applications of these techniques to integrity checking have been investigated in Leuschel and De Schreye (1998), where the authors describe evaluation of integrity constraints in terms of a meta-interpreter written in Prolog, which is then specialized for particular update patterns by a partial evaluator. Only explicit additions and deletions are considered.

The results produced by this method are difficult to compare with other approaches as they depend on heuristics inside the partial evaluator as well as in the meta-interpreter.

Finite Differencing to Database Integrity Control

Finite differencing designates a class of program transformation techniques described for imperative programming languages, which aims at replacing re-evaluation of complex expressions, when their arguments change, by smaller expressions applied for incremental updates. As described in Paige and Koenig (1982), this may be useful for expressions inside loops. For example, the following pseudo-code:

```
for (i=1, i++, i<= n) {E:= i^2; ...}
```

could be transformed in the following way:

```
E=0; for (i=1, i++, i<= n) {E:=E+i+i-1; ...}
```

With a simplified terminology as compared with Paige (1979) and Paige and Koenig (1982), we may say that subexpression "E+i+i-1" represent the difference of "i^2" with respect to update code i++. Supposing that addition is executed significantly faster than multiplication, this transformation may yield a significant speed up of the entire loop. Paige and Koenig provide a general framework for differencing and investigates a number of cases; however, no fully automatic techniques are considered.

Koenig and Paige (1981) and Paige (1982) have considered this principle for database integrity checking (by post-tests) in terms of incremental maintenance of views which, then, are used for simplified tests. Although the possibility of automatic techniques is indicated, the generality of the approach is difficult to judge. The work has had some influence on later research on integrity checking (see, e.g., Qian, 1988), even though only elementary updates (additions and deletions of single tuples) are considered. Paige (1982) includes interesting comparisons with Nicolas (1982) and earlier precursors of simplification techniques.

Methods Based on Rule Annotation

A common assumption in simplification methods is that the update is known during the simplification process. This is typically the case when simplification is done at run time. However, methods that do not need to access the fact base, such as those that are based on potential updates, are capable of producing simplifications also at schema design time, when only the rules and integrity constraints are known. Although it is inconceivable to predict specific updates before they are actually requested, it is reasonable to assume that they will match given *update patterns*. For example, given a relation p with, say, two arguments, one can expect updates such as "insert p(**a**,**b**)" or "delete p(**a**,**b**)", where **a** and **b** are not specific constants, but just placeholders, later to be instantiated by concrete update values. In Henschen, McCune, and Naqvi (1984), the authors propose a simplification method for relational databases allowing such unspecified constants (called *dummy constants*); we adopt here the terminology of Christiansen and Martinenghi (2003) that refers to those constants as *parameters*. The main advantage of simplifying integrity constraints with respect to foreseeable update patterns is that the simplification process, the computation of which typically is very costly, only needs to take place once, instead of each time an update is executed.

Most methods based on this approach consist of two phases. Firstly, there is a *semantic compilation phase* that, in general, produces parameterized templates of simplified constraints. Secondly, actual integrity checks take place at run time whenever an update that matches the pattern is executed. Then, the parameters in the simplified constraints are instantiated with the actual constants in the update, so that concrete instances of already simplified constraints are checked against the database.

Grant and Minker (1990) introduces a principle called *partial subsumption*, originally conceived for semantic query optimization, which is applied, among other things, to produce simplified integrity constraints. *Subsumption* is a well-known sufficient condition for entailment that can be checked with an SLDNF-based algorithm. In other words, it is easy to check whether a clause C subsumes a clause D, and if it does, then C entails D.

Partial subsumption roughly corresponds to the application of the subsumption checking algorithm with an integrity constraint taking the role of C and the body of a rule (or simply the head if the body is empty) as D. As can be easily shown, if an integrity constraint subsumes (the body of a) database predicate, say, p, this indicates the (odd) circumstance that any fact in the extension of p would violate the constraint. Hence, its extension is forced to be always empty. Therefore, instead of a yes/no answer to subsumption, one is rather interested in what remains in the resolution tree generated by the SLDNF procedure; such remaining clause fragments are called *residues* and indicate which other conditions should be met in order to violate the constraint. During the compilation phase, partial subsumption is applied to every predicate and every constraint. Predicates are then annotated with the corresponding residues thus generated. When an update to such a predicate occurs, instead of checking the original constraints, only the instantiated residues need to be checked.

Consider, for example, the constraint $\leftarrow$ student(X,Y), teacher(X,Y), stating that no student of a course is a teacher for that course. The partial subsumption algorithm generates the residue $\leftarrow$ teacher(X,Y) to be attached to the predicate *student*. When the insertion of, say, student(jack, db) is executed, then, instead of checking the original constraint, we only need to check the residue attached to student, instantiated to the constants in the update, for example, $\leftarrow$ teacher(jack, db).

This method applies to single additions and deletions and is described by examples for update transactions. The variable symbols in the residues can be regarded as parameters. However, multiple occurrences of the same parameter in the same relation, or in different relations within the same (transactional) update, are not considered. Changes are modelled as deletions followed by insertions, assuming that all deleted and inserted tuples are known in advance. However, this is not a reasonable assumption for many natural updates, such as, "move all computer science books from shelf 10 to shelf 11" (one should not have to list all such books to perform this update).

The simplification returned by the method described in Grant and Minker (1990) is a necessary and sufficient condition for the satisfaction of integrity in the updated state. In Lee and Ling (1996), the authors propose a different approach in which the output of the simplification procedure is a condition whose satisfaction guarantees the satisfaction of the constraints in the updated state — but not the other way round. In other words, if the generated condition is not met, nothing can be concluded about the consistency of the updated database. In that case, an additional check corresponding to a necessary and sufficient condition is needed. The advantage of using such a sufficient condition is that it may have, in some cases, a lower computational cost than a necessary and sufficient condition. The method calculates a set, called *relevant set*, of literals and attached conditions that may falsify the integrity constraints. If the update in question matches any of the literals in the relevant set and the attached condition succeeds, then the test fails. Otherwise, it is safe to conclude that the update cannot falsify the integrity constraints. For example, for the deductive rules $p(X,Y) \leftarrow a(X,Z), b(Z,Y)$, and $q(X,Y) \leftarrow p(X,Z), c(Z,Y)$, and the constraint $\leftarrow p(X,Y), c(X,Y), X>5$ (taken from Lee & Ling, 1996), the only possible falsifier using relation a is $a(X,Z)$ with the attached condition $X>5$. Therefore, it can immediately be concluded, even without accessing the fact base, that the insertion of $a(1,2)$ cannot violate integrity, since $1>5$ fails. This was not possible with any previously published method.

Some of the limitations common to methods based on induced or potential updates were identified and overcome in Seljée and de Swart (1999). The authors restrict their analysis to databases with no negation and updates consisting of a single insertion or deletion. For such cases, they identify different kinds of redundancies that occur in the three phases of integrity checking methods and show how to eliminate or reduce them. In particular, redundancies *by duplicates* consist in the repetition of certain steps, such as the generation of the same derived updates or the same instances of a constraint. Redundancies in intermediate results in the generation phase are caused by derived updates that eventually will not be needed, since they may be irrelevant or ineffective. Redundancies in the selection of relevant constraints may occur with methods based on potential updates, since some relevant potential updates may not correspond to any induced updates. This kind of redundancy can, of course, only be detected by accessing the fact base. Finally, the evaluation of the constraint instances might involve redundancies in the evaluation of intensional predicates. For example, consider the definitions $parent(X,Y) \leftarrow father(X,Y)$ and $parent(X,Y) \leftarrow mother(X,Y)$. Assume that, for some constraint, the insertion of $father(craig, john)$ generates the constraint instance $\leftarrow parent(X,Y), friend(craig,Y)$. Then, the evaluation of $parent(X,Y)$ would involve exploring both the branch $father(X,Y)$ and $mother(X,Y)$. However, the latter has not been affected by the update and, thus, its evaluation is unnecessary. The method produces (Prolog-like) meta-rules, called *inconsistency rules*, which indicate the optimized check that should be applied upon the execution of a given update. For the described example, the inconsistency rule is as follows:

$inconsistency(father(Z,T)) \leftarrow father(X,Y), friend(Z,Y)$

Pre-Tests and Weakest Preconditions

In this section, we describe methods that produce specialized integrity constraints to be checked *before* the update is executed on the database. In this way, inconsistent database states can be completely avoided. Thus, expensive rollback operations as well as repair actions become unnecessary. Methods featuring early recognition of inconsistency turn out to be particularly efficient for cases in which the update actually violates integrity, and even more so if the update is a complex transaction. More precisely, upon an illegal update, methods based on pre-tests just perform a check, whereas methods based on post-tests require executing the update, performing a consistency check and then rolling back the update.

The proposal of Henschen et al. (1984) brings forward the idea of a pre-test, but just for relational databases without views, not for the deductive case. The method generates, via resolution steps, a series of simplified checks from an integrity constraint I and an update U. If one of these checks succeeds, then U is legal with respect to I. Once the simplified constraints are generated, however, some strategies have to be employed to decide which specific checks are needed and in which order, in other words, redundancies are not eliminated from the generated constraints. Furthermore, and more importantly, failure of all checks does not necessarily imply inconsistency. This means that, in such a case, a sharper method must be used.

In Qian (1988), the author observes the relationship between Hoare's logic (Hoare, 1969; Dijkstra, 1976) for imperative languages and integrity checking. Qian identifies a simplified integrity constraint as a *weakest precondition* for having a consistent updated state. The general idea is as follows. Updates are regarded as a series of simultaneous assignment statements to the database state. For an integrity constraint I, one derives the weakest precondition I_w of I with respect to a given update U such that I is true after U iff I_w is true before U, that is, $D(I_w) = D^U(I)$, for any database state D. Then, I_w is transformed into the form $I' \wedge R$, such that I implies I'. With the hypothesis that I is true before U, one only needs to evaluate the possibly simpler formula R, instead of the original I. The transformation of I_w into $I' \wedge R$ is obtained via *formal differentiation* (Paige, 1979; also called finite differencing, cf. above), that is, a series of rewrite rules that decompose expressions of the relational calculus into simpler sub-expressions. Qian's method works for several kinds of updates; however, it does not allow more than one update action within a transaction to operate on the same relation. Furthermore, no parameterized compile time mechanism is described. Thus, Qian's simplification procedure needs to be run for each specific update.

The idea of integrity constraint simplification based on weakest preconditions was also adopted in Christiansen and Martinenghi (2003) and further extended in Martinenghi (2004). There, it is observed that both the generated weakest preconditions I_w and the original integrity constraints I refer to the database state before the update. Therefore, it is possible to *optimize* I_w by eliminating redundancies from it in two ways: by testing whether a denial in I_w is subsumed by any other denials in I_w or I; by testing whether any literal in I_w can be proved to be redundant. The authors devise a terminating proof procedure based on resolution that is used in the simplification process. The simplifications found in this way are in many cases minimal with respect to the number of literals and as instantiated as possible. It is worth noting that not only does the update language at hand include tuple additions, deletions, and changes, but it also supports parametric transaction patterns and bulk updates. In particular, any set of tuples that can be expressed as the result of a query can be added, deleted, or modified.

Aggregates, such as *sum, count,* and *average,* are not part of standard Datalog and are known to be not first-order expressible. In Das (1992), the author has described an infinitary axiomatization of aggregates that is compatible with the method of Lloyd et al. (1987). In Martinenghi (2004), following, in others words, Cohen, Nutt, and Serebrenik (1999), function symbols are used to express aggregates and denials are enriched with such function symbols and arithmetic operators. The optimization phase is then extended with rewrite rules that take care of these function symbols. Consider, for example, the constraint $\leftarrow$ quarantine(Y), Cnt[patient($\underline{X}$,Y)] > 10, expressing the hospital policy that, for any illness Y that requires quarantine, there must be at most 10 patients; for notational simplicity, we have underlined the variables that are not involved in the "group by" of the aggregate. For the insertion of a generic patient **a** with a generic illness **b**, the obtained simplification is $\leftarrow$ quarantine(**b**), Cnt[patient($\underline{X}$,**b**)] > 9, that is, if illness **b** requires quarantine, then there must be at most 9 patients affected by it before the insertion.

The Relationship Between
Simplification and Query Containment

The simplification problem is strictly related to the *query containment* problem. A query P is said to be contained in a query Q if the answer to P is a subset of the answer to Q in any database state. In principle, a perfect simplification process that eliminates all redundancies from the original integrity constraints can be reduced to a set of query containment decisions. However, query containment is known to be undecidable already for Datalog without negation (Shmueli, 1987). This means that no algorithm can be constructed that outputs a perfect simplification in all cases. The notion of "perfect", mentioned previously, could be based, for example, on the minimality with respect to the size of the simplified constraints, or as well on the size of the search space for checking the simplified constraints. In fact, any such criteria that identify "nothing to check" as the best achievable simplification, still lead to the mentioned undecidability problem. We note, however, that minimality criteria alone do not necessarily cater for more efficiency in all cases. For example, a syntactically minimal constraint does not necessarily always evaluate faster than an equivalent non-minimal constraint, since the amount of required computation may be reduced, such as by adding a join with a very small relation.

Conversely, the availability of a perfect simplification procedure in a given database class entails that query containment is decidable in that class. Query containment has been studied extensively in the literature, where a number of decidable sub-cases have been identified (Florescu, Levy, & Suciu, 1998; Calvanese, De Giacomo, & Lenzerini, 1998; Calvanese, De Giacomo, & Vardi, 2003; Bonatti, 2004). The tight correlation between query containment and simplification suggests that progress in the field of query containment can inspire the construction of even more refined simplification algorithms. However, it should be pointed out that, even if a perfect simplification procedure is unattainable in most contexts, simplifications that contain a slight amount of redundancies may prove very useful in practice too, and are anyhow better than non-simplified checking.

Integrity Maintenance

When updates that violate the integrity constraints are detected, a consistent database state must be restored.

The approaches based on the generation of pre-tests pursue a complete *prevention* of inconsistencies: integrity of the updated state is checked in the state preceding the update and, whenever an illegal update is detected, it is not executed.

When an inconsistency is detected by a method based on the generation of post-tests, integrity needs to be restored via corrective actions. Typically, such an action is a *rollback*, which simply cancels the effects of the unwanted update. Rollbacks usually require costly bookkeeping in order to restore the old state. In this regard, if the update has to be discarded, approaches based on prevention should be preferred.

In other circumstances, an update that violates the constraints can be considered as an operation that is not completely illegal, but that can only be accepted provided that other parts of the database are modified. In this case, a repairing action is needed to change, add or delete tuples of the database in order to satisfy the integrity constraints again. The obtained consistent database is called a *repair*.

Actions that Correct Integrity Violations

Whereas approaches based on prevention or rollback can be completely automated with the methods described in the previous section, repairs may require some intervention. Either the database designer, the user, or an application program may have to indicate how the database should react upon detection of inconsistencies. For very simple (yet common) cases, SQL itself provides some standard reaction policies, such as, for example, CASCADE for foreign keys. For more complex circumstances, the DBMS might need to calculate a corrective action according to given criteria corresponding to the preferences specified by the designer.

The generation of repairs has been considered in the seminal contribution Arenas, Bertossi, and Chomicki (1999) as well as in several subsequent works, such as Greco, Sirangelo, Trubitsyna, and Zumpano (2003), Wijsen (2003), Arieli, Denecker, Van Nuffelen, and Bruynooghe (2004).

Repairing a database means making an inconsistent database comply with the integrity constraints. Preferred repairs are typically those that require a minimal amount of modifications to the database. In Arenas et al. (1999), the possible modifications are deletions and insertions of tuples. In Wijsen (2003), tuple updates are also permitted as a repair primitive. This allows correcting an error within a tuple without deleting other consistent information contained in it.

Most works on repairs are concerned with the problem of answering a query in the presence of inconsistency. Consider, for example, a database containing the facts born(john, 1954), born(john, 1956), born(jack, 1954). Assuming that the birthday must be unique for every person, this database is inconsistent. Two repairs are obtained by dropping the first, respectively, the second tuple. Consider a query asking for all persons born in 1954. In the first repair, the answer only contains "jack"; in the second repair, it also contains "john".

A query answer is *consistent* (or trustable) if it belongs to the intersection of the query answers on *all* repairs. In the previous example, "jack" is a consistent answer, whereas "john" is not. The arising problem in consistent query answering is that, in general, a database can be repaired in infinitely many ways. However, for certain kinds of queries and integrity constraints (*conjunctive queries* and *full dependencies*), Wijsen (2003) has shown that there exists a condensed representation of all repairs, which permits computing all trustable query answers.

In Calì, Lembo, and Rosati (2003), the authors establish decidability and complexity results for the problem of obtaining consistent answers from inconsistent databases under key and inclusion dependencies. In particular, it is shown that the problem is in general undecidable in this context.

With a slightly different terminology, in Greco et al. (2003), the authors define a repair as a minimal set of additions and deletions that make the resulting database consistent. Since there may be several minimal repairs, a polynomial *evaluation function* is used to determine the *preferred repairs*, which are those that minimize that function. The number of preferred repairs may be considerably smaller than the number of repairs. Consequently, trusted answers based solely on the preferred repairs may be larger than those that are based on all repairs. The authors show that a preferred repair can be constructed in polynomial time if the integrity constraints are functional dependencies and the evaluation function measures the cardinality of the repairs. Besides, the repair is unique if the evaluation function measures the number of insertions (or deletions).

In Arieli et al. (2004), the authors reformulate the problem of repairing an inconsistent database in terms of *signed formulae*. In their approach, off-the-shelf applications, such as satisfiability solvers for quantified Boolean formulae (QBF) or constraint logic program solvers, can be used for efficiently computing the repairs. In particular, the problem of finding repairs with minimal cardinality can be converted to the problem of finding minimal Herbrand models for the corresponding *signed theory*. This can then be addressed by a solver, such as any of those described in Eiter, Leone, Mateis, Pfeifer, and Scarcello (1998) or Carlsson, Ottosson, and Carlson (1997). The problem of finding repairs that are minimal with respect to set inclusion corresponds to deciding the satisfiability of appropriate QBFs theories. It can, thus, be solved with tools such as those of Ayari and Basin (2002) or Cadoli, Schaerf, Giovanardi, and Giovanardi (2002). Consider, for example, a database D consisting of the fact p(a) and the integrity constraint I $\leftarrow$ p(X), ~q(X). Clearly, D is inconsistent and can be repaired by dropping p(a) or by adding q(a). For each ground atom p, the authors use a corresponding atom s_p whose intuitive meaning is "switch p". The integrity constraints are mapped into a formula containing such atoms, called the *sign formula*. The formula $s_p \vee s_q$ is the sign formula of I. Its minimal models are { s_p }, { s_q }; they induce, respectively, the updates "remove p(a)", "insert q(a)", which are the minimal repairs of D.

Active Rules for Integrity Checking and Maintenance

Active rules provide a flexible tool that encompasses checking as well as maintenance techniques. Active rules behave according to the event-condition-action (ECA) paradigm, which is commonly represented with the following pseudo-code: WHEN <event> IF <condition> THEN <action>. When a certain event occurs, the rule is *triggered* by that event. Then, the corresponding condition is checked (either before or after the event). Finally, if the condition is satisfied, the action is executed.

In the context of integrity checking and maintenance, active rules can be instructed to react upon given updates (the event), then to check the corresponding (possibly simplified) integrity constraints (the condition), and, finally, if the indicated condition is satisfied, to abort the transaction or repair the database (the action).

The idea of embedding integrity control in active rules is originally described in Ceri and Widom (1990) and has been reconsidered in Ceri, Fraternali, Paraboschi, and Tanca (1994). In the approach of Ceri and his collaborators, for each constraint, an active rule is generated in order to detect constraint violations and to execute database operations that restore consistency. The authors illustrate a framework for translating integrity constraints defined with an SQL-based language into active rules that maintain database integrity. Rule templates are automatically generated that enumerate all operations possibly causing constraint violation. The automation of this process addresses one of the main drawbacks of solutions based on active rules, in other words, that they are typically hand-coded and very difficult to maintain. However, the translation process is only semi-automatic, as the generated rules do not specify the compensating action, which must be added by the user.

In active rule systems, the action of a rule may trigger other rules. This can amount to potential difficulties. For instance, there may be ambiguities on the order of execution of rules, since several rules may be triggered by the same event. Furthermore, certain actions may determine cyclic or even non-terminating rule triggering. In general, it is undecidable whether a given set of active rules is going to terminate. The approach in Ceri and Widom (1990) addresses such situations.

In Ceri et al. (1994), the authors develop a framework for generating active rules that are guaranteed to always terminate in a consistent state. Furthermore, the repaired state is minimally distant from the state reached by the transaction. Significantly, the authors develop techniques for analysing the generated set of active rules, so as to avoid two kinds of unwanted situations. Firstly, they prevent redundant rules that would enforce the same constraint in different ways. Secondly, they avoid conflicting rules, whose action may cause the violation of other constraints.

A survey on different usages of active rules and their interaction with integrity constraints can be found in Ceri, Cochrane, and Widom (2000).

The approaches mentioned above lack, however, a *semantic optimization* phase. Similar to the simplification of integrity constraints for facilitating their evaluation at update time, also active rules can be simplified, based on the assumption that integrity is satisfied before the update. This aspect was considered in Decker (2002), where, from declaratively specified integrity constraints, simplified active rules are generated in the form of SQL triggers. The following example illustrates this approach. Let:

$$\leftarrow married(X, Y), married(X, Z), rel(X, R), legalBig(R), Y \neq Z$$

be an integrity constraint forbidding that some man X be married to two different women Y and Z if the religion of X does not legalize bigamy. First, this denial is re-written to the following normalized form, where variable bindings are expressed by equalities.

$$\leftarrow married(X, Y), married(X1, Z), rel(X2, R), X1=X, X2=X, Y \neq Z, legalBig(X3), X3=R$$

A denial in this normalized form is then translated into an equivalent NOT EXISTS SELECT statement, as follows. All positive literals go into an initial FROM clause of the SELECT statement. The equality literals and the built-in literals form a first group of conjuncts of its WHERE clause. For each of the negative literals, together with its added equations, a separate nested NOT EXISTS SELECT statement is added as a conjunct to the WHERE clause. Thus, we obtain the following SQL statement (we assume, for simplicity, that the i-th column of each relation is called c_i).

NOT EXISTS SELECT 'any' FROM married m1, married m2, rel

WHERE (m2.c1=m1.c1 AND rel.c1=m1.c1 AND m1.c2<>m2.c2 AND

NOT EXISTS SELECT 'any' FROM legalBig WHERE legalBig.c1=rel.c2)

Note that, as usual, the double occurrence of the married relation is normalized apart in SQL by the two identifiers m1 and m2. Also note that a sufficiently intelligent query optimizer will exploit that the NOT EXISTS SELECTs do not ask for all answers that satisfy the query, but just need to know whether any one such answer exists or none.

Next in the translation process, an SQL trigger for insertion or, respectively, deletion is generated, for each positive and each negative database literal in the normalized denial, in analogy to the method in Decker (1987). For our example, we obtain the following triggers:

CREATE TRIGGER ON married FOR INSERT AS

IF NOT EXISTS SELECT 'any' FROM inserted, married m2, rel

WHERE m2.c1=inserted.c1 AND rel.c1=inserted.c1 AND inserted.c2<>m2.c2 AND

NOT EXISTS (SELECT 'one' FROM legalBig WHERE legalBig.c1=rel.c2) ROLLBACK

CREATE TRIGGER ON married FOR INSERT AS

IF NOT EXISTS SELECT 'any' FROM married m1, inserted, rel

WHERE inserted.c1=m1.c1 AND rel.c1=m1.c1 AND m1.c2<>inserted.c2 AND

NOT EXISTS (SELECT 'one' FROM legalBig WHERE legalBig.c1=rel.c2) ROLLBACK

CREATE TRIGGER ON rel FOR INSERT AS

IF NOT EXISTS SELECT 'any' FROM married m1, married m2, inserted

WHERE m2.c1=m1.c1 AND rel.c1=m1.c1 AND m1.c2<>m2.c2 AND

NOT EXISTS (SELECT 'one' FROM legalBig WHERE legalBig.c1=inserted.c2) ROLLBACK

```
CREATE TRIGGER ON legalBig FOR DELETE AS
IF NOT EXISTS SELECT 'any' FROM married m1, married m2, rel
WHERE m2.c1=m1.c1 AND rel.c1=m1.c1 AND m1.c2<>m2.c2 AND
NOT EXISTS (SELECT 'one' FROM deleted WHERE deleted.c1=rel.c2) ROLLBACK
```

Clearly, the simplification is effected by using the built-in predicates *inserted* and, respectively, *deleted*, in place of the original relation names. In most cases, such substitutions reduce the evaluation space dramatically, since potentially huge tables are replaced by tables that only have a single element, viz. the inserted or deleted tuple.

Although not trivial, a careful analysis of the first two of the generated triggers will reveal that they are equivalent, hence one can be dropped. But even if this additional optimization step is not performed, it is clear that the simplified triggers are much less costly than their original form with joins involving potentially huge tables. Moreover, it is easy to see that, with the ROLLBACK in the action part of the trigger, their execution will always terminate properly.

Abductive Approaches to Integrity Maintenance

Instead of using event-condition-action rules or triggers for repairing the database in case it would otherwise be violated by a direct execution of an update request, there is an important alternative approach. It is based on the extension of SLDNF resolution by an abductive interpretation of negation, as described in Eshghi and Kowalski (1989). *Abduction* is a principle of reasoning which, roughly, takes rules and consequences thereof as input and hypotheses the conditions of the rules as facts. This inference principle is somehow inverse to, and in fact easily simulated by, resolution. It is elegantly used in Eshghi and Kowalski (1989) for hypothesising ground negative literals in queries to be true as long as resolution yields no evidence of the contrary. Such evidence is provided by violations of integrity constraints of the form ← P, ~P. These denials, by which the database is extended, express the classical logic law of contradiction, for most general atoms P of all predicates in the database.

Kakas and Mancarella (1990a) use an extension of that proof procedure for computing hypothetical repairs upon requested updates. The repairs consist of sets of ground positive or negative literals which ensure that, when interpreted as updates, the original update request is satisfied without violating integrity (which, as always, is assumed to be satisfied before the update). Similar to extensions of resolution procedures for integrity checking as described above, elaborations of the procedure of Kakas and Mancarella use the original integrity constraints as well as those that express the law of contradiction as additional candidate input clauses. In addition to the negative hypotheses in Eshghi and Kowalski's (1989) procedure, they also use positive ground instances of so-called *abducible* predicates as hypotheses. Intuitively speaking, an abducible predicate is one that has been defined by the database designer to be updatable for the purpose of satisfying update requests.

Further developments of abductive procedures in the lineage initiated by Kakas and Mancarella (1990a), for example, in Kakas and Mancarella (1990b), Toni and Kowalski (1995), Decker (1996), and others, interpret updates as ordinary queries. Upon such queries, the procedures compute answers, together with consistent hypotheses that, when applied to the database as updates, ensure the correctness of the answers that are consistent with the integrity constraints.

As a simple example which illustrates the abductive procedure in Decker (1996), consider the update request to insert p in a database containing the view definition p ← q, r and the integrity constraint ← p, s, where q, r, s are base predicates. The request is represented by the query ← p. Informally speaking, the procedure tries to satisfy this query (i.e., derive the empty clause in a search tree rooted at the query) by assuming suitable ground subquery literals as hypothetical updates. Hence, ← p is first reduced to ← q, r. Then, if both q and r are already present as facts in the database, they can both be resolved without any hypothesis, in other words, the request is already satisfied. If, however, q or r or both are absent, then they need to be assumed as hypothetical input. For example, suppose that q is already a fact in the database, but r is not. Then, q is resolved without further ado, and r is hypothesised as a fact which, when inserted to the database, will satisfy the given update request. However, since inserting r might violate integrity, a subsidiary computation is run in order to check whether integrity remains satisfied or not if r is inserted. To be successful, this consistency check must not end in the empty clause, since that would indicate inconsistency of the hypothesized root. The subsidiary computation in our example reasons forward from the root r ←, which represents the hypothetical update. It first resolves with p ← q, r, yielding p ← q as a resolvent. A further forward step, with the integrity constraint as input clause, yields ← q, s. Then, q is resolved like before, yielding ← s. Now, if s is absent in the database, then nothing more needs to be done, since the subsidiary computation which terminates with this non-empty clause has confirmed the consistency of inserting r. If, on the other hand, s is a fact in the database, then a subsidiary update request for deleting s must be run. Running this request starts at the root ← ~s, which in turn necessitates a subordinate consistency check rooted at the hypotheses ~s ←. This is then resolved against the denial constraint ← s, ~s, yielding the resolvent ← s, after which the consistency check terminates successfully, in other words, s has been consistently assumed to be absent from the database. Hence, the computed update for satisfying the update request of inserting p is to insert r and, if s is in the database, to delete s.

Similar to the use of active rules for maintaining integrity, the behaviour of all abductive procedures for integrity-preserving updates mentioned so far can be characterized as *reactive*, in the sense that these approaches react to impending violations of integrity by actions of repair. In further elaborations, Kowalski, Toni, and Wetzel (1998), Kowalski and Sadri (1999) and others have proposed resolution procedures which, in addition to reactive capacities, also show a proactive behaviour in the manner of programmed agents. Besides ordinary semantic integrity constraints and constraints for abduction, the underlying databases of such agent scenarios (which can be interpreted as shared or individual knowledge bases), may include semantic integrity constraints as in ordinary databases. The constraint denials may also be interpreted as particular goals of the agents, with which their decisions must be consistent, where decision making is implemented as an abductive query answering process that may involve corrective updates in case of integrity violation.

Future Trends

Integrity constraint specification and checking extend naturally to other contexts than relational and deductive databases. We discuss here the differences and peculiarities introduced by the added complexity of other paradigms.

In the next section, we show the difficulties introduced by the hierarchical structure of the data in XML databases. We survey recent results and indicate future lines of investigations in this context.

Later, we discuss integrity checking in databases in which data are not local to a single system, but decentralized and spread over local or wide-area networks of database nodes. The nodes may be homogeneous (e.g., all are relational databases with the same underlying schema) or heterogeneous (e.g., relational, object-oriented and legacy systems may be interconnected). In such database networks, integrity may be violated even when each node is consistent with its own local integrity constraints. We are going to discuss integrity checking strategies for distributed databases as well as data integration systems.

XML Databases

We assume, throughout this section, a basic knowledge of standard XML notions, such as element and path, and the corresponding syntax (Abiteboul, Buneman, & Suciu, 1999).

The study of integrity constraints has been recognized as one of the most important and challenging areas of XML research (Vianu, 2001). Not only are XML integrity constraints important for the same reasons they are in the relational case, but, in addition, XML is being used as a standard for data exchange and as a uniform model for data integration. This suggests several new applications of constraints, such as data semantics preservation during model transformation and detection of inconsistencies in data integration (Arenas & Libkin, 2004; Benedikt, Chan, Fan, Freire, & Rastogi, 2003; Vincent, Liu, & Liu, 2004).

In order to fully characterize integrity checking and maintenance in the context of XML databases, besides constraint verification and optimization tools, such as those that were described for the relational and deductive case, suitable languages for constraint specification, querying and update definition need to be introduced. All such languages and tools need to take into account the added complexity of XML documents, which is twofold. On one hand, XML structures must represent the containment relationship between a node element and its subelements. On the other hand, the position of a subelement relative to other subelements matters, contrary to the usual bag or set semantics of relational and deductive databases.

Constraint and Update Specification

Several proposals of constraint and schema specification languages for XML exist by now.

In current XML specifications, XML Schema definitions (Thompson et al., 2004) include type definitions, occurrence cardinalities, unique constraints, and referential integrity. However, a generic constraint definition language for XML, with expressive power comparable to assertions and checks of SQL, is still not present in the XML Schema specification. XML types, such as DTDs (Bray, Paoli, & Sperberg-McQueen, 1998), are regarded as extended context-free grammars that indicate restrictions on the element structure of a document, though not relating data values across elements. Conventionally, XML integrity constraints are intended as extensions of relational integrity constraints such as keys, foreign keys, and functional dependencies, which depend primarily on the equality of data values. It can be argued, as in the survey Fan (2005), that the difficulty introduced by XML types makes them more complex than relational schemata. Therefore, schema analyses that may be trivial for relational databases are intractable or even undecidable for XML. Works on XML types and typechecking are, for example, Alon, Milo, Neven, Suciu, and Vianu (2003), Buneman, Fan, and Weinstein (2003b), Fan and Libkin (2002), Klarlund, Schwentick, and Suciu (2003) and Vianu (2001). For example, satisfiability of DTD specifications has been studied in Fan and Libkin (2002) and shown to be NP-complete. Further complexity and axiomatization results are given in Fan and Siméon (2003).

In Fan, Kuper, and Siméon (2002), a unified constraint model (UCM) for XML is proposed that captures in a single framework the main features of object-oriented schemata and XML DTDs. In order to generalize relational constraints to XML, one should take into account the hierarchical nature of XML. Primitive keys and foreign keys are supported by XML DTDs through the use of ID and IDREF attributes, respectively. An ID attribute can uniquely identify an element within an XML document; however, unlike keys, one cannot use IDs to, for example, allow a <student> element and a <person> element to use the same SSN as an ID. Also, one can specify at most one ID attribute for an element type, while in practice one may want more than one key. Similar limitations apply also to IDREFs. Besides absolute constraints that hold on an entire XML document, relative constraints that only hold on sub-documents are also relevant. In this regard, key constraints for XML have been thoroughly studied in, for example, Buneman. Davidson, Fan, Hara, and Tan (2003a) and Buneman, Davidson, Fan, Hara, and Tan (2002), where the notion of *relative* key (i.e., key relative to a fragment) is introduced. To illustrate this, consider, for example, an XML document containing information about countries and provinces. The country name can be used as a key for country elements. However, the province name cannot be used as a key for provinces, since (in the real world) different provinces in different countries may have the same name. On the other hand, the province name is indeed a key of provinces relative to country elements, in other words, it is a relative key.

XPath (W3C, 1999) is a query language for XML that uses an *edge-labeled graph* model in which subelements are ordered and attributes are unordered. Paths can roughly be identified with expressions of the form *root/axisStep/…/axisStep*, where *root* specifies the starting point of the expressions (such as the root of a document) and every *axisStep* has the form *axis::nodetest[qualifier]**. An *axis* defines a navigation direction in the XML tree, such as *child, attribute, parent, ancestor, descendant, preceding-sibling* and *following-sibling*. All elements satisfying *nodetest* along the chosen axis are selected, then the *qualifier*(s) are applied to the selection to further filter it. Axes are commonly abbreviated; for example, *path/nodetest* stands for *path/child::nodetest* and *path/@nodetest* for *path/attribute::nodetest*.

The complexity of XPath query evaluation has been studied in, for example, Gottlob, Koch, and Schulz (2003) and Gottlob, Koch, and Schulz (2004).

XQuery (W3C, 2003) is a query language for XML that extends XPath, and is mainly enriched with "FLWOR" expressions (acronym for for, let, where, order by and return), which support iteration and binding of variables to intermediate results. For example, the following query reads "List cds by Decca with price below 20$, including their price and title":

```
<CDs>
{ for $b in doc("cd.xml")/CDs/cd
where $b/label="Decca" and $b/@price<20
return <cd price="{ $b/@price }">{ $b/title }</cd> }
</CDs>
```

General constraints for XML based on simple XPATH expressions interpreted as binary predicates were introduced in Deutsch and Tannen (2001) and referred to as XICs. Functional and inclusion dependencies, as well as (relative) keys and foreign keys can all be expressed as XICs, which is thus one of the most expressive constraint languages studied so far for XML.

Logical query languages based on the XML model are particularly suited for the application of simplification techniques. XPathLog (May, 2004) is an extension of XPath modelled on Datalog. In particular, the XPath language is extended with variable bindings and is embedded into first-order logic to form XPath-Logic. XPath-Logic formulas are built over path expressions, possibly extended to bind selected nodes to variables with the construct "→ Var". XPathLog refers then to the Horn fragment of XPath-Logic formulas. Thanks to its logic-based nature, XPathLog is well-suited for querying XML data and providing declarative specifications of integrity constraints. Furthermore, it can also be used as a rule-based update language.

XUpdate (Laux & Matin, 2000) is an update language for XML that makes extensive use of XPath expressions for selecting elements to be updated afterwards. Several update constructs are available for insertion, modification and deletion of elements.

Other proposals of XML update languages are discussed in Tatarinov, Ives, Halevy, and Weld (2001) and Sur, Hammer, and Siméon (2004), where XQuery-based implemented prototypes of XML update languages are described.

The diffusion of XML in most applicative fields poses a pressing need for providing a wide spectrum of professionals with the ability to handle XML data, including users with minimal programming skills. Intuitiveness and simplicity can be gained with the use of a graphical representation. To this end, the graphical framework of

Figure 1.

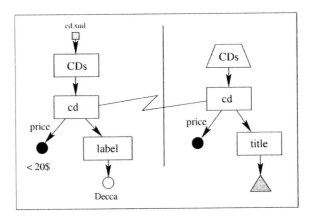

XQBE (XQuery By Example, Braga, Campi, and Ceri, 2005; inspired to Query By Example, Zloof, 1977) has been designed as a tool for querying, transforming, and updating XML data as well as for specifying integrity constraints. XQBE is based on annotated trees, so as to adhere to the hierarchical nature of the XML data model. The figure shows the XQBE version of the XQuery query shown above. The left part matches all the cd elements in the document cd.xml with a price attribute whose value is lower than 20 and a label subelement whose PCDATA content equals "Decca". In the right part, the paths that branch out of a bound node indicate which of its sub-items are to be retained, thus "projecting" the bound node. Only the title and price of the selected cd elements are retained. The grey triangular node below the title node expresses the inclusion into the result of the entire title fragments, obtained by means of projection from each cd element. The binding edge between the cd nodes states that the query result shall contain as many cd elements as those matched in the source part. The trapezoidal node above the cd node means that all the generated cd elements are to be contained into one CDs element.

The equivalent of denials can be specified with such a tool by binding the left part with an <inconsistency/> element in the right part. In this way, complex integrity rules can be specified by domain experts, who, however, may lack knowledge in data definition and manipulation languages. A number of applications can be envisaged, for example, in the medical domain, where health care professionals sharing information stored in clinical records may need to impose constraints, say, on compatibility between medicines and patients' profiles. A graphical framework such as XQBE would provide the domain specialist with a suitable and intuitive tool for the specification of integrity constraints.

Other graph-based languages that allow a natural representation of complex queries over XML data are, for example, XML-GL (Comai et al., 2001), QSByE (Query Semi-structured data By Example, Filha, Laender, & de Silva, 2001) and QURSED (Papakonstantinou, Petropoulos, & Vassalos, 2002).

Constraint Checking

As soon as integrity constraints are specified and updates that modify the state of an XML document collection arrive, integrity needs to be maintained. It should be noted that, in the XML context, constraint checking is also affected by the underlying representation of the data, in other words, whether XML data are stored in a native repository or shredded into relational tables.

Whereas constraint checking in XML has received little attention so far, the closely related consistency and implication problems have been addressed by a large body of research. The consistency problem is to determine, given a DTD and a set of XML constraints, whether there exists a document that both conforms to the DTD and satisfies the constraints. The implication problem (possibly in the presence of a DTD) is to determine, given a set of XML constraints F and another constraint C, whether for any XML document D, if D satisfies F then D satisfies C. In the context of XML, the interaction between XML constraints and DTDs is more complex than in the relational case, as was shown in Fan and Libkin (2002) and in the survey Arenas, Fan, and Libkin (2005). For example, the consistency problem in the presence of unary relative keys and foreign keys is undecidable.

The problem of incrementally validating XML documents with respect to DTD or XML Schema definitions was discussed, for example, in Papakonstantinou and Vianu (2003), where an algorithm is given for validation upon insertions and deletions of leaf nodes, and in Barbosa, Mendelzon, Libkin, Mignet, and Arenas (2004), where insertions of entire subtrees are also considered. In the latter paper, the complexity of document validation with respect to a DTD that includes ID/IDREF constraints has been shown to be low: in O(n log n) time and linear space; logarithmic bounds are achieved for specific classes of DTDs.

Validation of schema, key, and foreign key constraints is also considered in Abrão, Bouchou, Halfield Ferrari Alves, Laurent, and Musicante (2004), where the validator is represented by a bottom-up tree transducer; an update is performed only if it is first accepted by the validator.

An attempt to simplification of general integrity constraints for XML has been made in Benedikt, Bruns, Gibson, Kuss, and Ng (2002), where a code generator produces incremental checking code. The constraints are specified in a procedural fashion with an extension of XML Schema that includes loops with embedded <forbidden> elements that, analogously to denials, indicate what conditions should not hold. The method is based on Qian (1988).

As was previously mentioned, integrity constraint simplification can be reduced to query containment, since integrity constraints can be viewed as queries. To this end, relevant works on containment for various fragments of XPath that would foster a direct simplification approach for XML are, for example, Schwentick (2004) and Neven and Schwentick (2003).

We conclude this section by observing that, if the tree structure of XML constraints is mapped to a relational representation, the simplification techniques that were developed for the deductive and relational case can be applied to XML as well. The schema, the update patterns, and the constraints themselves need to be mapped from the XML domain to the relational model. Basically, each node type, as defined in the DTD, is mapped to a corresponding relational predicate. The representation needs to include information concerning the position of the element relative to the "siblings", since the XML data model is ordered. Furthermore, each element, except for the root node, must be connected to a parent element. The problem of representing semi-structured data in relations has been addressed in a number of contributions, for example, Shanmugasundaram et al. (1999), Deutsch, Fernandez, and Suciu (1999); for a survey see Krishnamurthy, Kaushik, and Naughton (2003).

Integrity in Data Integration Systems

The term *data integration* is applied whenever a collection of (perhaps distributed) databases, called *sources*, are used as a basis for construction of a virtual or materialized database, called *mediator*. With an alternative terminology, the sources are referred to as the *local* databases and the mediator as the *global* database. The mapping from schemata and data at the source to the mediator can be specified in different ways. This topic will not be covered in this chapter; we refer to Lenzerini (2002) for an introduction. Another interesting area in data integration is the automatic detection of similarities between schemata based on similar attribute names and relational structures. Methods that, based on such detections, allow the identification of a possible integration mapping are surveyed in Rahm and Bernstein (2001).

Integrity constraints may be specified both at the sources and at the mediator. Violation of integrity constraints at the mediator is likely to occur unless special actions are taken. A very simple case of data integration occurs when sources D_1, ..., D_n having a common schema (and integrity constraints) are taken into a common database formed as the union of their data $D = D_1 \cup ... \cup D_n$, and with the same integrity constraints. We observe that, even if the individual sources are consistent, the compound database D may not be.

This is the case, for example, when there is a key constraint on the first argument of a relation R, and R includes the tuple <a,b> in D_1 and <a,c> in D_2. Possible solutions are restoring consistency of D by disregarding one of these tuples (perhaps automatically, based on priorities), or relying on techniques for retrieving consistent answers from inconsistent databases, which were considered in a previous section. A recent such approach can be found in Cali, Calvenese, De Giacomo, and Lenzerini (2004); we may also mention de Amo, Carnielli, and Marcos (2002), in which paraconsistent logic is applied for this purpose. In fact, the translation of a query at the mediator level to queries at the sources is a nontrivial matter, and even more so if possible inconsistencies have to be considered; see, for examples, Lenzerini (2002) and Grant and Minker (2002).

Integrity checking for preventing inconsistencies in a database has not been given much attention in data integration, perhaps because in many applications the sources must be taken "as they are" and are not under the control of the mediator. As an exception, in Christiansen and Martinenghi (2004), the authors adapted their simplification technique (described above) to such cases. Under the assumption that the sources satisfy their integrity constraints, and given some integrity constraints to be satisfied at the mediator, simplified integrity constraints are generated for checking the consistency of the mediator, identifying those combinations of tuples across the sources that may produce inconsistencies. Consistency may be restored by applying changes at the sources (if possible) or maintaining at the mediator level a database of simulated deletions (or perhaps other modifications).

In the simple example above with identical schemata and a key constraint as indicated, each R tuple in source D_i needs to be compared to those of D_1, ..., D_{i-1}, D_{i+1} ..., D_n. This may be an expensive test in the general case, but it cannot be reduced any further. However, if each source (perhaps excluding D_i) is relatively small, these tests become manageable. Global assumptions about the combination of sources may lead to drastic improvements. If, for example, the key sets of R for the different sources are known to be pairwise disjoint, the test degenerates to *true*, in other words, the mediator is always trivially consistent.

Integrity Checking in Distributed Databases

In this section, we address some of the complications of integrity checking in distributed databases (abbr.: DDBs). First, we give a brief survey of the state of the art, particularly in fragmented databases. Then, we sketch some new ideas for approaching integrity checking in DDBs, particularly in replicated databases.

In a DDB, the stored data are transparently spread over multiple nodes in a network. (We do not consider non-transparent distribution such as in federated or mirrored databases.) The data in a DDB are either *fragmented* (sometimes: "partitioned") or *replicated* over several network nodes (mixtures of fragmentation and replication are also conceivable). Fragmentation means that different tables or disjoint sets of rows or columns of tables (respectively corresponding to horizontal and vertical fragmentation) reside on different nodes. Replication means that multiple copies of a data item exist, one at each node. For simplicity, we only consider *homogeneous* distribution in this section, in other words, all database nodes conform to the same schema. For a primer on motivations, advantages and potential problems of data distribution, we refer the reader to Özsu and Valduriez (1999).

Due to the complexity of managing data distribution, integrity checking in DDBs is highly complex as well. Apart from questionable recommendations to use triggers for integrity maintenance in the distributed case, it is hardly supported at all in commercial databases. Also research has brought forward relatively little, when compared to the non-distributed case. Many papers deal with problems of consistency of transactions, concurrency or replication in DDBs, such as, the synchronization of the evolution of data at different nodes. But relatively few thorough studies exist for the problem of maintaining semantic consistency in DDBs as specified by integrity constraints.

Transparency of distribution means that users and applications neither notice nor have to take into account that the underlying data actually are distributed. Integrity checking can be (and often is) conceived as an application on top of the DBMS. Thus, also the simplified evaluation of integrity constraints in DDBs could in principle take advantage of distribution transparency. However, to implement integrity checking in DDBs by transparently running simplified queries could easily induce an unnecessarily high burden of additional network communication and coordination. Also, possibly lots of redundant checking may occur if simplified integrity constraints were evaluated in each network node. Moreover, rolling back updates in the event of integrity violation would incur possibly unaffordable expenses of complex recovery actions at several or all network nodes.

Therefore, it is advisable to implement integrity checking not on top of, but as a module of the middleware that drives the data distribution. (We do not consider the alternative case that, instead of a middleware, distribution functionality would be embedded in the proprietary DBMS core code of a particular vendor.) Inside the middleware, knowledge about the given distribution structure can be taken into account for constraint simplification. Clearly, that would not be possible if distribution were transparent to integrity checking.

When data are fragmented over several nodes, the problem is not just to reduce the checking space, in other words, the amount of accessed stored data, as in the non-distributed case. Also the number of nodes to be involved in the evaluation process should be kept as low as possible, as well as the amount of necessary communication and coordination, such as, the data transferred across the network during integrity checking and maintenance. Each of these three dimensions needs to be minimized for simplifying integrity evaluation in DDBs.

Each of the dimensions just mentioned is minimized in Ibrahim's approach. Roughly, the idea is to first describe the fragmentation of tables, rows and columns by so-called *fragmentation rules*, otherwise known as, logical expressions which capture the structure of the data distribution. Then, the constraints are rewritten and split up into *fragment constraints*, in accordance with the fragmentation rules, such that they can be evaluated locally at the nodes where the corresponding data fragments reside, instead of having to evaluate integrity globally. Additionally, simplification methods as described in Nicolas (1982) and others can be applied to the fragment constraints, with regard to a given update or update pattern. Overviews and analytical discussions of Ibrahim's work can be found in Ibrahim (2001), Ibrahim, Gray, and Fiddian (2001), and Ibrahim (2002).

In Ibrahim's work, data replication in DDBs is not considered. In the remainder of this section, we describe a first attempt to design an approach to the maintenance of integrity in replicated DDBs.

Clearly, evaluating each relevant constraint, or rather simplified versions thereof, at each replica would yield an immense amount of redundant checking. Assuming that all replica are consistently synchronized, it should suffice to check integrity just in one of the replica nodes, for example, in the *primary copy*, in case there is such a designated node in the network. Synchronization of replica, however, may be eager or lazy, optimistic, or pessimistic, or of several other characteristics (cf. Muñoz, Irún, & Decker, 2005, for more). Therefore, it is tempting to intertwine a stepwise process of integrity checking with the particularities of the replication protocols at hand, for avoiding unnecessary additional rounds of protocol interaction in the network. But that would entail a very unpleasant dependency of integrity checking from the given protocols and would thus yield insular solutions which lack a sufficient degree of generality and portability.

A solution which is independent of protocols is to wait with integrity checking until the synchronization process has come to a halt, and only then evaluate simplified versions of relevant constraints, at some node. A particular advantage of this solution is that integrity checking can be elegantly parallelized, by assigning the evaluation of different constraints to different nodes which then can work simultaneously and complementarily on the evaluation of integrity. However, this solution is disadvantageous in case of integrity violation, since then, all of the synchronized new states in each replica have to be undone, and a reverse synchronization would have to take place for re-installing the old state.

A solution to the problem of having to undo the new state of all nodes in a replicated DDB in case of integrity violation is to install the new state only in one designated node (ideally, again, a primary copy or master replica), evaluate integrity in that same node and commit the update to be executed in the rest of the network only after integrity has been shown to be satisfied. If integrity is violated, then only the one updated node has to be reset. On the other hand, this solution does not allow the parallelization of integrity evaluation as sketched before. Moreover, doing integrity checking at the new state of one node before replicating this state to all others introduces an additional measure of laziness of replication, which may be unwanted in DDBs for which the eagerness of replication is crucial.

Thus the question is: What could constitute a practical compromise between the parallelization of integrity checking by assigning different constraints to different nodes, on one hand, and avoiding laborious rollbacks by doing all of integrity checking at a single node, on the other? In principle, the answer to that question is deceptively simple. If the DDB is not very update-intensive or note very prone to integrity violation but needs to be highly responsive and available also in case of undergoing updates, then parallelization is advisable. If not, then focusing integrity checking on a single site is preferable. Of course, mixed forms of both solutions are easily conceivable. For instance, integrity constraints (which may well be in the hundreds or more) can be assigned to a much more limited number of nodes, each of which could be the designated master for some region of the network.

Integrity checking in replicated DDBs is much more complicated, however, in case there is no single designated master copy which is the "owner" of (some region of) the networked database, but different tables (or even different rows or columns of tables) are assigned different owner nodes. Then, the evaluation of some constraint in one node may involve communication with other nodes that are the owners of data to be accessed. In general, the idea is to minimize the amount of additional network communication as much as possible. Hence, the assignment of a constraint I to a particular node should be such that this node can be expected to need less communication with other nodes for evaluating I than others. Fortunately, this probability can in many cases be conveniently determined already at schema specification time, assuming that the ownership of data is specified together with the schema and the specification of the data distribution structure. More generally, the evaluation of integrity constraints can be assigned to nodes also dynamically, which allows one to take into account the given update, the resulting constraint simplifications, the current network load, the present alive state of nodes, and other runtime parameters.

None of the ideas for integrity checking in replicated databases as sketched above have been investigated in detail yet, let alone implemented or tried out in practice. In other words, this section can also be read as a first outline of a research programme to be pursued in future work.

Conclusion

In this chapter we have reported on the main achievements obtained by research in the field of integrity checking and maintenance. We have shown that significant improvements can be achieved both in terms of efficiency and robustness with the application of the described methods. For the so-called simplification methods, we have emphasized the differences between compile time and run time approaches as well as pre-tests and post-tests. In particular, we have indicated the assumptions that characterize such methods. To this end, it is important to consider that the correctness of all integrity checking strategies addressed in this chapter relies on the common assumption that integrity is satisfied in the database state before the update. However, it should be interesting to investigate to which extent this assumption could be relaxed, perhaps in terms of a *paraconsistent* logic approach which would be able to work reasonably well even in the presence of contradictory information or in case integrity is not entirely satisfied.

We have shown the relationship between integrity maintenance and view updating. Also, we have discussed the relevant aspect of database repairs as well as possible implementations in terms of active rules.

Integrity checking and maintenance have reached a considerable degree of maturity for relational and deductive databases. However, up to now, commercial DBMSs are far from being fully equipped with general integrity checking/maintenance mechanisms.

In the emerging fields of XML databases and distributed databases, these research topics are, with few exceptions, still young and unripe.

We have addressed the general state of the art in the distributed case, distinguishing between the two main subcases of partitions and replications of relational tables. For the former case, the basic approach in the relational, non-distributed case has been generalized in some theoretical research contributions, but nothing at all has found its way into the products of commercial database vendors. In fact, not even foreign key constraints are supported by distributed databases in practice. For the latter case, hardly anything has been done yet in the research community, and even less so in database products, apart from work-related to replication consistency, which, however, is not expressible as a semantic integrity constraint in the usual sense. For the restricted case of full replication, we have outlined a first approach to reduce an unnecessary multiplication of integrity checking at each replica node of a distributed database network.

For XML databases, we have described different languages and paradigms for specifying integrity constraints, possibly with the help of a graphical tool, and we have provided a wide spectrum of references that report on complexity and tractability results for a number of problems related to integrity checking and schema validation.

The definition as well as the treatment of general integrity constraints would allow the specification of complex business rules directly on the schema of an XML document. However, no standard exists in this direction. In fact, there is still a substantial amount of research to be done in this area.

References

Abiteboul, S., Buneman, P., & Suciu, D. (1999). *Data on the Web: From relations to semistructured data and XML.* Morgan Kaufmann.

Abiteboul, S., Hull, R., & Vianu, V. (1995). *Foundations of databases.* Addison-Wesley.

Abrão, M., Bouchou, B., Halfeld Ferrari Alves, M., Laurent, D., & Musicante, M. (2004, August 29-30). Incremental constraint checking for XML documents. In *Proceedings of Database and XML Technologies, 2nd International XML Database Symposium, XSym 2004,* Toronto, Canada (LNCS 3186, pp. 112-127). Springer.

Alon, N., Milo, T., Neven, F., Suciu, D., & Vianu, V. (2003) XML with data values: Typechecking revisited. *J. Comput. Syst. Sci., 66*(4), 688-727.

Apt, K. R., Blair, H. A., & Walker, A. (1988) Towards a theory of declarative knowledge. In *Foundations of Deductive Databases and Logic Programming* (pp. 89-148). Morgan Kaufmann.

Arenas, M., Bertossi, L., & Chomicki, J. (1999, May 31-June 2). Consistent query answers in inconsistent databases. In *Proceedings of the 18th ACM SIGACT-SIGMOD-SIGART Symposium on Principles of Database Systems*, Philadelphia, PA (pp. 68-79). ACM Press.

Arenas, M., Fan, W., & Libkin, L. (2005) Consistency issues in XML databases. In *Inconsistency Tolerance* [result from a Dagstuhl seminar] (LNCS 3300, pp. 15-41). Spinger-Verlag.

Arenas, M., & Libkin, L. (2004) A normal form for XML documents. *ACM Trans. Database Syst, 29*, 195-232.

Arieli, O., Denecker, M., Van Nuffelen, B., & Bruynooghe, M. (2004, February 17-20). Database repair by signed formulae. In *Foundations of Information and Knowledge Systems, 3rd International Symposium, (FoIKS 2004)*, Wilhelminenburg Castle, Austria (LNCS 2942, pp. 14-30). Springer.

Ayari, A., & Basin, D. (2002). QUBOS: Deciding quantified Boolean logic using propositional satisfiability solvers. In *Proceedings of the 4th International Conference on Formal Methods in Computer-Aided Design (FMCAD'02)* (LNCS 2517, pp. 187-201). Springer.

Bancilhon, F. (1986). Naive evaluation of recursively defined relations. In M. L. Brodie, & J. Mylopoulos (Eds.), *On knowledge base management systems (Islamorada): Integrating artificial intelligence and database technologies* (pp. 165-178). Springer Verlag.

Barbosa, D., Mendelzon, A., Libkin, L., Mignet, L., & Arenas, M. (2004, March 30-April 2) Efficient incremental validation of XML documents. In *Proceedings of the 20th International Conference on Data Engineering, (ICDE 2004)*, Boston (pp. 671-682). IEEE Computer Society

Behrend, A. (2003). Soft stratification for magic set based query evaluation in deductive databases. In *Proceedings of the 22nd ACM SIGMOD-SIGACT-SIGART symposium on Principles of database systems* (pp. 102-110). ACM Press.

Behrend, A. (2004). Soft stratification for transformation-based approaches to deductive databases. PhD thesis, University of Bonn.

Behrend, A., Manthey, R., & Pieper, B. (2001, March 7-9) An amateur's introduction to constraints and integrity checking in SQL3. In *Datenbanksysteme in Büro, Technik und Wissenschaft (BTW), 9*. GI-Fachtagung, Oldenburg (pp. 405-423). Informatik Aktuell, Springer.

Benedikt, M., Bruns, G., Gibson, J., Kuss, R., & Ng, A. (2002). Automated update management for XML Integrity Constraints. In *Online Informal Proceedings of PLAN-X Workshop*. Retrieved from http://homepages.inf.ed.ac.uk/wadler/planx/planx-eproceed/papers/E00-1591816349.ps

Benedikt, M., Chan, C. Y., Fan, W., Freire, J., & Rastogi, R. (2003, June 9-12) Capturing both types and constraints in data integration. In *Proceedings of the 2003 ACM SIGMOD International Conference on Management of Data*, San Diego, CA (pp. 277-288). ACM.

Bernstein, P. A., & Blaustein, B. T. (1982, June 2-4). Fast methods for testing quantified relational calculus assertions. In *Proceedings of the 1982 ACM SIGMOD International Conference on Management of Data*, Orlando, FL (pp. 39-50). ACM Press.

Bonatti, P. A. (2004, June 14-16). On the decidability of containment of recursive datalog queries — Preliminary report. In *Proceedings of the 23rd ACM SIGACT-SIGMOD-SIGART Symposium on Principles of Database Systems*, Paris, France (pp. 297-306). ACM Press.

Braga, D., Campi, A., & Ceri, S. (2005). XQBE (XQuery by example): A visual interface to the standard XML Query Language. *ACM Transactions in Database Systems, 30*(2), 398-443.

Bray, T., Paoli, J., & Sperberg-McQueen, C. (1998). *Extensible Markup Language (XML) 1.0.* W3C.

Bry, F., Decker, H., & Manthey, R. (1988, March 14-18). A uniform approach to constraint satisfaction and constraint satisfiability in deductive databases. In *Advances in Database Technology — EDBT '88, Proceedings of the International Conference on Extending Database Technology*, Venice, Italy (LNCS 303, pp. 488-505). Springer.

Buneman, P., Davidson, S., Fan, W., Hara, C., & Tan, W. (2002). Keys for XML. *Computer Networks, 39*(5), 473-487.

Buneman, P., Davidson, S., Fan, W., Hara, C., & Tan, W. (2003a). Reasoning about keys for XML. *Information Systems, 28*(8), 1037-1063.

Buneman, P., Fan, W., & Weinstein, S. (2003b). Interaction between path and type constraints. *ACM Trans. Comput. Log., 4*(4), 530-577.

Cadoli, M., Schaerf, M., Giovanardi, A., & Giovanardi, M (2002). An algorithm to evaluate quantified Boolean formulae and its experimental evaluation. *Automated Reasoning, 28*(2), 101-142.

Calì, A., Calvanese, D., De Giacomo, G., & Lenzerini, M. (2004) Data integration under integrity constraints. *Information Systems, 29*(2), 147-163.

Calì, A., Lembo, D., & Rosati, R. (2003). On the decidability and complexity of query answering over inconsistent and incomplete databases. In *PODS '03: Proceedings of the 22nd ACM SIGMOD-SIGACT-SIGART Symposium on Principles of Database Systems* (pp. 260-271). ACM Press.

Calvanese, D., De Giacomo, G., & Lenzerini, M. (1998). On the decidability of query containment under constraints. In *Proceedings of the 17th ACM SIGACT-*

SIGMOD-SIGART symposium on Principles of database systems (pp. 149-158). ACM Press.

Calvanese, D., De Giacomo, G., & Vardi, M. (2003, January 8-10). Decidable containment of recursive queries. In *Database Theory (ICDT 2003), 9th International Conference*, Siena, Italy (LNCS 2572, pp. 330-345). Springer.

Carlsson, M., Ottosson, G., & Carlson, B. (1997). An open-ended finite domain constraint solver. In *Proceedings of the 9th International Symposium on Programming Languages, Implementations, Logics, & Programs (PLILP '97)* (LNCS 1292). Springer.

Carmo, J., Demolombe, R., & Jones, A. (2001). An application of deontic logic to information system constraints. *Fundam. Inform., 48*(2-3), 165-181.

Ceri, S., Cochrane, R., & Widom, J. (2000, September 10-14). Practical applications of triggers and constraints: Success and lingering issues (10-Year Award). In *Proceedings of 26th International Conference on Very Large Data Bases (VLDB 2000)*, Cairo, Egypt (pp. 254-262). Morgan Kaufmann.

Ceri, S., Fraternali, P., Paraboschi, S., & Tanca, L. (1994). Automatic generation of production rules for integrity maintenance. *ACM Trans. Database Syst., 19*(3), 367-422.

Ceri, S., Gottlob, G. & Tanca, L. (1990). *Logic programming and databases.* New York: Springer-Verlag.

Ceri, S., & Widom, J. (1990, August 13-16). Deriving production rules for constraint maintainance. In *Proceedings of the 16th International Conference on Very Large Data Bases,* Brisbane, Queensland, Australia (pp. 566-577). Morgan Kaufmann.

Chomicki, J. (1995). Efficient checking of temporal integrity constraints using bounded history encoding. *ACM Trans. Database Syst., 20*(2), 149-186,

Christiansen, H. & Martinenghi, D. (2003, August 25-27) Simplification of database integrity constraints revisited: A transformational approach. In *Logic Based Program Synthesis and Transformation, 13th International Symposium (LOPSTR 2003)*, Uppsala, Sweden, revised selected papers (LNCS 3018, pp. 178-197). Springer.

Christiansen, H., & Martinenghi, D. (2004, February 17-20), Simplification of integrity constraints for data integration. In *Foundations of Information and Knowledge Systems, 3rd International Symposium* (FoIKS 2004), Wilhelminenburg Castle, Austria (LNCS 2942, pp. 31-48). Springer.

Codd, E. F. (1972). Further normalization of the database relational model. In R. Rustin (Ed.), *Courant Computer Science Symposium 6: Data Base Systems* (pp. 33-64). Englewood Cliffs, NJ: Prentice-Hall.

Cohen, S., Nutt, W., & Serebrenik, A. (1999, May 31-June 2). Rewriting aggregate queries using views. In *Proceedings of the 18th ACM SIGACT-SIGMOD-SIGART Symposium on Principles of Database Systems*, Philadelphia, PA (pp. 155-166). ACM Press.

Comai, S., Damiani, E., & Fraternali, P. (2001). Computing graphical queries over xml data. *ACM TOIS, 19*(4), 371-430.

Cowley, W., & Plexousakis, D. (2000, September 10-14). Temporal integrity constraints with indeterminacy. In *Proceedings of 26th International Conference on Very Large Data Bases (VLDB 2000)*, Cairo, Egypt (pp. 441-450). Morgan Kaufmann.

Das, S. (1992). *Deductive databases and logic programming*. Addison-Wesley.

de Amo, S., Carnielli, W. A., & Marcos, J. (2002, February 20-23). A logical framework for integrating inconsistent information in multiple fatabases. In *Foundations of Information and Knowledge Systems, 2nd International Symposium, (FoIKS 2002)* Salzau Castle, Germany (LNCS 2284, pp. 67-84). Springer.

Decker, H. (1987). Integrity enforcement on deductive databases. In *Expert Database Conferences 1986 Proceedings*, Charleston, SC (pp. 381-395).

Decker, H. (1996, September 2-6). An extension of SLD by abduction and integrity maintenance for view updating in deductive databases. In M. J. Maher (Ed.), *Logic Programing, Proceedings of the 1996 Joint International Conference and Syposium on Logic Programming*, Bonn, Germany (pp. 157-169). MIT Press.

Decker, H. (2002). Translating advanced integrity checking technology to SQL, in Database integrity: Challenges and solutions (pp. 203-249). Hershey, PA: Idea Group Publishing.

Decker, H., & Celma, M. (1994, June 13-18). A slick procedure for integrity checking in deductive databases. In P. V. Hentenryck (Ed.), *Logic Programming, Proceedings of the 11th International Conference on Logic Programming*, Santa Margherita Ligure, Italy (pp. 456-469). MIT Press.

Deutsch, A., Fernandez, M., & Suciu, D. (1999, June 1-3). Storing semi-structured data with STORED. In A. Delis, C. Faloutsos, & S. Ghandeharizadeh (Eds.), *SIGMOD 1999, Proceedings ACM SIGMOD International Conference on Management of Data*, Philadelphia, PA (pp. 431-442). ACM Press.

Deutsch, A., & Tannen, V. (2001 September 15). Containment and integrity constraints for XPath. In M. Lenzerini, D. Nardi, W. Nutt, & D. Suciu (Eds.), *Proceedings of the 8th International Workshop on Knowledge Representation meets Databases (KRDB 2001)*, Rome, Italy.

Dijkstra, E., W. (1976). *A discipline of programming*. Prentice-Hall.

Eiter, T., Leone, N., Mateis, C., Pfeifer, G., & Scarcello, F. (1998) The KR system dlv: Progress report, comparisons and benchmarks. In *Proceedings of the 6th International Conference on Principles of Knowledge Representation and Reasoning* (KR'98), (pp. 406-417). Morgan Kaufmann Publishers.

Eshghi, K., & Kowalski, R. (1989, June 19-23). Abduction compared with negation by failure. In G. Levi, & M. Martelli (Eds.), *Logic Programming, Proceedings of the 6th International Conference,* Lisbon, Portugal (pp. 234-254). MIT Press.

Fagin, R. (1977). Multivalued dependencies and a new normal form for relational databases. *ACM Transactions in Database Systems, 2*(3), 262-278.

Fan, W. (2005, August 22-26). XML constraints: Specification, analysis, and applications. In H. Christiansen, & D. Martinenghi (Eds.), *LAAIC'05, Proceedings of the 1st International Workshop on Logical Aspects and Applications of Integrity Constraints. Included in Proceedings of DEXA 2005, International Workshop on Database and Expert Systems Applications,* Copenhagen, Denmark (pp. 805-809). IEEE Computer Society.

Fan, W., Kuper, G. M., & Siméon, J. (2002). A unified constraint model for XML. *Computer Networks, 39*(5), 489-505.

Fan, W., & Libkin, L. (2002). On XML integrity constraints in the presence of DTDs. *Journal of the ACM, 49*(3), 368-406

Fan, W., & Siméon, J. (2003). Integrity constraints for XML. *Journal Comput. Syst. Sci,. 66*(1), 254-291.

Filha, I. M. R. E., Laender, A. H. F., & da Silva, A. S. (2001, April 9-11). Querying semistructured data by example: The QSByE interface. In E. Simon, & A. K. Tanaka (Eds.), *Proceedings of the International Workshop on Information Integration on the Web* (pp. 156-163), Rio de Janeiro, Brazil.

Florescu, D., Levy, A., & Suciu, D. (1998, June 1-3). Query containment for conjunctive queries with regular expressions. In *PODS '98. Proceedings of the ACM SIGACT-SIGMOD-SIGART Symposium on Principles of Database Systems,* Seattle, WA (pp. 139-148). ACM Press.

Godfrey, P., Grant, J., Gryz, J. & Minker, J. (1998). Integrity constraints: Semantics and applications. In J. Chomicki, & G. Saake (Eds.), *Logics for Databases and Information Systems* (pp. 265-306). Kluwer.

Godfrey, P., Gryz, J., & Zuzarte, C. (2001). Exploiting constraint-like data characterizations in query optimization. In W. G. Aref (Ed.), *SIGMOD 2001 Electronic Proceedings.* Retrieved from http://www.acm.org/sigmod/sigmod01/eproceedings.

Gottlob, G., Koch, C., & Pichler, R. (2003, June 9-12). The complexity of XPath query evaluation. In *Proceedings of the 22nd ACM SIGACT-SIGMOD-SI-*

GART Symposium on Principles of Database Systems, San Diego, CA (pp. 179-190).

Gottlob, G., Koch, C., & Schulz, K. (2004, June 14-16). Conjunctive Queries over Trees. In A. Deutsch (Ed.), *Proceedings of the 23rd ACM SIGACT-SIGMOD-SIGART Symposium on Principles of Database Systems*, Paris, France (pp. 189-200).

Grant, J., & Minker, J. (1990). Integrity constraints in knowledge-based systems. In *Knowledge Engineering Applications* (Vol. 3, pp. 1-25). McGraw Hill.

Grant, J., & Minker, J. (2002). A logic-based approach to data integration. *Theory and Practice of Logic Programming, 2*(3), 323-368.

Greco, S., Sirangelo, C., Trubitsyna, I., & Zumpano, E. (2003, July 16-18). Preferred repairs for inconsistent databases. In *7th International Database Engineering and Applications Symposium (IDEAS 2003)*, Hong Kong, China (pp. 202-211). IEEE Computer Society.

Grefen, P. W. P. J. & Apers, P. M. G. (1993). Integrity control in relational database systems — An overview. *Data Knowl. Eng., 10*, 187-223.

Griefahn, U. (1997). *A uniform approach to the implementation of deductive databases*. PhD dissertation, University of Bonn.

Gupta, A. & Mumick, I.S. (1999) *Materialized views: Techniques, implementations, & applications.* MIT Press.

Henschen, L., McCune, W., Naqvi, S. (1984). Compiling constraint-checking programs from first-order formulas. In H. Gallaire, J. Minker, & J. Nicolas, (Eds.), *Advances in database theory* (Vol. 2., pp. 145-169). New York: Plenum Press.

Hoare, C. A. R. (1969). An axiomatic basis for computer programming. *Communications of the ACM, 12*(10), 576-580. ACM Press.

Ibrahim, H. (2001). An overview of integrity constraints enforcement for a distributed database. In *Proceedings of the International Conference Parallel and Distributed Processing Techniques and Applications (PDPTA)* (Vol. 2, pp. 822-828). CSREA Press.

Ibrahim, H., Gray, W. A., & Fiddian, N. J. (2001). Optimizing fragment constraints — A performance evaluation. *Int. J. Intell. Syst., 16*(3), 285-306.

Ibrahim, H. (2002). A strategy for semantic integrity checking in distributed databases. In *Proceedings of the 9th International Conference on Parallel and Distributed Systems (ICPADS 2002)* (pp. 139-144). IEEE Computer Society.

Jones, N. D. (1996). An introduction to partial evaluation. *ACM Comput. Surv., 28*(3), 480-503.

Jones, N. D., Gomard, C. K., & Sestoft, P. (1993). *Partial evaluation and automatic program generation.* Prentice Hall International.

Kakas, A., & Mancarella, P. (1990a, August 13-16). Database updates through abduction. In D. McLeod, R. Sacks-Davis, & H.-J. Schek (Eds.), *16th International Conference on Very Large Data Bases*, Brisbane, Queensland, Australia (pp. 650-661). Morgan Kaufmann.

Kakas, A., & Mancarella, P. (1990b, August 6). Knowledge assimilation and abduction. In J. P. Martins, & M. Reinfrank (Eds.), *Truth maintenance systems, ECAI-90 Workshop*, Stockholm, Sweden (LNCS 515, pp. 54-70). Springer.

Klarlund, N., Schwentick, T., & Suciu, D. (2003). XML: Model, schemas, types, logics, and queries. In J. Chomicki, R. van der Meyden, & G. Saake (Eds.), *Logics for Emerging Applications of Databases [outcome of a Dagstuhl seminar]*. Springer.

Koenig, S., & Paige, R. (1981, September 9-11). A transformational framework for the automatic control of derived data. In *Proceedings of the 7th International Conference of Very Large Data Bases*, Cannes, France (pp. 306-318). IEEE Press.

Kowalski, R., & Sadri, F. (1999). From logic programming towards multi-agent systems. *Ann. Math. Artif. Intell., 25*(3-4), 391-419.

Kowalski, R., Toni, F., & Wetzel, G. (1998). Executing suspended logic programs. *Fundam. Inform., 34*(3), 203-224.

Krishnamurthy, R., Kaushik, R., & Naughton, J. F. (2003, September 8). XML-SQL query translation literature: The state of the art and open problems. In Z. Bellahsene, A. B. Chaudhri, E. Rahm, M. Rys, R. Unland (Eds.), *Database and XML Technologies, 1st International XML Database Symposium*, Berlin, Germany (LNCS 2824, pp. 1-18). Springer.

Laux, A., & Matin, L. (2000). *XUpdate working draft.* Retrieved from http://www.xmldb.org/xupdate

Lee, S., & Ling, T. (1996, September 3-6). Further improvements on integrity constraint checking for stratifiable deductive databases. In T. M. Vijayaraman, A. P. Buchmann, C. Mohan, & N. L. Sarda (Eds.), *VLDB'96, Proceedings of 22nd International Conference on Very Large Data Bases*, Mumbai, Bombay, India (pp. 495-505). Morgan Kaufmann.

Lenzerini, M. (2002, June 3-5). Data integration: A theoretical perspective. In L. Popa (Ed.), *Proceedings of the 21st ACM SIGACT-SIGMOD-SIGART Symposium on Principles of Database Systems*, Madison, WI (pp. 233-246). ACM.

Leuschel, M., & De Schreye, D. (1998). Creating specialised integrity checks through partial evaluation of meta-interpreters. *J. Log. Program., 36*(2), 149-193.

Lloyd, J. (1987). *Foundations of logic programming* (2nd ed.). Berlin: Springer.

Lloyd, J., Sonenberg, L., & Topor, R. (1987). Integrity constraint checking in stratified databases. *J. Log. Program., 4*(4), 331-343.

Martinenghi, D. (2004). Simplification of integrity constraints with aggregates and arithmetic built-ins. In *FQAS'04 Proceedings* (LNCS 3055, 348-361). Springer.

May, W. (2004). XPath-Logic and XPathLog: A logic-programming-style XML data manipulation language. *Theory and Practice of Logic Programming, 4*(3), 239-287.

Mayol, E. & Teniente, E. (1999, November 15-18). A survey of current methods for integrity constraint maintenance and view updating. In P. P. Chen, D. W. Embley, J. Kouloumdjian, S. W. Liddle, & J. F. Roddick (Eds.), *Advances in Conceptual Modeling: ER '99 Workshops on Evolution and Change in Data Management, Reverse Engineering in Information Systems, and the World Wide Web and Conceptual Modeling,* Paris, France (LNCS 1727, pp. 62-73). Springer.

Muñoz, F., Irún, L., & Decker, H. (2005). An overview of different approaches to database replication. In J. H. Doorn, V. E. Ferraggine, & L. C. Rivero (Eds.), *Encyclopedia of Database Technologies and Applications.* Hershey, PA: Idea Group.

Neven, F., & Schwentick, T. (2003, January 8-10). XPath containment in the presence of disjunction, DTDs, and variables. In D. Calvanese, M. Lenzerini, & R. Motwani (Eds.), *Database Theory — ICDT 2003, 9th International Conference,* Siena, Italy (LNCS 2572, pp. 315-329). Springer.

Nicolas, J.-M. (1982). Logic for improving integrity checking in relational data bases. *Acta Informatica, 18,* 227-253.

Nilsson, U., & Małuzyński, J. (1995). *Logic, programming and prolog* (2nd ed.). John Wiley & Sons Ltd.

Özsu, M. T. & Valduriez, P. (1999). *Principles of distributed database systems* (2nd ed.). Prentice-Hall.

Paige, R. (1981). *Formal differentiation.* Ann Arbor, MI: UMI Research Press.

Paige, R. (1982, December 14-17). Applications of finite differencing to database integrity control and query/transaction optimization. In H. Gallaire, J.-M. Nicolas, & J. Minker (Eds.), *Advances in data base theory* (Vol. 2), based on the *Proceedings of the Workshop on Logical Data Bases,* Centre d'études et de recherches de Toulouse, France (pp. 171-209). New York: Plenum Press.

Paige, R., & Koenig, S. (1982). Finite differencing of computable expressions. *ACM Trans. Program. Lang. Syst., 4*(3), 402-454.

Papakonstantinou, Y., Petropoulos, M., & Vassalos, V. (2002, June 3-6). Qursed: Querying and reporting semistructured data. In M. J. Franklin, B. Moon, & A. Ailamaki (Eds.), *Proceedings of the 2002 ACM SIGMOD International Conference on Management of Data,* Madison, WI (pp. 192-203). ACM.

Papakonstantinou, Y., & Vianu, V. (2003). Incremental validation of XML documents. In *Proceedings of ICDT* (pp. 47-63).

Qian, X. (1988, February 1-5). An effective method for integrity constraint simplification. In *Proceedings of the 4th International Conference on Data Engineering* (pp. 338-345). Los Angeles, CA: IEEE Computer Society.

Rahm, E., & Bernstein, P. A. (2001). A survey of approaches to automatic schema matching. *VLDB Journal, 10*(4), 334-350.

Sadri, F., & Kowalski, R. (1988). A theorem-proving approach to database integrity. In J. Minker (Ed.), *Foundations of Deductive Databases and Logic Programming* (pp. 313-362). Morgan Kaufmann.

Schwentick, T. (2004). XPath query containment. *SIGMOD Record, 33*(1), 101-109.

Seljée, R., & de Swart, H. (1999). Three types of redundancy in integrity checking: An optimal solution. *Data Knowl. Eng., 30*(2), 135-151.

Shanmugasundaram, J., Tufte, K., Zhang, C., He, G., DeWitt, D., & Naughton, J. (1999, September 7-10). Relational databases for querying XML documents: Limitations and opportunities. In M. P. Atkinson, M. E. Orlowska, P. Valduriez, S. B. Zdonik, & M. L. Brodie (Eds.), *VLDB '99, Proceedings of 25th International Conference on Very Large Data Bases*, Edinburgh, Scotland, UK (pp. 302-314). Morgan Kaufmann.

Shmueli, O. (1987). Decidability and expressiveness aspects of logic queries. In *Proceedings of the 6th ACM SIGACT-SIGMOD-SIGART Symposium on Principles of Database Systems* (pp. 237-249). ACM Press

Sur, G., Hammer, J., & Siméon, J. (2004). UpdateX — An XQuery-Based Language for processing updates in XML. In *Programming Language Technologies for XML (PLANX04)* (pp.40-53).

Tatarinov, I., Ives, Z., Halevy, A., & Weld, D. (2001). Updating XML. *Presented at the SIGMOD Conference.*

Thompson, H. et al. (2004). *XML Schema. W3C Recommendation.* Retrieved from http://www.w3.org/TR/xmlschema1

Toni, F., & Kowalski, R. (1995, June 13-16). Reduction of abductive logic programs to normal logic programs. In L. Sterling (Ed.), *Logic Programming, Proceedings of the 12th International Conference on Logic Programming*, Tokyo, Japan (pp. 367-381). MIT Press.

Ullman, J. D. (1988). *Principles of database and knowledge-base systems I & II.* Computer Science Press.

Van Gelder, A., Ross, K., & Schlipf, J. (1988, March 21-23). Unfounded sets and well-founded semantics for general logic programs. In *Proceedings of the 7th ACM SIGACT-SIGMOD-SIGART Symposium on Principles of Database Systems*, Austin, TX (pp. 221-230). ACM.

Vianu, V. (2001, May 21-23) A Web odyssey: From Codd to XML. In *Proceedings of the 20th ACM SIGACT-SIGMOD-SIGART Symposium on Principles of Database Systems*, Santa Barbara, CA. ACM.

Vincent, M., Liu, J., & Liu, C. (2004). Strong functional dependencies and their application to normal forms in XML. *ACM Trans. Database Syst., 29*(3), 445-462.

W3C. (1999). *XML Path Language (XPath)*. Retrieved from http://www.w3.org/TR/xpath

W3C. (2003). *XML query use cases*. Retrieved from http://www.w3.org/TR/xmlquery-use-cases

Wijsen, J. (2003, January 8-10). Condensed representation of database repairs for consistent query answering. In D. Calvanese, M. Lenzerini, & R. Motwani (Eds.), *Database Theory — ICDT 2003, 9th International Conference*, Siena, Italy (LNCS 2572, pp. 378-393). Springer.

Zloof, M. (1977). Query-by-example: A data base language. *IBM Systems Journal, 16*(4), 324-343.

Chapter XI

Predictive Approach for Database Schema Evolution

Hassina Bounif

Ecole Polytechnique Fédérale de Laussanne, Switzerland

Abstract

Information systems, including their core databases need to meet changing user requirements and adhere to evolving business strategies. Traditional database evolution techniques focus on reacting to change to smoothly perform schema evolution operations and to propagate corresponding updates to the data as effectively as possible. Adopting such a posteriori solution to such changes generates high costs in human resources and financial support. We advocate an alternate solution: a predictive approach to database evolution. In this approach, we anticipate future changes during the standard requirements analysis phase of schema development. Our approach enables potential future requirements to be planned for, as well as the standard, determining what data is to be stored and what access is required. This preparation contributes significantly in the ability of the database schema to adapt to future changes and to estimate their relative costs.

Introduction

Information systems, including their core databases, need to meet changing user requirements and adhere to evolving business strategies. Roughly 90% of data-driven applications undergo changes during their lifecycles. These changes affect the applications, the schema and their corresponding data.

Schema changes are complex; schema evolution is implemented either by restructuring, versioning, or modifying the original schema using restricted evolution primitives or adopting views on the top of it. These database evolution techniques are *a posteriori* solutions — they react to changes rather than plan ahead for them. Adopting such solutions to implement this process of change generates high costs in human resources and in financial support: when the schema has to be changed, much work is required. Besides managing the changes on the schema, applications and data linked to it need to be adapted as well. Thus, due to the high cost, schema evolution is often avoided. There are a number of consequences of this, including:

1.   Evolution is put off until later, which sometimes results in applications that are inefficient, or even incorrect, until that change is made.

2.   Been pushed off until absolutely necessary, the evolution may wind up causing considerably more problems in the end; for the users will have to make really wide scale changes for having waited so long for the evolution.

Fortunately, there is another solution to solve these problems: design for schema evolution a priori. This is the solution presented in this chapter. Specifically, we suggest an original approach for schema evolution, in which the change factors are taken into consideration and incorporated in the design phase of the schema before the database is created. Therefore, our approach is called an *a priori* schema evolution solution in contrast with existing a posteriori solutions. This new a priori approach is multidisciplinary, that is, it involves several fields such as data mining and ontology to study and analyse the requirements on which the schema is developed and that are classified into two categories: current and potential future requirements. In addition, this approach is compatible with any data model, facilitates the work of designers and helps them save time and fund on the evolution of their databases.

This chapter explains briefly the articulation of this new approach for database schema evolution. It comprises four main sections. The following section reviews schema evolution background. The next section, gives an overview of the predicting approach and presents the preliminary results to demonstrate the feasibility of the proposed approach. A section on future trends are then presented; and the final section is a summary of the important points established in this chapter and introduces perspectives on the future work.

Background

The concepts in an application are not static; as the application use changes, the meaning of the concepts changes as well. However, the schemas in which these concepts are encoded are often very difficult to change because the data models used for schema modelling produce structures and data integrity, that are specific for applications running at the present time on the top of these schemas (Spyns et al., 2002). As a result, schemas are often inappropriately seen as invariable.

Change statistics have shown that change on database schema is an important issue independent of the data model. According to Sjoberg (1993), in a one year survey on a large set of relational database schemas for HMS (a health management system), the number of relations and fields increased significantly. Every relation on the schema was modified and there were 35% addition operations more than deletions. For example, of the total of 148 relations, 1646 fields have been added; whereas in 116 other relations belonging to the same schema, 1158 have been deleted.

Changes on the database occur during both its creation and its maintenance for several reasons, such as:

- The perception of the real world and its modelling are complex tasks to cope with, especially if the real world is continuously evolving.

- The part of the real world that is of interest keeps on expanding because of the new user or application requirements have arisen.

- Another important reason is the technological cause of database evolution, such as changes in the functionality of the supporting computer infrastructure, or internal system reorganization tailored for improvement in performance.

Intuitively, schema evolution means the ability of a database schema to undergo changes over time without any loss of the extant data. System evolution is categorized into two main groups: vertical evolution within a single database system and horizontal evolution involving the integration of two or more cooperative database systems at the same time. An example of horizontal evolution is the research work presented in McBrien and Poulovassilis (2002) that considers the evolving of a global schema derived from a set of schemas belonging to heterogeneous database architectures.

The vertical evolution, the focal point of this research work, is a complex operation in which the schema changes, while keeping the consistency of its corresponding data, includes the study of how that change influences:

- Earlier database schema

- Data already stored in the database

- Existing applications running on the early schema

When carrying out an evolution operation, existing database evolution approaches tend to accept the changes by introducing modifications on the databases systems instead of preparing the database for evolution in order to minimize both modifi-cation operations and costs. The proposed solutions for schema evolution can be categorized mainly by following one of these approaches: *modification, versioning, views* and *combining the approaches*.

Modification

The original schema and its corresponding data are replaced by a new schema and new data. This approach does not adhere exactly to the schema evolution definition because it may lead to loss of information (e.g., some existing data may no longer be relevant in the new setting and may therefore be discarded) and makes the applications that use the original schema inconsistent with the new database schema. This makes the approach unsuitable in most real cases, and increases the intervention of a database administrator to handle the changes. Yet it remains the most popular method with existing DBMS (database management systems). There are three techniques in the way the modification is performed: the immediate, the deferred, and the mixed. The cost of the modification corresponds to the number of schema components to be changed. A case of modification operation on the schema: before and after modification operation is illustrated in Figure 1. The attribute Host is deleted and the attribute location is replaced by table which name is location. This new table holds two attributes: Id_location and Address. Consequently,

Figure 1. An example of the modification approach

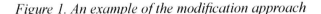
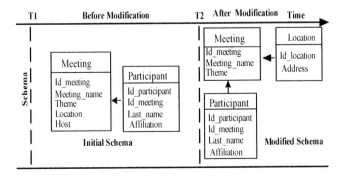

after modification, existing applications are incompatible with the new schema and information is lost.

Versioning

The original schema and its corresponding data are preserved and continue to be used by existing applications simultaneously with the new version. The new schema incorporates the desired changes. There are many different techniques that help organize schema versions such as sequential versions and parallel versions; accordingly applications can access data in a versioned schema environment. The storage of the versioned schemas is realized by either (1) versioning by copy or by (2) versioning by difference (Loomis, 1995). The versioning by copy consists of creating a new version of the schema that contains both the modified parts and the parts that do not undergo changes during the evolution process. Whereas, in versioning by difference, the new version retains only the parts of the initial schema that have been changed.

Generally, the versioning approach presents performance problems. It generates high costs and requires much memory space as the database evolves, which is difficult to support in the long term. A case of versioning by copy operation on the schema is illustrated in Figure 2. The old schema and the new version are both accessible to the users and existing and new applications running on top of them. Although, the table Meeting has been changed, there is no loss of data. It is still possible to access data before and after the evolution of the schema. The table Participant exists with the same structure in both versions. However, to make queries on this table, the DBMS (dtabase management system) has to detect on which schema, the current or the version, the table Participant has to be acceded for processing. This slows down performances.

Figure 2. An example of the versioning approach

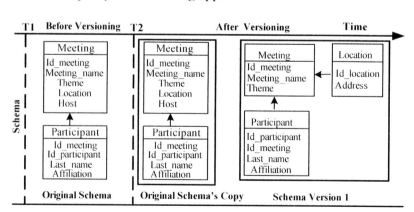

Views

A view is a derived table; that is, it is a saved query. It can be derived either from database tables or from other views created on the schema. It is a mechanism which enables a virtual reconstruction of the schema, in other words, it makes possible to change the schema without stopping the database and without destroying its coherence with existing applications. However, view supports limited kinds of evolution; for example, they can only handle restructuring and deletions, but not additions. A view cannot be a sub-schema in order to allow the extension operations of the schema (Bertino, 1992).

Bellahsène (1996) proposes an approach using a view mechanism to simulate schema modification without the reorganisation of the database. The views, called virtual schemas, are a set of virtual classes that evolve separately from the core schema and guarantee the access to existing applications. The union of the views and the core schema form a federated schema. This underlines the autonomous character of the views. In Figure 3, some attributes such as theme, duration, and location belonging to the tables Meeting and Participant have been masked but not deleted. As a result in the view, there remains only the attributes required by the user which are Meeting_name and Last_name.

Combining the Approaches

Evolution mechanisms provided by the previous described three approaches (modification, versioning, and views) are complementary to each other. Therefore, some works on database evolution develop approaches that combine them. For example, Benatallah (1999) proposes an approach that combines modification and version-

Figure 3. An example of views approach

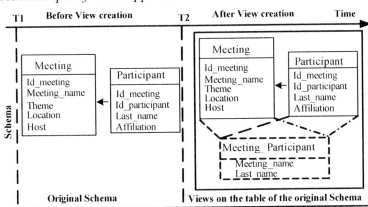

ing approaches to benefit from their positive aspects for better management of the database schema evolution. In his work he uses either the modification or the versioning depending on the type of changes required on the schema. If the schema loses properties such as the case of a suppression operation, a new version of the schema is generated. Otherwise the schema is modified. In his solution, a technique for adapting instances to the schema after an evolution is proposed. It is based on the importance evaluation of an object version existence in a schema; in other words, if an object is important vis-à-vis of existing applications, then a version of it is created. Otherwise it is modified. He also developed a language that describes the relationships between two consecutive schema states. Finally, his approach allows the reorganization of the database by removing old versions that are not any more relevant for the applications.

All existing approaches complement each other, but are insufficient solutions to schema evolution. For instance, in the modification approach, changing the schema, may lead to loss of information. Whereas in the versioning approach, replication of the schema avoids data loss, it however creates complex navigation through the different generated versions and slows down the DBMS (database management system). Whereas combining solution allows avoiding the above mentioned problems, it is at the same time, characterized by the complexity and the onerous mechanisms to be executed. Instead, if these solutions anticipated the changes, they would have studied and adapted storage structures and access methods, as well as avoided heavy mechanisms. In short, these approaches are a posteriori solutions. They allow us to track changes done on the database in order to understand the evolution process that occurred.

Database Refactoring

Some people confuse schema evolution with schema refactoring while there is an important distinction between them. Database refactoring is to make simple changes on the database schema in order to improve its design while retaining both its behavioural and informational semantics. However, these changes do not extend the schema with additional features (Ambler, 2005). The refactoring technique was initially applied on the code (Fowler et al., 2001). Database refactoring is a part of agile methodologies in which requirements are not fixed at the system up-front. The design phase of the system is extended and the changes are allowed to occur even late at the development phase. There are several types of database refactoring grouped in a catalog called *Database Refactoring Catalog* (Ambler & Sadalage, 2005) which are respectively:

- Stored procedure refactorings such as *Add Parameter*
- Structural refactorings such as *Merge Columns, Merge Tables, Rename Columns*
- Architectural refactorings such as *Encapsulate Table With View*
- Performance refactorings such as *Add Mirror Table*
- Data quality refactorings such as *Apply Standard Codes* and *Introduce Lookup Table*
- Referential integrity refactorings such as *Introduce Cascading Delete*
- Transformations (non refactorings) *Introduce View* and *Update Data*

Predictive Schema Evolution Approach

The predictive approach for database schema evolution suggests a new perspective on the problem of schema evolution that consists in preparing for evolution by anticipating changes before they occur: potential changes are inspected and integrated into the schema for future use. The reason that no one offered this solution before is because it is based on prediction and people used to think that prediction was not always certain and realizable. But with the new prediction techniques especially in data-mining field, this judgment is not present anymore. The following two examples compare the predictive approach with a classical approach in which potential future requirements are not considered. The first example is illustrated in Figure 4; it represents the modelling of a simple case of scientific meeting in which

Figure 4. Modelling a simple case of scientific meeting with both classical and predictive approaches

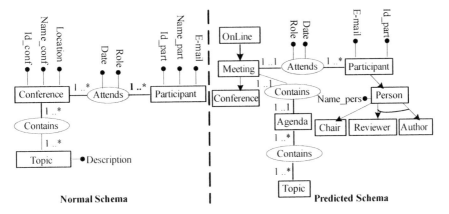

Figure 5. Second example of modeling a simple case of scientific meeting

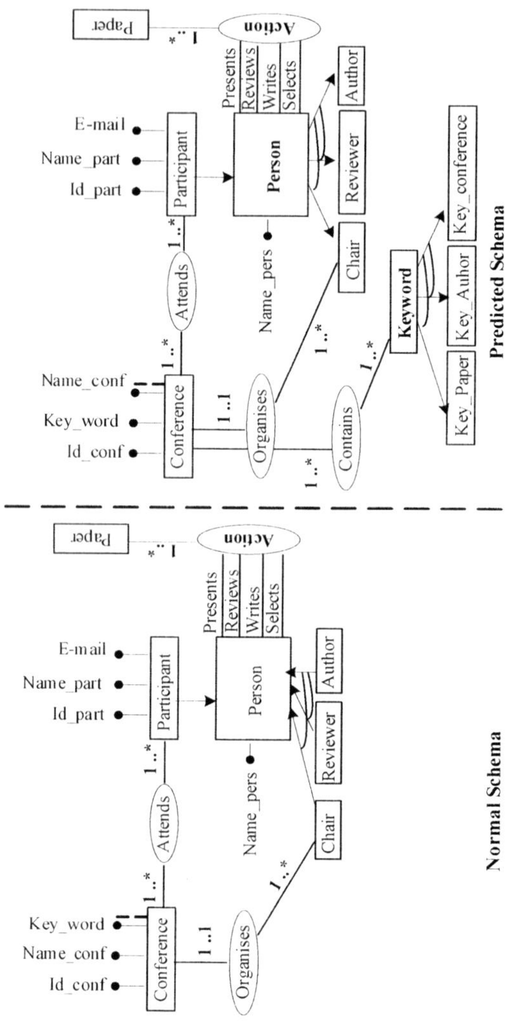

the requirements are both to determine (1) the people participating to a conference and (2) the topic of the considered conference.

Conception in a classical approach is realised with three entities and two binary relations, whereas in the predictive approach, conception entails ten entities and three binary relations. The difference in conception between the two approaches shows that in the predictive schema, entities are already prepared for future use. The sources of the anticipated information are the requirements ontology used in the requirements analysis phase.

In the second example, Figure 5 represents the modelling of the same case. The requirement is to determine the topic of a conference using key words. In a classical approach, key word is a multi-valued attribute that belongs to the entity conference; whereas in the predictive approach, key word is not considered as an attribute. It represents an entity whose name is KeyWord having three sub-entities Key_Paper, Key_Author and Key_Conference that inherit its properties. Consequently, KeyWord conceived as an entity allows retrieving more information from the database.

From the last two examples, we can see that people will still use the normal schema because it translates their current requirements. However, anticipating a predicted schema that supports additional requirements is as useful as important for both the users and the designers. The predictive approach is based on three modelling levels: the ontological level, the conceptual level and finally the logical level. To illustrate this point, we consider the previous example that represents the model-ling of a simple case of scientific meeting in which the requirement is to determine the people participating to a conference. This is illustrated in Figures 6, 7, and 8 respectively.

Figure 6. The ontological level of the predictive approach

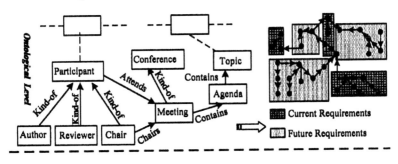

Figure 7. The conceptual level of the predictive approach

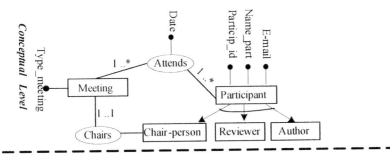

Figure 8. The logical level of the predictive approach

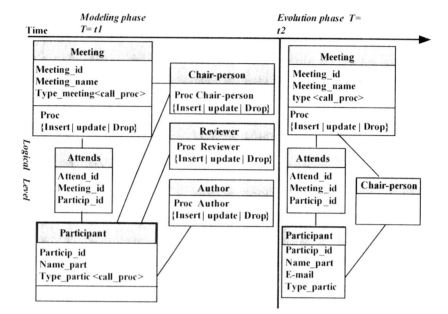

- **The ontological level:** at this level, several design suggestions about the entities, attributes and relationships are provided to the database designers.

- **The conceptual level:** these suggestions, called potential future requirements, are included into the conceptual schema of the database to be modelled.

- **The logical level:** the conceptual schema is converted as it is into a logical schema. However, the tables and attributes that correspond to future requirements are not functional yet. They are included in the schema but cannot be acceded by the DBMS. However, in the evolution phase, these accompanying structures are accepted or rejected based on their relevance with the future state.

Classes of Users

When elaborating this approach, two main categories of database designers have been taken into consideration. The first category is designers who carefully conceive a database schema. Currently, such designers use tools such as computer-aided design (CAD) and CASE tools for schema design such as DBMAIN and they invest a considerable time in the design process. Their main objective is to obtain a schema that accepts changes with a minimum of modification on it. Such users are thinking of such possibilities as part of their design process. Thus they would be amenable to create their system using the predictive approach. By formalizing the thought process they are going through anyway, these designers can avoid the redesign process.

The second category is designers that might not initially spend time in the database design; we accommodate them by allowing them to use our predictive approach when they redesign the schema. First, they employ reverse engineering to understand the database schema before launching any changes on it. The data model produced is called a reverse engineered (RE) data model (Kroenke, 2004). This model cannot be considered as a conceptual schema because it converts all the logical schema tables to entities without making distinction between data tables and the other tables of the schema whose function is to join tables. This model is not a logical schema because some important schema information is lost during the conversion process such as in the case for foreign keys. Then a dependency graph is used to show the dependency among schema components. For example, a change in a table might affect relationships, views, triggers, stored procedures and existing applications. These impacts need to be known before changing the schema (Kroenke, 2004). With the predictive approach, designers do not need to build such a graph because the requirements ontology allows recognising all those dependencies.

Predictive Approach Objectives

The main objectives are:

- Investigating potential future requirements
- Determining a schema in which possible changes are already integrated
- Evaluating the cost of changes to be assigned to a database schema that includes potential future requirements
- Reducing schema evolution process at the logical level to modifications operations that the DBMS is able to achieve
- Adapting the schema to the changes without loss of data

Predictive Approach Advantages

The predictive approach is beneficial for both designers and end-users even if it requires from them to change their behaviour. From the side of designers, it reduces

Figure 9. The three main phases of the predictive approach

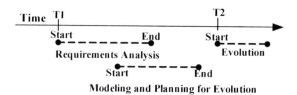

considerably their efforts and time in designing a flexible schema. From the side of end-users, it saves the funding reserved for schema changes.

The process is divided into three main phases (requirements analysis, modelling and planning for evolution, and finally evolution) which we study briefly in the following sections. The two first phases overlap: the initial conceptual database schema produced in the modelling phase is used in the requirements analysis phase.

Requirements Analysis

Traditional information system design begins with a requirements analysis phase. In this phase, the designer of the system defines what the requirements are for the system, both in terms of what data are to be stored, and what access is required.

Our approach for schema evolution works in the same way. However, this a priori schema evolution solution in contrast with existing a posteriori solutions differs by explicitly including in the analysis to be performed besides the current requirements, additional requirements called potential future requirements.

These new requirements are potential future needs that might emerge during the lifecycle of the database. Similar to the use of foresight scenarios in commercial and non-commercial organizations—that managers have adopted to project and explore significant opportunities in order to ensure the success and growth of their organizations—our idea is to find out possible future requirements to ensure an anticipated evolution of the database schema. This investigation operation is performed within the organization to be modelled, within the relevant external knowledge that may be found in domain ontology and database schemas that, at some extent, describe the activity domain of the organization to be modelled. Finally, Web pages that are connected to the activity domain are also worth being explored.

We propose to model requirements with a structured method based on domain ontology called a requirements ontology because in this approach, several complex tasks with data mining techniques need to be accomplished and several challenges such as the definition of potential future requirements, have to be surmounted as well.

We are not interested in the requirements process and its associated specification templates that are applied usually in the construction of a new system. However, we require that the resulting output of these tasks is to be defined in terms of requirement ontology.

The word "ontology" comes from philosophy in which its purpose is the metaphysical description of the existence of beings. However, in computer science, several research communities define the ontology as a formal specification of the conceptualization of the real world and therefore, are using it in information systems integration, evolution, and management of changes that could occur on them. We summarize the reasons for the choice of ontology in our research as follows:

1. Formulating requirements in natural language often leads to ambiguity in terms' meanings; an ontology is machine-readable and provides concepts that are clearly defined with a precise semantics.

2. The knowledge conveyed by the domain of ontology, is vast and propitious in modelling the perception of the real-world: the designers, who use ontology in the process of their database schemas modelling at developing time, increase the quality of conceptual analysis (Guarino & Schneider, 2002a, 2002b)) and decide the changes orientation taken by the schemas.

3. Domain ontology represents a generic knowledge that can be reused by different kinds of applications related to the domain definition.

4. Domain ontology has the advantage of describing and explaining a whole domain and not just the part(s) related to given running applications.

5. Conceptual schemas and ontologies are quite similar in the sense that both consist of conceptual schemas and rules that manage them (Jarrar et al., 2003). However, for databases, conceptual schemes are intended to be used during design phase, whereas ontologies are used and accessed at run time with applications (Jarrar et al., 2003).

6. An ontology provides a domain theory independently from the structure of the applications. Consequently, an ontology is categorized between a knowledge base (KB) and a database schema.

7. Ontology often reuses and extends existing ontologies.

So far, we have presented the direction, the priority and the reasons of this research work. The next step is to go forward and explain the proposed solution.

Requirements Ontology Definition

A requirement ontology (RO) is a domain ontology that represents a new way to model user's requirement for a database schema to be modelled and evolves over time. Intuitively, it is defined as a set of metadata schemas for the database to be modelled. It consists of two kinds of partitions, the ones representing current requirements and the ones corresponding to potential future requirements, called respectively Current Domain and Future Domain. This is illustrated in Figure 10.

In this ontology, requirements are expressed with concepts and their relationships, the components of domain ontology. For example, if a database designer needs to create a database for meetings, the requirement ontology associated to this database is containing concepts and relations such as MEETING, PARTICIPANT, ROOM and AGENDA concepts and IS, HAS relations types and so on. The set {C, R, S, F} expresses respectively concepts, relations, constraints, cost function.

- **Concepts and constraints:** C represents a set of concepts {c1, c2,..., cn} that belong to the domain ontology, and each concept has one or several attributes with one or several values. However, one attribute is devoted to identify the nature of the concept whether it is a concept that belongs to current requirement or to potential future requirements. This attribute is called nature_concept and can take one of the two values: c for current and f for potential future. S describes explicit semantic constraints applied on concepts and instances, such as allowed domain values and cardinalities. A concept cannot be repeated on the requirements ontology. Each concept is unique with its attributes and constraints. For example the meeting concept has the following attributes nature_concept, name, theme, meeting_date, duration, location, and host. As constraints on attributes, for example, duration belongs to a float type whereas the attribute meeting_date belongs to date type.

Figure 10. The requirements ontology partitioned into current and potential future requirements

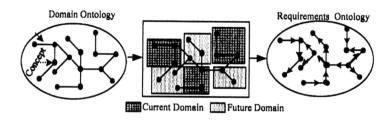

- **Relations:** R is a set of relations between two concepts of C, and each relation between two concepts equals to 1. There are four kinds of relations: hierarchic identified by the label "kind-of" which expresses the specialization of one concept regarding another and inherits attributes from this super concept, composition identified by the label "has" which expresses that a concept is a part of another concept, descriptive in which is possible to define several types of relations and is identified by a verb form and finally reflexive, that allows self-loops in which an arc whose endpoints are the same concept. For example: kind-of (meeting, conference) is a hierarchic relation, has (meeting, utterances) is a composition relation, lives (Person, Country), originates (Person, Country) and represents (Person, Country) are descriptive relations and finally invites (Person, Person) is a reflexive relation.

- **Cost function:** Similar to larger object classes, larger concepts are generally more costly concepts since they need more time and effort to be modified. The cost function, F, estimates the costs related to the selection of concepts and their relationships from the requirements ontology. It is a function of input concepts size, and their relations weight and output quantity. Its value is the cost of making that output giving those input size and weight.

Methodology for Building this Ontology

There is no absolute way to model and build an ontology. A range of techniques and approaches have been reported in the literature (Corcho & Fernández López, 2003; Gomez et al., 2003; Gruber, 1993; Mirzaee et al., 2004; Uschold et al., 1996). However, the best method depends on the purpose of the ontology and the goals that is expected to be fulfilled. The requirements ontology has two functions:

1. Aiding the requirements determination
2. Supporting the design and the evolution of the schema

Our methodology for building it consists of four main phases (see Figure 11):

- **Knowledge acquisition and pre-processing:** consists of schemas collection and preparation
- **Data mining algorithms and informal conceptualization:** in which semantic relations are extracted from schema data sets repository in an unsupervised way and used as output for the informal conceptualization of the ontology from scratch.

Figure 11. The process of building requirements ontology is divided into four main phases: Phase 1, from specifications to the construction of data-sets repository, Phase 2, data mining algorithms, Phase 3, refining or revising the resulted knowledge and Phase 4, the formal conception

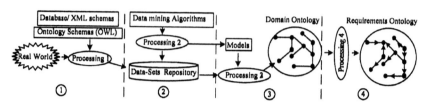

- **Evaluation for refinement or revision:** means testing the validity of the concepts belonging to the taxonomy and taking decision to keep or reject them using qualitative and quantitative methods.
- **Formal conceptualization:** consists in building formally the requirements ontology using OWL and description logic.

Knowledge Acquisition and Preprocessing

Like (Madhavan et al., 2005) in knowledge acquisition step, we use schemas that model similar concepts to benefit from their modelling variations and generate modelling statistics. We acquire these schemas having several formats (e.g., XML, OWL,) from three kinds of resources: (1) within the organization to be modelled, (2) within the relevant external knowledge that may be found in domain ontologies and database schemas that, at some extent, describe the activity domain of the organization to be modelled. Finally, (3) Web pages connected to the activity of the domain are also worth being explored.

Pre-processing consists of two stages:

1. Construction of the data sets repository
2. Preparation of data in order to be used for pattern discovery

The first stage of data pre-processing involves data assembling and cleaning in order to build a data sets repository from varied kinds of schemas. A number of heuristic metrics are used for the schemas selection process such as their similarity with the domain to be modelled and their semantic diversity. Therefore, the data sets repository is composed of:

- 40% of schemas belonging to the same domain as the domain of the database to be modelled.
- 40% of schemas from a similar domain.
- 20% of schemas from domains similar to the similar domains.

However, it is used, manipulated and referred as a whole. It uses a meta-schema that offers a flexible structure to store different kinds of schemas and to facilitate afterwards the manipulation and the analysis of the stored data in the mining phase. The data sets repository meta-schema consists of five tables as displayed in Table 1.

For relational, object and object-relational schemas, additional process is accomplished: they are translated into conceptual schemas by means of reverse engineering techniques in order to be easily added in the datasets repository. The second stage of data pre-processing involves three tasks:

1. Retrieve concepts from the data sets repository and the conceptual schema of the system to be modelled. (The conceptual schema of the system to be modelled represents the current schema of the database).

2. Classify these concepts according to two labels: *Current* for concepts belonging to the conceptual schemas of the system to be modelled and *Future* for concepts extracted from the data sets repository and representing potential future requirements.

3. Construct of contingency matrixes A and B that are used during the data analysis process.

    - Matrix A is a bi-dimensional matrix, in which the raw corresponds either to a schema coming from the datasets repository or to the schema of the organisation to be modelled and each column corresponds to a concept extracted from these schemas. The value 1 represents the presence of a certain concept in a certain schema.

Table 1. Data sets repository meta-schema tables

Versioned Schema	Represents a version of the schema to be stored
Schema	Represents the initial schema
Concept	It could be a class in the object schema, a class in an ontology schema or a node in xml schema
Attribute	Represents the properties of a concept
Relationship	Represents a set of relations between two concepts or a concept with its own

- Matrix B in which the raw corresponds to the type of relation that is attached to a concept and each column a concept. We have defined three generic relationships *Has*, *Kind-of* and *Verb* (see the definition of the requirements ontology to have the meanings of these relations).

Data Mining Algorithms and Informal Conceptualization

The goal of this phase, divided into two main steps, is to set up a primary informal conceptualization of the requirements ontology by determining the terminology of concepts necessary for building its domain ontology as well as the semantic relations that link these concepts in an unsupervised way. An architectural overview of the discovery processes is given in and described in the following sections.

Clustering Step

In this phase, clusters are generated respectively from the processing on the matrix A and then on the matrix B. The dissimilarity measure employed between concepts in each processing is different. In the first case in which the matrix A is the input, the distance calculation is based on concepts occurrence on the schemas, whereas in the second case, in which the matrix B is employed, the distance calculation is based on the category of relations and their occurrences.

Rules Mining Step

In this phase, the resulted clusters in the form of sets such as {c1, c2, c3}, {c1,c3,c5,c6}, and so on, are given as input for the rule mining process in order to build rules to

Figure 12. Presentation of the mining process steps

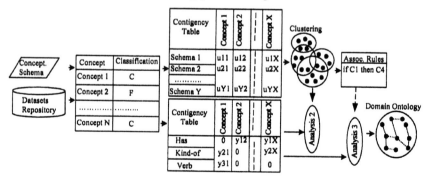

link requirements ontology concepts. A modified version of the Apriori algorithm (Agrawal & Srikant 1994) is used for the identification of these rules.

Evaluation for Refinement or Revision

The evaluation for refinement or revision consists of two steps:

- The first step is realised straight away after the rules mining process. It is a semi-automatic step in which redundant and contradictory rules are removed using a set of heuristics.
- The second step of evaluation is done in the phase of conceptual formalisation using Description Logic formalism.

Formal Conceptualization

The formalisation of the requirements ontology is done with description logic (DL) formalism. Such formalism, a descendant of semantic networks, is convenient for the representation of and reasoning about ontologies as well as for database schema integration and evolution. The basic elements of a DL language are concepts, Roles (binary relations between concepts) and Individuals (constants). A DL KB is composed of both a TBox (intensional knowledge or taxonomy) and an ABox (assertional knowledge). TBox describes the structure of the domain; therefore it contains concepts definitions and axioms whereas ABox describes specific instances and therefore contains concepts and role assertions (Baader & Nutt 2003). The role of DL in the requirements ontology is both (1) to formalize it in order to derive database schemas from it (2) to evaluate with the reasoning task if the description of its concepts and their relationships is consistent and satisfactory in other words, non contradictory.

Modelling and Planning for Evolution

In this phase, one or several sub-domains of the requirements ontology are chosen by the database designer to be turned into (1) a design evolution catalogue that translates the future requirements and (2) a database schema that translates current requirements. This initial schema supports database operation till the next evolution phase. An evolution catalog is a set of structures such as tables and attributes representing the evolution of the database schema at the logical level.

Evolution

In this phase, from the design evolution catalog, the database designer accepts or rejects the structures representing the possible future requirements and defined in the schema. It is expected that several evolution structure might be defined as evolution can follow different paths corresponding to different evolution strategies of the organization. If alternative structures exist for achieving the same evolution process, then the cost strategy built in the requirements analysis phase enables choosing the best evolution strategy with respect to the situation that actually exists at the time evolution has to be performed.

Future Trends

Schema evolution remains an active research area, even though considerable advances have been made in: data, rules, constraints, schemata, models, and meta-models. All existing solutions are complementary to each other in the issues and principles that are taken into consideration for the resolution of the evolution problem. In Roddick et al. (2000), a group of researchers from a wide range of disciplines but with a common interest in the evolution of information and database systems, proposed a set of areas, as excellent sources to elaborate future solutions. These sources include spatial and spatial-temporal change, semi-structured data, conceptual modelling tools, workflow management, and mining the change.

Similarly to weather forecasting solutions based on prediction with mathematical models, the future solutions for the evolution of information and database systems will have a tendency to anticipate possible future changes that could occur on a database schema and to create sophisticated structures such as accurate metadata schemas to manage them. Another important point about these solutions is that they are multidisciplinary. Although, they are devoted to database schema evolution, they are combining several disciplines such as databases, artificial intelligence, ontologies, networking, statistics, and so on.

Conclusion

In this work, we have presented a completely new approach for schema evolution called the *predictive approach* that implies the investigation of potential future requirements besides the current requirements during the standard requirements analysis phase of schema development and their inclusion into the schema. Those requirements are determined with the help of domain ontology, "a requirements ontology" using data mining techniques. This preparation contributes significantly in the ability of the database schema to adapt to future changes, to estimate their relative costs, and to facilitate the work of designers and help them save time and funding on the evolution of their databases. Two kinds of database designers were taken into consideration, the category of those who design a schema from scratch and the category of those who redesign the schema from existing schemas using reverse engineering and dependency graphs. Unfortunately, this new approach is not without problems. Predictions of potential future requirements might not turn into effect. The changes that have been included might never be used; however they can be removed completely without any alteration on the database schema. The predictive approach has several objectives and advantages that are useful and important for both the users and the designers. Moreover, the consequences of this approach are also considerable. This predictive modelling opens perspectives in the way requirements that are inspected and integrated into the schema. The next step in this research work is to test this approach significantly through several case studies with the use of a prototype that is under development.

Acknowledgment

The author would like to thank Rachel Pottinger for her comments and her many suggested improvements.

Note

This work is carried out as part of IM2 (Interactive Multimodal Information Management) (http://www.im2.ch), Swiss National Competence Centre in Research (NCCR), supported by the Swiss National Research Fund.

References

Agrawal, R., & Srikant, R. (1994). Fast algorithm from mining association rules. In *Proceedings of the 20th International Conference on Very Large Databases (VLDB 94)*, Santiago, Chile. Morgan Kaufmann.

Ambler, S. W. (2005). *The process of database refactoring*. Retrieved from http://www.agiledata.org/essays/databaseRefactoring.html

Ambler, S. W., & Sadalage, P. (2005). *Database refactoring catalog*. Retrieved from http://www.databaserefactoring.com/catalog

Baader, F., & Nutt, W. (2003). Basic description logics. In F. Baader (Ed.), *The description logic handbook: Theory, implementation and application* (pp. 43-45). Cambridge University Press.

Bellahsène, Z.(1996). View mechanism for schema evolution. *Advances in Databases, 14th British National Conference on Databases (BNCOD 96)*, Edinburgh, UK.

Benatallah, B. (1999). A unified framework for supporting dynamic schema evolution in object database. In *Proceedings of the 18th International Conference on Conceptual Modelling (ER99)*. London: Springer-Verlag.

Bertino, E. (1992). A view mechanism for object-oriented database. In *Proceedings of the 3rd International Conference on Extending Database Technologies (EDBT92)*, Vienna, Austria. Springer.

Corcho, Ó., M. Fernández-López, et al. (2003). Methodologies, tools and languages for building ontologies: Where is their meeting point? *Data Knowledge Engineering, 46*(1), 41-64.

Fowler, M., et al. (2001). *Refactoring: Improving the design of existing code*. Boston: Addison-Wesley.

Gómez-Pérez, A., Fernández-López, M., et al. (2003). *Ontological engineering*. London: Springer-Verlag.

Gruber, T. R. (1993). Toward principles for the design of ontologies used for knowledge sharing. *International Journal of Human-Computer Studies, 43*(5-6), 907-928.

Guarino, N. & Schneider, L. (2002a). Ontology-driven conceptual modelling. In *Proceedings of the 21st International Conference on Conceptual Modelling*, Tampere, Finland. Springer-Verlag GmbH.

Guarino, N. & Schneider, L. (2002b). Ontology-driven conceptual modelling: Advanced concepts. In *Proceedings of the 21st International Conference on Conceptual Modelling*, Tampere, Finland. Springer-Verlag GmbH.

Jarrar, M., J. Demey, et al. (2003). On using conceptual data modelling for ontology engineering. *Journal Data Semantics, 1*, 185-207.

Jarrar, M., & Meersman, R. (2002). Formal ontology engineering in the DOGMA approach. On the move to meaningful internet systems. In *Confederated International Conferences (DOA/CoopIS/ODBASE 2002)*, Irvine, CA. Irvine, CA:Springer.

Kroenke, D. M. (2004). Database redesign. *Database processing*, (pp. 265-275). Upper Saddle River, NJ: Prentice Hall.

Loomis, M. E. S. (1995). *Object databases — the essentials*. Reading, MA: Addison-Wesley

Madhavan, J., Bernstein, P. A., et al. (2005). Corpus-based schema matching. In *Proceedings of the 21st International Conference on Data Engineering (ICDE'2005)*, Tokyo, Japan.

McBrien, P., & Poulovassilis, A. (2002). Schema evolution in heterogeneous database architectures, a schema transformation approach. In *Proceedings of the 14th Conference on Advanced Information Systems Engineering (CAiSE 2002)*, Toronto, Canada. Springer-Verlag.

Mirzaee, V., Iverson, L., et al. (2004). Towards ontological modelling of historical documents. In *Proceedings of the 16th International Conference on Software Engineering & Knowledge Engineering (SEKE 04)*, Banff Alberta, Canada.

Roddick, J. F., et al., (2000). Evolution and change in data management — Issues and directions. *SIGMOD Record, 29*(1), 21-25

Sjøberg, D., (1993). Quantifying schema evolution. *Information and Software Technology, 35*(1), 35-44.

Spyns, P., Meersman, R., et al. (2002). Data modelling versus ontology engineering. *SIGMOD Record, 31*(4), 12-17.

Uschold, M., & Grüninger, M. (1996). Ontologies: Principles, methods and applications. *Knowledge Engineering Review, 11*(2).

About the Authors

Zongmin Ma (Z. M. Ma) received his PhD degree from the City University of Hong Kong in 2001 and is currently a full professor in College of Information Science and Engineering at Northeastern University, China. His current research interests include intelligent database systems, knowledge management, Semantic Web and XML, life science data management, knowledge-bases systems, engineering database modeling, and enterprise information systems. Ma has published over 40 papers in international journals, conferences, edited books, and encyclopedias in these areas since 1998. He also edited and authored several scholarly books published by Idea Group Publishing and Springer-Verlag, respectively.

*   *   *   *

Yubin Bao received his BE degree from Centralsouth University of China in 1990, and his ME and PhD degrees from Northeastern University of China in 1993 and 2003, respectively. Now he is the associate professor of Northeastern University. His research interest includes data warehousing, online analytical processing, and data mining. He has published more than 20 papers on academic journals and conferences.

Cláudio de Souza Baptista is an associate professor in the Department of Computer Science and Director of the Information Systems Laboratory at the University of Campina Grande, Brazil. He received a PhD degree in computer science from the University of Kent at Canterbury, United Kingdom (2000), a MSc in informatics, and a BSc in computer science from the University of Paraiba, in 1991 and 1989, respectively. His research interests include database, decision support systems, geographical information systems, and digital libraries. He has authored more than 25 papers in international conferences and journals. He is a member of the ACM SIGMOD.

Hassina Bounif received the MS degree in computer science from the University of Geneva, Switzerland. She is currently at the end of her PhD studies at the EPFL — Ecole Polytechnique Fédérale de Lausanne — Swiss Federal institute of Technology. She is working on a multidisciplinary approach for database schema evolution. Her current research interests include database schema evolution, multimedia databases, ontologies, data-mining, and XML technologies.

Henning Christiansen is full professor of computer science at Roskilde University, Denmark. His research interests cover a range of topics such as logical aspects of databases, intelligent query systems, logic and constraint logic programming with applications for automated reasoning and natural language processing, and computer science teaching methodology. He is active in promoting international conferences and workshops including the Flexible Query Answering Systems' series, and he is coordinator for international student exchanges at Roskilde's Computer Science Section.

Hendrik Decker has been at the forefront of advancing integrity checking methodologies since 1984 when he started working in the knowledge base group of the European Computer-Industry Research Centre (ECRC) in Munich, Germany. There he continued to pursue his research and application interests in database technology with Siemens from 1990 until 2001. From then until the present, he moved on to become a senior researcher at the Instituto Tecnológico de Informática (ITI) in Valencia, Spain. Besides the integrity, consistency, and paraconsistency of stored data, his current interests also include distributed databases, in particular their high availability.

Tzung-Pei Hong received his BS degree in chemical engineering from National Taiwan University in 1985, and his PhD degree in computer science and information engineering from National Chiao-Tung University in 1992. He was an associate professor at the Department of Computer Science in Chung-Hua Polytechnic Institute from 1992 to 1994, and at the Department of Information Management in I-Shou University (originally Kaohsiung Polytechnic Institute) from 1994 to 1999. He was a professor in I-Shou University from 1999 to 2001. He was in charge of the whole computerization and library planning for National University of Kaohsiung in Preparation from 1997 to 2000 and served as the first director of the library and computer center in National University of Kaohsiung, Taiwan, from 2000 to 2001. He is currently a professor at the Department of Electrical Engineering and the Dean of Academic Affairs in National University of Kaohsiung. His current research interests include parallel processing, machine learning, data mining, soft computing, management information systems, and WWW applications. Hong is a member of the Association for Computing Machinery, the IEEE, the Chinese Fuzzy Systems Association, the Taiwanese Association for Artificial Intelligence, and the Institute of Information and Computing Machinery.

Ioannis N. Kouris received a five-year BE degree from the University of Patras, Greece, Department of Electrical Engineering and Computer Technology in 1999 and a MSc degree in decision sciences with specialization in E-commerce from Athens University of Economics and Business in 2000. Currently he is a PhD candidate at Patras University, Department of Computer Engineering and Informatics. He is a research staff at the Department of Computer Engineering and Informatics at Patras University, and a member of research unit 5 at Computer Technology Institute (CTI). He teaches computer programming in Technological Educational Institute of Patras. Major research interests include data mining, Web mining, collaborative filtering, and information retrieval.

Christos H. Makris graduated from the Department of Computer Engineering and Informatics, School of Engineering, University of Patras, Greece, in December 1993. He received his PhD degree from the Department of Computer Engineering and Informatics, in 1997. He is now an assistant professor in the same department. His research interests include data structures, Web algorithmics, computational geometry, data bases, and information retrieval. He has published over 40 papers in various scientific journals and refereed conferences.

Davide Martinenghi received his PhD degree in computer science from Roskilde University, Denmark, in 2005 with a dissertation on integrity checking for deductive databases. His main interests are data integrity maintenance, data integration, logic programming, knowledge representation, and, in a broad sense, applications of logic to database systems. Recently he focused on the development of visual paradigms for the representation of data and actions in XML. He is also interested in software engineering and object-oriented programming and design.

Rosa Meo is professor at the Department of Computer Science at the University of Torino, Italy. She holds a DrIng degree in electrical engineering and a PhD in computer engineering, both from Politecnico di Torino. Her research interests are in the field of databases, in particular active databases, XML, and data mining. She has been serving as a reviewer for several international conferences and journals such as *ACM TODS*, *AI Communications*, *Integrating Data Mining*, *Databases with Information Retrieval*, *Logical Aspects* and *Application of Integrity Constraints (DEXA Workshops)*. She participated to some European funded projects in data mining, such as Mietta (on Multilingual Information Extraction) and cInq (consortium on knowledge discovery by Inductive Queries).

Fabiana Ferreira do Nascimento is an informatics master student in the Department of Computer Science at the University of Campina Grande, Brazil. Her research interests include database and decision support systems. Fabiana received a BSc degree in computer science from the University of Campina Grande, Brazil, in 2003.

S. A. Oke graduated in industrial engineering from the University of Ibadan, Nigeria with bachelor and master's degrees in 1989 and 1992, respectively. He is currently a doctoral candidate of the same department. He worked for the Comcraft Group (Nigeria operations) as a consultant. Oke lectures in the Department of Mechanical Engineering, University of Lagos, Nigeria. He is a member of the Nigerian Society of Engineers. His research interests include decision analysis, quality, safety, performance, and maintenance management.

Giuseppe Psaila is assistant professor at the Faculty of Engineering at University of Bergamo. He obtained the degree in electronic engineering from Politecnico di Milano, and the PhD in computer engineering from Politecnico di Torino. His research interests are in the field of databases, in particular active databases, data mining, XML and workflow systems. He participated to several European funded research projects in the database field, such as the IDEA Project (development of an active, deductive and object oriented database system), Mietta (on Multilingual Information Extraction) and cInq (consortium on knowledge discovery by Inductive Queries).

Marcus Costa Sampaio is an associate professor in the Department of Computer Science at the University of Campina Grande, Brazil. His research interests include database, data warehousing, data mining, and decision support systems. He received his doctorate in computer science from the University of Montpellier — France in 1995, and his MSc degree in computer science from the University of Campina Grande in 1984. He has authored more than 30 papers in conferences and journals. He is a member of the Brazilian Computer Society.

André Gomes de Sousa is an informatics master student in the Department of Computer Science at the University of Campina Grande, Brazil. His research interests include database, data warehousing, geographical information systems, and spatial data warehouse. André received a BSc degree in computer science from the University of Campina Grande, Brazil, in 2004.

Huanliang Sun is an associate professor in the School of Computing Science at Shenyang Jianzhu University. He got his PhD degree in computer software and theory at Northeastern University, China. His research interests include data mining and data warehouse, particularly clustering, and data streams clustering. He published his papers on data mining fields, such as on proceeding of RIDE-SDMA'05, WAIM'04, and *Journal of Software* (China).

Athanasios K. Tsakalidis is a computer-scientist, and professor of the University of Patras, Greece. His degrees include a diploma of mathematics, University of Thessaloniki, a diploma of informatics, and a PhD in informatics, University of Saarland, Germany. From 1983-1989, Tsakalidis was a researcher in the University of Saarland. He has been student and cooperator (12 years) of Professor Kurt Mehlhorn (Director of Max-Planck Institute of Informatics in Germany). From 1989-1993, he was associate professor, and since 1993, he has been professor in the Department of Computer Engineering and Informatics of the University of Patras. From 1993-1997, and 2001-today, Tsakalidis has been chairman of the same department. From 1993-today, he has been member of the Board of Directors of the Research Academic Computer Technology Institute (RACTI). Also, from 1997-today, he has been Coordinator of Research and Development of RACTI, and from 2004-today, he has been Vice-Director of RACTI. He is one of the contributors to the writing of the *Handbook of Theoretical Computer Science* (Elsevier and MIT-Press 1990). He has published many scientific articles, having an especial contribution to the solution of elementary problems in the area of data structures. Tsakalidis' interests of study include data structures, computational geometry, information retrieval, computer graphics, data bases, and bio-informatics.

Ching-Yao Wang received his BS degree in information management from Chang-Jung University in 1998 and received his MS degree in information engineering from I-Shou University in 2000. He is currently a PhD student of Institute of Computer and Information Science in National Chiao-Tung University, Taiwan, where he has been working on research of data mining. His interests include data mining, data warehousing, expert systems, artificial intelligence, soft computing and internet applications.

J. Gerard Wolff is Director of CognitionResearch.org.uk. Previously, he held academic posts in the School of Informatics, University of Wales, Bangor, the Department of Psychology, University of Dundee, and the University Hospital of Wales, Cardiff. He has held a research fellowship with IBM in Winchester, UK, and he has worked for four years as a software engineer with Praxis Systems plc in Bath, UK. His first degree at Cambridge University was in natural sciences (specializing in experimental psychology) and his PhD at the University of Wales, Cardiff, was in the area of cognitive science. He is a chartered engineer and member of the British Computer Society (Chartered IT Professional). Since 1987 his research has focused on the development of the SP theory. Previously, his main research interests were in developing computer models of language learning. He has numerous publications in a wide range of journals, collected papers and conference proceedings. Further information may be found at: www.cognitionresearch.org.uk.

Ge Yu received his BE degree and ME degree from Northeastern University, China in 1982 and 1986, respectively, PhD degree from Kyushu University, Japan in 1996. He is a professor of Northeastern University of China. He is the member of IEEE, ACM, IPSJ (Information Processing Society of Japan), and the senior member of CCF (China Computer Federation). He is the vice-chair of CCF Database Society, and the vice-chair of CCF Office Automation Society. He is the member of steering committee of WAIM Conference. He was the member of many international conferences like ICDE'2002, WISE20'05, ER'2004, DASFAA'05. His research interesting includes database theory and technology, distributed and parallel information systems, embedded software, network information security. He has published more than 130 papers on academic journals and well-known conferences like ICDE, DASFAA, and more than 130 papers were indexed by SCI, EI and ISTP.

Gian Piero Zarri was awarded a MSc in electronic engineering (University of Bologna, Italy) and then a PhD in computer science (University of Paris XI-Orsay, France). He is known internationally for combining methods from knowledge-based systems and natural language processing, as well as databases and information retrieval systems: for example, he defined and developed NKRL, the "narrative" knowledge representation language used in several European Commission-funded projects. He is the author of more than 160 refereed papers and, among other things, the co-author of a recent success book, *Intelligent Database Systems* (2001). His teaching activities have concerned, mainly, a post-graduate course on "Knowledge Representation". He has co-operated intensively with industry, as a consultant and, as an expert, with international bodies like the European Commission and UNESCO.

Faxin Zhao is a PhD student in the School of Information Science and Engineering at the Northeastern University, China. His research areas include intelligent database systems, knowledge management, data warehousing, and data mining. He received his master's degree from the Northeastern University of China and bachelor's degree from the Jilin University of China.

Index

T

traditional ontologies 138
transaction identifier (TID) 6, 73
transformation 152
tree-shaped structure 118
tree 202
truth table 212, 214
tuple constraint 242
type definition 205

U

unsupervised learning 199
update 244, 245, 252, 269, 272
update pattern 252, 269
update propagation 245

V

variable 205
versioning 289, 290
view definition 241, 249, 263
view 240, 289

W

weakest precondition 254, 255

X

XML 61, 62, 63, 70, 203, 239, 264
XML for data mining (XDM) 61, 63, 70
XML-schema 63
XML databases 264
XPath 266
XQuery 266

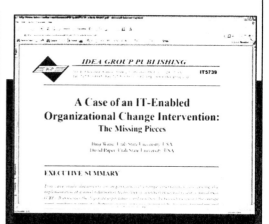